THE JAPANESE THREAD

Also by John K. Emmerson

Arms, Yen & Power: The Japanese Dilemma (1971)

Will Japan Rearm? A Study in Attitudes (1973)
with Leonard A. Humphreys

THE JAPANESE THREAD

A Life in the U.S. Foreign Service

JOHN K. EMMERSON

Holt, Rinehart and Winston
New York

Library of Congress Cataloging in Publication Data

Emmerson, John K.
The Japanese thread.
Includes Index
1. Emmerson, John K.   2. Diplomats—United States—
Biography.   3. United States—Foreign relations—Japan.
4. Japan—Foreign relations—United States.   I. Title.
E748.E45A34   327'.2'0924 [B]   77-26624
ISBN 0-03-041646-9

*Portions of this book have previously been published
in the following magazines:*

Foreign Service Journal: "Tokyo 1941," Part 1, April 1976;
"Tokyo 1941," Part 2, May 1976; "Japanese and Americans
in Peru, 1942–43," May 1977; "China-Burma-India," Part 1,
October 1977; and "China-Burma-India," Part 2, November 1977.

Asia Mail: " 'Egg Diplomat' in Taihoku," April 1977.

Epoch, Report of U.S. Affairs: "Peru no Nihonjin to Amerikajin" [Japanese and
Americans in Peru], in Japanese, No. 2, 1977.

Designer: Amy Hill
Printed in the United States of America
10 9 8 7 6 5 4 3 2 1

To Dotty and Don
who have lived much of this life

The end of the white thread of the
  Waterfall of Takio,
A bond from one generation to another—
Forever.

. . . From an old book.

*(Signpost at the foot of the Waterfall
of the White Thread, near Takio
Shrine, Nikkō.)*

Contents

Illustrations appear on pages 241–248.

Acknowledgments

In the course of writing this book, I have incurred indebtedness to many friends, who have given generously their encouragement, suggestions, reminders, and corrections. Their help has been indispensable.

During a visit to Harvard University some ten years ago, John K. Fairbank, professor of Chinese studies and an old friend from China–Burma–India days, urged me to write a book, or "two books," as he insisted, and put his thoughts on paper to remind me. In Palo Alto I met William Abrahams, an enthusiastic editor who followed the evolution of a manuscript from its beginning to its end, with prodding, helpful hints and faith. To him I owe much. Others who spared time to read the whole book and therefore merit recognition are Harrison Salisbury of *The New York Times;* Professor Gordon A. Craig, Stanford historian; Professor Robert E. Ward, also of Stanford and chairman of the Center for Research in International Studies; and Professor Roger Dingman of the history department, University of Southern California. John S. Service, a foreign service colleague since prewar days, read the *Thread* with his professional eagle eye for slips and errors. Professor Edwin O. Reischauer of Harvard read the chapter on the embassy during the period of our service together, 1962–66. Others who gave me the benefit of their comments on pertinent parts of the book include Claire Paradis, a member of the 1927–28 Delaware Group in France; John Paton Davies, who figures prominently in the Burma and China chapters; Henry Gosho, the "Horizontal Hank" of the China–Burma-India theater of war; Proctor Mellquist, editor of *Sunset Magazine* and a Burma "psychological warrior"; Clarke Kawakami, also a colleague from Burma days; Charles Taylor of Toronto, Canada, author of an essay on Herbert Norman; Raymond Ickes, formerly of the Department of Justice; former ambassador to France Amory Houghton; Brewster and Ellen Morris, he a former minister in Berlin and ambassador to Chad, she a friend from prewar days; and Robert A. Fearey, who served in prewar and occupied Tokyo. Daisuke Ishikawa, now in the American embassy, Tokyo, whose friendship has spanned the entire thirty years of my foreign service, recalled incidents and read pertinent passages. Very special gratitude is due to Stella E. Nicholson, who served as my steady and dedicated secretary in five consecutive posts: Beirut, Paris, Lagos, Salisbury, and Tokyo.

Many others, both in Japan and in the United States, whose names would fill many pages, gave unstintingly of their advice and assistance.

Needless to say, none of the above is responsible for anything that I have written.

I should like to thank the Center for East Asian Studies at Stanford University for research grants, which greatly facilitated the preparation of the book. Furthermore, I owe appreciation for the generous help and cooperation that I received from the staffs of the archives in the Hoover Institution at Stanford, the Foreign Affairs Document and Reference Center of the Department of State, and the National Archives in Washington.

Finally, a word to Dorothy, my wife, who provided the patience, sensitivity, and serene confidence without which this work would never have come about.

Japanese personal names are written according to Japanese custom: surnames first.

THE JAPANESE THREAD

1

Colorado to Japan

I entered the foreign service feet first, on a stretcher.

The pain had begun at midnight, a sharp, persistent, and very inconvenient pain. The Pullman porter brought ice packs. I thought irritably of what we had to do in the morning, in San Francisco, and concentrated hard on wishing away this pulsing ache. Nothing must block our catching that boat for Yokohama. This was to be the beginning of our new life, our new career, the alien experience in a mystic country, which only Lafcadio Hearn had understood. The train clacked rhythmically through the Feather River canyon and on to its morning appointment in Oakland, where we were to board the ferry for the crossing to San Francisco.

I was clutching my side as we sat near the prow of the ferryboat, staring in troubled wonderment at the jagged San Francisco skyline while the Ferry Building, then the outstanding landmark, grew taller as we approached. It was Friday, December 13, 1935, and the S.S. *President Cleveland* sailed at four.

Dorothy and I needed some routine inoculations so we sought out the civic health center. The pain had not gone away; the gnawing became more insistent. We asked, tentatively and incidentally, whether a doctor would examine me. The staff seemed surprised that we should expect a doctor to be on duty, and professional ethics restrained them from recommending one by name. Instead they sent us to the offices of the San Francisco Medical Association in another part of town. Arriving at the association's headquarters, which were located in what seemed to be a private stone mansion—my side now feeling like a fireball churning inside a raw wound—we were politely advised to seek help at the nearby Stanford University Hospital. The hospital authorities were considerate; they showed us a list of five doctors who were then available. With some exasperation and a little hurry, we pointed to a name—Dr. Scarborough it happened to be—and were ushered immediately to his office. He took one look at me, told me to sit down, then to lie down, and by early afternoon he was removing my appendix.

Instead of departing on Friday the thirteenth, we took the next weekly boat to Japan, the deliberate old *President Monroe*, which was to sail for twenty days, not to Yokohama but to Kobe. I like to think of my boarding as my official entry into the foreign service— on a stretcher. I wrote my father afterward, "You should have seen my dramatic embarkation! The ambulance wheeled up to the dock, the attendants carried me out on the stretcher (covered with sheet and strapped down—with towel over my head) and up the gangplank with the passengers and crew looking on curiously." I remember rather enjoying the drama of the situation and managed to look woebegone as Dorothy walked by my side.

Like marriage, the moment of starting a career can establish the direction of a whole life. Or so it was for me. But the chain of circumstances which had led me to the foreign service had begun many years before.

I was born in Cañon City, a small, mountain town in Colorado situated in a prehistoric lakebed, opening to the Royal Gorge. I grew up frustrated that I had never seen the sea. Perhaps it was an ancestral urge for change that in boyhood dreams I was always traveling on boats or trains. Ours was one of those American families that had migrated ever westward, from New England in the seventeenth century to Colorado in the twentieth. My father's grandfather moved in the early years of the nineteenth century from Kentucky to what later became Illinois in a migration of pioneers who "brought their feuds and their long rifles with them." His ancestors had lived in Virginia, and their forebears had somehow worked their way south from Boston where the first American Emersons (our southern branch later added an extra *m)* had arrived from England sometime after 1600 but not on the *Mayflower.* My mother, also born in Illinois, came from English and New York Dutch parentage, but had a grandmother who was French. It may have been Great-grandmother Bezier, pictured as a smiling, dark-eyed beauty, who first inspired my dreams of France.

I was ten years old when the armistice bringing World War I to an end was signed in a railroad car at Compiègne in France. In November 1918 the great influenza epidemic occurred—it had taken more lives than had the Germans—and the Cañon City schools were closed. For the pupils, it was the longest, most eagerly enjoyed vacation ever. The month of November I spent at home, pecking away at the family L. C. Smith typewriter, producing my single-sheet, daily newspaper *The Cañon City Daily Moon,* whose motto was "The Shining Light in the Darkness." As I recall, it ran for thirty issues and reported momentous events: the flu, the midterm elections (President Wilson had called for a Democratic Congress and got a whopping Republican majority), and the termination of the war. Our family was rock-ribbed Republican; the *Moon* advised its readers (my sister, my father and mother, and a few uncles and aunts) quite directly, "The editorial policy of this newspaper is Republican, and the editor does not care whether any Democrats read it or not."

France, which was much in the newspapers (including my *Moon)* became my fascination. I romanticized the French; they lived far from Colorado, across an ocean, in what I was sure was a beautiful country, and spoke a different language. I bought a French flag and hung it in my bedroom. Later, when I was in high school, one of the teachers who happened to know some French, started a beginners' course. Five adventurous students enrolled. I doubt that French had ever been taught before at Cañon City High School and wonder whether it was ever taught there again. My teacher, Miss Lulu Cuthbertson, had a brother who had fought the war in France and became acquainted with a family in the Midi. Armed with their address, and with slow but enthusiastic effort, I carefully composed a letter in my Colorado French, announcing that I was fifteen years old and that I would like to correspond with a French boy of my own age. After I waited interminably for trains and boats to go and come, a reply arrived. From Montpellier, it apologized, "I am not a boy but a girl. Still I would like to correspond with you." It was signed "Louisette." Inspired, I almost wore out my dictionary looking up words to use in describing life in Cañon City and later, in relating student experiences when I entered Colorado College in Colorado Springs. For five years, from 1923 to 1927, we wrote to each other, exchanging photographs, postcards, and mementos.

Like Moscow for the women of Chekhov's *Three Sisters,* Paris became my dream and my goal. During my freshman year, the *Colorado College Tiger* announced routinely that the Institute of International Education in New York offered scholarships to enable students to spend their junior year in France. I made a mental note and exactly a year later searched each issue of the *Tiger* to confirm that, indeed, the offer was open for 1927–28, when I would be a junior. I applied, convinced that an unsophisticated boy from Colorado with the minimum four years of uncertain French had no chance for such a prize. I told my family nothing, sure that they would oppose my going so far from home, above all to Paris, a city of temptation and sin.

Consternation gripped the household when the letter from New York informed me that I had been awarded a thousand dollars, donated by Felix Warburg, a New York banker, and that I should join the University of Delaware Foreign Study Group, due to sail for France on July 16. My sister thought it great; older than I and a born teacher, she had taught me to read before I entered school and took a special interest in my education. My mother was shaken, imagining that I might sink into an unknown and frightening slough of depravity. My father was likewise apprehensive, but his satisfaction at my achievement overcame his qualms. Eventually both became at least outwardly reconciled and sent me off to the French ends of the earth with pride and tears.

When I try to recall what it was like in 1927, I see double and triple exposures. My memory mixes what I experienced and what I later read about the twenties—the decade of jazz, flappers, normalcy, and Coolidge cool. The Paris of 1927 in reality must have been a much more glamorous place than I ever knew it to be. I lived for eight months on the Left Bank without being touched by the society of artists, musicians, and authors who were making the Paris of that day a nostalgic dream for generations to come. Just two months before our arrival, Charles Lindbergh had landed at Le Bourget and been idolized by all of France. His image was so fresh in the popular mind that, lean and lanky as I then was, I happily basked in the aura of an imagined resemblance.

Le Groupe Delaware consisted of thirty-seven college juniors: twenty-seven girls and ten boys, and our two teacher-advisers, George Brinton of the University of Delaware and Dorothy Dennis of Wellesley College. We were to live in French families, learn French, and become acquainted with the history and culture of France. Within the limitations of our 1920s college junior mind-set (a combination of chauvinism, naïveté, and wonderment) it was a good year.

Life in France was one unending bout with the French language. The leaders of the Delaware Group set out to make us speak, read, write, think, and dream in French. By fiat we were to speak only French among ourselves. Apart from a few faithful members who struggled to obey the rule, most of us animatedly brutalized the sacred Gallic tongue when our mentors were near but instantly reverted to college American when danger had passed.

We spent August through October in Nancy, the old capital of the dukes of Lorraine, built around the central square, Place Stanislas, which recalled the city's Polish heritage and traditional independent spirit. Since we were to live with the French, Nancy had been deliberately picked for being off the beaten American tourist path.

Claud Strong and I were assigned to the Pension Schouller. I later described our arrival for a college composition class:

> Our taxi rattled over cobblestones down a long, crooked street. We passed under an old arch (every city has its Arch of Triumph) and wheeled to a stop at No. 23, rue de Strasbourg. At the left of a huge door opening on the street was a brass plate with

dim lettering: MADAME MATHIS-SCHOULLER. We opened the huge door, entered a court, turned to the left, climbed three flights of spiral stairs, and rang.

Yes, we were the two new American *pensionnaires*. No, we didn't speak very well the French. These were our rooms? Merci. Madame Mathis was fat, motherly, with yellowish white hair. We would like her. Her smile and her chuckle welcomed us wholeheartedly.

Was there anything we wished? We looked at each other, I at Claud, Claud at me. Mental telepathy must have functioned—a bath! So, stammering and stuttering, we proceeded to try to make known the serious fact that we were dirty and tired; please, where might we take a bath?

"*Eh bien, alors ...*" commenced Madame Mathis in her creaky but rhythmical French voice. "Follow the rue de Strasbourg under the Porte Saint Nicolas, then continue on the rue Saint Dizier about six streets. You will come to a jewel shop; you will see an alleyway opening to the right; you will turn. You will see a sign: Bains du Casino."

We followed directions, entered, gave the lady at the counter five francs each, received towels and soap, sat down to await our turn, and were finally shown to our baths. Life had begun in France.

The Pension Schouller was right out of Balzac. It had no parlor, no living room, no salon. Life went on in the dining room, crowded with a table seating twelve, a roomy old buffet along the wall, a tall, square, green porcelain stove with potted plants on top and, in the corner, a table bearing big spreading ferns. All manner of geegaws pendant from the walls were disparaged by Madame Mathis: "*Mon dieu, ce ne sont que de petits machins.*" There were frail, inlaid wooden letter holders; odd pieces of old porcelain; a picture of the basilica of Lourdes done in mother-of-pearl; and an inlaid wooden plaque, the *marqueterie,* for which Nancy was famous, depicting the cherubic figures of an Alsatian boy and girl, she wearing her big, black bonnet and he with his fat, red umbrella. Along the walls and over the patterned green wallpaper were stretched cloth hangings with hunting scenes embroidered in red outlines. The room smelled of soup and wine, and the closeness of a place seldom aired.

The *pensionnaires* gathered around the board at mealtime played out scenes of French provincial life quite unselfconsciously before the wondering eyes of the young Americans. Copious old Madame Mathis presided with genial authority over the soup tureen. Mademoiselle Laure sat at her right, a fiftyish *vieille fille*, with piled hair that was too black, jet eyes that snapped and popped fire when excited. She usually wore a faded maroon, knit jacket brightened by a conspicuous amethyst brooch, and always wore a narrow, black velvet choker. She liked to sing opera in a dried, quavering voice: the "Jewel Song" from *Faust*, the *Carmen* "Habanera," or "My Heart at Thy Sweet Voice."

The other table companions were no less memorable: Monsieur Rassiano, the brisk and imperious doctor, whose stiff, black whiskers bristled from beneath his chin like the ruffs then worn by well-groomed bulldogs, and whose manner matched his whiskers; Monsieur Petit, a fitting name for the quiet, sober bank clerk with a round head, smooth, unremarkable face, and slightly stooped shoulders; and Monsieur Vautrin, a bank colleague who seemed inseparable from Monsieur Petit. Together they entered the dining room, together ate in silence, and together departed on their way. Then there was dainty Monsieur Colin, "the little one" from the south of France, pink faced, beardless, mustacheless, and with a recurrent, tinkling giggle. Monsieur Garagnon, who sat next to me, was swarthy, heavily moustached, rolled his *r*'s sonorously in a heavy Lyon accent and sputtered French at a speed which left us—Claud and me—totally uncomprehending. The group was completed by Monsieur Gardiet, he of the purple suit and sallow complexion, of dark, Latin temperament, fiery, excitable, nervous, high-strung, and a talker of ceaseless volubility. Serving the table was Jeanne, the maid, with rosy, chapped cheeks, looking always scared. Once she collapsed after spilling soup down the prim vest of Monsieur Rassiano.

At the table of the Pension Schouller, Claud and I were treated to the daily gossip of these youngish, unmarried Frenchmen—the sly jokes about scandals and love affairs and their emotional outbursts.

Sometimes our relative impassivity in the face of these displays of temperament exasperated them. Even the meek Monsieur Petit was roused to tell us once, *"Que vous êtes froids, vous autres Américains!"* And cold we were, to them, and materialistic and rich. I fear that in our youthful insensitivity we did little to disabuse them of these illusions. As I look back, I think we rather relished startling them by comparing salaries and prices in France and the United States. They gasped when we told them that congressmen received $7,500 a year, which turned into the colossal sum of 187,500 francs. I enjoyed their reaction to my account of earning $.65 an hour working in the post office, when a French boy would be lucky to get $.65 a day.

Surprisingly, there was little talk that I remember about national or foreign affairs. World War I, ended nine years before, still lived in their minds. Alsace and Lorraine, the lost provinces of France mourned since 1871, had been German before that war. No chance was missed to curse the *boches*. Madame Mathis showed us photographs of her son who had been killed in action. America, to the Nancy boarders, was a gigantic country overflowing with riches. Charles Lindbergh had personified the daring of young America. His picture decorated the walls of many French classrooms. We learned that French youth was beginning to assert its independence and freedom. Suzanne, a girl who joined our pension, typified this new generation. Athletic, boyishly bobbed, loud voiced, Suzanne idealized Americans, went to classes with boys, and talked with great animation at mealtimes. Madame Mathis and Mademoiselle Laure frowned restlessly when Suzanne would joke with the loquacious Monsieur Garagnon and the simpering Monsieur Colin. After we left Nancy, we heard from Mademoiselle Laure that Suzanne had gone. "To be truthful," she wrote, "we are not sorry. She was not at all a *jeune fille bien élevée.*"

Our three months in Nancy were to prepare us to enter classes at the Sorbonne in November. To us, it seemed that the administration of the Delaware Group had planned our lives so that the sheer absence of time would keep us out of mischief and away from fun. Mornings, spent at the University of Nancy, began with a written examination related to the previous week's work. Grammar followed, then dictation, and lectures in the geography and history of France. In the afternoons we had private lessons, and the rest of the time was for study. Each week we had to memorize one poem and read one novel; detailed tests checked our devotion to duty: "What did Héloise wear when she first met Abélard?"

As weeks went by, we felt put upon. The touted gaiety of Parisian life passed us by while we packed our minds with French names, dates, rules of grammar, and passages from the romantic poets. Many years later, when I had to face the Japanese language, these battles with irregular verbs and drills in approximating the French *r* in "around the rough and rugged rocks the ragged rascal ran," seemed blissfully simple exercises.

Once in Paris, we lived with a French family in a fifth-floor apartment at number 12, rue de Babylone, on the Left Bank. The building faced a tiny triangular park, with the Au Bon Marché department store across the street to the right and the Hotel Lutétia over to the left. The entrance to the Métro station, Sèvres–Babylone, opened at one corner of the park, as it still does. Black-bearded Monsieur Couderc and short, round Madame were both lame and walked with rocking limps. They were Protestants, believed in strict norms of behavior, and were constantly solicitous of our welfare. Three boys made up the family—Daniel, about twenty; Yves, seventeen; and Samuel, thirteen. Samuel had dimples, a flashing smile, and loved to play tricks. The older boys were so serious and knew so many facts and figures that our own store of American knowledge just didn't stack up.

As in Nancy, there was neither bath nor running water for washing *chez la famille Couderc*. In my room, a generous, white porcelain basin stood on an oilcloth-covered washstand. I can still feel myself balancing the heavy basin, as I emptied the dirty water into the tin bucket below, which was ordinarily hidden by a blue-checked curtain. Madame Couderc filled the basin each morning from an immense enameled pitcher. Saturday nights were bath nights. Taking turns, one stood in what I remember as a shallow, immense piepan. Splashing water over oneself, one soaped and rinsed as best he could. Since I drank water abundantly at mealtimes—decidedly *not* a French custom, even for the Coudercs who were prohibitionists as well as Protestants—and daily drained the final drop of my quota of washing water, Madame used to hold up her hands in hopeless surrender, *"Monsieur, quelles masses d'eau vous consumez, dehors et dedans!"* ("What masses of water you consume, outside and inside!")

The routine of study, lectures, dictation, private lessons, and examinations continued in Paris. We were subjected to double discipline. As foreign students enrolled in the *Course de Civilisation* at the Sorbonne, we had to follow the French system of oral and written examinations, but as juniors working for college credits from the University of Delaware, we had to satisfy the traditional American requirements for class recitations, frequent quizzes, and especially, assigned papers. The French experience sometimes seems now a kaleidoscope of mind-stuffing (almost resulting in a protest revolt against too much work)—visiting cathedrals and museums, seeing a few plays and operas, carrying on mealtime discussions at our pension in Nancy and with our family in Paris, and experiencing long, exhilarating walks through the streets of Paris. Also, Claud and I were always complaining about the food: the soup and the sameness, the cabbage, the chicory, the Jerusalem artichokes, and the *haricots verts*, the latter more stringy than *verts*, or so we thought.

We took trips, to the French Alps and to the Midi. It was during the latter spring excursion that I met my pen pal Louisette, in Montpellier. I told her to look for my collegiate yellow slicker, and she didn't miss me at the station. There was just time for lunch with Louisette and her family and a little stroll about the city with her alone, before I rejoined the group as they came through on a later train. Louisette's father and mother welcomed me like Lindbergh. The meal was a banquet, with every *spécialité* of the region spread, one after another, before me. I tried to eat and praise the food to the limits of my stomach and my language. Louisette was, as I had anticipated from her photographs, very good-looking, with large, dark eyes and black hair. She was animated but shy at meeting her first American. We talked rapidly as she proudly showed me Montpellier. But the moment ended. We had to go back to the station. The Delaware group was lined up along the windows of the railroad car, straining to glimpse the girl they knew I was meeting.

Louisette and I shook hands gravely and said "Au revoir." The train pulled out. There seemed little chance of our meeting again. Our regimen in Paris, let alone my meager allowance, permitted no personal travel. And her world in Montpellier was alien to mine. Our correspondence lapsed. We never saw each other again. I have never been back to Montpellier.

France became an important part of me. Study was not all drudgery, and something of Victor Hugo's sweep (his *souffle,* as our Sorbonne professor called it), of Molière's zany irony, and of Verlaine's music in words, invaded me. It was a beautiful and sentimental time of life. I had my twentieth birthday in Paris, and on a crisp, sunny March morning walked from the Sorbonne down the Boule Miche to the Seine, across to the Tour Saint-Jacques and Saint-Germain-l'Auxerrois, and then along the riverbank. I wrote in trite, awkward but conscientious French, *"L'horizon de la vie parait toujours attirant."* I romanticized over Paris sunsets. I wrote poetry that I blush to read today. One day I decided to be a writer, on another to be a musician. Once I wrote about the frustrations of my inadequacies, and at yet another time confided, "Nothing is impossible!" I discovered art in Paris. In Colorado painting, sculpture, and architecture had been only photographs in casually leafed volumes of the *World Book Encyclopedia.* While in France I wrote effusive tributes to Rodin's statues, to the Victory of Samothrace, and to the rose windows of Notre-Dame.

The only world-famous pianist I had ever heard was Ignace Jan Paderewski who played at the municipal auditorium in Denver. At age fifteen, so transported was I by this ethereal music heard from the cheapest and topmost balcony seat, that upon return to Cañon City I immediately bought for fifteen cents a Century Edition copy of Paderewski's Minuet in G, announcing to Miss Catherine Hendrickson, my indomitable piano teacher, that I was going to play it. With sarcastic impatience she advised me to return to the "Robin's Refrain." To spite her, I learned the Minuet. Miss Hendrickson's recitals were agony. As the only boy among at least fifteen girl pupils, I awaited my turn to play my piece from memory under the fierce eyes of "Old Hen," as we disrespectfully called her, and before the set smiles of the adoring mamas. Much later I realized that I owed my love of music to Miss Hendrickson and Paderewski.

In Paris I heard Wilhelm Backhaus play Rachmaninoff and Liszt, and Vladimir de Pachmann celebrate his eightieth birthday by playing Chopin. Throughout the concert, he talked intimately to the audience: "Only de Pachmann can play Chopin like this!" At the Comédie Française we saw *La Fontaine* with Sacha Guitry and his stunning wife Yvonne Printemps, who sang a delicate, eternally haunting air by François Lully, *"Revenez, amours, revenez."* Madame Couderc played the piano, and in the living room together we would hammer out a four-hand arrangement of Beethoven's Fifth Symphony. I entertained the family with the "Golliwog's Cake-walk," the "Juba Dance," and "At the Donnybrook Fair."

It may seem strange, for someone who was to become a foreign service officer, that the political and economic issues of the time so completely passed me by. My forced preoccupation with Villon, Verlaine, Lamartine, de Musset, the golden age of Louis XIV, and the rise and fall of Napoleon left little room for concern over the political problems then facing France. Our French hosts would tell us in their speeches of welcome how gratified they were that representatives of a young and growing America were now seeking in France the cultural heritage they had missed at home. As Frederick Lewis Allen noted in his *Only Yesterday*, the United States, in artistic matters, had almost become a French colony. The emphasis in the courses of civilization arranged for foreigners at the Sorbonne was on the grandeur and the glory of historic France. We learned little about the workings of the Third Republic or about France's international relations. However, we did become aware that Gaston Doumergue was president and that Aristide Briand was foreign minister. We visited the League of Nations in Geneva and learned of Briand's forensic triumphs there.

Our year in France was just past midpoint in the period of Coolidge prosperity. Henry Ford and Charlie Chaplin represented America to the French, that is, until Lindbergh flew into Paris. The Model A Ford was introduced in December 1927. Also in 1927, Sacco and Vanzetti, the two Italian radicals who had been arrested for murder seven years before, were denied their last appeal and executed. The case had stirred up worldwide protest; twenty people were killed by bombs exploding during demonstrations in Paris. Some small fracases took place, even in Nancy.

One event that penetrated my general political unawareness was the negotiation of the Kellogg-Briand Pact (the Pact of Paris), the treaty that we thought would ban forever the scourge of war. Its inspiration and signature bracketed our stay in France. The leonine Aristide Briand had addressed a message to the American people on April 6, 1927, the tenth anniversary of the entry of the United States into World War I, in which he proposed that France and the United States join in an engagement to "outlaw war," a phrase he confessed was not directly translatable into French. (In the course of his message, Briand referred to the "pious pilgrimage" that the American Legion was about to make to France for its annual convention. The so-called pious pilgrimage happened while we were in Nancy, and the drunken antics of the pilgrims, vividly reported in the Paris press, stimulated some lively conversation at Madame Mathis's dinner table.)

The Americans persuaded Briand to include the whole world in his pact, which he unenthusiastically agreed to do. Just after we left Paris, on August 27, 1928, the plenipotentiaries of fifteen nations, including Japan, signed, in the Salle de l'Horloge of the Quai d'Orsay, the Pact of Paris outlawing war. In intervening exchanges, it had been agreed by all signatories that the pact would not limit the inalienable right of self-defense. The United States declared in a note of June 23, 1928, that the right of self-defense "is inherent in every sovereign state and is implicit in every treaty." (Many years later, when Japan had become a major part of my life, these same questions of war, peace, and self-defense were to arise. Motivated by the ideals of the Kellogg-Briand Pact, General Douglas MacArthur and Prime Minister Shidehara Kijuro were to agree in 1946 on a "no-war clause" for the postwar Japanese constitution. Subsequent Japanese governments and courts maintained consistently that Japan's renunciation of war did not impair the nation's inherent right of self-defense.)

Several wars later, the Pact of Paris appears as a futile gesture, a "letter to Santa Claus," as someone termed it at the time. Yet in the complacent, carefree, pre-Depression years, when anything seemed possible, the Kellogg–Briand agreement was part of the happy innocence of the time. Japan's outlawing of war, coming in a different age and in a different setting, so far has shown amazing durability. But that is to get ahead of the story.

Back in the United States I returned to Colorado College for my senior year. The problem was my major. The Delaware Group experience pointed me in the direction of French. But a career? Would I be a French teacher for the rest of my life? Edith Bramhall, the dominating, irascible, demanding, yet utterly unselfish head of the political science department, settled it for me. Brammy, as we called her, believed anything was possible if you were ingenious and had imagination and industry. Frugality was a way of life for her, but it interfered with none of her personal projects. When she discovered that corpses shipped across the country by rail required an accompanying passenger traveling on a paid ticket, she cultivated the acquaintance of the local morticians, who were glad to notify her when a body was to be shipped to the East. She regaled us students with experiences in getting bodies to their destinations. It was one way to travel free, and she recommended it.

"Who wants to teach French as a career?" Brammy asked me rhetorically and derisively, "Obviously you should join the foreign service—and major in political science." Her tone of voice showed no iota of doubt. I had never met a foreign service officer; I had no idea of what one did or what he needed to know. We had never entered the American embassy while in Paris. My conception of diplomats was the conventional one of spats and cocktail parties, languages and travel. The languages and travel lured me. Despite frustrations, homesickness, and lost opportunities, the year in France had drawn me toward foreign sights and sounds and people. Probing into the requirements for government service abroad, I read with trepidation about the three-day examinations in history, law, politics, economics, geography, and general information. Economics was a dark, unknown, and forbidding land; I had not managed brilliantly Miss Bramhall's political science course, and my knowledge of history was laced with imprecisions. My sophomore year was crowded with English courses, and my junior year had been French. But nothing daunted the tenacious Miss Bramhall, who felt that turning out a political science major in one year would be simple. The more I thought about it, the more her determination on my behalf made sense. The foreign service—unknown and frightening as it was—appealed to all my childhood visions, now sharpened by my taste of France. I decided to major in political science and to take the examinations for admission to the foreign service.

Brammy also made the first dent in my Republicanism. She loved England and the Labour party. She traveled often to London where she had friends among the Labourites and met Ramsay MacDonald, her idol. She taught us about the Industrial Revolution and the struggles of British workers for their rights, and inculcated in us a sympathy for the underdog. We read Jeremy Bentham, a biography of Francis Place, the British radical reformer, and Arnold Bennett's novels about the pottery towns of England. My own life had included no urban or industrial experience. So-called coal camps clustered around the outskirts of Cañon City, where miners lived, many of Italian origin, but I knew nothing of their society. As a small boy, I remember that once they struck against the Rockefeller-owned Colorado Fuel and Iron Company, and the citizens of Cañon City were shocked and feared violence. I think the original John D. Rockefeller came to look at the situation and, as was his custom, passed out shiny dimes to waifs who gathered around him. Somehow I had missed the occasion and my dime.

I met Dorothy McLaughlin at Colorado College, a girl with deep, lively eyes, keen interests in everything, and great energy and initiative. In those days no one thought of getting married while going to school, and both of us had graduate study in mind. Fortunately for our growing attachment, we were both in New York, she at Columbia and I at New York University. That year the stock market crashed and the Depression era began. The New York effort to distill humor out of disaster came through in a song I remember hearing with Dorothy at Harlem's Cotton Club: "Everything is Coming Down," sung with the variations and implications one can easily imagine. By the spring of 1930 my fellowship ran out, and I had to earn money. It was still too early to face the State Department inquisition, in spite of my master's degree from NYU. Luckily, a fellow resident at International House, who was principal of a school in Nebraska, asked me to join his faculty. For a year I taught civics and history and coached debate at the Nebraska School of Agriculture, a specialized high school in the western part of the state, affiliated with the University of Nebraska. NSA was in Curtis, a tiny town halfway between North Platte and McCook. The students came from farming families, and most intended to return to farming as a life's career. The experience sent me back to smalltown America, where I again came into firsthand contact with the innate decencies, as well as the petty jealousies and covert capers, endemic to the American Main Street.

Saving my salary was not difficult in Curtis in those days. Room with a town family and board at the school were reasonable, and there was little else to spend money on. Some of the teachers had cars and a wild weekend would be a movie in North Platte or McCook, or a picnic near some creek or tree in the limitless, flat land which surrounded us. It was not difficult to refuse an offer for a second year of teaching. I took my hoarded savings and set out for Washington, D.C., in order to enter the School of Foreign Service at Georgetown University, for my final preparation for those fate-deciding tests. I had expected to spend a full academic year at Georgetown before offering myself to the State Department in the spring or summer of 1932. But during the fall rumors circulated in Washington that the examinations scheduled for January 1932 might be the last ones for a long time. The Depression showed no sign of ending; government employees were being laid off, and my prospects for employment by the State Department were beginning to dim. It was now or never. So I decided to cram faster and harder and to make my try in January.

At Jesuit Georgetown I got a shot of conservatism. Father Edmund A. Walsh, director of the School of Foreign Service, was well known as a Russian expert. At that time his cause was to prevent the United States from recognizing the Soviet Union. I took his course on the Russian Revolution and found Marx and Lenin so dull that little of the significance of their teachings penetrated my consciousness. A conflicting impression had been made on me by a professor of sociology at Colorado College who, along with his wife, had visited the Soviet Union in the early twenties during its "workers' paradise" period. Upon their return he had communicated enthusiasm over the accomplishments of the Soviet regime in bringing Russia into the modern world.

I chose courses at the foreign service school which would prepare me for the State Department exams: American foreign policy, diplomatic history, international law, maritime law, and commercial law. James Brown Scott, then a venerable and distinguished authority on international law, gave a seminar whose members included diplomats from some of the foreign embassies in Washington. I wrote a paper on U.S. foreign policy in which I referred to America's "manifest destiny," not with approbation but to identify a policy. When I read the paper to the class, a Chilean diplomat, misunderstanding my meaning, bristled at the phrase, protesting vigorously at the mere mention of an outmoded and discredited slogan. Professor Scott rubbed his bald head circumspectly and said quietly, "Mr. Emmerson has put *quotation marks* around 'manifest destiny.'" My reputation with the Latin Americans was saved.

During the three days of foreign service examinations, we marked true-false statements and wrote essays. There were long lists of words to test on geography and general knowledge. The examiners had excised whole hunks of the pronouncing gazetteer in the back of Webster's unabridged dictionary and demanded identification of each proper noun, whether river, lake, mountain, city, country, or man. There were separate essay questions on American and world history from 1776; on economics; on international, maritime, and commercial law; on diplomatic practice; and on foreign policy. There may have been others that I have forgotten. Facing the economics section terrified me the most, so I prepared by memorizing a current college-level economics textbook.

Somehow I passed the written tests and became eligible to take the oral examination. These thirty minutes were more unsettling than the three days of writing. One of the examiners asked me the current price of wheat. I had no idea of the price of wheat but made a wild guess, which miraculously was not too far off. Another, who happened to be from my home state, asked me to relate pertinent facts in the life of James J. Moffatt. All I knew about Moffatt was that a tunnel was named for him and that he must have been a prominent citizen in the early days of Colorado. I stumbled through an evasive answer. The clue to pass or fail was a summons to take the physical examination. If no summons came, it was a bad sign. I remember only that, after a long time, somebody came out to the corridor, where I had expectantly hesitated, to instruct me to proceed to the Navy Department on Pennsylvania Avenue, where the medics awaited me.

Passing the examinations did not mean a job. All appointments were indefinitely postponed because of the Depression. My Nebraska nest egg soon disappeared, but I still had to eat. Looking for a job when panhandlers and street apple sellers were the legendary signs of the times was not the happiest of prospects. Fortunately, I had learned typing and shorthand in Cañon City and, as insurance, had taken the clerical civil service examination a few days after answering questions for the State Department. I applied to an employment agency, where the kindly lady, impressed by my typing speed, sent me to Senator Steiwer of Oregon. I managed his dictation without too much trouble but, not being from Oregon, I could hardly expect a permanent job with him.

Next, I joined the American Taxpayers' League, a lobbying organization headed by short, energetic, nervous Pappy Arnold, who was always on the road raising funds, and by Lydia Popkins, a big-boned, red-haired, red-faced lady with a loud laugh and a good heart. Lobbyists had not previously been a part of my experience and the Taxpayers' League was a discovery. Sponsoring lower taxes was a cause everyone favored, but the fact that the league never succeeded in reducing anybody's taxes seemingly bothered no one. Senators and representatives were delighted to speak gratis on nationwide radio hookups and did not mind the plug at the end for a modest contribution to the Taxpayers' League. On Mondays we would open up the morning mail and pour out the dollar bills. But we depended on Pappy to bring home the big contributions from his forays around the country. Sometimes even his persuasive powers failed, and there would be no salaries for a week; when a windfall came, we would all get raises. During the horse-racing season, Lydia Popkins and her friends would lock themselves in the boss's office and, with the assistance of a little refreshment delivered by Butch, the bootlegger, would place their bets by telephone. As the afternoon wore on, the shouts and laughter, or groans and wails, as the case might be, would emerge in crescendo from the inner office. Finally, the money-raising petered out, and the low-ranking employees—which included me—were summarily fired.

Being a stenographer for the Taxpayers' League was a job—and jobs were scarce in 1932. At one time I was making the enviable sum of thirty-five dollars a week. I regaled my Washington friends with tales of Pappy and Lydia Popkins and the other hangers-on in this enterprise for milking the public. Personally I felt detached from it all (too tolerant perhaps, because the characters were likable), but certainly was disillusioned about causes and the motives of the so-called perpetrators of the public good. Compared with these goings-on, bureaucracy appeared then to be a satisfying and stimulating haven.

Next, I drew on my civil service status and found a job in the sanitation division of the District of Columbia Health Department. It was an easy job. I manned the complaint desk and listened by telephone to the reports of garbage in the streets, unlawful smoke belching from chimneys, stopped-up toilets, nuisance-creating dogs, and whatever the citizens had on their minds. The complaints were duly recorded and distributed to the sanitary and food inspectors who made their daily rounds within their assigned sectors of the city. A big map on the office wall indicated by pushpins the location of every outdoor privy existing in the District of Columbia. In 1932 there were quite a few.

I became eligible to vote for the president of the United States. Four years previously I had argued for Herbert Hoover in a college debate. But in the Washington of the Depression, some of us who became friends, either students or searchers for careers, found our champion in Norman Thomas. He represented for us idealism, morality, and social justice. We knew he couldn't win, and we were not much interested in socialism, but he appealed to our instincts for the improvement of humanity—handsome, articulate, the man who cared. I cast my first presidential ballot for Norman Thomas.

My career in the sanitation division was short-lived. A classmate at Georgetown, Robert Strumpen-Darrie, was the son of the president of the Berlitz School of Languages of America, and through him I was offered a job in the Berlitz New York office. Since the work would be a little nearer to my career ambitions than a lobbying organization or a local sanitation office, and because Dorothy was still in New York, I accepted with alacrity.

The pay was fifteen dollars per week, but by standards of the Depression years, it was not to be disdained. I lived at the YMCA for five dollars a week, ate my breakfast at two stops on my way from Twentieth Street to Thirty-fourth Street: orange juice at a Nedick's stand, coffee and croissants at the DeWitt Clinton Hotel (luxury!), and managed without pain. Dates were sometimes expensive, but Dorothy and I both worked and we established a dutch-treat relationship, unusual in those pre-women's-lib days, but workable and agreeable.

After I had been but a few months in New York, the president of Berlitz transferred me to the Chicago school, of which my friend Robert was then director. Our association was a deeply happy one. Not being a native speaker, I could not, by Berlitz rules, teach French, but I could do translations. Robert and I shared many adminstrative duties, and I organized courses in public speaking and Effective English, the latter to appeal to Americans who worried about their grammar and yearned for social poise and business advancement through an ability to think and speak correctly while on their feet. I wrote the courses as I gave them, and we made great plans for storming the country with Effective English.

Teaching public speaking and English appealed to my performing instincts. As a child I had been urged to recite poetry at family gatherings and church events, and as a teenager I had studied elocution as well as piano. In college I earned trivial sums of money by playing during dinner at the Colorado Springs Elizabeth Inn, by broadcasting a half-hour program over the local radio station as the "Monomotor Oiler," and by traveling to high schools around the state presenting concerts advertised as "EMMERSON—Entertainer Extraordinary." One review in the *Colorado College Tiger*, written by

Dorothy, as I later learned, described the performer as having "reduced his audience to a state of helpless laughter." Planning courses for adults wanting to speak and write better English meshed nicely with my natural exhibitionism. Human communication—although I never analyzed it at the time—is an important aspect of life. Holding an audience, whether by music or monologue, was great fun. The personal expression of inner feelings and emotions was something else, however, and I had to wait for Japan to discover that the bottling-up of my feelings, my propensity for nonverbal communication, was in reality very Japanese.

In August 1934 Dorothy and I were married, and she joined us in Chicago as receptionist, secretary, coffee preparer, administrative assistant, and general watcher over the state of our health and morale. Office hours were from nine to nine. On the walk home along Michigan Avenue we would sometimes tarry at a little oasis. Once or twice I found myself playing the piano at a dark little bar near the bridge or at the Ranch on Oak Street. I had a few things I could play: Beethoven's "Turkish March" from the *Ruins of Athens,* some easy Chopin preludes, and the good old Minuet by Paderewski. How these classical warhorses blended into the atmosphere of friendly stopovers along the avenue, I cannot remember; at any rate, I was never hooted down.

Our idyllic existence in Chicago was shattered one morning in September 1935 by the arrival of a piece of what looked to be junk-mail advertising. The letterhead read "Horace F. Clark and Company, Bonding, Washington, D.C." Dorothy was about to throw it in the wastebasket when a single, typed-in sentence at the bottom of the page leaped out at me. It read something like this: "This letter soliciting your bond as a government official is sent in reference to your recent appointment as a foreign service officer, Department of State." This was it! Three years and nine months had passed since those examinations in Washington. Our minds by now were set in a different direction. Bob, Dorothy, and I were immersed in the world of Berlitz. We were propagandizing the slogan "Learn Another Language," thinking up new ways to advertise, planning new courses, new publications, dreaming about the further expansion of Berlitz Schools throughout America and throughout the world. Foreign policy, economics, the exigencies of the diplomatic service—these had become the concerns of another earlier age. Suddenly I was brought up short, Was it to be languages or diplomacy?

A decision that should perhaps have been easy plunged me into searching self-examination and conflicts of intellect and emotion. I knew that I was truly choosing my life, that the way stations and the destinations of the two paths stretching ahead would bear little resemblance to each other. In Chicago our relationship was compatible; the three of us had achieved the kind of rare understanding that may come once in a lifetime. We were reveling in the satisfactions of applying ingenuity, imagination, and concentration to exciting tasks. Pretty much on our own, we were indulging in responsibility and looking ahead to opportunities and rewards for individual initiative and application. When the week's receipts were good, we exulted, and when the thin margin of profit began to disappear, we were despondent. Still, our enthusiasm for the future was boundless. For us, education and business and challenge and reward were combined in Berlitz.

Dorothy shared my enthusiasms and turmoil, but with supreme sensitivity she knew that this was a decision that I must make alone. On a bright, crisp, fall day, I walked north from the school on Michigan Avenue, to Lake Shore Drive, and on out to Lincoln Park. There, sitting on a stone bench, and then pacing about in the shadow of the statuary, I knew I had to make up my own mind. Was it to be languages or diplomacy, business or bureaucracy, life at home or abroad, probable financial success or lifetime security, the known or the unknown? With my vague notions of the obligations and lifestyle of the career foreign service officer, I doubted my abilities to negotiate with foreigners, to cope with strange situations, and to meet the required social standards. In my mind at the time, that year in France had not been enough of an intellectual preparation for the foreign service; I had taken only one brief course at the Sorbonne on French government, and it had not inspired me. At Berlitz I had gained self-confidence; I could do a French translation and could criticize a stammering young businessman who wanted to improve his poise. Our time in Chicago had been so brief, yet it had been a continuing honeymoon. Our little apartment on the near Northside, the "bucket of blood" where gangster hideouts and sleazy pleasure joints huddled beside the swank apartment houses and hotels for the rich, was warm and hospitable when we returned from the school at night. We had soon acquired a secondhand, unclaimed Kimball grand piano from a friend whose father owned a warehouse; the rest of the furniture didn't matter.

One day I found a doodled drawing on Bob's desk: a forest with two trees cut down, below which was printed the hoary phrase that had come to punctuate our daily banter, *sic transit gloria mundi*. Arguments about the transience of life were frequent among the three of us. Whatever the subject—friends, associations, or events—Bob and I would bait Dorothy with, "Two years from now, will it really matter?" Thoughts about our motto *sic transit gloria mundi* must have surged through my mind in Lincoln Park, thoughts about breaking the happy cocoon of our life in Chicago. Excruciating wrench though it would be, life would go on, and "two years from now" the pain of disruption would be healed.

So, as the pros and cons piled up in my mind that day in Lincoln Park, the influences of Great-grandmother Bezier and of my wayward, world-traveler Uncle Harry, a family legend; images of sunset-on-the-Seine; and my boyhood dreams of seeing the sea all began to win over the comforts and satisfactions of the status quo. In the end, I knew that the prospect of unknown adventure was irresistible, that I had to join the foreign service. I walked away from Lincoln Park with my eyes turned toward a new career. Dorothy and Bob were not surprised, I am sure. Dorothy felt this would be the outcome but had determined to say nothing to influence me; our understanding was enough. Nevertheless, momentary gloom enveloped us, as we contemplated the breakup of a happy association. (Bob soon married an old friend we had all known in Washington. Later, he became president of the Berlitz schools.)

Correspondence with the State Department crawled in those days. It took the bureaucracy several weeks to notify me officially by letter that I had been offered an appointment. Fortunately, *The New York Times,* in a minuscule paragraph deep inside its pages, confirmed the letter from Horace F. Clark. Sometime later a circular letter arrived informing all new appointees that several assignments would be made to Japan and China for language study. Anyone interested should apply. Quite separately, I heard from U. Alexis Johnson (my close friend and Georgetown classmate, who was then in Washington working for Call Carl, an automotive service company) that he was going to Japan, that the language assignment looked like a good deal, and why didn't I come along?

Until that time, the Orient for me had been the legendary exploits of an Uncle Harry I never knew, and a short course in Far Eastern history, taught at Georgetown by a bubbling world traveler and irrepressible raconteur, Dr. Boyd-Carpenter. Of my father's four brothers, Uncle Harry, the eldest, was the restless one who left the southern Illinois farm to see the world. He arrived in California in 1878, worked in Hawaii, then ruled by King Kalakaua, became a trader in the South Seas, and built railroads in the Straits Settlements, Siam, Tonkin, the Philippines, China, and Siberia. We had a photograph of Uncle Harry standing near the King of Siam, alongside the train that made the initial trip over the first railroad built in Siam. He was in Manchuria when the Boxer Rebellion occurred and received one hundred pounds from the British government for helping to guard British property in Newchwang. I remember staring in boyish awe at his photographs of Boxers before and after their heads were chopped off. He was supposed to have bought a Chinese gold mine; I dreamed of the gold that would any day pour in to make us rich. My Uncle Frank once whispered to me confidentially that Uncle Harry had left a "wife" in a remote village in the South Seas, and that very probably a cousin of about my own age lived somewhere out there.

Neither Chinese nor Japanese was then in the curriculum of the Chicago Berlitz School, and I had not the slightest sense of the nature or the structure of these languages. But my battles with French as a member of the Delaware Group and the siren song of far-off places, enhanced by Uncle Harry's exotic adventures in the Far East, left no doubt in my mind. I answered the State Department, yes. In due course the orders came posting me to the embassy in Tokyo, as third secretary and language officer.

We bid our farewells to Chicago. The government would pay for the transportation of household effects, but we had no household effects, except our grand piano and a radio-phonograph. Dubious that a grand piano would be considered as a household effect, I was pleased to learn from the State Department that a piano indeed qualified and could be shipped at government expense. After a graceful wind-up for the public speaking and Effective English classes, and after a brief introduction to the gray, old State Department in Washington, we traveled by train to Colorado in order to say good-bye to our families, before boarding the Denver and Rio Grande and the Western Pacific to San Francisco.

We were to arrive in San Francisco on Friday morning, December 13, 1935.

2

Prewar Japan 1936–39

At six-thirty, on the cold, dark morning of January 10, 1936, I roused myself and climbed out on the deck of the homey, lumbering old *President Monroe* to glimpse for the first time—Japan! The air was sharp and clean and the water quiet, as the ship carefully sought its way through green, wooded islets and along the grassy points of land. The full moon splashed light across the water at the same time that the redness of a morning sun was beginning to appear out of the opposite, shadowy horizon. This unusual combination of moonlight, sunrise, and lapping water struck me as a good omen for the beginning of our life in Japan.

Again, State Department communications had failed, and the consulate in Kobe, unaware of our arrival, had sent no one to meet us. But a local Dollar Line employee efficiently and courteously gave us, as I wrote my father, "a wonderful introduction to the Japanese people." After a courtesy call at the consulate, we boarded Japan's finest and fastest train, the Tsubame ("Swallow") for the eight-and-a-half-hour trip to Tokyo. We were gratified to learn in the dining car how reasonable life was going to be. The yen was worth twenty-eight cents: in the diner, dinner cost one yen fifty sen or forty-two cents and went from soup through fish, meat, salad, dessert, and fruit, to coffee.

Our friends, Alexis and Pat Johnson (he would become ambassador to Japan in 1966), who had preceded us, welcomed us at the Tokyo station and took us to the Sannō Hotel, where we spent our first night in our new country. The historic Sannō, in the Akasaka district not far from the American embassy, became famous a month later when rebel soldiers seized it as their headquarters.

Much further along in history, the Sannō was again occupied by the military, this time by the Americans. As a transient officers' billet, it has housed for more than thirty years successive generations of uniformed officers traveling in and out of Tokyo. Structurally little changed since 1936, the Sannō, classified as one of the diminishing U.S. military bases in Japan, has continued to provide the strictly American housing, dining, drinking, and PX privileges expected by our armed services personnel stationed overseas. The Japanese owners of the property tried to recover it for their own use, but the foreign office has championed the military, less out of pro-Americanism than out of reluctance to spend the money for obligatory alternative facilities.

The embassy, in 1936, stood on a hill, dominating the mixture of modest commercial establishments and private homes that surrounded it. The American Bakery was just across the street. Within the walled compound, the ambassador's residence looked down from its wooded eminence onto the chancery and two apartment houses, which Ambassador Grew called dormitories. The buildings, white with modest blue tile decorations, were grimy when we saw them first. Built in 1930, before the American government constructed its own facilities abroad, the Tokyo embassy became known in Washington as "Hoover's folly." Those who served in Tokyo during the turbulent periods from the thirties to the seventies grew attached to these graceful buildings, with the barest suggestion of an oriental tilt—some called it Moorish—at the edges of their roofs. We were among those who cringed when the wrecker's ball swung in 1974 to demolish the swimming pool, the apartments, and the chancery in order to make way for the high-rise box, which would commemorate the contemporary proliferation of personnel and the high price of land.

I called on Ambassador Joseph C. Grew at the first opportunity.

Tall and imposing, distinguished by his dark, bushy eyebrows and his gray-streaked hair, he epitomized the classic diplomat of the old school. I had been warned that he was partially deaf but resented people who shouted at him, and also had been told that one should speak distinctly but without raising one's voice. He encouraged me in my language study, but remarked that he, although fluent in German and French, had deliberately decided not to learn Japanese. He feared that the dangerous hazards of ludicrous wrong usages would impair the dignity and esteem of the president's representative.

Mr. Grew was right about not trying to learn Japanese. Already fifty-six, and with his heavy responsibilities as chief of mission, the ambassador could at best have gained a collection of polite phrases that might have amused the Japanese he met but would not truly have won him respect. Living in Japan, we soon learned that the people of the Yamato race have a peculiar feeling about the language they speak. They regard it as unique, personal, and almost sacred—a method of communication that should be reserved only for themselves. A foreigner speaking Japanese is for them like Samuel Johnson's definition of a woman's preaching: ". . . a dog's walking on his hinder legs. It is not done well; but you are surprised to find it done at all." Soon after arriving in Japan, we heard a story widely circulated among missionaries. An American preached a sermon to his local flock in flawless Japanese; a parishioner came up to him afterward to remark respectfully, "I never knew before that I could speak English but today I understood every word you said." All of us who get along in Japanese have had the experience, usually when traveling in the countryside, of trying to penetrate the mental block that stops communication because the person you meet refuses to believe that you can speak his language. Only after you, the *gaijin* ("outside person"), have firmly established your credentials of comprehension and fluency can a two-way conversation proceed.

Ten officers made up the core embassy staff. These included the army, navy, and commercial attachés, and the consul general, but not the State Department or military language officers. Because of the sudden post-Depression influx, eight foreign service officers had been assigned to study Japanese, the largest number ever in Japan at one time. The total personnel of the embassy reached about sixty-five. Mr. Grew wrote after the New Year's reception by the emperor in 1936: ". . . the extent of our own Embassy was rather staggering. Our commissioned personnel and their wives total thirty-five persons and most of them were there." In 1974 the embassy telephone directory listed 271 Americans and 407 Japanese, a modest roster, in fact, and reduced from the proliferation during the postwar years.

Indeed, the business of an embassy was simpler in those more relaxed times. In 1940, as the most junior third secretary (third was as low as you could get) handling miscellaneous odds and ends, I was given an inquiry to answer. A Japanese citizen wrote to express interest in the United States and to request any information we might have available. My reply, prepared on the basis of established policy, in the accepted State Departmentese, read something like this: "Dear Mr. Tanaka: The Embassy acknowledges receipt of your letter and regrets to inform you that the Embassy cannot accede to your request since the United States government does not engage in propaganda." The enormous operations of the United States Information Agency in the postwar period make our studied smugness hard to fathom.

In the less complicated days of 1936 we had no administrative apparatus to look after the creature comforts of embassy families, no government-owned apartments or houses (except the ambassador's residence and the two apartment buildings in the embassy compound), no general service officers, commissaries, or post exchanges. We had a pouch clerk and a budget and fiscal officer. Dorothy and I beat the pavements looking for a house to rent. Finally, we were lucky to hear of a Japanese diplomat who would leave his house while he served abroad. Our stay at the Sannō Hotel was thus brief and we missed its February encounter with history.

Establishing a household in Tokyo was immensely facilitated by Dorothy's teacher, Elisa Vaccari, a vivacious, enthusiastic Japanese lady married to an Italian linguistics professor. The Vaccaris became famous from the stream of Japanese–English dictionaries, grammars, and conversation texts that poured from their pens over the succeeding years. My wife proofread some of the early Vaccari books. In return she achieved immortality in the exercise sentence: *Emahson-san no okusan wa machi e ikimashita* ("Mrs. Emmerson went downtown"). I was told that when Ralph Waldo Emerson's works were first translated into Japanese, his name was pronounced *Emahson* with the accent on the *ah*. Therefore, since the New England essayist and poet was widely known in Japan, my *Emahson* would be quickly understood, which proved indeed to be the case.

Ambitious to speak as much Japanese as possible, we deliberately sought servants who knew no English (our superb Chinese cook, Ming-san, was an exception). With Elisa Vaccari's help, we advertised in the *Asahi* newspaper for a non-English-speaking maid to serve in a foreign household. On the appointed day and hour, fifty kimono-clad young women clogged our entranceway and part of the narrow street beyond. Mrs. Vaccari patiently screened each applicant. Two or three offered to pay us for the chance to live in a foreign home and to observe the etiquette and strange social customs of foreigners. After a few unsatisfactory trials, we finally settled down with Suzu-san, who was from a little country town, Komoro, in mountainous Nagano prefecture. Suzu-san had chapped cheeks and hands and was frightened and shy at her first encounter with foreigners.

She worked for us three years but suddenly disappeared one night from our home in Shukugawa, near Osaka, where I was then assigned as a vice-consul. We had returned home late from a dinner party to find the house lights blazing but no one at home. On the dining table was a note in Japanese, which by then I could read. Suzu-san wrote that she had made an irreparable mistake, that since there was no way she could ask our forgiveness, she was going to end her life. Closer inspection of the dining room revealed that she had been writing at the table and had inadvertently brushed the ink bottle to the floor, leaving splotches of ink on the Chinese rug that I had brought from Peking only a few weeks before. She had obviously gone out into the night taking none of her belongings with her.

Only later did we learn that Suzu-san fortunately had thought better of sudden death and instead had sought refuge with relatives in Tokyo. Again, our indispensable friend, Mrs. Vaccari, found

Suzu-san and assured her on our behalf that all would be forgiven and forgotten if only she would come back. For her, as we might have known, this was unthinkable, and we never saw Suzu-san again. With successive applications of milk, the rug eventually returned to its original state. Many years later, foreign anthropologists and sociologists began to study Japan's "shame culture" and the Japanese ways of communication and avoidance of confrontation. Suzu-san was our introduction to some of these traits.

The Japanese language was for two years my absorbing occupation and preoccupation. Unlike the year in France, there was no living in a Japanese home or boarding house, and it took effort to meet and know Japanese. Bachelor language officers with the advantages of more freedom of association occasionally betrayed in their speech the feminine origins of their instruction. Some of them acquired "Japanese head" from overconcentration on memorizing the Chinese characters, or lost their perspective by deliberately excluding non-Japanese contacts from their daily environment. Others, however, related superficially to foreign surroundings. The ideal diplomat, guarding his precious national identity, looks in on a foreign society as through an open window (if his hosts permit) with unblemished sight, acute listening capacity, and a canny ability to communicate when necessary, with insight and understanding, to his government and to the people among whom he lives. For this, language is a required instrument.

The embassy ran no language school but employed private tutors who came to our homes to give us lessons. One teacher appeared in the morning and another in the afternoon, all selected and supervised by Professor Naganuma Naoe, who, in his smart leather puttees, roared on his motorcycle from one to another of our houses to inspect what was going on. With about twenty language officers to instruct, of whom eight were State Department foreign service officers, Naganuma-sensei did a thriving business. His seven textbooks had been written originally for military students and were later amplified to suit the vocabulary needs of diplomats. Before Naganuma wrote them, the only beginners' readers were the primers for Japanese schoolchildren, with words for flowers and animals but few for government and diplomacy. Naganuma's *tokuhon* ("readers") were copied and used throughout the war by the U.S. Navy Language School in Boulder, Colorado. I had the opportunity, in September 1945, to express appreciation to their author for his contribution to the American war effort. His immediate and natural reaction was, "What about my royalties?"

The Japanese language! A German writer has observed that the *kanji,* or "Chinese characters," which make it up, must have answered "to the Japanese preference for what is hazy, well-shrouded, capable of more than one meaning and to the technique of a patriarchal government which would feel much embarrassed if everybody could read everything with as much ease as the western alphabet allows." In our prewar period we had to memorize 2,500 *kanji*; after the war the Japanese government reduced the number of official characters (that is, those to be used in newspaper type) to 1,850. Baffling at the beginning, the *kanji* reveal themselves each to be a graceful vignette of art and history, of sight and meaning. Based on 217 radicals, which are clues to concepts (earth, fire, water, heart, hand, grass, tree, man, sound, etc.), the characters have both beauty of line and the strength of ideas. *Kanji* present not the only difficulty. One learns that there can be as many as thirty expressions for the pronoun *I,* that a Japanese sentence hides its meaning until the end, that there are men's words and women's words, multiple gradations of politeness and status, and an infinite number of ways to avoid categorical affirmations. But there we enter the realm of culture and communication. A Japanese has written an article entitled "Sixteen Ways to Avoid Saying 'No' in Japanese." My first probing of just a few of the mysteries of communication began with my language study in 1936.

In the fall of the year a naval language officer friend had advertised in a Tokyo newspaper for a student to live in an American home and assist in Japanese instruction. He received so many replies that he asked me whether I would be interested in one of his applicants. The idea seemed a good one and so Ishikawa Daisuke, an eighteen-year-old middle-school student came to see me. He was a slight boy, quiet, uncertain, but anxious to study English and to discover what Americans were like. Ishikawa-san lived with us, wrote my character cards, helped me during my struggles with vocabulary and grammar, went on long walks with us wherever we were at the time, and talked Japanese exclusively with me. This was an uneven bargain, but he accepted it. He studied English in his spare time, listening attentively to our conversations with each other and with American friends, and picking up in the process a good knowledge of our language.

Two years later, after the language study had ended and Ishikawa-san had left our home, he wrote me an eleven-page letter in crowded, tiny, but plainly readable, characters. He expressed with embarrassing frankness his reactions to life with Dorothy and me. He wrote about his feelings when we first met: "At that time I was—probably most Japanese are that way—a worshipper of Europe and America. When I think of it now, I was intoxicated with western civilization to a ridiculous degree." He described his hesitations at coming to work for me, the objections of his family, who feared the "bad influences of an association with foreigners," his shock at first hearing my wife speak strange Japanese with an American accent. Yet he became "addicted to this blue dream of delight," which he experienced when he started to work in my "exotic" study. In 1938 (Year of the Tiger and of continuing war in China), looking back to those earlier years, he felt guilt over his satisfaction, calling it "the ugly pride of someone who has lost the national spirit." He remembered 1936 as the "year that I lost my self." He described the conflict of his emotions: a Japanese boy living with foreigners, sacrificing his schooling, and worrying about the future. He apologized for his apparent melancholy ("Japanese are said to be prone to melancholy") and for confiding in me his disappointments, pessimism, troubles, and anxieties for the future, "like a younger brother telling an older brother without any kind of pride." Until I received his letter, I had not truly realized how unalterably we had changed the life of this Japanese boy.

The woman who was to become the closest friend of the language officers was Countess Watanabe Tomeko, daughter of Field Marshal Ōyama Iwao of Russo-Japanese War fame. The countess's mother had been one of the five brave Japanese girls who had accompanied Japan's first diplomatic mission to the United States in 1872. Only twelve years old at the time, Yamakawa Sutematsu lived with the family of a Christian minister in New Haven, Connecticut, and remained in the country for ten years, later becoming the first Japanese girl to graduate from Vassar College. After her return to Tokyo in 1882, she married Field Marshal Ōyama, then minister of war. The countess must have felt, although she never said so, that perhaps she might repay some of the hospitality accorded her mother in America by inviting our group of eager, young American foreign service officers into her home. Tea with the countess on Wednesdays became a happy ritual. She corrected our halting Japanese and, with sparkling humor, kept us enthralled with stories of her life, her family, and Japan. Her husband, then deceased, had been an official of the Yokohama Specie Bank and they had been stationed in London, although she had never visited the United States. The countess spoke English well but decreed that Japanese would be the language at her teas. Years later, when one of our group, U. Alexis Johnson, became ambassador to Japan, the countess recalled her association with us in an interview with the press, in which she commented with warmth and frankness on our varied aptitudes for the Japanese language.

Nineteen thirty-six, Year of the Rat, a symbol of wealth and prosperity, opened with barbed exchanges between the United States and Japan. The first five years of the 1930s had been an uneasy period for America's Asian relations. The Manchurian incident, in 1931, had aroused American opinion; a doughty secretary of state, Henry L. Stimson, had tried but failed to get the British to join him in stopping the Japanese advance. The end result had been a Japanese walkout from the League of Nations and a Japanese-dominated Manchukuo. Meanwhile, a series of assassinations and attempted coups d'etat in Japan had eroded American confidence in the peaceful motives and intentions of an aggressive nation propounding the military virtues and the destiny of an expanding Japanese empire. American pro-Chinese sentiment had been strong since the Boxer Rebellion and John Hay's Open Door Policy, and now Americans were sympathetic to the Chinese underdog, suffering from what appeared to be a bullying military tyrant.

Franklin D. Roosevelt's 1936 New Year's message to Congress

was termed "plain speaking" by the *Japan Weekly Chronicle* and "courageous statesmanship" by Ambassador Grew. The president did not mention Japan by name but pointedly criticized nations who were reverting to a belief in the law of the sword, or in FDR's words, to the "fantastic conception that they alone are chosen to fulfill a mission." FDR commented that his words would not be popular with any nation that might choose to "fit the shoe to its foot." Grew thought this phrase a master stroke and noted prophetically in his diary that the speech "won't stop the Japanese push into China—nothing can stop that except defeat in war—but it may conceivably exert a moderating influence on their methods and tactics: it may possibly tend to slow up the movement temporarily."

Ambassador Grew drew the same kind of satisfaction from a bristling anti-Japanese speech delivered in the Senate on February 10 by Key Pittman of Nevada. Assailing Japan's foreign policy as a threat to the United States, Senator Pittman denounced her venture in Manchuria as a flagrant violation of the covenant of the League of Nations, the Kellogg Pact, and the Nine Power Treaty. The senator concluded that there were only two ways of protecting peace—one through respect and obedience to treaties and the other through a sufficient naval and air force. Reacting to the speech, the *Asahi* expressed alarm over the growth of anti-Japanese opinion in America, citing President Roosevelt's message to Congress, a *New York Daily News* editorial that discussed a Japanese–American war as inevitable, and Senator Pittman's open condemnation of Japan. Grew asserted that the Pittman speech was "utterly jingoistic" and agreed with the American editorialists who excoriated it, but he thought its net result helpful, rather than harmful, since it might serve to modify the American outcry against big military budgets and, at the same time, serve as warning to the Japanese that "when slapped in the face often and hard enough, a time might come when we wouldn't turn the other cheek."

These gathering clouds little affected our daily life in Tokyo, which was more concerned with the mechanics of settling into our house and the mysteries of the Japanese language than with matters of international politics. We spent our first days in the fruitless exercise of calling on all the embassy officers and their wives who outranked us; since we were at the bottom of the list, this meant everybody. We found we could do about five calls in an afternoon, and with thirty-five senior officers it required more than a week's work.

As any visitor knows, Tokyo streets are not named; after World War II, the Occupation tried valiantly to put up signs for First Street, Second Street, and so on, which the Japanese ignored. The signs stayed up, though, until the weather beat them away. Kurt Singer, in his sensitive book *Mirror, Jewel, and Sword,* mentions the "anomalous character of Tokyo's streets symbolic of the Japanese city; a cluster of villages grown to immoderate proportions." To make our calls, we hired a taxi (fortunately the fare for a whole afternoon was only seventy cents) and set out on a hunt-and-find expedition, starting with the city ward *(ku),* narrowing our objective to the district *(chō),* the block *(chōme),* and finally, to an elusive number. Houses were numbered not consecutively but in the order of their construction; in those days the taxi driver uncomplainingly appealed to the grocer (the "eight hundred things" shop), the tobacconist, or to the policeman stationed in his little box. Invariably the people to be called upon were not at home, but the formality of leaving cards at the door accomplished our obligation.

Dorothy complained of the "honey sweet" social life, with its rule of "being nice to everybody." We were, however, spared much of the Tokyo diplomatic social frenzy; first, because we were so junior in rank, and second, because England's King George V died. The government went into mourning for a month, which meant a black dress for Dorothy and a black tie for me and fewer parties all around.

The winter of 1936 was unusually severe, with the lowest temperature in nine years being registered in the capital city. A blizzard of record proportions hit the nation in early February, paralyzing Tokyo where stranded theatergoers huddled overnight in bitter cold and darkness. The snowfall was reported at 10.4 inches, a fifty-four-year record.

Snow fell again on the evening of February 25. In the early dawn of the next day a group of zealous young army officers dedicated to restoring the emperor to his rightful position and to bringing about a Shōwa * restoration, assassinated the finance minister, the lord keeper of the privy seal, the inspector-general of military education, and the brother-in-law of the prime minister, the last by mistake. The officers tried, but failed, to murder Prime Minister Okada Keisuke, the Grand Chamberlain Admiral Suzuki Kantarō (who would be prime minister at the time of Japan's surrender), Count Makino Nobuaki (former lord keeper of the privy seal and father-in-law of Yoshida Shigeru, Japan's famous postwar prime minister), and Prince Saonji Kimmochi, the last of the elder statesmen. The mutiny—for it was a mutiny in which some 1,400 soldiers followed their officers—became known in Japanese history as the *Ni-ni-roku Jiken* (the "Two-Two-Six Incident"), and shook the nation and its structure as no crisis had done in Japan's modern period.

February 26 was a Wednesday, our weekly day for tea with Countess Watanabe. This day, however, rumors were flying, and those of us who nonchalantly kept the appointment found an agitated countess who sensibly thought the time was not for tea.

Although the War Ministry issued an official announcement of the incident at 8:15 on the night of the twenty-sixth, it was not until Thursday, the twenty-seventh, that the public read in the newspapers the first bare outlines of what had happened. The foreign-edited, English-language *Japan Weekly Chronicle* was not even allowed to print the first bulletin, a discrimination that the paper later protested editorially. By early Thursday morning, the city had been placed under martial law and government troops were beginning to move toward the central area of Tokyo (which included the prime minister's residence, the War Ministry, the Diet, the Metropolitan Police Headquarters, and the Sannō Hotel where the rebel soldiers were entrenched).

Since our house was far from the affected district and our news most fragmentary, Dorothy and I decided on Friday, the twenty-eighth, to pick up our mail at the embassy, which was in viewing distance of the scene of activity. We boarded a tramcar and on our way passed directly in front of the Sannō. Soldiers with drawn

* *Shōwa is the era name for the reign of the present emperor, Hirohito, 1926–.*

bayonets lined the streets. We later learned that foreign residents of the Sannō had been given an hour's notice to evacuate by soldiers who were polite and considerate, but firm. At the embassy, everyone was rushing about in tense confusion. Several Japanese army officers were surveying the building, preparing to organize an evacuation to military barracks should fighting become dangerous. The embassy officers were horrified to see Dorothy and me calmly walk in to complicate their situation. They wasted no time in instructing us emphatically to go home—*if* we could get home. The streets were calm, almost deserted, since citizens had been advised to stay indoors. Tramways were still moving, however, and we returned home without difficulty and without embarrassing the embassy. By that evening, the government troops prepared to storm the rebels' positions. On the twenty-ninth all communications were stopped: streetcars, trains, and telephones. A friend came by the house at 5:30 on that afternoon to tell us that the rebels had surrendered and the incident had ended. The leader, a Captain Nonaka, and one other officer managed to commit suicide; seventeen others, including several civilians, were later tried, convicted, and executed.

Japanese have linked the assassinations of February 26 to two other dramatic events in their history: the vendetta of the forty-seven ronin in 1703 and the murder of the regent, Ii Naosuke, by a band of samurai in the last days of the Tokugawa shogunate in 1860. All three occasions were snowy mornings, and the deeds were done out of professed determination to serve lord or emperor. The forty-seven ronin avenged their lord, who had suffered public insult and been forced to kill himself; they then gave themselves up to the authorities and were sentenced to commit *seppuku* themselves. The samurai from Mito who killed Ii opposed Japan's opening relations with the West. The regent had signed treaties with the United States, England, and France and had dispatched to the United States a mission, which, upon returning to the port of Uraga, heard the news of his assassination six weeks after it had occurred. Of the Mito men, five managed to commit suicide, and the others were executed. One of the young officers who participated in the February 26 incident recalled in his final testament the death of Ii, "When we thought about the snow falling as it did also at that time and knew that we were about to repeat that act at the same place, our hearts were filled with great joy." The heavy snowfall, which formed a backdrop for each of these three events symbolized for the Japanese the serenity of the perpetrators' souls and the purity of their motives.

Scholars have probed deeply into the causes of the February rebellion. They find them in the poverty of the countryside, from which most army men were recruited, in the traditional rivalry between the army and the navy, and in the bitter split within the army—between the Imperial Way *(Kōdō-ha)* and the Control *(Tōsei-ha)* factions. Although the mutiny failed and the responsible young officers were executed, the army emerged more powerful than ever. Officers in dominating positions, including Gen. Tōjō Hideki, took advantage of the menace of so-called radical fascism demonstrated by the incident and thoroughly purged the army of those who had sympathized with the young officers' cause. The new controlling group proceeded to consolidate its military influence over politics.

It would be, however, a mistake to interpret Japanese history of the 1930s as a military conspiracy pointed toward inevitable war with the United States, or to signal Two-Two-Six as marking an abrupt shift in national goals. The fundamental principles of Japan's foreign policy had been set by the Meiji founding fathers, who declared the national aims to be "rich country, strong army." Throughout the prewar period successive governments followed courses consistent with these aims. They determined that Japan must maintain a dominating position in East Asia (in order to make the country rich, through access to materials and markets), a strong enough defense to meet any threat, and equal relations with the Western powers through diplomacy. Policymakers recognized that pursuit of these goals might bring war with either the United States or Russia, but they did not deliberately aim for war. One of the first magazine articles that I ever translated while still a language officer was an essay in the *Diplomatic Review* on the question of whether Japan should expand to the north or to the south: a northward advance would risk war with the Soviet Union, while extension of power in the south would clash with interests of the United States. Once domination over Manchuria had been secured, fate seemed to lead Japan ever farther into China and into resulting conflicts with the American principle of support for the sovereignty and territorial integrity of China.

The young officers' dream was to restore to the emperor the prerogatives that they contended had been abused and distorted in his name by evil, corrupt, and cunning advisers, both civilian and military. They took their inspiration from the Meiji restoration, which had established Japan as a modern state and yet restored Emperor Meiji as the rightful sovereign. They hoped to carry out a Shōwa restoration that would reestablish and reinforce the unique essence of Japan's national polity, restore moral order, improve the lot of the peasantry, and rescue the common people from the twin tyrannies of capitalism and communism. The principles were vague and any concrete program of reform nonexistent. One of the participants wrote from prison, while awaiting execution, that he and his fellow patriots could never have accomplished their scheme if they had "indulged in private fancies about the actual structure of the government." He went on to say, "The punishment of evil men and restoration are the same thing." To those who murdered Japan's leaders in the early dawn of February 26, their acts were dictated solely by their love of country and loyalty to their emperor. As another wrote from prison, "Killing traitors is not a crime, but the duty of the patriot."

Mishima Yukio, Japan's most universally recognized modern novelist, would be fascinated with the February 26 incident. He wrote about it extensively, abundantly revealing his dedication to the national Japanese values that he saw manifested in emperor worship and the act of suicide for a noble purpose. His brief novel *Yūkoku (Patriotism)* was based on the actual suicide of Lieutenant Aoshima Kenkichi and his wife Kimiko, which occurred on the night of February 28. The officer was a member of the Imperial Bodyguard Division who had been given permission to return to his home that Friday night. According to Mishima's story, the lieutenant, married only six months, had not been invited to join the revolt although his best friends had planned it. Out of compassion for his newly married state, his superiors had given him leave for this one night, but on the following morning, the twenty-ninth, the unit under his command would be ordered to attack the rebels to bring the mutiny to an end. He tells his wife that he cannot follow this order, which would pit imperial troops against imperial troops. He determines to commit *seppuku,* and his wife asks permission to accompany him in death. Together they prepare to carry out their pact.

Mishima wrote *Yūkoku* in 1960 and a few years later produced a film based on the story, in which he played the lieutenant's role. No words were spoken: the entire drama, leaving nothing to the imagination, took place in the young couple's apartment, the two-character word *sincerity* in calligraphy on the scroll hanging in the alcove behind them, while the music of Wagner's *Liebestod* is played in the background. The two say their farewell in a torrid love scene; then, deliberately and with impeccable attention to detail, the lieutenant performs the ritual of *seppuku* before the eyes of his adoring wife. She, in Mishima's words, "sensed that at last she too would be able to taste the true bitterness and sweetness of that great moral principle in which her husband believed," and thrust the blade of her own short dagger deep into her throat. The youthful audience in the Tokyo theater where we saw this film in 1966 stared with rapt attention, their eyes fixed on the screen, during the unfolding of the tragedy.

Mishima made a cult out of the beauty of youth and death. He found the ugliness of present-day Japan to be as intolerable as the corruption that impelled the young officers to assassinate the country's leaders in 1936. He professed his belief in the infallibility of the emperor and glorified the taking of one's life for the emperor. Yet Mishima found fault with the present Shōwa monarch.

In his book *Voices of the Heroic Dead* the ghosts of the executed young officers, as well as those of wartime kamikaze pilots, deplore Hirohito's renunciation of divinity during the American Occupation as a betrayal of their acts done for his sake. In actual fact, the emperor had been furious when he heard the news of the murders on February 26. He called the Righteous Army an "insurgent army," telling his closest adviser, Marquis Kido Kōichi, that, regardless of the question of spiritual motivation, the acts had "damaged the glory of the national polity." He instructed the war minister, "I will give you one hour to suppress the rebels," and speaking of them in uncompromising terms, he said, "Any soldier who moves imperial troops without my orders is not my soldier, no matter what excuse he may give."

In the late 1960s Mishima posed at playing army through a privately drilled corps of youths; his calls for a return to the pristine beauty of imperial rule were fruitless, as he undoubtedly expected them to be. I talked with him at length in Tokyo in the summer of 1968. We had met him and his wife during my service at the embassy in the early 1960s. They had been to dinner in our home and had attended our farewell reception. I wrote to him, suggesting an interview, and he telegraphed an affirmative reply. Always an exhibitionist and intensely conscious of his physique, he appeared wearing an immaculate white suit, with white shirt, tie, and shoes. We conversed over whiskeys-and-soda in the Men's Oak Bar of the Okura Hotel. He was worrying about the defeatist attitudes of Japanese youth, deploring the rebellious university students who were saying that if Japan were attacked by an enemy, they would bare their chests and refuse to lift a finger in defense of their country. Mishima told me that he was visiting as many schools as he could, trying to instill in the students some of the love and loyalty for country, which he saw so starkly lacking.

Mishima was gracious, intent, positive in his opinions, and seemingly delighted to talk with me. He shifted easily from Japanese to English and back again. He was a man with a planned, determined mind. I think he must have laid out the denouement of his own life, his dramatic *seppuku* in November 1970, long ahead of time, just as he would plot his next novel. From our conversation, I could catch a glimpse of the complexity of his character: Japanese to the core but with a disarming Western exterior; his ardent patriotism, focused on the emperor as idea and ideal, was set against overweening personal pride in physical beauty and sexual prowess (generally reputed to be homosexual in its nature). He possessed dazzling creativity but also bravura and showmanship; an obsession with violence and the craftsmanship of its literary expression were combined, as it turned out, with the will to prove publicly his creed that Beauty is Death.

Neither we who were living in Tokyo in February 1936 nor foreigners outside of Japan truly understood the mix of motives and circumstances which produced the *Ni-ni-roku Jiken.* Americans learned most about it from a facetious article in the *Saturday Evening Post* by the well-known journalist J. P. McEvoy who reported the events "from an armchair" in the Imperial Hotel. He was able to include the text of the rebels' statement, which he had had translated before catching a ship to the United States. The embassy saw the incident as strengthening the military group in Japan, and Hugh Byas, the serious *New York Times* correspondent, set it in the context of "government by assassination." Puzzling to foreigners was the fact that the rebels had no program, no reforms, nor a revolution to impose. Theirs seemed a futile, desperate, and emotional gesture. Yet such gestures have occurred repeatedly in Japanese history, stemming from the warrior codes that had been established in Japan's feudal ages.

But the February 26 incident was more than a gesture. It represented a culmination of confused frustrations and dissensions: the perpetrators were proproletariat but anti-Communist, anti-big business but supported by some industrialists; they were military officers, but they denounced certain of their military masters; they were dedicated to saving the emperor, but the emperor condemned them, while his brother Prince Chichibu gave them sympathy. They accomplished none of their ideals; they did not cleanse the body politic; they did not bring about a Shōwa restoration; and, except for two of them, they did not even win the privilege of self-destruction, which had made the forty-seven ronin heroes for all time. The immediate effect was a tightening of military control. General Terauchi, the new minister of war, promptly revived the principle that only active officers could serve as ministers of war and navy, thus effecting military predominance in the Cabinet-making process. In the longer run, the expressed ideals of the rebels won admiration from Japanese mesmerized by the repeated slogans proclaiming Japan's "sacred mission."

Everyone knew, however, that the boasts of "a hundred million Japanese of one heart" were empty. Free parliamentary elections—the last ones until the war ended—had been held February 20, 1936, forty days after we had arrived in the country and six days before the young officers' mutiny. The two major parties, Seiyukai and Minseitō, won 80 percent of the seats, although, surprisingly, the leftist Social Masses party increased its representation in the House of Representatives sixfold, from three to eighteen elected members. A liberal journalist of the time remarked, "The people elected you gentlemen because they want you to fight for the cause of parliamentary government." One Diet member, Saitō Takao, whom I was to meet after the war, had the courage to strike at the military in a so-called slip-of-the-tongue speech delivered on May 7. Others—including the famous Ozaki Yukio, historically known as "father of the Japanese parliament"—continued their courageous struggle against military domination. During this same period university professors and journalists were bravely publishing denunciations of the military until, one by one, they were dismissed or arrested. Two weeks after the February 26 incident, a professor at Tokyo University wrote, "Even if force dominates the world for a time, it will inevitably destroy itself." From 1936 on, parliamentary democracy weakened and died, the power of the military increased, and it became less likely that Japan's leaders would deviate from the course of expansion, which they had already set.

After the first year in Tokyo, which included a summer in the mountain resort of Karuizawa and a trip through the Inland Sea to Kyūshū, it occurred to me that I could learn more Japanese away from the distractions of the capital. Even though we were at the bottom of the diplomatic list, ranking after third secretaries, and had no responsibilities in the embassy, we were inevitably swept into the diplomatic social whirl and found ourselves dutifully performing the inevitable chores of taking guests off the reception line and gently pushing them to circulate—ever circulate—at the official parties given in the residence by Ambassador and Mrs. Grew. This social life, pleasant as it might be, was contributing little to our understanding of Japan or to our knowledge of Japanese. A colleague and I therefore proposed to our mentor at the embassy, Cabot Coville, the second secretary, that we be permitted to travel around Japan, accompanied by a tutor who would instruct us, as in Tokyo. Cabot assented immediately, stipulating sternly, however, that we return to the embassy every three months to be tested on our progress.

Cheerfully, in early January of 1937, we set off for Nikkō ("light of the sun"), the mountain site of the resplendent shrines built to memorialize Japan's first shōguns of the Tokugawa period, but a holy place since the eighth century. There we spent two cold, snowy, beautiful months in a Japanese–foreign-style house built at the turn of the century. It was named Kami Akamon ("Upper Red Gate") for the gates that swung apart to reveal the zigzagging stones, leading up through the trees and azalea bushes to the veranda above. The old two-story house, painted red with a green metal roof, faced a moss-covered slope, across which a little brook gurgled its way from a fall at the back, over carefully placed rocks to a pool at the bottom of the garden. The house was surrounded on its acre of land by trees: maples, ginkgoes, cryptomerias. We learned later that white mountain lilies bloomed in profusion in the spring, azaleas in the summer, and that maples turned crimson in the fall. At the edge of the property was a precipice overlooking the Inari ("Fox God") River and across to mountains where the pointed, shrine-topped peak of Toyama ("Outside" Mountain) stood out. The house was open to the garden with sliding *shoji,* some of paper, others of glass, which could be parted wide to let the sunshine in or closed to keep *some* of the cold outside.

Our household in 1937 included Ishikawa-san, Beppo Johansen (another language officer), Ming-san and family, and an opinion-ated woman recruited from the neighborhood to do washing and cleaning. She told us about the bell ringer at the Buddhist temple, which, incidentally, owned our land, who heaved his suspended log at the giant hanging bell to mark each two-hour period from eight in the morning until six at night. We should not set our clocks by his ringing, she advised, since he was a little crazy and pulled the log when the spirit moved him. For us, the deep tones of the temple bell were part of our idyll, and the hours they signaled were of no matter.

The winter of 1937 was severe. Snow covered the ground, and long icicles hung down from the protruding eaves. The rough stone lantern in the garden wore a constant white cap. We asked Ming-san to use the icicles to make ice cream. He looked at us in consternation: "Ice cream in winter!" The unhappy groans from the kitchen, as he ground the crank of the old-fashioned freezer, were audible in the living room. Ishikawa-san remembered the episode, and years later informed us that Japanese now ate ice cream in wintertime!

Our tutor lived at the nearby Kanaya Hotel, established in 1872. We studied with him until one, then took walks in the woods and trips to the hills in the afternoons. We discovered not far from our house, near a three-hundred-year-old stone path, lined with towering cryptomeria trees and leading up to the red-lacquered Takio shrine, the Waterfall of the White Thread. I could not dream then how this thin, splashing cascade would come to represent the Japanese thread in my life and how many times in later years I would watch it, sensing its cool beauty. We did not know then that Kami Akamon would become the symbol of our life in Japan.

Reluctantly leaving Nikkō in early spring, we moved to Kyoto, Japan's 1,100-year-old capital of "peace and tranquility." We knew we could never be officially resident in Kyoto, where no American consular representation was established, so this would be our only chance to live in the center of Japan's traditional culture.

Each day in Kyoto we would walk to a different part of the city and pay respects to a different shrine, temple, pagoda, garden, waterfall, or a quiet, leafy glen. One of my favorite places was Kiyomizu-dera, "the Temple of Pure Water," in the southeastern part of the city, hugging Higashi-yama, "the East Mountain." The temple is built on a hill with a protruding platform, sustained by an enormous web of great timbers, like scaffolding, overlooking the deep valley with the panorama of the city in the distance. Below, a jet of water from the mountainside forms a waterfall under which pilgrims would bathe while chanting prayers; the colder the weather and the icier the water, the more efficacious the supplication.

Twice in history Kiyomizu temple was associated with critical Japanese decisions, both disastrous. At the end of the sixteenth century, Toyotomi Hideyoshi, one of the architects of Japan's unity, went to Kiyomizu to seek solace after the death of a beloved son. As he stood on the terrace looking toward the western sky, he is said to have exclaimed to an attendant, "A great man ought to employ his army beyond ten thousand miles and not give way to sorrow." Hideyoshi then launched his ambitious campaign to conquer Korea and China, which ended in utter failure for Japan and planted ineradicable outrage among the Koreans. Nearly two and a half centuries later, in October 1941, General Tōjō Hideki and Prime Minister Konoye Fumimaro were discussing the prospects of war with the United States. Tōjō said, "A time may come in a man's life when he must shut his eyes and jump off the veranda of Kiyomizu temple." Konoye replied that an individual could do this, but for someone who shouldered the responsibility for a nation with 2,600 years of history, it would be impossible. Tōjō's jump, when it came, brought tragedy that even Konoye could not have sensed.

The China Affair began with the skirmish at the Marco Polo Bridge in North China on July 7, 1937. We were then spending the summer at Lake Nojiri, an exhilarating mountain resort in Nagano prefecture on the way to the Japan Sea. It was there we heard the news of the death in a bombing raid on Shanghai of Robert Reischauer, already a well-known scholar of great promise and the elder brother of Edwin O. Reischauer, whom we had come to know well in Kyoto. Before long, the burst of telegraphic traffic generated by the China war overwhelmed the embassy code room, which called for help. As a result, we language officers were torn from our books and our mountains to do emergency code duty in Tokyo. This was boring but intense work. With the gray and brown codes, which soon became compromised, it was a matter of looking up words in books, but a more highly classified strip-cipher method involved matching and pasting, which was tedious and eyestraining. The more sophisticated and more secure machines came later.

Our first child, Dorothy Louise, was born in Kyoto in the Year of the Tiger, when the cherry blossoms were at their height. The day, April 3, was a national holiday, *Jimmu Tennō-sai,* the death date of

Japan's first emperor who, according to the *Chronicle of Ancient Things (Kojiki)* passed away at the hearty old age of 127, in 585 B.C. Later, our son, Donald Kenneth, made his debut in Tokyo. In Japanese tradition, Kyoto is a woman's town, while Tokyo is for men. A Japanese saying, which I repeat whenever I meet a Japanese, expresses the ideal combination; "A Kyoto girl and a Tokyo boy" (*"Kyō onna, Azuma otoko"*).

The language study ended in early 1938, and I was assigned to my first consular post, Osaka. We tried to continue living in our beloved Kyoto, not a long commuting distance, but the technicalities of the bureaucracy prevented it, and instead we found a house in Ashiya, between Kobe and Osaka, also a long daily commute from the office, but in a different direction. In those days—and still today—very few foreigners ever lived in Osaka, a dirty, crowded, sprawling industrial metropolis of more than three million inhabitants.

The Osaka consulate general introduced me to the demands of my chosen profession. Already a foreign service officer for two years, I had yet to do a day of strictly official work. The serene life of a student, with only the ever-absorbing mysteries of the Japanese method of communication to challenge my endurance and imagination, had spoiled me for office routine. But the shock had to come. I learned the duties of a vice-consul. I issued invoices—every shipment to the United States had to have an invoice signed by a consular officer. I made out passports—the Kansai ("Western Japan") had an unusually large population of American citizens, many of Japanese ancestry—there was at least one town in Hiroshima prefecture dubbed Amerika mura ("America town") by its citizens. I issued visas—the consul has the authority to grant or deny entrance to the United States; the tears, the agonies, the pleas, the ruses, and the deceptions all make visa work a very human, nerve-racking, and conscience-searing responsibility. I made out documents for ship's captains and investigated sailors who had got drunk or jumped ship.

And then I wrote reports—on hides and skins, the market for machine tools (unlimited), and on cases of copyright and patent infringement (Japanese often copied American trademarks). Trying to pry out information about the state of heavy industry in Osaka was, in 1938, like trying to steal the emperor's sword, mirror, and jewel. But brash and ambitious as I was, and anxious to try out my new store of Japanese, I knocked on company doors, asked lists of questions, and learned precious little about Osaka's production of big machines. The State Department, however, glad to receive *any* report with heavy industry in the title, gave me an "excellent" for my effort. The worst task was to prepare the monthly accounts. I remember with revulsion those long sheets of lined paper, extending over the length of my desk, on which every yen, sen, dollar, and cent had to be recorded in the right column, with the right addition and the right subtraction at the right place. Then I had to count the money in the tin cashbox and the fee stamps in their drawer, and somehow make what I found in the box and the drawer jibe with those mixed-up numbers on the sheets. Being five yen short was a prolonged and terrifying agony, especially if the inspector was about to arrive.

Then I discovered Chikamatsu. Someone told me that this seventeenth-century playwright was the Shakespeare of Japan, that he had been born in Osaka, and that the Bunraku Puppet Theater in Osaka produced his plays.

Chikamatsu had lived in the latter part of the seventeenth and the early years of the eighteenth century, in the Genroku period, the golden age of Japanese popular literature, theater, and art.

Chikamatsu became my escape from the boredom of the office routine and from the barriers and tensions of 1938 Japan. I joined the Chikamatsu Study Society, which met every month at the Hōmyōji temple, where one of several of Chikamatsu's tombs could be found. Presiding over the society was Kitani Hōgin, one of those Japanese living national treasures (although the Japanese were not so designating individuals at the time) who dedicate an entire lifetime to perfecting one art. For Kitani-sensei, Chikamatsu was life. He had edited the complete works of the playwright and knew the last detail of every text. In 1938 I was one of the few foreigners to show an interest in Chikamatsu. The first Sunday I attended a meeting of the study society, I was ushered into a huge tatami room in the temple precincts, where the Japanese members, all in kimono, were sitting in normal fashion on the floor. My gaze suddenly stopped in the middle of the room where, towering above the kneeling group, there was one straight wooden chair. I was motioned toward it. Somehow, with much deferent bowing and gesturing and mumbling of what I hoped were polite expressions of humility, I succeeded in getting the chair removed, insisting that I could tuck myself on the floor along with everybody else.

The puppet theater was a revelation, a marvel of technical skill, refinement of expression, and perfection of coordination—of gesture and movement, of action, words, and sound. To someone who has never seen a performance, it seems impossible that the puppeteers, three of whom manipulate each doll—three-quarters life size—can vanish in the mind of the beholder so that only the puppets remain, their humanness more convincing than their reality. Chikamatsu himself put it well when he discussed the theatrical art as lying in the "slender margin between the real and the unreal." "It is unreal," he wrote, "and yet it is not unreal; it is real, and yet it is not real. Entertainment lies between the two."

Like so many arts in Japan, the medium of puppetry is perfectionism incarnate. Traditionally, the puppeteer entered his profession as a boy; his first task was to manipulate the feet; as he gained experience he graduated to the left arm; and finally, in his mature years, as the culmination of his career, he was entrusted with the right arm and the head.

The leading puppeteer at that time was Yoshida Eizō, whom I met backstage at the Bunraku-za. Eizō, with his thin face, sunken cheeks, missing teeth, and close-cropped head, impressed me as an ancient one although he was only sixty at the time. He had entered the Bunraku at the age of twelve and deplored animatedly the new compulsory education law that would require boys to spend eight, instead of six years, in school before they could start a career. To start working with puppets after fifteen years of age was much too late.

The puppet art requires the perfect union of five men: the three puppeteers, the reciter, and the samisen player. The samisen is the banjolike, three-stringed instrument that accompanies the action, expressing by its agitated strumming, plaintive plucking, or jubilant twanging, the changing emotions of the puppets. The reciter is, however, the key to the performance. He takes all the parts and gives a running commentary on the action. I also met at the Bunraku-za the leading reciter, Tsudaiyu I, who told me about his art. Feodor Chaliapin, the world-renowned Russian baritone, had just visited Japan and had met and discussed with Tsudaiyu their respective professions. Tsudaiyu was pleased to discover that for both the great singer and for himself, tones came from the abdomen. "But," added Tsudaiyu with open pride, but no touch of arrogance, "Chaliapin has only to open his mouth and let the tones come out. My art is much more difficult. I must express the feelings and emotions of hundreds of different personalities—men, women, the young, the old, villains, heroes, children—and I must portray the whole scale of human passions." While talking with me, Tsudaiyu illustrated what he meant by reciting snatches from the puppet plays.

Among Chikamatsu's numerous plays was one being presented at the Bunraku-za which offered yet another illumination of Japanese ideas of life and death: *The Love Suicides at Amijima* (Net Island). I talked to Professor Kitani about it and decided to try my hand at translation. This would bring surcease from visas, passports, and drunken sailors, as well as from the gloomy portents of war, which continually forced themselves upon our consciousness. The love-suicide theme was a popular one with playwrights of the Genroku period, and Chikamatsu was the master of the genre. The story shocks the moral standards of our Western heritage but the writing was so beautiful and the emotions, as lived by the puppets on the stage, so poignant that I became absorbed in the challenge of trying to render this classic prose, filled with untranslatable allusions and plays-on-words, into understandable English.

The plot was simple. Jihei, a paper dealer with a wife and two children, falls in love with a courtesan of the gay quarter, Koharu. Their love presents an insoluble dilemma: he must either renounce her or desert his family for her. His adoring wife, Osan, is conscious of the unfolding tragedy; her husband is squandering the family fortune and neglecting his business to finance his philanderings with Koharu. Understanding her husband's feelings and ready to sacrifice everything for him, Osan prepares to sell her own prized kimonos so that he can ransom Koharu from the house where she is indentured. Finally Jihei and Koharu see that suicide is the only way out of their dilemma and take the long walk over the myriad bridges that cross the Yodo River in central Osaka. Jihei asks his beloved, "But why do we grieve? Though in this world we could not live together, in our life to come—and in the future's future and until far beyond that future, shall we remain united. That we might share one fate, have I each summer copied parts of sutras, the scripture of great mercy and compassion, of the lotus of the wonderful law." Finally, they reach Daichō temple by the waters of a stream where they carry out their vows of death. He prays, "My fate is within the lotus—*Namu Amida Butsu.*" Then he kills her with his sword and hangs himself in the stream. The play concludes: "In the morning fishermen going to their work see through the meshes of their nets: 'Someone has died! Someone has died! Come! Come!'

"From voice to voice the tale is spread and tears fill eyes that a love-suicide has come about at Net Island, where caught in nets of vows, two lovers found salvation in Nirvana."

The Love Suicides at Amijima, as so many of the other domestic tragedies of Chikamatsu, was presumably based on fact, and in 1939 and 1940 most of the places named in the play still existed in Osaka. A bronze plaque on a modern building commemorated the site of the teahouse where Jihei and Koharu kept their tryst. One could still walk to the temple where the suicide had taken place.

With Kitani-sensei's advice and assistance, the translation was finally finished, but by that time it was the spring of 1940 and I was transferred from Osaka to Tokyo where more pressing duties took me away from Chikamatsu and his love suicides.

Personal happiness provided a kind of immunity to the growing tensions in relations between Japan and the United States against a background of impending war in Europe. In 1939, after three years in Japan, we returned to the United States for home leave. Alex Johnson and I thought it would be an educational experience to return to Japan by way of Europe and the Trans-Siberian Railroad. When we appealed to the powers at the State Department for permission, Loy Henderson, then in charge of Soviet affairs, thought it a splendid idea, a unique opportunity. The chiefs of the Far Eastern Division, Stanley K. Hornbeck and Maxwell Hamilton, were far less enthusiastic. What if war should break out while we were en route? This risk of unknown danger only fired our enthusiasm. But our timid, bureaucratically cautious bosses prevailed, and we missed the once-in-a-lifetime adventure of traversing Europe on the eve of war. Instead, I was sent temporarily to Taiwan, which was militarized for a possible southward advance and therefore known as Japan's "aircraft carrier pointed south." I was to take charge of the one-man consulate which the U.S. government maintained in the capital city of Taihoku, later to be known by its Chinese name, Taipei.

3

Taiwan 1939

Terry's Guide to the Japanese Empire Including Korea and Formosa 1928 enticed the curious visitor to Ilha Formosa ("the beautiful isle"), as the sixteenth-century Portuguese adventurers called it, or Taiwan ("terraced bay"), as it became known to the Chinese and Japanese:

> The island is one of rare beauty and charm; a bizarre blend of civilization and savagery; of snow-clad mountains and the lush vegetation of the semi-tropics; of the sixteenth century Orient and the twentieth century Occident. In one respect it offers the blasé traveller an unusual thrill—that of hob-nobbing with savage head-hunters who secretly covet the visitor's head but are prevented from taking it unless the traveller is willing.

By 1939, when I saw it as vice-consul, Taiwan had been ruled by Japan for forty-four years and out of a total population of nearly six million, more than one hundred thousand were Japanese. The guidebook's headhunters, or Takasago tribes, as they were more euphemistically called after an old Japanese designation of Taiwan, numbered some one hundred and fifty thousand and inhabited the more remote mountain areas.

Taiwan was Japan's first colonial experiment. Wrested from China after war in 1895, the island was to be a model of how Japanese could govern and assimilate the Chinese. It would contribute to Japan's rice bowl and to Japanese appetites for sugar and tropical fruits; it would be a beautiful object of Japan's beneficent rule. In 1939 Taiwan was becoming the staging area for Japan's southward advance. The navy regarded it as a special preserve; its southern port of Takao (now Kaohsiung) was a key in the navy's plans. The Japanese saw the Taiwan experiment as a pattern for Japan's mission to bring "sincerity" to mainland Chinese. Their success in transforming Formosan Chinese into true imperial subjects would demonstrate the benefits to be bestowed when the new order, the Co-prosperity Sphere, became established in East Asia. A few high-minded Japanese truly believed in Japan's civilizing mission and were convinced that the great Japanese empire could confer the advantages of its achievements since the Meiji restoration on the less privileged peoples of Asia, for the mutual profit of both the Japanese and the other Asians. To live in Formosa in 1939 was to sense this complex generation of motives and forces—venal, idealistic, contradictory, and incompatible. The Japanese were forcing the Chinese to be Japanese; the military was winning ascendancy, and World War II was about to start in Europe.

Assignment as vice-consul to Taihoku (now Taipei), the capital of Taiwan, was considered before the war to be the penance every Japanese language officer had to do at some time. Taihoku was a hardship post, where service counted as time and a half toward retirement. During the summer months Taihoku's semitropical climate was hot and humid, with temperatures averaging about ninety degrees for days on end. The annual rainfall at Keelung, the port just eighteen miles from the capital, was 289 inches, and I came to feel that it couldn't be much less in Taihoku. The American doctor at the mission hospital warned that human energy in Taiwan was diminished by a third; you had to work harder to obtain your required oxygen. After I had been at the post for a while, I decided it wasn't as bad as its reputation. We had those creaking, turning ceiling fans in the offices, and beautiful beaches were not too far away. The fall and winter months brought cool weather, and also typhoons (about six a year). But climate was a small part of the environment.

For one thing, being in charge of your own one-man post was a heady experience for a young "egg diplomat," still unhatched, as the Japanese used to call us. The consulate building, an imposing two-story stucco structure with a pillared portico and a walled garden around it, was situated on Taihoku's main thoroughfare, which led up to the Taiwan Shrine on the hill, the principal object for patriotic devotion by the citizenry. The offices were on the ground floor, and living quarters were upstairs. Figuratively, I could slide down the banister and immediately begin to officiate as the one American vice-consul. I had four employees to boss: Matsuo Chūhei, the Japanese chief clerk, who had already worked for the American government for twenty-three years, and who knew everything about the office that was to be known; and three Formosan Chinese—Chin, who did typing, filing, and office odd jobs; Ong Bok Seng, the rickshaw puller; and the gardener-messenger, whom we called Ueki-san. Government transportation was the official rickshaw which Bok Seng pulled.

The consular corps consisted of the British consul, a stiff, protocol-conscious civil servant, who lived in an imperious, renovated seventeenth-century Dutch fort at Tamsui, on the sea about thirteen miles from Taihoku; the Italian consul, a pale, tubercular, intense professor of literature at Taihoku University; the Netherlands consul, who in real life was a bright, enthusiastic English businessman working for the Rising Sun Oil Company, a subsidiary of Shell; and me. The small foreign community also included several well-seasoned British tea merchants, representatives of trade and oil companies, and a few missionaries, mostly Canadian. My American constituents, who for protection had to look to their consul, in other words, to me, were engaged in business, missions, or education.

A social center for part of the tiny foreign community—not the missionaries—was the Twatutia Club, named after the old foreign settlement in Taihoku, which I believed at the time to be the oldest foreign club in that part of Asia. Boasting all of twelve members, the Twatutia Club was housed in an ancient brick building surrounded by a weedy garden. The library walls were lined with hundreds of old books exuding the musty, mildewed leather smell which ancient, undusted, unread tomes possess. The tile-and-brick floors were uneven. Bits of plaster occasionally wafted downward from the ceiling and exploded silently in puffs of dust as they broke on the floor. The Chinese caretaker-bartender looked as old as the building. One ironclad rule prevailed: no woman was ever allowed to enter the bar.

The two senior pillars of the foreign community were Francis Hogg and "Chibbie" Orr, both British tea merchants who spent the tea season in Taiwan and the rest of the year in England. They were the presiding elders of the Twatutia Club. Clinging tightly to their Victorian standards, they deplored the rush of modernity and remained solid, genial defenders of Britain's colonial empire on the eve of its last moment of glory. Francis Hogg, whose circumference almost equaled his height, lived in one of the rambling, thick-walled Chinese houses that provided the living quarters of the China-coasters. He still ventilated his vast dining room by the punkah, the wide strip of cloth suspended from the ceiling over the table that was agitated gently back and forth by the patient Chinese coolie who sat just outside the door, holding his finger, or his foot, on the attached string. When, during the long lunch, the motion of the punkah would slow drowsily to a stop, Francis would shout out, and the punkah would be impelled by the suddenly awakened menial into immediate, spasmodic jerks. This western, foreign fringe of some fifty people lived apart from the society of the islanders, glimpsing it distortedly through contacts with servants, middlemen, and the ubiquitous Japanese police.

I spent the first two months alone in Taihoku; we oversolicitously thought the heat would be bad for the baby. The social life was generally confined to foreigners; there was little opportunity, in the gathering tensions of Japan's war in China to meet either Japanese or Formosans except in official business circumstances.

The consulate was a sleepy little office. There was not much official business: shipments of tea and camphor to invoice, and consular services (visas, passports, notarials) to perform, but the American community was small and its interests limited. This left time for travel, always under police surveillance, and for reporting. I became interested in the history of Taiwan, in the nature of the Japanese administration of the island, and in its growing importance to Japan's southward advance policy.

The first humans to visit Taiwan probably arrived two thousand or more years ago and were Malayan or Indonesian peoples. Proximity encouraged Chinese pirates and fishermen to touch at its coast, and Japanese seafarers found the island at an early date. Old Chinese records, which refer to Taiwan as Liu-ch'iu, the name for the Ryukyus (Okinawa), date from the seventh century. The Portuguese discovered and named Formosa around 1557, and, during the succeeding centuries of exploration and discovery, Spanish and Dutch ships came to the island. Some of these Westerners met unfriendly and discouraging receptions from the native inhabitants. Nevertheless, the undaunted Dutch, in 1622, established themselves in forts and for thirty-eight years maintained one of the most profitable bases in Asia for their East Indies Company.

In 1680 a romantic trader-adventurer known to westerners as Coxinga, who had built up his own sea power fighting China's Ch'ing rulers, invaded Formosa and captured it from the Dutch. Coxinga, born in Nagasaki of a Japanese mother and a Chinese merchant prince who had supported the Ming Dynasty, was educated in Nanking and fell heir to his father's mercantile empire and military prowess. Coxinga, as a part-Japanese, romantic adventurer, became a legend in Japan. His dramatic exploits served Chikamatsu as inspiration for one of his most popular and finest period plays, *The Battles of Coxinga,* first performed in 1715, when it enjoyed a then-unprecedented run of seventeen months.

Coxinga lived only a year after the Dutch had surrendered to him, but his successors held Taiwan for another two decades until they, in turn, gave in to superior Manchu forces from the Chinese mainland. Chinese rule then lasted until 1895, when Meiji Japan defeated China and brought Taiwan into the fledgling Japanese empire. Recording this event ten years later, a Japanese historian recalled with unembarrassed chauvinism the legacy of Coxinga, "... Thus the island, which China had torn from Coxinga's descendants by intrigue, bribery and brute force, passed again into the hands of the Japanese, in whose veins flows the same blood as filled those of Coxinga."

Migration to Taiwan from the Chinese mainland was almost continuous in spite of a temporary ban by the Ch'ing government. The population, a few thousand in 1600, increased to two million by 1895. Most of the first Chinese came from Canton and its vicinity; later settlers originated in Fukien province just across the Formosa strait and were to form the majority of the inhabitants. Periodic troubles arose during the two hundred years of Chinese administration, between the Chinese and the aborigines, and between the two Chinese groups from Kwangtung and Fukien. Li Hung-chang, the Chinese negotiator at the peace conference that ended Sino–Japanese hostilities, warned the Japanese that administration of the island would cause them no small difficulties, not only because the people "were deeply addicted to the vicious habit of opium-smoking," but also because "it is not an uncommon thing for the people of Formosa to rise and murder their officials." Troubles did, indeed, eventuate, including the proclamation of two short-lived democratic republics of Formosa by groups of open opponents of Japanese rule. For six months, the Japanese contended with armed warfare and, although the guerrilla resistance was suppressed by 1902, four revolts occurred between 1907 and 1928.

Late on the scene, and thus without colonial experience, the Meiji government could fall back on no traditions or precedents in ruling a foreign people. At the age of forty-one, Gotō Shimpei, later baron and subsequently count, one of the amazing coterie of young, able Meiji leaders who brought the Japanese nation into the mainstream of modern life, was appointed civil administrator of Taiwan under Governor General Kodama Gentarō in 1898. Seized with a prideful zeal to make this first colonial experiment of an Asian nation succeed, Gotō set about with General Kodama to institute a major series of reforms in security, law, and land. He deplored the handicaps of Japan as a colonial power, its lack of knowledge and preparation, particularly the absence of a Japanese religion as an inspirational and civilizing influence. He observed that the colonies of other nations had invariably prospered due to the driving force of religion. Japan had no such colonizing tool. As it turned out, of course, Japan's substitute for religion became nationalism, which, by the 1930s, had captured imperial policy.

The first requirement of the colony's new overlords was law and order. Once active and incipient revolt among the Formosan Chinese had been eliminated, the problem of the Takasago people remained. Divided into nine tribes and differing in physical characteristics, languages, and customs, these so-called savages lived in very primitive societies, mainly in the mountain districts on the eastern side of the island. Their vaunted headhunting proclivities inspired caution and awe. Members of the Taiyal tribe of the northern mountains looked upon headhunting as "the most glorious thing in their life." The taking of a human head was required for rites and ceremonies, to decide a dispute (the one who gets the head wins), and as a young man's formal admission into the company of adults. In 1939 the Taiwanese government managed its native sons through a network of five thousand policemen stationed at five hundred locations in the savage areas. The local Japanese police officer was not only guardian of the law but supervised the economy, education, health, and welfare of his charges, as well as being their doctor, agricultural adviser, and religious guide—in short, their father-confessor as well as their disciplinarian. Policy was supposed to combine suppression and development, severity and kindness, and force was generously used.

A headhunting spree had occurred as recently as October of 1930 at Musha, a mountain village in the center of the island not far from Sun and Moon Lake. Although the censored reports were confused at the time, some 1,500 aborigines, armed with spears, cudgels, and swords, suddenly pounced upon Japanese police stations and in the resulting melee killed more than 200 people, of whom about 130 were Japanese. "Many bodies were headless," read a news report of the event. Police retaliated swiftly and brutally, mobilizing airplanes and armed troops to bombard and execute the fleeing rebels. The causes—although no one ever knew for sure—were resentment over the low wages paid for requisitioned coolie labor, anger over love affairs between Japanese policemen and native girls, and the indiscriminate felling of trees near native villages during construction of the hydroelectric project at Sun and Moon Lake. The

British-edited *Japan Weekly Chronicle* pointed to the police as the central object of hatred by the rebels, proving "how complete has been the failure of the method of pacification used." The editorial, courageously for that moment in history, asserted that the only way to deal with the aborigines was to leave them undisturbed. "But this is not Japanese policy . . . the Chinese seem to be able to compromise; with the Japanese it is a case of either living according to Japanese ideas or perishing."

By 1939 the aborigines were living quietly in their still-primitive villages. Government authorities had sought to modernize them by encouraging them to come down to the plains and farm the land. Movement from mountain to lowland had been underway, and by 1939 more than 40 percent of the total number of aborigines were classified as plains dwellers. Their passage toward civilization was measured as a maturation process; certain of the tribes won designation as "half-ripened," while only more time and effort could bring the final accolade—"fully ripened."

In numerous trips into the interior, we frequently met these true natives of Taiwan on mountain paths. Most of them were of the Taiyal tribe, formerly spread over the mountainous northern half of the island. With high cheekbones and regular features, they were frequently tattooed, the women with blue diagonal lines on their cheeks, the men with black marks on their foreheads, chins, and, sometimes, arms and legs. They walked erect, with handsome dignity. They would stop, bow respectfully, and greet us in carefully articulated Japanese. It was hard to associate the ferocity of headhunting with such serene docility. On several occasions we were escorted into aboriginal villages, always by their police guardians. The huts were entered through low doors, the interiors were blackened by smoke and the air was acrid. Always on the shore of Sun and Moon Lake the villagers would dance delightedly for visitors; a group of girls would surround a large, flat, circular stone embedded in the ground, and each, holding a tall, wooden pole, would beat on the stone, producing an orchestrated harmony of complex vibrating rhythms and tones.

Japan's first objective was to make its new colony a successful enterprise, and in this the government succeeded. Within less than ten years, Taiwan was completely self-supporting and was soon to be called the most profitable place for a Japanese investor. The island supplied Japan with her needs for sugar, and its two-crop season contributed handsomely to the insatiable Japanese appetite for rice; rice and sugar made up 70 percent of Taiwan's exports. Government monopolies of camphor, opium, salt, tobacco, and liquor added to official revenues. Tropical fruits, bananas and pineapples, flourished. On the eve of the Pacific war half of the island's population was engaged in farming; the total area under cultivation had multiplied two and a half times since the beginning of the century. After 1930, 90 percent of Taiwan's foreign trade was carried on with the mother country, including Manchuria and Korea. Unmistakably, Taiwan existed for the benefit of Japan and the Japanese.

Mindful of the Meiji slogan, "rich country, strong military," its early administrators regarded Taiwan both as "the greatest and richest treasurehouse of the Empire" and as a fortified bastion between the Ryukyu Islands and the Philippines, a stepping stone to the South Seas. Coxinga had boasted that he "would lay a bridge of boats from Formosa to Manila" and subdue the Philippine Islands. Thinking of similar possibilities, General Kodama, in 1901, purportedly suggested Taiwan as a springboard for attacks on French possessions in Southeast Asia. By the 1930s Japanese interest in the raw materials of the South Seas had intensified. Moreover, warfare in China and the evolving concept of a Japanese "civilizing" mission for other Asians put new emphasis on a strategic role for Taiwan. On the fortieth anniversary of Japanese rule (1935), civilian officials met to discuss the relationship of Taiwan to the policy of southward advance. This policy took on more concrete meaning when, on February 10, 1939, the Japanese navy occupied Hainan Island off the coast of South China, and on March 30 took over the Spratly Islands near Indochina. Both of these territories became wards of the Taiwanese government. By this time the navy had already begun to dominate the affairs of Taiwan; from 1936 until the end of the Pacific war, every governor-general of the island was an active admiral. The basic points of view of Japan's army and navy differed on the direction of imperial thrust. The army believed that the greatest threat came from the north and that, therefore, Japan must confront Russia before undertaking a destined southward march. The navy, on the other hand, judged the riches of the south to deserve immediate attention, particularly since only sea power could gain them for the empire.

I discovered upon my arrival in Taiwan in June of 1939 that Admiral Kobayashi Seizō, already governor-general for three years, had announced that the three elements of his policy would be (1) the Japanization of the Taiwanese, which he called *kominka,* literally "turning-into-imperial-subjects"; (2) the industrialization of Taiwan; and (3) expansion to the South Seas. It therefore seemed natural to focus on these problems during my brief assignment to Taihoku and, within the limits of censorship and surveillance, to report my findings to the State Department.

Of Admiral Kobayashi's three policies, the one that interested me most (and that he placed first on his list) was *kominka.* From the beginning of the Japanese colonial period, administrators had emphasized education for the purpose of assimilating the Taiwanese as Japanese subjects. Recognizing communication to be the first principle of assimilation, authorities decided that Formosans must speak Japanese. According to the Taiwan Yearbook of 1939, 2.5 million Taiwanese, or about 45 percent of the population, were then speakers of Japanese (surely an inflated figure, since the criteria for determining who spoke Japanese were flexible, to say the least). In the course of trips and walks, I found that I could communicate in Japanese mainly with schoolchildren and teenagers; relatively few Formosan Chinese adults could go beyond polite phrases of greeting. The aborigines learned Japanese more readily than did the Chinese, and even today many Takasago families have preserved their use of the language. To enforce Japanese learning, only Japanese was permitted in banks and government offices. If a Formosan customer addressed a Formosan clerk, he was required to use Japanese or to call an interpreter. Insignia bearing the legend THIS HOUSEHOLD SPEAKS JAPANESE were placed over the doors of designated Formosan homes, and signs were prevalent in buses and public places reading SPEAK ONLY THE NATIONAL LANGUAGE. An official in a press interview called for the mobilization of the motherland of Taiwan under the slogan: "Raise our children in Japanese." He added that to use Taiwanese "did not befit a 'soldier of the Imperial Army.'" In towns and villages the police maintained blue books, in which the names of all Japanese speakers were recorded. Whenever a villager applied for a license, permit, or wished to take up any legal, personal, or business matter with the authorities, reference would invariably be made to the blue book, and if the applicant's name was not listed, his chances for satisfaction of his claim diminished rapidly.

As for general education, about half the eligible Taiwanese children were in primary schools. The Japanese far outnumbered the Taiwanese in secondary and higher institutions. Out of the 580 students in the university, only 178 were Formosan, and of these, 148 were studying medicine, the only field in which they could expect to compete with the Japanese. Thus education was directed toward instructing the younger generation in the Japanese language but not toward higher studies, which might encourage undue ambition and too aggressive leadership.

Kominka, which began as an official movement only with the China Affair in 1937, was designed to permeate every aspect of Formosan life. It was intended, as the word itself suggested, to advance the Taiwanese people to the enviable status of true Japanese nationals. To accomplish this, traditional Chinese language, culture, religion, and custom had to be eradicated and replaced by a Japanese value system. Instruction in the schools was in Japanese, and all publications in Chinese—books, magazines, and newspapers—were prohibited. Chinese theatrical performances and puppet plays were outlawed.

We did succeed in obtaining official permission for the production of a puppet show, with all of its dash and cacophonous orchestral accompaniment, in our living room in the consular residence with an audience strictly limited to a few foreign friends. The puppeteer-reciters and the musicians put their hearts and souls into this performance, so unique was the opportunity to display their skills. Probably never had the puppet emperors and court officials gesticulated with such abandon nor had the classical songs and sounds reverberated with such penetrating emotion as on that night in our living room. Our baby awoke in terror, as the actors warmed to their tales. Since the handmade, colorfully costumed, hand puppets were outlawed, some of us acquired a few for our personal collections. Chinese festivals were likewise prohibited, and the wearing of Chinese costumes was discouraged. The Japanese fixed upon the cloth buttons and the traditional Chinese gown as symbols of disobedience, and policemen often took delight in publicly snipping the buttons from the gown of an unsuspecting Taiwanese.

Kominka was designed, among other things, to cultivate the national spirit, spread knowledge of the national language (Japanese), and develop the psyche as well as the physique of imperial subjects. To accomplish these ends, mobilization programs were established throughout the island, with emphasis on youth groups, or the *Seinendan,* which in 1938 had a reported 113,000 members.

If the Japanese pioneers of colonialism worried about their own lack of religion as a civilizing tool, they were at the same time unnerved at the "bewildering tangle of corrupt superstition" that they found in the confusing Formosan mixture of Confucianism, Taoism, and Buddhism. A Japanese historian, writing in 1905, quoted with approbation the horrified revulsion of a long-time resident Canadian missionary, expressed in a flight of self-righteous eloquence, "For twenty-three years I have been in the midst of heathenism, brushing against its priests and people and I know the poison of its sweets, the fatal flash of its light, and the stagnant foetor of its life."

Temples were still prevalent in 1939, and the old religious practices persisted. Once we visited Shinangū, a temple in the countryside not far from Taihoku. With some poetic license, I described at the time the "thousands of steps" that led up the mountain, rising "from landing to landing, until at last you perceive the grandiose brick balustrades (four of them) curving up to the temple itself.... The fog was heavy and covered the tops of the mountains but the tier upon tier of paddy fields cut in their ornate figurings and lush green, with brown farmers' huts set here and there, made the landscape picture." We looked down from the plaza before the *betsu-den,* a building where worshipers could spend the night, and out into the green rice, where hundreds of *shiro-sagi* ("white herons") darted in flashes and arcs of stark white against the green background. We learned from the priests that those who wish to know their future sleep in the *betsu-den* where their dreams are the answers to their prayers. They also clasp in their hands pieces of wood resembling ears or kidneys, which they throw to the floor while mumbling prayers. If the sticks fall in a certain pattern, the prayer is answered; if not, the believer repeats the process until the right pattern appears and satisfaction is obtained. A comfortable religion, it seemed to me.

The Japanese blatantly attempted to force the Taiwanese to turn into imperial subjects. This was to be the religion Baron Gotō missed. The cult of the emperor was to take the place of the Formosan gods. Ingeniously, the Japanese rationalized their campaign against traditional religion and their moves to destroy the Taoist temples: the ancient Formosan deities had immediately become Japanese when Japan took over the island. Thus, the Taiwanese had for forty years unknowingly worshiped Japanese gods in Chinese temples. At dedication ceremonies for a new Shintō shrine, the old Taoist guardians were duly recognized before their images were carted off to Taihoku Imperial University's Department of Literature and Politics. *Taiwan Nichi-Nichi Shimpo,* unofficial organ of the Government-General, solemnly proclaimed the established doctrine:

> Gods have a vast world view and can see into the future a thousand, ten thousand years. At the time Taiwan became Japanese, the temple gods, with foresight, determined the course which the people of Taiwan must follow. From the standpoint of protecting the race, they determined that this people should live as a Japanese people, that this was the road they must travel. Thus the gods, protecting the Formosan people as Japanese, have built the society which exists today.

Foreign observers in 1939 were skeptical about the success of *kominka.* I talked about it with Kuna-san, our Taiwanese major-domo who ran the household, a bright, handsome, young man with keen ambitions for the future. He conceded that Formosan youths had lost the old religion of their parents and had not yet accepted "in their hearts" the teachings of *yamato-damashii,* the "soul of Japan." They were thus left with no moral staff to cling to. For down-to-earth economic reasons they did not resist Japanese indoctrination. The young Formosan admired the vitality of the industrialized, expanded Japan to which he owed allegiance, whereas his view of his ancestral land across the strait was filtered through the propaganda screen of the empire's "holy war." Yet he remained a second-class citizen in his homeland.

The real purposes of *kominka* were to wipe out any trace of potentially rebellious Chinese or Formosan nationalism, to facilitate the smooth administration of the colony, to mobilize support and participation in Japan's economic and military penetration of China and the south, and to establish a pattern that could be followed by Japan in China.

All vestiges of home-rule movements disappeared in the early 1930s. A system of local "self-government" was established in 1935, and the second election in the history of Taiwan was held during my service in Taihoku, in November 1939. But elections were limited indeed. Half the local legislators were appointed, and most of these were Japanese. Taiwanese were minorities in provincial and municipal assemblies. The press played up the fact that a village with only eight Japanese inhabitants had nevertheless overwhelmingly elected a Japanese to be their representative. Provincial governors, mayors, and town and village heads were all appointed by the governor-general, and all acts of local assemblies were subject to the veto power. Town and village councils could do no more than submit opinions to government offices on request and were subject to dissolution at any time by the governor-general.

The Japanese utilized the traditional Chinese system of administration to mobilize support for the war in China. Organized groups of households could stage parades and meetings quickly and efficiently throughout the island. They prodded farmers to produce assigned amounts of hay for army horses, to grow castor beans (designated a patriotic crop, since their oil could be used by airplanes), and to send water buffalo off to war, each with a red ribbon tied around its middle.

The scheme with greatest appeal to Japanese leaders facing

onerous and expanding responsibilities on the continent was the use of Formosan personnel for the occupation and administration of China. Provided they were in truth Japanese with Chinese faces, their contribution could be uniquely valuable. Already by 1939 Taiwanese had been sent to areas under Japanese military occupation, to participate in Japan's southward advance, but never for combat. Trust did not extend that far. According to Governor-General Kobayashi, by May of 1939, nearly 10,000 Formosans had been sent to the front to do manual work for the Japanese army; 8,000 were in Amoy, Canton and Hainan Island, of whom 850 were actively cooperating in medical, educational, and other fields. Their knowledge of both Chinese and Japanese was a special advantage. More than thirty years later, a Taiwanese looked back on those of his compatriots who had been mobilized for war duty as part of an "appendix of human resources," who, expecting to escape injustices known at home, found themselves also second-class citizens on the China mainland and in the South Seas, where they, in turn, took on the aspects of "threatening tigers" and applied to those in their power the same insults and discrimination that they themselves had suffered in Taiwan.

The governor-general had stated that since agriculture had already been developed to a saturation point, the island's economic future rested in industrialization. The value of manufactures had increased sharply after 1935 and, by 1939, was beginning to surpass that of agriculture. Government policy was designed to speed this process, in order to enhance Taiwan's position as a viable unit in the Japan–China–Manchukuo economic bloc.

Coal and waterpower were the colony's precious assets, although, as in Japan, substantial quantities of oil, iron, and other critical minerals were lacking. When James Davidson wrote in 1903 that "the island possesses a supply of fuel almost unlimited," he was thinking only of coal, the production of which in 1938 amounted to more than two million tons. The Japanese then anticipated that coal in the ground was sufficient for a hundred years, even with an annual consumption of several million tons. (This estimate was reconfirmed in 1974, when Taiwan's coal production reached four million tons, and reserves were still estimated to last at least another fifty years.) Three and a half tons of gold and ten thousand tons of copper were being mined in 1939, and local production met a tenth of the island's oil requirements. Concerned from the beginning with the development of electric-power generation, Japan's administration established in 1919 the Taiwan Electric Power Company and built both thermal and hydroelectric power plants in succeeding years. The most ambitious undertaking was the dam and power plant located near Sun and Moon Lake in the center of the island. In 1937, J. P. Morgan & Co. floated a $22 million bond issue, which together with a Japanese issue, financed the dam and power station, both designed by the American J. G. White Engineering Corporation. Additional hydroelectric projects were completed or were under way when war broke out.

Industrialization, Governor-General Kobayashi's second policy, was to link the Taiwanese economy closely to Japan's developing interests in south China and Southeast Asia. Since Japan controlled the mandated islands of the Pacific, she could bring raw materials, such as bauxite, to Taiwan for processing. An important aluminum plant was operating in Takao (present-day Kaohsiung) in 1939, and a second one was projected for the developing port of Karenkō (Hualien) on the east coast. Stimulated by military demands, the government was planning to produce pig iron and steel out of raw materials from Indochina, nickel and cobalt out of ore from Rhodesia, and magnesium out of magnesite from Manchuria. Much activity was going on in the development of port facilities, new industrial areas, and in the improvement of transportation and communications. In carrying out their ambitious programs of industrialization, Taiwan's rulers faced serious problems, not only the lack of oil and iron, but an undeveloped transportation system and a critical shortage of labor. The aborigines might have been recruited, but no one regarded them as competent for factory labor. Out of forty-five thousand members of the Ami tribe in the Karenkō district, only a thousand were considered fit workers. Their efficiency was estimated to be only 60 percent of that of the Formosan Chinese.

Taiwan was best suited for light industry, such as textiles, yet as Japan's economy shifted into a military gear, the island was being forced to meet the demands of production for war. The shift toward industrialization and the construction of a base for industry (parts, power plants, and processing) gave the Chinese a significant start when they took over Taiwan at the end of the war. It is incorrect to affirm, as does a 1974 publication of the Institute of International Relations in Taipei, that "the Japanese made no serious effort to industrialize the island during their occupation period."

We learned least about Japan's third ojective in Taiwan, the southward advance. Military secrets were zealously guarded, particularly from the eyes of foreigners, and in those days America had no Central Intelligence Agency. Incidents had been frequent. A secretary in the military attaché's office in Tokyo, traveling on a ship that touched at a Taiwanese port, had been detained and interrogated. While I was vice-consul, the wife of an American tea merchant was slapped while walking near a railroad track in what was apparently a prohibited area. Police surveillance was naïvely assiduous but a challenge to a conscientious foreign service officer. We tried to see as much of the island as we could. At inns, a policeman would invariably occupy the adjoining room; although in plainclothes, he made no pretense of hiding his identity. We would draw him into conversation, which was good for our Japanese, and he could record a mass of trivia to report to his superiors. His assignment to watch us must have been so dull that I am sure he welcomed a chance to drink sake and chat with the suspicious foreigners.

I decided to visit Takao, the largest naval base near the southern tip of the island. Uniformed representatives of four security services—the regular police, military police *(kenpeitai)*, army, and navy—met and scrutinized me at the railway station. They firmly informed me that I might pay my respects at the Shintō shrine, located on top of a hill overlooking the harbor, but I would not be allowed to take photographs. The admonition was unnecessary since I have always been a hopeless photographer and seldom carry a camera. With appropriate escorts, I was driven up to the shrine, well marked by conspicuous No Photography signs, and driven back to the station to take the next train north. My hosts were taciturn and not about to describe the wonders of Takao. The view from the shrine was scenically impressive, but I was too far away to count or identify warships at anchor.

There were other brushes with the police. One day a furtive young Japanese slinked into my office to whisper an offer to sell to the U.S. government the plans of the naval base at Maizuru on the coast of the Japan Sea. Fortunately, even with my inexperience, I was not duped by this crude proposal and, summoning up suitable disdain and outrage, I summarily rejected the proffered intelligence. From my navy friends I later learned that the Japanese secret police frequently dispatched agents to offer undercover services or plans of naval bases in order to compromise American officials.

During my stay on Taiwan I decided to ask Ishikawa Daisuke, the student who had helped me with Japanese in Tokyo and Kyoto, to come to Taihoku. Only many years later did he tell me of his experiences in reaching Taiwan. He was first interrogated by the special police *(tokkō)* in Tokyo, who grilled him about his association with me. He told them he had helped me with Japanese, including assistance in translating Chikamatsu's *The Love Suicides at Amijima.* The police had apparently never heard of Chikamatsu or his plays and were incensed, "This is no time to talk about stories of lovers' suicides! Don't you know that Japan is fighting on the China mainland? We are at war!" Naïvely, Ishikawa had brought in his luggage a secondhand copy of Karl Marx's *Das Kapital,* which was of course promptly confiscated. I doubt if he ever read it; he never showed the slightest interest in communism. After instructing him to report unusual happenings, the Tokyo police let him proceed. At Shimonoseki, where he was to board a ship for Taiwan, Ishikawa was detained for two days, part of the time in a hot, damp cell full of bedbugs. On the boat he had a police escort; he told me he felt "like a VIP." He was not molested in Taiwan and returned to Tokyo without further trouble.

One of my more pleasurable experiences in Taiwan was making the acquaintance of Chiba Shin-ichi, the representative of the Japanese Foreign Office assigned to the Taiwan colonial government. He was an experienced diplomat with great personal charm and integrity but was restricted in what he could do. He had served in Poland, Spain, and France; his French was fluent, and we spoke it instead of Japanese or English. I had appealed to him at the time of the slapping incident. He had been understanding and sympathetic and had promised an investigation, but his final answer was, *"Il n'y a rien à faire."* Since the lady in question had suffered no injury, except to pride, and knowing the embassy's preoccupation with hundreds of more serious affronts being continually perpetrated on Americans in China, I hesitated to add another cause célèbre to the bulging dossiers in Tokyo and decided to let my little slapping incident die quietly.

One evening Chiba invited me to have dinner with him in a good Japanese restaurant, and the two of us sat for a long time on the tatami, drinking sake and arguing about Japan and Asia and the growing tensions between our countries. Such a circumstance was rare in that time and place; few Japanese officials would associate informally and socially with Americans or talk frankly and earnestly about serious questions. Chiba was a nationalist but also an idealist; he believed that Japan had a mission to fulfill in East Asia, a mission that would bring advantages to Asians as well as to Japanese. He did not condemn Japan's military actions, but I sensed that he regarded them as regrettably necessary to the achievement of Japan's higher aims. I could not accept a justification of Japanese brutality in China, but I respected Chiba's vision of an economically advanced Japan sharing benefits with other Asians and his conviction that such could be possible were Western powers not to intervene.

Twenty-one years later, during the celebrations for the independence of Nigeria, I met in Lagos a young Japanese foreign service officer who was a member of his country's delegation to the ceremonies. When I learned his name was Chiba, I asked him whether by any chance he was related to the foreign office representative I had known in Taiwan in 1939. The young man replied, "He was my father." I told Chiba Kazuo, the son, that I would always remember his father with esteem and affection; he had been considerate to me at a most difficult period in Japanese-American relations. The young Chiba looked at me and said softly, "I will burn a stick of incense for you in my father's honor when I return to Tokyo."

Later I heard the rest of his father's story. In 1941 Chiba Shin-ichi had been appointed minister to Portugal and, afterward, chief of mission in German-occupied Paris. Recalled to Tokyo in late 1943, he and his wife were in Istanbul awaiting a Soviet transit visa when, on February 28, 1945, Turkey declared war on the Axis. They were interned in Ankara and on the day of the issuance of the Potsdam Proclamation calling on Japan to surrender, July 26, 1945, together they committed suicide. Chiba Kazuo, whom I was to meet many times during his foreign service career, in Tokyo, Washington, and once in Moscow, wrote of his father:

> His strong samurai nationalism tempered by immersion in Europe during the between-war years of depression and slow recovery, then firsthand observation of Japan's economic struggles in an increasingly hostile world environment to free trade, convinced him of Japan's destiny to be the breaker of Western hegemony in East Asia. Yet his cultivated and sensitive albeit manly mind apparently saw Japan's role in terms of a *mission civilisatrice,* not raw and naked physical domination and exploitation.

Their son believed that the self-sacrifice of his father and mother came about largely from despair over their beloved country's fate and from his father's "profound sense of historical and personal doom together with his remembered samurai ethos." I believe there were many Japanese who held this idealistic conception of their country's destiny.

The one serious case in Taiwan was the arrest, after I left my assignment to Taihoku, of our faithful and loyal Matsuo Chūhei. For years, the consulate had prepared for Washington a routine report, among many boring, nonessential, routine reports, on the market for American automobiles in Taiwan. The answer could have been written in one word: none. But the bureaucracy demanded statistics on cars and dealers. Matsuo had checked his sources and prepared the report each year. Knowing that any commercial information was sensitive, he first cleared his action with the military police and, while I was still in Taihoku, made his usual inquiries but, as could be expected, failed to get any information. He was arrested in May 1940, accused of industrial espionage, and in September sentenced to three years' imprisonment. Nothing the State Department or the embassy could do, including Ambassador Grew's personal intervention with a succession of foreign ministers, moved the Japanese authorities. Only after his sentencing did the U.S. government learn for the first time the true reason for Matsuo's arrest and punishment.

It developed that since 1938 the Japanese military police had pressed him to deliver to them the consulate's code book (to which he did not have access), office keys, records, and safe combinations. Matsuo repeatedly refused these requests. He maintained unflinchingly his conviction that his loyalty as a Japanese subject did not license him to betray the employer he had served during a great part of his adult life. By recorded testimony of every one of the fifteen principal officers for whom Matsuo had worked since he entered the Taihoku consulate in 1917, he had been a totally dedicated, conscientious, high-principled employee of the United States.

Matsuo came out of prison at the height of the war, in 1943, broken in health and fearing that he would be liquidated should the Americans invade Taiwan. Fortunately, there was no invasion and Matsuo survived. The State Department tried to extend him what help was possible; his wife and six children were supported by the U.S. government during the war, money being transmitted through the Swiss who looked after American interests, and he was reemployed at the war's end. He died in 1952. Perhaps his character is best summed up in two poems he wrote while in prison. One referred to his red prison garb:

> The red uniform I wear for the sake of my country and
> for the sake of the world
> Is in my mind of gold brocade.

The other expressed his loyalty to the two countries he believed he had served:

If ties between Japan and the United States can be
  made stronger
My own sacrifice is as nothing.

In Europe, Munich had happened in 1938, Hitler and Mussolini were brandishing their swords, and millions of men were under arms waiting for the spark that everyone knew would ignite the war. Ribbentrop and Molotov signed their nonaggression pact in August while I was in Taiwan. For me personally, the war was far away, but I understood the feelings of my two very good British friends in Taihoku, John Hurden and Francis Culpin, both working for the Rising Sun Petroleum Company. John and I (he a bachelor and my wife not yet in Taiwan) spent the weekend of September 2 at Sun and Moon Lake. Looking out from the veranda of the Green Hotel over the windless waters of the lake, the mountains on the other side becoming shadowy as dusk advanced, we felt spellbound by peace and silence. Early the next morning, Sunday, September 3, we heard a voice speaking English downstairs. John recognized it. "King George!" We leaped down the steps to listen, through the sputtering static of shortwave radio, to King George of England announcing solemnly, "We are at war."

4

On the Way to War 1940

While I was energetically probing into *kominka* and serenely swimming in the rhythmic waters off Tamsui, the great world outside our little island was rocked with tremors portending bigger quakes to come. The China Affair was entering its third year. Japanese troops were on the march on the continent, their successes celebrated in their homeland by lantern parades, mass rallies, and ever more frequent send-offs at the railway stations for soldiers departing for the China front. Americans had been shocked two years before by the bombing of the U.S. gunboat *Panay* and by the rape of Nanking, unknown to the Japanese people at the time. China's capital had been moved twice by 1938, first to Hankow and then to Chungking, where it remained until 1945. Japanese troops had engaged the Russians in two trials of strength, at Changkufeng, near the Manchukuo–Korea–USSR border, in the summer of 1938, and at Nomonhan, near the Mongolian People's Republic, in May 1939. The Russians showed their superiority in armor and tactics in both encounters, but especially at Nomonhan, and sobered the Japanese, who had fifty thousand casualties at Nomonhan, into second thoughts about their advance to the north.

The leitmotiv of the Japanese–American relationship during the decade of the 1930s was the dissonant, contrapuntal theme of principles and power. From the time of John Hay's famous 1900 proclamation to the nations with interests in China, American policy in East Asia had been dedicated to the principles of the Open Door policy and the preservation of the territorial and administrative integrity of China. Yet, it was always clear, as George F. Kennan so accurately observed, that "in no instance would we be prepared to use force to compel compliance with these principles."

The 1922 Nine Power Treaty embedded in its first article an agreement to respect the sovereignty, independence, and territorial and administrative integrity of China. The word was *respect* and not *defend.* The United States was not legally bound to defend these principles against all comers. Ten years later, following Japan's subjugation of Manchuria and attack on Shanghai, Henry L. Stimson, then secretary of state, telephoned (an unusual method of trans-Atlantic communication in those days) to Sir John Simon, the British foreign secretary, to persuade him to join in citing Japan as a violator of the Nine Power Treaty. Economic sanctions and embargoes were discussed in the United States, and Stimson favored them, but he was sure that invocation of the treaty was necessary to spur Congress into action. The British refused to cooperate. Stimson's failure meant that the forum of discussion remained with the powerless League of Nations in Geneva. The only results achieved there, in February 1933, were unanimous condemnation of Japan (Siam abstained and Japan opposed), a walkout from the League by the Japanese Foreign Minister Matsuoka Yōsuke and his delegation, and the recommended nonrecognition of the state of Manchukuo. Four years later when the Manchurian Incident *(Manshu jiken)* had expanded into the China Affair *(Shina Jihen),* the League of Nations again met, again condemned Japan, and, again, failed to stop the war.

One early October morning in 1937, while I was assigned to the embassy for temporary code duty, Duncan Laing, in charge of administration, came out of the ambassador's office looking solemn. He had just handed over to Grew the morning's telegraphic take from Washington, including the report of President Franklin D. Roosevelt's speech advocating a "quarantine" of aggressors. "The Old Man is sure upset," Laing reported; "he said when he read the speech, 'There goes everything I have tried to accomplish in my entire mission to Japan.'" Even Secretary of State Cordell Hull, whose associates in the State Department had drafted the speech, without, however, the quarantine idea which was a last-minute FDR brainstorm, was shocked and guessed that his educational campaign for international cooperation had been set back six months. American reaction to the quarantine idea was explosive, with public outcries for impeachment of the president and quickly organized signature campaigns petitioning to keep the United States out of war. Hull believed in firmness and a stern policy toward Japan, but the U.S. had to be led carefully out of its isolationist mood. "Quarantining" the Japanese "patient," no matter how ridden with aggression-disease he might be, was too drastic. Japan must first be exposed before the world as an aggressor. Resolutions were cheap and riskless. The day after the speech, October 6, 1937, the League of Nations pronounced Japan's actions in China to be in violation of the Nine Power Treaty and the Kellogg-Briand Pact, and the U.S. government declared its support of the League's resolution.

Grew's view of Japanese–American relations differed frequently from that of Washington. With his New England heritage, no one possessed convictions deeper than his over moral principles and the rights and wrongs of human actions. Yet he had lived in Japan long enough to question whether all the rules for dealing with European nations strictly applied in Asia and, also, whether the high-minded policies being pursued by the United States were always based on cold appraisals of the realities of power. In 1936 Grew had recognized that moral and legal principles would not deter Japan in China; furthermore, Japan's interests in the area were vital, while those of the United States were peripheral. He had great faith in diplomacy, his chosen profession, and he thought that we should "explore every avenue which might lead to some variety of political agreement with Japan."

But it was in the fall of the next year, the time of the quarantine speech and Grew's spontaneous burst of feeling, that—as Waldo Heinrichs has noted in his perceptive biography of the ambassador— the first open disagreement between the embassy and the Roosevelt

Administration occurred. In August Grew had recommended that we seek to solidify our relations with Japan, for which he was soundly rebuked in a personal cable from Hull. The ambassador saw the mobilization of world opinion against Japan as a negation of his own efforts to improve the Japanese–American relationship, in the full knowledge that we had no intention of backing our morals and our ethics with force. Grew believed very simply, as he wrote in 1939, that the principal duties of the embassy were to protect and promote American interests to the maximum and to maintain and further good relations between Japan and the United States. He was convinced beyond any doubt that a Japanese–American war would be a catastrophe that could be avoided. Until the very last minute, he clung to that belief, although with diminishing confidence as time went on.

In Washington both Secretary of State Cordell Hull, and his chief advisor on Far Eastern affairs, Dr. Stanley K. Hornbeck, were personally biased in favor of China and morally outraged over Japan's continuing expansion on the Asian continent. Hull confessed that when he took office in February 1933 he had "two points on the Far East firmly in mind." One was the American interest in maintaining China's independence and preventing Japan's overlord-ship of the entire Far East. The other was the definite conviction that Japan had no intention whatsoever of honoring treaties and would regulate her conduct by the opportunities of the moment. He described Japan's diplomatic record as "that of a highway robber."

Stanley Hornbeck, whose Far Eastern experience had consisted of four-and-a-half years' teaching in government schools in China, had early on developed critical judgments of the Japanese. In a study written in 1914, he had concluded that Japan had already made a sham of the Open Door and was threatening China's integrity. In a book written two years later, he defended the American Monroe Doctrine ("defensive") and our acquisition of the Philippines ("accidental") but denounced Japan's professed Monroe Doctrine ("aggressive") and annexation of Korea ("premeditated"). Hornbeck brought to the job of chief of the Division of Far Eastern Affairs in the Department of State, a position he assumed in 1928, a first-class mind, a good academic reputation, and a conviction that

Japan was a threat to peace and that the United States should forge a special relationship with China.

This relationship with China was the crux of our troubles with Japan. Throughout the marathon of talks, which engaged Japanese and Americans during the spring, summer, and fall of 1941, ran the recurring theme of the American side, Cordell Hull's "four principles." First handed to the Japanese ambassador by Hull, on April 16, they were (1) respect for the territorial integrity and the sovereignty of each and all nations; (2) support for the principle of noninterference in the internal affairs of other countries; (3) support of the principle of equality, including equality of commercial opportunity; and (4) nondisturbance of the status quo in the Pacific except as the status quo may be altered by peaceful means. The word *China* did not appear in the principles, but China was the understood beneficiary of each one of these four goals. The United States was proclaiming in words the liberation of China.

My family had left Taiwan ahead of me and returned to our home between Osaka and Kobe in the fall of 1939. I arranged to return on Christmas Eve like Santa Claus, bearing gifts. When I learned that I was soon to be transferred to the embassy in Tokyo, I hurried to finish my translation of Chikamatsu's play and to study more intensively for the optional examination in Japanese, which was supposed to bring an extra promotion if I passed it.

Ambassador Grew, on leave in the United States during most of that summer, was startled by the depth of anti-Japanese feeling which he found among Americans. It is difficult to comprehend how isolated we were in the embassy in those days before airplanes had become international buses, when only the most urgent business was reserved for the telegram and when one reached rarely for the trans-Pacific telephone, remembering that someone else doubtless listened to every word. Fingering archives today reveals the long and leisurely dispatches and personal letters which floated back and forth across the ocean, taking weeks in transit. A November idea would get a January or February response.

Only by being present in the United States was Grew able to discover how universal had been American approval of the denunciation of our commercial treaty with Japan and to sense how much the sentiment for an embargo of trade with Japan was mounting among Americans. He feared that his fellow citizens did not understand the implications of their instinctive reactions. He tried to warn them that a policy of sanctions could lead to war.

The Japanese also should be warned, Grew concluded. He felt that we should let them know that the United States would not back down, and to do this "some sort of major operation was necessary." It occurred to him that a public speech would be more effective than one more futile note to the foreign office. The result was the famous "horse's mouth" speech, delivered on October 19, 1939, before the two hundred members of the America-Japan Society, half of them Japanese.

The original draft was prepared in Washington, but Grew worked over it many times, exerting great care to get just the right tone, one which would impress but not embarrass. He believed that "brass tacks" were needed, not "Jovian thunderbolts." In the course of his speech, he argued that the cardinal principles of American policy transcended any purely legalistic approach to foreign affairs. This public emphasis on principle did not seem inconsistent to Grew, who never deserted principles, even when he appealed to Washington for "realism" instead of intransigence in support of principles. The speech was daring for an ambassador and doubly for a Japanese audience. Grew, indeed, spoke from the horse's mouth:

> ... The American people ... have good reason to believe that an effort is being made to establish control, in Japan's own interest, of large areas on the continent of Asia and to impose upon those areas a system of closed economy. It is this thought, added to the effect of the bombings, the indignities, the manifold interference with American rights, that accounts for the attitude of the American people toward Japan today.

The conviction of Grew's Boston accent communicated his deep sincerity.

Many Japanese were shaken by such unusual, unexpectedly direct talk, but they believed this American envoy when he said that he bore neither a dagger nor a dove concealed in his bosom but only a desire to work with all his mind, heart, and strength for Japanese–American friendship. He was encouraged when told that the prime minister and other top leaders of the government had studied the speech carefully and that it had made a "very deep impression" upon them.

On December 1, the embassy reported that "the outlook for the future relations between the United States and Japan does not now appear to be bright." Grew's November diary, which, as usual, incorporated a summary of the month's events, a detailed section of chronologically itemized personal notes, copies of dispatches, paraphrases of telegrams, and an entertainment schedule, listing guests at the residence and the ambassador's social engagements, was not sent from Tokyo until December 23, due to irregularities in pouch mailings. Hornbeck, as usual, read it meticulously, wielding his red pencil generously, in underlinings, exclamation points, question marks, and pithy comments. He found much to disagree with this month.

The ambassador had analyzed American policy, the probability of Japan's defeat, Japan's desiderata, and had posed the question, What do we do bout it? If the two considerations for American policy in the Far East were (1) the fundamental principles of international policy (our respect for legal commitments and expectations that others would respect theirs); and (2) a sense of realism; should we compromise when principles clash with realism, and, if so, how much? Grew believed that "nothing can be more mathematically certain (if anything in international affairs is ever certain) than [the fact that] Japan is not going to respect the territorial and administrative integrity of China, now or in the future, has not the slightest intention of doing so, and could be brought to do so only by complete defeat." Hornbeck crossed out the word *complete* and added at the end of the sentence, "of her Army."

Grew continued, "Observance in practice of the Open Door is and will continue to be a matter of degree governed by expediency, not by principle. Herein lies the point of realism."

To answer the question, Can Japan be defeated? Grew was convinced that, given war in Europe, there was no immediate likelihood that any nation or set of circumstances would inflict defeat on Japan. He envisaged setbacks, pressures, hardships, belt-tightening, but no defeat. He pointed out the characteristics of the Japanese, their samurai do-or-die spirit, their traditional stoicism in the face of earthquakes, hurricanes, floods, epidemics, the blighting of crops, and almost constant wars within and without the country.* "They are inured to hardship," wrote Grew, "and they are inured to regimentation."

Hornbeck objected. To Grew's statement, "of an overwhelming debacle there is little present outlook," he countered, "No. But a squeeze out, a freeze out, perhaps—and definitely possible. No one anywhere, so far as I know, has suggested a 'debacle.' " The majority opinion in the embassy, as Grew stated, rejected the contention that an embargo, even if it embraced total exports and imports to and from Japan, would cause a debacle or would force the Japanese to relinquish their program in China.

Grew listed Japan's fundamental desiderata: (1) strategic protection against Soviet attack, particularly in Manchuria; (2) economic security through control of raw materials in China; and (3) eradication of anti-Japanese and Communist activities and propaganda in China. Hornbeck in his bold red pencil added, "(4) Power, profit, empire."

Finally the ambassador confronted the dilemma of principle versus realism. He saw two possible courses, one, "complete intransigence"; that is, the refusal to negotiate a new treaty of commerce and navigation and the imposition of an embargo. Hornbeck, his anger showing in the breadth of his red mark, crossed out *intransigence*. Then Grew posed his "wiser course," that the United States recognize no compromise with the Nine Power Treaty but aim for good relations with Japan. These would be contingent on concrete evidence, such as respect for American rights and a cessation of the bombings. Then the United States would enter into negotiations for a new treaty with the understanding that ratification would depend on future developments. In the meantime

---

* *The latter statement was an exaggeration. Japan enjoyed two hundred and fifty years of relative peace during the Tokugawa period (1616–1868).*

the question of an embargo would be held in abeyance. SKH (the familiar initials known so well to all who worked in the State Department's Far Eastern Division) vigorously penciled in the margin, "We should *not* say this."

This exchange between Grew and Hornbeck goes to the heart of the issue finally resolved only by Japanese bombs on Pearl Harbor. Grew believed that some concessions had to be made to realism, that Japan was determined to win influence in China and would not be deterred by the termination of a treaty or by an embargo. He saw an intransigent attitude on our part as driving Japan toward war. "In the long run, we ourselves also shall have much to gain by avoiding a break with Japan, much to lose if a break occurs. . . . Intransigence on our part will accelerate the trend toward such a break."

SKH again crossed out *intransigence*. Hornbeck was sure that one could freeze out Japan although he never drew a blueprint for action. Commenting on the embassy's dispatch cited above, he complained, "Takes no account of other (than embargo on exports) methods of bringing pressure. Assumes that Japanese army cannot be pushed or frozen out of China."

Finally, Mr. Grew returned to his article of faith, the efficacy of diplomacy. He concluded his dispatch, "There will be time enough to speak of sanctions when the resources of diplomacy have been exhausted. At the moment of this writing, those resources have not yet been exhausted. By nature not a defeatist, I believe that those resources may yet win the day."

The State Department did not accept Grew's recommendations and was not prepared to negotiate a new treaty. Hornbeck wanted to "put the screws on the Japanese," and the ambassador had to turn the screw by telling the Tokyo government that the discriminatory treatment accorded American interests in China constituted a serious obstacle to the conclusion of a new agreement with Japan. Grew saw Admiral Nomura Kichisaburō, then foreign minister, on December 22. Nomura was crushed, according to Grew, and did not, as had been his custom, see the ambassador to the door. Two days before, Grew had written in his diary, "The important thing is to avoid an open rebuff to Admiral Nomura's patient efforts."

On New Year's Eve Joe Grew seemed less immediately concerned over war with Japan; from his particularly murky crystal ball, he prophesied that before the decade of the 1940s was out, Great Britain, France, Germany, and Japan would unite to fight the Soviet Union! He was sure that Hitler, however, would not be on board at that time. He signed off, "A Happy New Year to all."

By March of 1940 I was in Tokyo, looking for a summer beach house for the family and for a house in Tokyo for the next two or three years. I also took my examinations, in Japanese economics and politics and in the Japanese language, with written and oral translations to and from Japanese and English. I passed and won my promotion to the exalted rank of foreign service officer, Class 8. Until then I had been unclassified and on probation, but I could not complain since I had galloped from unclassified C through B and A in four years and was now ready to become a regular, which happened on August 1. Of course, there were still seven steps ahead, since Class 8 was the lowest.

My first job in the embassy was in the commercial section, where I wrote reports on lumber, hides and skins (*always* hides and skins), and whatever other commodities might come my way. Our offices were in the basement of the chancery, while the enviable political officers dwelt in a superior realm of their own, clustered around the ambassador on the second floor.

Every day the news was bad, both from China and from Europe. The embassy's pile of protests over Japanese injuries to American citizens and properties grew; the ambassador had, in November, presented to Foreign Minister Nomura a compilation of the embassy's written representations since the China conflict had begun. There were 382, of which 256 had never been acknowledged by the Japanese government.

One day the telephone rang. "Grew speaking. Will you come up to see me?" I mumbled a gasping assent and trembled all the way up the stairs. He asked me if I would like to come up to the political section to do press reporting. Overjoyed, I thanked him and thus gained my real promotion, to the upper regions of the embassy. I read the daily Japanese newspapers, supervised the two Japanese translators in an adjacent office, did some summaries of editorials myself, and wrote the daily press telegrams to the department. When the Japanese Foreign Office *did* reply to our notes of protest, I frequently did the translations. The formal style of Japanese then used for official correspondence, *sōrōbun*, was very different from the conversational language; it took a knack to figure out the inverted word order and to render the substance into accurate and understandable English. Fortunately, Naganuma's course had included a brief introduction to *sōrōbun*. As time went on, I had a chance to draft political telegrams and voluntary reports—then a feature of foreign service duty—on subjects that interested me.

The year 1940 was a year of consolidation for Japan, both internally and externally. In order to better effect the spiritual mobilization of the nation, which had been a slogan since the beginning of the war in China, the Japanese government sponsored the formation of a new structure, designed to forge the unity of the government, Diet, and people. The last political party was dissolved in August, and the New Structure became, therefore, Japan's unique brand of authoritarianism. While this was happening inside the country, Hitler's dazzling blitzkrieg was elating Japanese supporters of the Axis and, in September, the emperor, by imperial rescript, associated his country with Germany and Italy in the Tripartite Pact. While Japan tightened controls on the civilian population and charted a new course in international affairs, Ambassador Grew changed his viewpoint on the future of developing Japanese–American relations. His so-called green-light telegram of September 12 made diplomatic history.

It was this swift succession of events that those of us privileged to serve in the American embassy in Tokyo witnessed during 1940. I say *witnessed* advisedly, because it became increasingly clear and frustrating as time passed that there were serious limitations, both in Tokyo and Washington, on what we could do to influence the course of Japanese–American relations.

At the beginning of the year the ambassador found some grounds for optimism. On January 16, Admiral Yonai Mitsumasa became prime minister, which, in Grew's view, was good news. He was to feel later that we missed perhaps a last chance in not more aggressively seeking an agreement with Japan during Yonai's administration. It was Yonai who consistently sought to avoid war with the United States and who, on January 14, assured Grew that he need have no further anxiety that Japan would join an alliance with Germany.

The date of the termination of the treaty of commerce and navigation, January 26, passed, in Grew's words, "without too many local fireworks." Yet this was the date that, in November, he had thought might usher in "the most critical period in the entire history of American–Japanese relations." By February he was still confident that Japanese efforts toward conciliation were "on an upward curve and should be encouraged, not rebuffed." And in March he believed that the futility of the war in China was "steadily coming home to the great majority of thinking Japanese."

We in the embassy tried to follow the developing New Structure movement *(Shintaisei Undō)* designed to establish a kind of Japanese-style totalitarian regime to replace the dissolved political parties. The idea of a Shōwa Restoration had inspired reformers of both the right and the left ever since the murders of February 26, 1936. The first person to draft a plan for a New Structure was Ozaki Hotsumi, a journalist, consultant to Prince Konoye, China researcher, and, as became known later, a close collaborator of Richard Sorge, the notorious Soviet spy. Ozaki had a Leninist model in mind; he and several liberal intellectuals who discussed the movement during Konoye's first administration (1937–39) thought of it as a bulwark against militaristic domination. Ultranationalists joined in the effort for their own opposite reasons and succeeded in turning the New Structure into a project for national consolidation. Prince Konoye resigned his position in the privy council in June 1940 to head the movement, and in October it was formally inaugurated as the Imperial Rule Assistance Association (IRAA or Yokusan Kai). Konoye, who became prime minister on July 22, denied any intention of establishing a one-party state or a Nazi-type totalitarian regime. The Diet continued to exist, since the constitution had not been abridged, and a very vigorous debate ensued within its chambers on the character and merits of the IRAA. As reported in an embassy dispatch written in February 1941, some members called the organization Red and compared it to the Soviet system; others jumped on the provision that the prime minister should lead the association and accused the government of setting up a Hitler-type führer system. Ozaki Yukio, the old fighter for democracy and founding member of Japan's parliament, likened the IRAA to an illegitimate son who usurps the prerogatives of his father (the Diet). The IRAA never did, in fact, become a Nazi-type party. Japan's leaders tried to produce through it a defense state by organizing the citizenry and controlling education and public opinion. But its essence was propaganda, not politics. As the embassy defined it, "What is evolving is totalitarianism, if one insists on using that term, but it will be totalitarianism *sui generis*."

Since those of us living in Tokyo at the time were able to maintain very few contacts with knowledgeable Japanese, our impressions of the New Structure and the IRAA came largely from lively newspaper accounts and from our observations of daily life. Under the all-embracing rubric of the New Structure came regulations to close dance halls, to designate geishas as "national policy girls," to abolish golf trophies, to stop the sale of jazz records, to remove telephones from concubines' houses, to close theaters producing plays "not in keeping with the times," to ban off-color jokes (stories must have spiritual value), to *gradually* eliminate brothels, and to prohibit the painting of nudes. Foreign influences were to be rooted out: signs in English and in Roman letters disappeared; baseball terminology, which from the beginning had been English, was translated into awkward Japanese equivalents; and bars called Miss Tiger and Black Cat were ordered to change their names.

On May 27 the members of the embassy staff gathered to celebrate Ambassador Grew's sixtieth birthday in the apartment of Marshall Green, then the ambassador's young private secretary, later to rise high in the foreign service. Eugene Dooman, the embassy's second in command, delivered a congratulatory speech, interlaced with classical quotations and recitations of poetry. The ambassador went him one better, quoting more Latin sentiments and declaiming longer poems. Both loved their Latin phrases and set examples in the frequency with which their dispatches were laden with *pari passu, sui generis, fidus Achates, infra dignitatem,* and the like. Junior officers, intent on getting good marks in efficiency reports, vied with each other to work into their dispatches an eye-arresting Latin phrase. Grew always thought that "twenty-seven," his birthdate, was a lucky number for him and throughout his diary are references to the coincidences of good fortune on days numbered twenty-seven. His feelings on his sixtieth birthday were sensitively reflected in the verse by the T'ang dynasty poet, Po Chu-i, which he inserted in his diary for the month of May 1940:

> Between thirty and forty one is distracted by the Five Lusts;
> Between seventy and eighty one is a prey to a hundred diseases.
> But from sixty to seventy one is free from all ills;
> Calm and still, the heart enjoys rest.
> I have put behind me love and greed; I have done with
>   Profit and Fame;
> I am still short of illness and decay and far from decrepit age.
> Strength of limb I still possess to seek the rivers and hills;
> Still my heart has high spirits to listen to flutes and strings.
> At leisure I open new wine and taste several cups.
> Mellow, I recall old poems and sing a whole volume!

As spring worked itself into summer there was little time for champagne and poetry. We had for a long time been concerned over Japan's flirtation with the Berlin–Rome Axis, and the accumulating news of Hitlerian triumphs deepened our anxiety. When Admiral Yonai, who had assured Grew that Japan would not join the Axis, resigned and was replaced by Prince Konoye on July 18, there was no rejoicing in the embassy. The ambassador confided to his diary that a typhoon could hardly have more effectually demolished the foundations of Japanese–American relations that had been laid while Yonai was prime minister. He saw the Konoye government as going "hell-bent toward the Axis." Convinced that the United States had missed an opportunity to strengthen the hand of those Japanese who wanted a rapprochement with the United States, Grew was despondent, ". . . Now the process of 'teetering' so often described in my telegrams appears to be over, and all indications point to Japan's having definitely decided to prepare to shape its course toward the totalitarian camp." Hornbeck, with his usual acerbity, underlined twice on his copy the word *over* and put a huge red question mark at the side of the passage. Grew told the State Department that any "talk of principle" would not likely influence Japanese policy at a time when Axis victories in Europe were flaunting such golden opportunities before the eyes of the country's leaders.

By September the embassy had reluctantly come to the conclusion that the time for holding back was over. In his famous green-light telegram, Grew reluctantly recommended the gradual, progressive application of countermeasures against Japan. Of course, a moral embargo on the export of airplanes and aeronautical equipment had been in effect since 1938. Now, contrary to his previous judgments, Grew was prepared to recommend embargoes, but he warned that "drastic" embargoes would likely meet Japanese retaliation. This retaliation, he again reminded Washington, might take the form of a "sudden stroke" by the military. He counseled the U.S. government to face squarely the consequences of any actions it might take. "A firm policy will inevitably involve the risk of war." This time Stanley Hornbeck agreed enthusiastically; he underlined the sentence, wrote "Concur," and added "But it may make greater or make less an already existing risk."

In my foreign service experience, I can think of two telegrams that were landmarks in the policy-making process. One was Grew's green light, the other, George F. Kennan's red light, the latter cabled from Moscow on February 22, 1946. The purposes of the two messages were different but both shook their Washington readers. Grew and Kennan, who in 1946 was in charge of the Moscow embassy, were marking the beginnings of new eras in our relationships with Japan and with the Soviet Union. Grew was abandoning his total reliance on diplomacy and recommending the use of economic force. Kennan was warning that the era of Stalin's wartime cooperation was over and that the very premise of the Soviet system presaged a continuing adversary relationship with the United States. Kennan began his telegram by citing the Soviet contention that the USSR lies in "antagonistic 'capitalist encirclement.'" Japan, in 1940, was lamenting its own encirclement by the ABCD (America, Britain, China, and the Dutch). But Stalin's encirclement was more imaginary than real; Japan's more real than imaginary. Russia's vast resources sufficed for its livelihood, but Japan lived at the mercy of the outside world. *Strangulation* was a word seriously and often used by the propagators of a Greater East Asia Co-Prosperity Sphere, although the idea of a Japan going to war over strangulation seemed senseless to most Americans in 1940. Although comparisons are dangerous, the word had a curious echo to it when Henry Kissinger used it thirty-five years later to hint at the awesome possibility of American armed forces being used to break the strangulation that could choke our access to the oil of the Middle East.

As the September typhoon season ended, gloom deepened in the embassy corridors. Japan joined the Axis on September 27, not a Grew lucky twenty-seven. Pressed by the fiery Matsuoka, Konoye's foreign minister, Japan's leaders took the decision after duly deliberating in the Noh-style,* elliptic, agonizingly calm Japanese manner. Much of the discussion in the Imperial Conference, made up of the top civilian and military leaders of the government, centered on how Japan could withstand war with the United States, should it come, and where she could get oil. All present agreed that oil from the Netherlands East Indies was indispensable and was to be obtained by peaceful means if possible, by force if necessary. While Grew was telling Washington that firmness was the way to deal with the Japanese, Matsuoka was telling his colleagues that firmness was the only way to succeed with the Americans. The conference approved Japan's joining the pact, but Hara Yoshimichi, president of the privy council, plaintively and with excessive sangfroid—since he was discussing the life or death of his country whether he knew it or not—pled only for more time, "Even though a Japanese-American clash may be unavoidable in the end, I hope that sufficient care will be exercised to make sure that it will not come in the near future."

Prince Konoye, writing at the end of the war, defended Japan's joining the Axis in 1940, since at that time Germany and the Soviet Union were on good terms, and it appeared that Germany would control Europe. Japan's hand would be strengthened and a

* *Noh is the classical, slowly moving, stylized Japanese drama.*

settlement of the China Affair facilitated. He confessed that, by 1941, the Axis alliance had become a liability since Germany and the Soviet Union were then at war with each other, and Japan's Axis affiliation hindered an accommodation with the United States and Great Britain. However, the army, according to Konoye, was pro-German in sentiment and insisted on sticking with the Tripartite Pact.

In view of the abnormal situation prevailing in the Far East, the State Department, on October 3, advised American men not required for urgent reasons and the dependents of American citizens in Japan, China, Hong Kong, the Kwantung Leased Territory, Korea, and Formosa, to return to the United States. To set an example, American government officials took the initiative to send their families home. By November most dependents had already obtained passage on the available ships and were on their way. Faced with an indeterminate separation, Dorothy and I decided in early December to have a last look at Peking. We left our children with our dedicated, trustworthy servants and traveled by train and ship to the Chinese port of Taku, where vessels were always getting stuck in the mud when the tide was not just right, then to Tientsin, and finally, to Peking. There we stayed in a small, comfortable old Chinese boarding house, taking rickshaws to see the sights of the city, still beautiful in spite of the swarms of Japanese soldiers and military trucks further filling the already crowded main streets. Our friends in the embassy greeted us with controlled enthusiasm. Their wives and children had all been sent promptly to the United States in compliance with the department's order. To see me, an officer of the Tokyo embassy, which they regarded in some degree as the protagonist of the enemy country, flaunting my wife before their enforced bachelorhood, did not inspire the warmest feelings of welcome.

The foreign service officers who formed the China and Japan services had traditionally lived their separate existences. Except for Korea and Manchuria—where Japanese language officers were needed to deal with the local authorities—few of us ever served in the other's territory. The result was a parochialism that, unfortunately, was not conducive to the broader view of U.S. policy interests. While we from Japan did not defend Japan's actions in China, we thought that we understood some of the reasons motivating Japanese foreign policy. The officers in China, facing daily the vexations of Japanese bureaucratic obstructionism, the stubborn cruelty of the Japanese soldiery, and the ever-accumulating incidents of injury and depredation inflicted upon Americans, their property, and their interests, viewed Japan and the Japanese with indignant antagonism, if not with emotional hatred. Arguments with fellow foreign service officers were long and hot. On this occasion, the chargé d'affaires of the embassy, Bob Smythe, announced that he would deal with our temporary presence in Peking by inserting in the social column of Peking's English-language newspaper an item informing its readers that Mr. and Mrs. Emmerson of the Tokyo embassy were visiting for a few days in Peking but that Mrs. Emmerson and her two children had reservations to sail from Yokohama to the United States on the S. S. *President Coolidge* on January 4, 1941. On this condition, our visit was tolerated.

The oldtime foreign residents of Peking bemoaned the passage of the era before the Japanese came. But we, who had never lived in China, responded with fresh joy to the rhythms of the shouting, trotting rickshaw pullers, the loud cries of the competing hawkers of wares, the confused mixtures of sounds and colors, and the incessant bustle. Bicycling in the early morning to the Temple of Heaven, bargaining in the Street of Jade or in the flea market, dazzled before the Dragon Wall and the Marble Boat—this was head-turning stuff in the days before so many people had become used to easy travel and bored with native markets and exotic sights.

Two events of historic importance to Americans living in Japan occurred in November: the election to a third term of President Franklin D. Roosevelt, and the celebration by the Japanese of the 2,600th anniversary of the founding of their nation. We were invited to an election night dinner by Frank Williams, the embassy's commerical attaché, and his wife; Ambassador and Mrs. Grew were guests of honor. Since Roosevelt's victory was already certain, there was no suspense to the evening. After dinner, the host persuaded me to do my piano act, imitations with variations on "When You and I

Were Young, Maggie," together with "The Three Trees," which even then had become my trademark in the foreign service. Many years later I discovered that I had made Mr. Grew's diary. Under "Entertainments," the item for November 6 reads: "Election dinner at the Williams'—but we knew the result of the election before dinner started and the radio returns were simply addenda. Emmerson did some very clever skits on the piano. He is a serious type and I had no idea that he possessed such a light touch and so much fun and humor." Unsurprisingly, Mr. Grew thought of me as a serious type. I had seen him usually in his study up at the residence whence I delivered telegrams for his approval. Unendowed with the gift of punning, which made Marshall Green famous in the foreign service, I must have been grim, solemn, and abashed when the bushy eyebrows tightened and their owner, deserting momentarily his venerable Corona, applied the ambassadorial pencil to my efforts of the day. For me, it was not a time to josh.

For the subjects of his imperial majesty, the celebration of the 2,600th anniversary of the founding of Japan by its first emperor, Jimmu Tennō, in 660 B.C., was to symbolize the unity of their hundred million hearts in dedication to the national polity and the service of their emperor. We were invited to the great assemblage on the plaza before the imperial palace, in morning coats, silk hats, and long dresses—where fifty thousand invited guests witnessed the ceremonies, which included speeches by the emperor and by Ambassador Grew, as dean of the diplomatic corps. Each guest was given an imperial lunch box, including a bottle of sake and a cup with the imperial crest. No one ate the lunches; we each properly wrapped the food and sake in a crested *furoshiki,* or cloth scarf, and respectfully took the package home.

In December Grew wrote a "Dear Frank" letter to President Roosevelt. He was direct, "It seems to me to be increasingly clear that we are bound to have a showdown someday, and the principal question at issue is whether it is to our advantage to have that showdown sooner or to have it later." He was convinced that under prevailing circumstances no Japanese leader or group of leaders "could reverse the expansionist program and hope to survive." Still, although he conceded that those Japanese who opposed the government's adventures abroad were inarticulate and powerless, he could not entirely repress the irrepressible, his congenital optimism, and in the same letter to the president, Grew glimpsed the possibility of so discrediting the present leadership of Japan that a "regeneration of thought" might occur, which would permit a return to normal Japanese–American relations and lead to a readjustment of the Pacific problem. He returned to his disconsolate mood at the end, however, noting, "This, indeed, is not the Japan we have known and loved."

As in 1939, the ambassador determined he would end the year on a hopeful note. So on New Year's Eve he put aside his anxieties for the future, his conviction that the Japanese would not change the course they had set for themselves, and his premonitions of war, and forced himself to believe that all would come out well in the end. A lover of good music from his youth (he told me he had practiced the piano an hour every day for many years), Grew this night listened to Beethoven's Ninth Symphony broadcast from Tokyo, with obviously imperfect playing and less than desirable broadcast quality, ". . . I can never hear that inspiring 'Ode to Joy' without a degree of inspiration no matter how inadequately it is rendered. It conjures up visions of better things to come. My insuperable optimism leads me to believe that they will come in 1941. This time I believe that good ground for optimism is offered by the facts. Anyway, a Happy New Year!"

The year 1940 ended with the rest of the embassy staff unable, as was the ambassador, to convince ourselves that war would really come. We talked about it among ourselves interminably, agreeing on the British fleet and Britain's victory in the war as essential to American security, and the inevitability of the United States someday doing more for the British. Meanwhile, Japan's war in China continued to contradict American principles and American statements. And Germany and Japan were now allies. Yet war between Japan and the United States seemed then so cataclysmic, so unthinkable, that, although rationally we saw it ahead, in our bones we could not feel that it would ever happen.

5

Tokyo 1941

The American embassy in Tokyo during 1941 was a bachelor establishment. Most of the wives and children had sailed for the United States by the first part of the year, and from June until after Pearl Harbor only Mrs. Grew and the wife of the naval attaché remained. There were ninety-nine of us when we posed for a formal photograph in the embassy courtyard in April. This number included foreign service officers, clerks, secretaries, and Japanese employees.

Eugene Dooman was counselor, second in command, and the ambassador's principal advisor. He was swarthy, pudgy, a BIJ (born in Japan), and by that time one of the most senior Japanese specialists in the service. He spoke fluent Japanese and was positive and sure in his opinions. Grew had great confidence in him and in his judgments. Dooman drafted many of the embassy's telegrams, and the ambassador invariably consulted him before dispatching any messages or making any recommendations to Washington. Fancying himself a gourmet, Dooman took pride in the cuisine prepared in his household and knew the best and most out-of-the-way restaurants in Tokyo and the extraordinary dishes that they could serve. He had a recently imported and expensive Capehart phonograph, at that time the acme in instruments for recorded music, and exulted in treating his after-dinner guests to selections from his rich classical record collection. Like Grew, he respected both the Latin and English languages. He corrected sentences—the words *reportedly* and *contact* (as a noun) were his pet hates—and he liked to remind junior officers that the clarity and accuracy of their drafting should be a source of pride, since someday their handiwork would be displayed before posterity in published State Department documents.

Among the senior officers were Edward S. (Ned) Crocker and Charles E. (Chip) Bohlen. Neither was a Japanese language officer, but both had come to the embassy with sound reputations from their previous posts. Ned Crocker was buoyant, a man of recherché tastes, and with a great zest for living life. After the families had gone, Ned would stop in for a nightcap at any hour on his way home from the late-night parties, which by that time had become epidemic in Tokyo. In a time of serious scarcity and regimented austerity, he was the one who always managed to import odd and palate-titillating delicacies from the best sources in Europe. His exuberance carried him often to the golf course, on one of the earliest trans-Pacific flights of the Pan Am Clippers—just for the ride—and on a boat trip to and from San Francisco when his wife left Japan, to spend a total of only six days in the United States.

Chip had come directly from Moscow and was making his first encounter with the Orient. To our amazement, he found the freedoms and comforts of wartime Japan—harassed as life often was by the amateurish obstructionism of self-important minions of the law—refreshing and exciting in contrast to the grimly closed Soviet society he had left. Since I had a large house and no family with me, I invited him to move in. For ten months we shared the big house at Hirō-chō Go-banchi, which otherwise would have given me only space, silence, and too many imagined echoes of infants' voices. Chip was ebullient, curious about Japan, and always willing to share his inexhaustible fund of uproarious stories and, at a party, his inimitable Russian songs. In addition, I luckily and incidentally received from him an unparalleled course in the enigma-wrapped mystery of the Soviet system.

I was the most junior of the third secretaries, ranking after several experienced and competent Japanese language officers. My job was to watch the press, which, in spite of rigid censorship and control, revealed nuances of opinion and trends in official policy that were discernible in no other way. There was a newspaper for almost every household, although the total countrywide circulation of 11 million would roughly equal that of only one of Tokyo's leading metropolitan dailies today. The repetitious jargon of journalistic writing in 1941 was numbing: the exhortations to patriotic fervor, the encomiums to the holy war, the self-righteous pride in the New Order, the Co-Prosperity Sphere, and the Eight Corners of the Universe under One Roof. Somehow all of these phrases, including those used to depict the ever-bogging war in China—*direction-shift* to mean retreat and *breaking jewel* to mean battle death—seemed to a foreigner more fanciful and more solemnly and pathetically ludicrous when expressed in the stylized lines of the Chinese ideographs. Sophisticated Japanese readers, one knew, pushed away the detritus of official verbiage and were able to perceive some of the realities underneath. One had to try to do likewise, but being of a different culture and having to communicate my findings to a skeptical Washington bureaucracy did not ease the task. Many years later, when I tried to read *Pravda* and *Izvestia* in Moscow, I experienced a similar feeling. Kremlinologists became geniuses at this kind of cryptanalysis.

By this time most of our Japanese relationships, except with officials in the Foreign Office, had been cut. Even our oldest friend, Countess Watanabe, who, in a courageous gesture of friendship, had come to the house to say good-bye to Dorothy, did not get in touch with us now. Nor did we embarrass her by communication. The embassy tended to become an ingrown society. We saw each other at work, and we saw each other outside of work. We stayed late in the office: my telegrams were usually ready to show to the ambassador by 6:00 or 6:30 in the evening, but late developments would extend the hours. And with no waiting wives and children at home, we made our own social life at each other's houses and apartments. Fortunately, most of us had placed generous orders for food and drink with supply houses in San Francisco and Copenhagen so that when shipping stopped, as it did in the summer, we had ample stores to draw on. All of this meant a very frantic, impulsive, and convivial life. I once wrote to Dorothy, "You must yawn at this long recital of social events in Tokyo. They sound inconsequential, especially in view of all that is important, which has been going on. But of course I can't write about that. .... Funny part is that none of us feel any danger or think much about it, except that the hilarity may be a little too hilarious."

We discovered that the word *bever* in Webster's *Unabridged Dictionary* meant "a light repast between meals." This was inspiration enough for the Bever Club, which met promptly at 11:00 o'clock every morning in Ned Crocker's office. He always had special cheeses from Holland or Denmark, sausages or salami, crackers or pumpernickel, and Danish beer. Officers and secretaries, in a very casual impromptu manner, would happen to drop in and be urged to sample the bever. Grew may never have discovered the Bever Club, it being one of those little things an ambassador would prefer not to know, like the fact that almost everyone in the embassy bought yen at favorable rates in China and somehow managed to get them into Japan.

Most of the embassy officers, except me, played golf. Grew loved the game but was not very good at it. He was amused and pleased when his golf became a political barometer. A day on the course, even at a most critical moment, demonstrated calm in the face of storm. When everyone played golf, I found myself in charge of the embassy. One day Houstoun-Boswall, the British chargé d'affaires, panted breathlessly up the stairs of the chancery to discuss with the ambassador a most urgent matter. Grew was out playing golf. Might he then see the counselor? He was out, playing golf. What about a first secretary? All out, playing golf. To his harumphing dismay, Houstoun-Boswall had to bluster his business to me, who earnestly promised to do the necessary and to bring his representation to the highest embassy authority as soon as the golfers returned. Stanley Hornbeck managed to restrain his enthusiasm for the ambassador's golfing propensities. When he read Grew's happy description of the long Memorial Day weekend at Kawana on the Izu peninsula, "We played golf daily ... for four days," he penciled icily alongside his heavy red underlines, "*We* worked."

Embassy officers were slaves to the pouch, our only link with the department, except for telegrams. Normal weekly intervals length-ened as American ship sailings became more irregular. Grew complained to his diary on March 20 that twenty-one pouches had just arrived after a lapse of twenty-nine days, "probably a record." Pouch day, when it came, produced a paroxysm of activity, to meet our deadlines for dispatches, letters, and enclosures. The day after was the letdown—to be spent at golf, on the beach, or in sleep.

The problem was one not only of time but of security. Governments needed to protect their confidential communications. The United States had come a long way from Secretary of State Stimson's indignant and immortal dictum of 1930, "Gentlemen do not read each other's mail." The embassy was never told that, through the system known as MAGIC, top officials in Washington were reading Japan's daily diplomatic and military messages. MAGIC's most spectacular success was the shooting down in April 1943 of Commander in Chief of the Combined Japanese Fleet Admiral Yamamoto Isoroku, whose airplane's location for a certain day and hour was pinpointed by an intercepted message.

Japanese efforts to break American codes have been less publicized than has MAGIC. On August 6 I had dinner at the home of Herbert Norman, a Canadian foreign service officer whom I had met because of our mutual interests in Japanese history and politics. Norman had been born in Japan of missionary parents and was a known scholar of things Japanese. He had published an excellent book, which had already earned him a sound reputation, *Japan's Emergence as a Modern State.* One of the guests that evening was Ushiba Tomohiko, then private secretary to the prime minister, Prince Konoye. After dinner we sat in the garden, drinking coffee and liqueurs, conversing in the warm semidarkness. Ushiba became very serious and talked to me with surprising candor. He believed, he said, that the last hope for adjusting Japanese–American relations rested with Prince Konoye, who would like to talk oftener with Ambassador Grew but feared leakages and publicity. Then Ushiba dropped his bombshell. Embassy reports sent to Washington were being read by Japanese authorities. We did, he understood, have "one confidential code."

Mr. Grew had earlier expressed concern about the safety of our communications. When he once heard that a Japanese had credited him with inside knowledge of behind-the-scenes events, he wondered whether the source of such judgment came from reading our telegrams. He was confident that our top-secret codes were secure and was somewhat reassured by Ushiba's remark that one at least was unreadable. I remember the ambassador remarking, after reading my telegram, "Salman's hair will stand on end when he sees this." David A. Salman was in charge of the department's code room.

In fact, the Japanese army, navy, and Foreign Office each maintained code-breaking organizations. Neither the army nor navy was particularly successful in reading American military messages, but the Angō Kenkyū-han (Code Research Section) in the Foreign Office had for some time been able to decipher the less sophisticated State Department cryptographic systems. The Gray Code was used to save telegraphic expense rather than to protect security, since we assumed it was unsafe. Numerous frequently used phrases and sentences could be expressed in one word. President Roosevelt sent his last-minute message to the emperor on December 6 in Gray Code: "Saves time—I don't mind if it gets picked up." The Brown Code was more recent and more respected but still a mere dictionary. All of our names were in it, and I can remember the secret pleasure in discovering the name *Emmerson* with two *m*'s, the code word for which I cannot now recall.

Due partially to inhibitions over message security, the State Department limited its communications with the Tokyo embassy. Not only were we ignorant of MAGIC, but Washington seldom bothered to inform us of policy positions—if indeed there were any—or even of conversations with representatives of other governments on matters pertaining directly to Japan. In April, Grew was humiliated to learn from the British ambassador, Sir Robert Craigie, of conversations by American officials in London and Washington, "How *infra dignitatem* it is to receive such information from a foreign colleague concerning the intimate affairs of my own government." In a July cable to Sumner Welles, "strictly confidential to the Acting Secretary," Grew related with injured pride that Craigie had shown him "most secret" British messages reporting what Welles had told the British ambassador and what the director of U.S. naval intelligence had said to the British naval attaché. He asked that Welles explain to the president "the great discouragement and handicap with which I as his ambassador am confronted. Unless a motor is hitting on all cylinders it cannot function effectively." This feeling of blind groping in the dark, without guidance or even comment on his telegrams, persisted through Grew's assignment to Japan. Reflecting, in 1951, he recalled the embassy's isolation of ten years before, "Our telegrams, save when specific instructions were asked, seldom brought response; they were rarely even referred to, and reporting to our Government was like throwing pebbles into a lake at night; we were not permitted to see even the ripples."

My later foreign service experience confirmed that of Ambassador Grew. Almost invariably, my British colleagues were better informed than I; London faithfully repeated pertinent messages to all interested posts. Often I learned of events in Washington from British diplomats who freely shared their confidential messages with me. As chargé d'affaires of the embassy in Pakistan, for example, I had a close relationship with the British High Commissioner, and we consulted frequently. On one occasion, when the policies of our respective governments were compatible, we consorted in drafting parallel messages to London and Washington.

During all of 1941 the problem of peace or war between Japan and the United States was ever uppermost in our minds. Looking back over the experience of that year, and reading the voluminous and confusing record of the official and unofficial conversations, telegrams, dispatches, memoranda, letters, diaries, and minutes of conferences, I am appalled at the wasted words, the talking past each other, and the helpless yielding of decision to fate. We in the embassy were convinced—and Ambassador Grew remained so to the end—that a Japanese–American war was unnecessary and that enough common points of national interest existed to make mutual accommodation possible—"constructive conciliation," was his phrase. Yet as observers on the spot, we also watched Japan's progressive enmeshment in a New Order she could not successfully construct, being denied access to raw materials, and suffering frustrations the depth of which the United States was not prepared to understand.

Some theories of history minimize the role of humans who are said to be swept along by the inexorable tides of economics or politics. Perhaps this was the case in 1941, that the developments of the ten previous years led inevitably to war, or, as the War Crimes Tribunal solemnly decided in 1948, that war resulted from a major Japanese conspiracy to dominate all countries bordering on the Pacific and Indian oceans, or that Emperor Hirohito plotted it all for years. We who lived this history may be myopic judges, but I cannot myself accept the "irresistible tide" or "conspiratorial" theories. I think, perhaps too much, of the patriotic, dedicated, but fallible, human beings in both Japan and the United States in whose hands rested much of the responsibility during this period. Perhaps I was influenced by the attitude of Grew, my first boss in the foreign service, about whom his biographer, Waldo Heinrichs, has written, "Precisionist that he was, diplomacy was for him essentially a matter of personal relationships, the intercourse of nations being governed best by the code of gentlemanly conduct." And the personal relationships were important in 1941.

On the American side, Franklin D. Roosevelt had set his eyes on Europe and hoped to avoid a clash with Japan, or at least to stave it off as long as possible. The army and navy, by 1941, supported Plan Dog, an Atlantic-first outline of military strategy, which stipulated that, even if forced into war with Japan, no major operations would be conducted in the Pacific until the British Isles were safe. FDR hoped to keep Japan quiet, and he greatly admired and respected his friend Joe Grew, his man in Tokyo.

In the State Department, Cordell Hull, Tennessee lawyer turned secretary of state, stuck to his moral principles, his outrage against Japan, and his faith and concern in China, and acted out, during the summer and fall of 1941, often with distaste and exasperation, the long series of encounters with Admiral Nomura Kichisaburō, the Japanese ambassador. Hull's chief adviser on Far Eastern affairs, Stanley K. Hornbeck, in turn looked to Maxwell Hamilton, then chief of the Division of Far Eastern affairs and to the principal Japanese expert in the department, Joseph Ballantine. Hornbeck and Hamilton were both China-oriented. Documents that found their way to Hull had wandered over the desks of Ballantine, Hamilton, and Hornbeck, acquiring deletions, emendations, and rephrasing on the way. For an officer assigned to Far Eastern affairs, getting a piece of paper as far as Hornbeck, let alone beyond, was a moment of minor triumph. Fearful of his chief's eagle eye for error, Max Hamilton would fix on every phrase, every word, and every comma to achieve the perfection that could pass the Hornbeckian judgment. He often failed. The two-way paper traffic, up the line for approval, back the line for correction, and up and back and up again, made business a crawl.

Still, with all of Hornbeck's stern standards and Hamilton's careful, subservient gravity, both men thought an occasional night on the town would do the staff good. The routine was an annual visit to the Gayety Burlesque in downtown Washington where the male staff members without wives would temporarily forget the questions of war and peace in Asia and, like little boys at a peephole show, would stare self-consciously at the bumps and grinds of the Gayety's tired and shopworn strippers.

On the Japanese side, the leading characters in Tokyo were Prince Konoye, prime minister until General Tōjō took over in October, and Matsuoka Yōsuke, the American-educated foreign minister who was replaced in July by Admiral Toyoda Teijirō. Grew, in 1940, called Konoye "a man of weak physique, poor health, and weak will." Born into a prestigious noble family, Konoye toyed with radicalism in his youth but later cultivated relations with intellectuals on the one hand and ultranationalists on the other. It was said of him that he kept "many masks beside him." He was prime minister when the China Affair began in July 1937, and again in 1940, when the New Structure and Imperial Rule Assistance Association came into fruition, and yet again, in September 1940, when the Tripartite Pact was signed. Still, Grew was convinced in the summer of 1941 that Konoye represented the best and last chance for a settlement with Japan. The Americans gave the prince little help, and he himself lacked courage and determination. He seemed impotent before destiny; he weakened before opposition and sought escape from crisis in illness or flight. He was, in the words of a Japanese diplomat, a "complex and contradictory character ..." "a shy squirrel sheltered in the deep forests." Herbert Norman,

Canadian scholar-diplomat, called him "congenitally a hypochon-driac, a melancholic given to hesitations, indecision, and pro-crastination."

If Konoye was a vacillating hypochondriac, Matsuoka was a compulsively loquacious, emotionally disturbed man. Grew was at first pleased to deal with the first Japanese foreign minister with whom he could speak English. When Matsuoka took over the Foreign Office in 1940, Grew described him as "a loose talker but a man who is patently straightforward and sincere according to his lights." But as acquaintance progressed, judgments changed. Mat-suoka talked incessantly, wrote letters and notes to Mr. Grew in English, and then became incensed when he learned that the ambassador had reported his remarks, which were intended, he insisted, as comments to his friend Mr. Grew and not to the American ambassador. Grew noted how dangerous it was to have in office a foreign minister who "by all criteria can only be considered as mentally ill-balanced." We in the embassy, viewing Matsuoka's very un-Japanese antics through Grew's and Dooman's reports and in the press, could not help wondering what had happened during that Oregon-spent youth. Perhaps some American quirk, some wounding emotional experience, or some insidious inciting influence had warped his Japanese character.

In Washington the Japanese were represented by the admiral-ambassador, Nomura Kichisaburō, a genial seadog who had met Franklin Roosevelt in 1915, when FDR was assistant secretary of the navy and Nomura a naval attaché at the Japanese embassy. Nomura was proud of the letters he had received from Roosevelt in the intervening years, in 1929, 1933, and 1937, and printed them as frontispieces for his memoirs. Hull's first impression of Nomura was "solemnity," his "mirthless chuckle," and his bowing. Hull was often perplexed by what Nomura was trying to tell him in his halting Japanese-English. Conversations were frequently tête-à-tête with no interpreter present. Throughout the succeeding months of informal U.S.-Japanese conversations—they never became negotiations—Nomura showed himself as an earnest peace-seeker but inex-perienced, bumbling, imprecise, and with amazing lapses of good judgment. He frequently withheld or delayed urgent communications that he was instructed to deliver, altered texts to make them more palatable to Hull, and inaccurately reported to Tokyo conversations with FDR and Hull. Grew, in August, wrote that he had "too much evidence that the Japanese embassy in Washington was half the time asleep at the switch either in failing to understand statements made by our government or in failing to report them promptly, accurately, and comprehensively." Ushiba, Konoye's private secretary, told me in our August conversation that the staff of the Japanese embassy in Washington was "painfully weak." The Foreign Office would have preferred to hold the conversations in Tokyo, removed from the fumbling hands of the good admiral, but the State Department, doubtless wary of giving Ambassador Grew too much initiative, or apprehensive that he might be too "understanding" of Japan, insisted that the locus be Washington.

Acting quite outside the official channels of governmental communication—the Foreign Office, the State Department, and the two embassies—were several private citizens, Americans and Japanese, self-seized with the mission of finding a way out of the Japanese–American impasse.

One of the Japanese was Hashimoto Tetsuma, a former member of the nationalist Black Dragon Society, who had organized the Shiunsō (Purple Cloud Society) and been known to the embassy since at least 1939 when, in a half-page advertisement replying to the "horse's mouth" speech, he had castigated the United States for the conquest of its overseas territories (Hawaii and the Panama Canal) and for perpetuating these unscrupulous methods in its recent attitude toward Japan. In 1940 Grew had a chance to tell Hashimoto what he thought of him, but Dooman assured the ambassador that the leader of the Purple Cloud was having a change of heart and was genuinely working for improved Japanese–American relations. In early January 1941, Hashimoto turned up in Washington and presented his plan for peace at the State Department. Ballantine wrote that Hashimoto was visionary and impractical and that his proposals offered no basis for an affirmative response from the United States. He continued to visit the embassy after most other Japanese friends had feared to call. Dooman respected him and duly reported his confidential revelations to Washington. Twenty-one years later Hashimoto and his Purple Cloud were to appear again in my life. But that is another story.

The Americans involved were Bishop James E. Walsh and Father James M. Drought of the Catholic Maryknoll Mission who, from the time they were introduced to President Roosevelt by Postmaster General Frank C. Walker on January 23, until the following November, worked with secrecy, gall, and supreme confidence to prevent a war they naïvely believed their efforts could stop. Their two Japanese associates were Wikawa Tadao, a Christian and an executive of a cooperative bank, and Colonel Iwakuro Hideo, an energetic military man who had conducted political activities in Manchuria and China and, in 1941, was supposed to be influential in the Japanese army. Wikawa and Iwakuro collaborated with Walsh and Drought, busily carrying messages to and from their highly placed friends in Tokyo and purposefully handling the gullible Nomura in Washington.

Known as the John Doe Associates, "their backdoor diplomacy"— in the words of Robert Butow, author of the definitive history of their efforts—"made an amicable settlement of the Far Eastern crisis harder to obtain." Drought drafted documents out of his head, which were then passed off as the positions of Japan, or, as occasion demanded, of the United States. Hull and Hornbeck were skeptical of the priests' activities, but felt they should not ignore such earnest proposals for peace. Nomura was completely taken in by Drought and Wikawa and seemed at times unable to distinguish between his government's policies as communicated from Tokyo and the persuasive-sounding language of Drought's drafts. Butow concludes, "From start to finish this prolonged search for peace in Washington and all corresponding contacts in Tokyo were consistently under the pernicious influence of the misbegotten actions of the John Doe Associates operating behind the scenes." *

* *I met Wikawa and Iwakuro later under very different circumstances. During the Occupation, Wikawa was active in establishing a cooperative political party and called on me in the political adviser's office in Tokyo in the fall of 1945. He recalled at that meeting his efforts for peace in 1941. Iwakuro, who had subsequently become a general, turned up in 1966 at the embassy in Tokyo,*

The record of the Japanese–American diplomatic conversations of 1941 is long and tortuous. The details have been published in official documents and in the numerous accounts of historians and will not be repeated here. Apart from the issues, which in the end proved impossible to reconcile, one can imagine the difficulties of communication, understanding, and agreement among the diverse players who were acting out the drama: the moralistic Hull, the dogmatic Hornbeck, the cautious Hamilton, the hopeful Grew, the well-meaning but weak Konoye, the irrational Matsuoka (succeeded by the calmer, saner Toyoda), and the eager conspirators for peace, the John Doe Associates. And behind the Americans was Franklin D. Roosevelt, intent on staving off war in the Pacific in order to concentrate on Europe, subjected to the conflicting pulls of numerous special interests, yet intrigued by the sheer theater of a battleship meeting with Konoye to save Pacific peace. Behind the Japanese was the emperor, whose inclinations were pro-British and pro-American, whose rescripts would be unchallengeable, whether to join the Axis or to guarantee peace with America, but who, beyond reading poems to express his perturbation, could not step outside the bonds of his advisers. And behind all of the diplomatic palaver were the chiefs of the armies and navies of Japan and the United States, concerned with their respective degrees of preparedness and power. Still further behind, yet inseparable from the foreign policies of the two contenders, were the allies of Japan—Hitler and Mussolini—and those of the United States—Churchill and Chiang Kai-shek. Small wonder that diplomacy failed.

In January 1941 Grew had recovered from his New Year's Eve moment of euphoria and wrote in his diary that "the outlook for the future of relations between Japan and the United States has

---

offering his services to bring peace to Vietnam. He enthusiastically related his experiences in China and Indochina during World War II, his acquaintance with key Vietnamese in both Saigon and Hanoi, and described his particular qualifications for undertaking secret and delicate missions for peace. His ardor for peace had not cooled with the years; he actually went to Vietnam in 1966 but found that problem even more baffling than the one that had faced his country and the United States in 1941.

never been darker." He was troubled over Japan's developing stranglehold on Indochina and by the threat to Singapore, which he considered vital to the defense of the British Isles. He was impressed by the views of Hugh Byas, the astute correspondent of *The New York Times,* who saw in Japan "the growing avalanche-like strength of the aggressive forces." At the same time the ambassador was disheartened to hear from home that Americans believed that sending the fleet to Asiatic waters would be suicidal and would never support a war to save Singapore.

On the twenty-seventh of the month (again Grew's special date!) the Peruvian ambassador, Ricardo Rivera Schreiber, whispered to an embassy officer that he had picked up a rumor that Japan had planned a surprise mass attack on Pearl Harbor in case of trouble between Japan and the United States. This sounded fantastic to all of us, but Grew took it seriously enough to telegraph to Washington. We were not particularly perturbed; as the ambassador recorded in his diary, "I rather guess that the boys in Hawaii are not precisely asleep." When I stopped in Honolulu in October, I was told that since the receipt of our telegram, reconnaissance patrol flights around Oahu had been stepped up.

Eight years later Rivera Schreiber was to recall more details of the rumor he had passed to us. In a press interview in Lima, the former ambassador to Japan related that his valet had come to him in an agitated state to reveal that Japan was going to war and would destroy the American fleet "in the middle of the Pacific." The valet's source was a Japanese interpreter in the Peruvian consulate in Yokohama. Later, according to Schreiber, a Tokyo Imperial University professor named Yoshida had told him that Admiral Yamamoto Isoroku had formulated a plan to attack the U.S. fleet at Pearl Harbor and that maneuvers in preparation for such an operation were then in progress. The Peruvian ambassador recalled that he had made an urgent appointment to see Ambassador Grew and had related to him every detail of the rumors he had heard. According to Schreiber, "The gravity of my revelations were [sic] grasped by the United States diplomat who immediately sent a cable to President Roosevelt." Grew recorded at the time that not he but a member of his staff had received the report.

We now know that Admiral Yamamoto, in December 1940, had asked for a study of an air attack on Pearl Harbor. We should have taken the rumor more seriously, although, curiously enough, the Japanese Naval General Staff at first rejected the proposal, and the admiral who had developed it tried until October 1941 to persuade Yamamoto to give up the idea. The Pearl Harbor rumor was one of many constantly filtering into the embassy; usually, however, the targets of predicted Japanese attacks were Singapore, Hong Kong, the Netherlands East Indies, or Indochina.

Matsuoka was busy with Axis diplomacy. He agreed with Grew in January that Japanese–American relations "couldn't be worse," and by April was off on his triumphal tour to Moscow, Berlin, Rome, and back to Moscow. The then-as-now hyperactive Japanese press reported his every move and his every word (including the moxa treatments he received during the train journeys), and Japanese citizens shared pride in the receptions accorded their representative by Hitler, Mussolini, and Stalin. The dramatic and sudden signature in Moscow of a neutrality pact took everyone by surprise, including, by his own admission, Matsuoka himself. Ambassador Grew in February had seen "no probability" that Japan and the Soviet Union would join in a nonaggression pact or any other kind of agreement. Actually, the treaty was apparently a sudden, unpremeditated, last-minute inspiration by Stalin. The Japanese public was treated to all the details of the dramatic send-off at Kazan station by Stalin himself, who delayed the train's departure by an hour. In the alcoholic glow produced by some kind of "red drink" which Matsuoka zestfully described when he returned home, Stalin bear-hugged the Japanese minister and, remembering his Georgian heritage, exclaimed with feeling, "We understand each other. We are Asiatics."

Matsuoka seldom faced the issues or weighed coldly the risks or the consequences of war with the United States. While in Moscow, he met by prearranged chance at a performance at the Moscow Art Theater, the British ambassador, Sir Stafford Cripps. During an intermission Cripps managed to hand him a communication from Winston Churchill, posing eight extremely pertinent questions, relating to such matters as the prospects for German conquest of

Britain, the transformation of British and American industry to a war footing, the effect on the United States of the Axis alliance, the naval superiority of the two English-speaking nations vis-à-vis Japan, and the inadequacy of Japan's seven million tons of steel production contrasted with an expected British-American total of ninety million tons in 1941. Churchill ended his message with a plea, "From the answers to these questions may spring the avoidance by Japan of a serious catastrophe and a marked improvement in relations between Japan and Great Britain, the great sea power in the West." Matsuoka ignored the questions and replied with astonishing nonchalance that Japan was determined to fulfill the lofty concept of *hakkō ichiu* by bringing about universal peace. This policy would be carried out, according to Matsuoka, "resolutely but with complete circumspection, having in mind every detail of changing circumstances." Grew noted wryly in his diary, "Altered circumstances! That is the loophole which Japan always leaves herself."

The Japanese–American conversations of 1941 were so confidential that no one in the embassy was supposed to know about them except Grew and Dooman. For months, Grew referred cryptically in his diary to messages too secret to record. But in the embassy the circle of the witting—to borrow vocabulary from the CIA—inevitably widened, and I read most of the telegrams being exchanged with Washington. On May 27, again a lucky day, the ambassador composed "perhaps the most important telegram" of his service in Japan. He drafted it "early in the morning after a night of most careful and prayerful thought."

The message was Grew's response to the department's question whether any Japanese government could or would carry out the commitments of an agreement reached with the United States. The ambassador unhesitatingly answered in the affirmative, stressing that a bilateral undertaking approved by the cabinet, the privy council, and the emperor would be executed in good faith. Sanction by the army and navy would be assumed; furthermore, Grew believed the military ministers favored a settlement. He saw much for the United States to gain from an agreement with Japan, and judged the alternative to be a "progressive deterioration of American–Japanese relations leading eventually to war."

Hornbeck, as can be guessed, held an opposite view. Writing about the same time, he analyzed the motives of "these Japanese" who were promoting bilateral conversations intended to lead to agreement. They had not had a change of heart but were still bent on imperial expansion, still hoped to control China, and still sought power, prestige, privilege, and a paramount position in the Far East (Hornbeck's alliteration). To contradict Grew's belief in Japanese good faith, Hornbeck recalled Japan's violation of its pledge to support the independence and integrity of China, made in the Root–Takahira agreement of 1908, and asked what reason there was to expect Japan to "pay more or better attention to the provisions of a new treaty with us, if concluded now?"

The embassy's next surprise came on June 22, when Germany attacked the Soviet Union. I heard the news in Kyoto at the Miyako Hotel, a stopover on my way to Tsuruga on the Japan Sea to meet Allen Lightner, Jr., who was arriving from Moscow on his way to the United States. The embassy did not expect this attack, although Washington had apparently received inklings of it earlier in the year. Most of us were pessimistic about the Russians' chances: speculation ran from a few weeks to two or three months, and few thought that the Russians could hold out indefinitely. Even Chip Bohlen, our Soviet expert, was not too confident of Stalin's prospects. In a special memorandum prepared for Grew, he wrote somewhat equivocally on June 25:

> While most military observers in Moscow, including the German military attaché, have estimated that the campaign against the Soviet Union would require approximately two months for the destruction of the Soviet armed resistance ... there is, however, the possibility that the German estimate of the time required is too long. The Soviet structure ... might, although most competent opinions hold the contrary view, disintegrate completely within a few weeks.

Grew was elated at the attack, thinking it the best thing that could happen. "Dog eat dog," he wrote. "Let the Nazis and the Communists so weaken each other that the democracies will soon gain the upper hand or at least be released from their dire peril." Matsuoka lost his credibility by this new war and by July was out of office. Konoye formed a new cabinet with Admiral Toyoda Teijirō as foreign minister.

After MAGIC had revealed that Japanese forces were about to make another southward move, imperial troops occupied southern French Indochina. I wrote to Dorothy, "On July 26 things happened. It was Saturday. The announcement of Japanese entry into French Indochina was made at noon and by 2:00 we heard that the United States government had frozen Japanese assets in the United States. There was much flurry in the *taishikan* [embassy] as you can imagine. At 7:30 that night the ambassador remarked that it was quite unusual to find the whole staff of secretaries in the office at 7:30 on a Saturday night!"

Freezing meant the termination of all financial transactions, the virtual cessation of trade, and the ending of direct Japanese–American steamship service. In Tokyo we knew that this was the beginning of the end. No move by either government had so shaken the other. The Japanese recognized that time was not on their side.

Prime Minister Konoye made one more serious effort to find a way toward peace and at the same time to preserve something of the Japanese position in China and the East Asia Co-prosperity Sphere. He proposed a personal meeting with President Roosevelt to lay the foundation for an agreement. Father Drought and his friends had suggested such a dramatic encounter months before, but it now appeared as an official demarche of the Japanese government. FDR was intrigued with the idea. He had met Churchill to produce on August 14 an Atlantic Charter, and the drama of a conference in the Pacific appealed to his imagination. To Konoye's suggestion that they meet in Hawaii, the president countered with a battleship off Juneau, Alaska; his time away from Washington would be fifteen days instead of twenty-one. The Japanese agreed and proposed to announce that the two heads of government would meet "somewhere in the Pacific." FDR encouraged the Japanese by telling Nomura that he was "very hopeful," that he would be "keenly interested in having three or four days with Prince Konoye." Grew and Dooman revived their sagging hopes by energetically endorsing the proposed Konoye–Roosevelt conversation. Grew reaffirmed his conviction that an agreement would stick. After all, the prime minister had assured him at a secret dinner in his private home, with all the servants sent away, that responsible high-ranking officers of the army and navy would be with him on the battleship and would sign whatever he signed. As could have been expected, however, when the bureaucratic skeptics Hornbeck and Hamilton got their hands on the proposal, they proceeded, with encouragement from Hull, to tear it to pieces bit by bit. Their objections were multitudinous but boiled down to insistence that a general agreement must be achieved *before* the risks of a summit could be faced.

The Japanese were overwhelmed by the constant reiteration of principles by the Americans. For them, the realities were China, raw materials, and military power. For principles, they could always bring forth their *hakkō ichiu* and their New Order in East Asia. These were as inspirational to them as were Hull's famous four axioms to the United States. But while nations preached principles, they acted on realities. Hull's list seemed vague, moralistic, and irrelevant, and the Japanese were not sure the Americans had always lived up to their own preachments or would fight for them in the future. Still, Konoye had accepted the four principles at the secret dinner with Grew, or so Grew and Dooman thought. Konoye's own version was agreement to the principles "in principle," which was a subtle Japanese way of misting the primary colors.

The Japanese had a defensible argument for hesitating to come to specific agreements in advance of an Alaskan meeting: decisions would inevitably leak, and the diehard nationalists would act to stop the accommodation. Assassination attempts had already been made on both Konoye and Hiranuma, the latter a former prime minister. Grew urged Washington not to be so insistent on prior understanding. Konoye could make concessions at a meeting with FDR that he could never make at home. Besides the awesome prestige of an imperial rescript, sealing the agreement, would destroy all opposition. But Hull and Hornbeck stood firm. The United States never rejected the Pacific meeting but never approved it. The futile exchange of memoranda continued, with John Doe and Company contributing to the confusion to the last.

By September the Japanese leadership had agreed that the time for decision had come; the likelihood of war with the United States had to be faced. An imperial conference, convened on September 6, resolved that if Japan's demands were not met by the first ten days of October, the government would then make the decision to open hostilities with the United States, Great Britain, and the Netherlands. The reader of the record of this conference, as well as those of later meetings in October and November, and finally on December 1 and 4, cannot fail to be astounded at the calm, almost trancelike character of the flat, fatalistic statements which seemed to move Japan irresistibly and irrevocably toward the catastrophe that all wished to avoid. It was like a slow, agonizingly prolonged playing out of a collective ritual *seppuku*. Only the emperor hinted at the impending tragedy, when he gravely intoned in his thin, jerking voice, the poetical question of his grandfather, Emperor Meiji, which was left unanswered, "Why, then, do the winds and waves of strife rage so turbulently throughout the world?" Moved by the emperor's words, the representatives of both the government and the supreme command agreed that precedence should be given to diplomatic negotiations over preparations for war.

Due for home leave, at my own expense, I had expected sometime during the summer to join the family in Colorado, where they had established temporary residence. I made reservations on the *Hikawa Maru* sailing in August, but the freezing order canceled that. Ambassador Grew talked seriously to me, "I can't imagine your wanting to leave the embassy now when you have this opportunity of a lifetime to see history made." He and Dooman flattered me that my job was important; after words like these, there could be no question of my taking home leave. But by mid-September gloom was accumulating. The Japanese were pressing for an American reply to the proposal for a Konoye–FDR meeting, and Grew was worrying about what would happen on the first anniversary of the Tripartite Pact on September 27 (again, an unhappy twenty-seven). He remembered Konoye's urgency on September 6, "Time is of the essence." The ship was ready, the prime minister's suite of twenty was chosen, weather off Alaska would worsen if the meeting continued to be put off. The Japanese suggested September 9–20, then September 21–25, then early October—obviously keeping in mind the deadline set by the secret imperial conference. Meanwhile, in Washington Nomura achieved another gaffe in the transmission of documents, and Hornbeck took two weeks' leave, informing a correspondent that nothing would happen while he was away. The positions of the two governments were as far apart as ever.

Finally, Dooman advised me, with the concurrence of the ambassador, to take my leave. There was little more that could be done at the embassy. I spent most of the month of October traveling to the United States. Chip Bohlen and David (Tommy) Thomasson, another embassy officer, were due to make the courier run to Shanghai, so the three of us set off together, to Nagasaki by train and to Shanghai by a crowded, bobbing Japanese shuttle ship. Shanghai was a city of impulsive revelry, taking a last wild fling before the curtain fell. After the deadly slogans and drab discipline of Tokyo, Shanghai was a whirling blur of lights, rickshaws, shouts, Russian, Chinese, and Japanese music, crowded nightclubs, restaurants, bars, and starved bodies on the streets. Everything was cheap; everything was frenzy.

I boarded the S. S. *President Coolidge* on October 8, on what was to be her last sailing for the United States. I walked down the gangplank in San Francisco sixteen days later, on October 24.

After my reunion with the family and a brief leave in Colorado, I reported for duty at the State Department in mid-November. By that time the situation looked indeed bleak, and no one had much hope for resolution through negotiations of the issue with Japan. I was immediately put to work on routine problems of shipping, injuries to American citizens and their interests, and the vast numbers of problems resulting from the freezing order of July.

In due course, I paid my respects to Hornbeck, as was the custom for officers returning from the field. Square-jawed, balding, unsmiling, he fixed me with his penetrating gaze and, with some cold condescension in his voice, asked the routine question to which he clearly did not expect a satisfactory answer nor any information that he did not already possess. "What do you people in the embassy think about war with Japan?"

I answered without hesitation, "We think Japan wants to dominate East Asia and hopes to do so without war. But if this looks impossible, Japan will go to war in desperation."

The furrows in the redoubtable Hornbeck's brow deepened, and he spoke as a schoolmaster setting his pupil right. "Name me one country in history which ever went to war in desperation!" No apt example came rushing to my mind to save me from my predicament, and, without protesting further, I made my exit from the office as gracefully as possible.

I had of course only parroted what Grew had been telling Washington for years. He had warned repeatedly of the Japanese do-or-die spirit, of their willingness to risk national *hara-kiri* rather than submit to foreign pressure, and of the national psychology of desperation, which develops into a determination to risk war. Some weeks before I met Hornbeck, on November 3, Grew had cabled that "action by Japan which might render unavoidable an armed conflict with the United States may come with dangerous and dramatic suddenness."

Hornbeck had long disparaged the embassy's view that Japan might act in desperation. In a long "reviewer's review" of Grew's thesis, he wrote in January 1940 that he did not expect Japan "to go insane," that he saw no likelihood that action by another nation or combination of nations would "drive the Japanese state suddenly to a point of extreme desperation." Hornbeck saw no need to "baby" Japan, to fear Japan, or to pay blackmail to Japan. He excused Grew to some extent for his arguments about intransigence and realism because he was functioning in the Tokyo environment of strain, uncertainties, apprehension, and tension. The day before Pearl Harbor he reverted to this view of the warped outlook of the embassy, "working in the turbulent and stifling atmosphere of Tokyo and subjected constantly to the impact of messages borne by, and comments offered by, Japanese 'friends' and 'go-betweens' who purvey a product made in Japan, of Japan, by Japan, and for Japan." He was right that our outlook was restricted and our contacts limited, but perhaps we were better judges of Japanese psychology than was Hornbeck, functioning in his own Chinese-made, bureaucratic straitjacket.

One learned in the foreign service to be wary of predictions. The fear of being wrong usually stayed the hand of the cautious bureaucrat and inspired the well-worn weaseling phrases: "The situation may develop in this way, but *on the other hand . . .*", or "While the outlook is grim, *certain mitigating factors may . . .*" Always leave a way out. Hornbeck must be given credit for having the courage to record his convictions. On November 27, ten days before the attack on Pearl Harbor, and a few days after he had spoken with me, he wrote a memorandum, which he urgently called to the attention of Secretary Hull in a covering note, "If you have a minute, you might find it worthwhile to look at the marked portion of this memo . . . before or while speaking to the president."

The marked portion read:

In the opinion of the undersigned, the Japanese Government does not desire or intend or expect to have forthwith armed conflict with the United States. The Japanese Government, while launching new offensive operations at some point or points in the Far East, will endeavor to avoid attacking or being attacked by the United States. . . . So far as relations directly between the United States and Japan are concerned there is less reason today than there was a week ago for the United States to be apprehensive lest Japan make "war" on this country. Were it a matter of placing bets, the undersigned would give odds of 5 to 1 that the United States will not be at "war" on or before December 15. . . . stated briefly, the undersigned does not believe that this country is now on the verge of "war" in the Pacific.

After the war had begun, Hornbeck tried to explain his faulty prediction in his draft autobiography,

In my putting on paper the statements which I made in the memorandum I addressed to Mr. Hull on November 27, I made the mistake of yielding to an emotional urge and committing myself on the record in terms of wishful thinking and gratuitous predicting. Both my thinking and my predicting were, however, based on my scrutiny of materials which emanated from "intelligence" services, some British and some American.

Hundreds of thousands of words have been written to analyze how and why it all happened. Hull insisted on his four principles, and the Japanese—while accepting the principles in principle—found it impossible to wipe out four years of national sacrifice and to withdraw their troops from China.

Both sides had mistaken images of each other. Many Japanese could not believe that Americans would fight to preserve the integrity of China and the faraway countries of Southeast Asia. A leading Japanese industrialist expressed his opinion in April 1941, "The United States would hesitate to fight in the Pacific." Even the Japanese navy, although reluctant to make war on the United States, gambled that Americans, subjected to a knockout blow at Pearl Harbor, would not cross the Pacific to fight in Asia. Yet the Japanese never really hated the Americans; in spite of government-inspired propaganda, the virulent press, and zealous antiforeign insults by the police and *kempeitai,* and even in spite of the American wartime bombings, goodwill for the United States was never completely eradicated. We would find it still there when we returned during the Occupation.

Anti-Japanese feeling was, however, strong in the United States at the time and with it went a racist contempt for the weakness, ineptness, and untrustworthiness of the Japanese. J. N. ("Ding") Darling, the then-famous newspaper cartoonist, put it all in a drawing: a little Japanese soldier on the other side of the Pacific, sweating to blow up a tremendous balloon with painted, scowling, piano-keys teeth, horn-rimmed glasses, military cap, and tag "Japanese Bluff." Uncle Sam stands on his own shore, wearing a navy cap, readying a slingshot behind him and smiling slyly, with satisfaction.

By late November the issues had been largely narrowed to Japan's obligations under the Axis pact, the withdrawal of troops from China and Indochina, and the principle of equal commercial opportunity. Nomura and Ambassador Kurusu Saburō, who had been sent to assist him, persisted in trying to satisfy Hull on the Axis.

Japan was obviously unable to publicly renounce her German ally. Hornbeck commented on the irony of the United States, "the world's foremost advocate of respect for treaties," urging Japan to disregard the Axis pact and make an agreement with us that would prove her faithless to her allies. Still, the Japanese sought diligently to convey to Grew and Hull the assurance that membership in the Axis would not automatically mean war with the United States should German–American hostilities develop. Nomura asked Hull not to insist upon specific language but to "read between the lines." The Japanese agreed to withdraw their troops from China within a period of two years after the restoration of Sino–Japanese peace, except for some forces in certain specified areas. Ambassador Kurusu told Hull, on November 18, that about 90 percent of the troops would be pulled out, but he could not specify how long the remaining 10 percent would be retained. The Japanese were also prepared to move all troops from southern to northern Indochina and to withdraw all forces from Indochina when the China Affair was settled. Furthermore, the Japanese government was ready to recognize the principle of nondiscrimination in international commercial relations, applicable to all Pacific areas, including China, as well as the whole world.

At the last minute, having learned through MAGIC that, after November 29, "things are automatically going to happen," Hornbeck, Hamilton, and Ballantine set to work to produce a *modus vivendi*, which would provide a breathing spell of three months and thus gain needed time for our army and navy. This document went far to meet previous proposals made by the Japanese and accepted their offer to withdraw from southern to northern Indochina with the proviso that Japanese forces in Indochina would not exceed twenty-five thousand, and no replacements would be made. In return, the United States would modify the freezing regulations and permit some trade. While the two parties would mutually refrain from military advancement in any part of East Asia or the Pacific, no mention was made of forces in China. Hull insisted on consulting the British, Australians, Dutch, and Chinese before presenting the offer to Japan. Chiang Kai-shek's reaction was explosive, and Churchill sent a cable to the president, asking whether Chiang Kai-shek would not be "having a very thin diet."

Hornbeck recounts that the decision to scrap the *modus vivendi* was made in the afternoon of November 25, in the light of the "emphatic objections, arguments and pleas of the Chinese" and of Churchill's pointed query. That evening what was to be the final note to the Japanese was prepared, and Hull won the president's approval of it early the next morning, November 26.

The *modus vivendi,* even at that late date, had a chance, albeit a small chance, for acceptance. The Japanese had earlier made a similar proposal themselves, and decisions of the imperial conferences had clearly provided for calling off the Pearl Harbor operation, even at the last minute, if an agreement were achieved. Whether the Japanese military could indeed have been halted in their tracks is, of course, a debatable question, but like the Konoye–FDR meeting, it was another missed chance by the American decisionmakers at the time. We were paralyzed by China, and for how many years in the future was this paralysis to affect American foreign policy in East Asia.

The *modus vivendi* could never have been characterized as an "ultimatum" as was, with justification, the note delivered to Nomura and Kurusu on November 26. The latter document asked Japan to do the impossible; in addition to enumerating Hull's four principles as well as five more economic principles, the United States called upon Japan to withdraw forthwith *all* military forces from China and Indochina, to support *only* the Chinese Nationalist Government against which Japan had been fighting since 1937, and to make a formal commitment, which would in effect nullify Japan's adherence to the Tripartite Pact.

By the time Nomura and Kurusu were able to deliver the Japanese answer to Hull on Sunday afternoon, December 7, at 2:20 P.M., bombs had been falling on Pearl Harbor for an hour. The tension in the secretary's State Department office can be imagined. Hull had read the intercepted message, which Nomura was about to deliver, and had just heard from Roosevelt the unconfirmed report that the Japanese had attacked Pearl Harbor. His first instinct was to refuse to see the Japanese envoys, but he changed his mind and let them in, keeping them standing while he pretended to read the note Nomura handed to him. When he finished reading Hull angrily said that in all his fifty years of public service he had never seen a document more crowded with "infamous falsehoods and distortions."

The Japanese note—intended in effect to be a declaration of war, although it did not mention war—was contentious and emotional. It reiterated the well-known justifications for Japan's policies in East Asia but revealed again that the core of the issue was China, against the background of Grew's often-posited principles versus realities. For Japan, the American demand for "wholesale evacuation" of troops from China and support of the Chungking government "ignored the actual conditions of China" and shattered the "very basis" of the negotiations. Also, for the Japanese, "always holding fast to theories in disregard of realities" was difficult to understand. To force their immediate adoption of such principles seemed "only a utopian ideal." With such total failure of mutual comprehension, war was inevitable.

Every American then alive and old enough to understand remembers precisely the spot and the moment. Pearl Harbor in one instant made everything different from everything that had come before: a new boundary for history. General George C. Marshall, chairman of the Joint Chiefs of Staff, was riding horseback in Rock Creek Park. Dorothy and I were spending the weekend in New York with our old friends from Chicago and Washington days, Bob and Bae Strumpen-Darrie. When the news came, we left precipitously, the champagne bottle unopened, and listened to radio reports on the train all the way to Washington. Grew was right. War had indeed come "with dangerous and dramatic suddenness."

In Tokyo, Ambassador Grew and his staff were interned in the embassy compound. The Grews accommodated the senior officers in their residence on the hill, and the rest of the Americans lived in the two apartment buildings and in chancery offices, which had been turned into makeshift bedrooms. During the six months of waiting for diplomatic exchange arrangements to be completed, embassy officers, including the Grews, played continuous poker and bridge games, devised a tiny golf course on the grounds between the buildings, and amused themselves the best they could within the strictures of confinement and the whims of the Japanese police bureaucracy. The ambassador, with the assistance of Dooman,

Bohlen, and others, wrote his version of the immediate pre-Pearl Harbor history, as seen by the embassy. The report eloquently argued the case for a Konoye–FDR meeting and presented a point of view fundamentally opposed to the positions taken by the State Department.

When the day of departure finally arrived, on June 18, 1942, the embassy employees and a few additional Americans boarded the *Asama Maru* in Yokohama. Grew had worried about how he would get his report of some sixty pages out of the country without risking inspection by Japanese authorities. It had been typed in six copies and the pages were divided among several of the embassy officers and worn, beneath their shirts, strapped to their torsos. The Japanese made no searches, and the report was carried on board intact. After exasperating delays and an exchange with the Japanese diplomats returning from the United States and other countries at Lourenço Marques, Mozambique, the Americans arrived in New York on August 25 aboard the *Gripsholm*. The ambassador and his private secretary, Robert A. Fearey, took the first train for Washington ahead of the other passengers. That evening at his home on Woodland Drive, Grew received the welcome and respects of numerous friends and ranking officers of the government, including Harry Hopkins.

The next morning, accompanied by Fearey, Grew called on Secretary Hull, carrying in his briefcase the embassy's report. He was ushered into Hull's office, Fearey remaining just outside the oaken doors. Soon the rising tones of angry Tennessee profanity penetrated the door. After a time, Grew emerged, obviously shaken. He asked Fearey to accompany him to the Metropolitan Club for lunch. There, he related the details of the interview. He had handed his report to the secretary, describing it as the embassy's view of the attempts to reach agreement with Japan. Hull picked up the paper and, as he leafed through its pages, his face flushed with mounting anger. Finally, he threw the report on the desk before him and exclaimed, "You will either destroy every copy of this report, or you and I will fight this issue out in public!" Grew remonstrated that he could not retract his convictions but neither could he be a party to a public controversy in time of war when national unity was essential.

Hull insisted that Grew select one of the two alternatives and come back the next morning with his choice. The ambassador told Fearey over lunch that he was determined to reject both alternatives. To Grew's surprise, when he returned to Hull's office the next day, the secretary made no mention of the report and strongly supported Grew's plan to undertake a nationwide speaking tour designed to awaken the American people to the fighting strength and tenacity of the Japanese enemy.

Ten years later in his autobiography, *Turbulent Era,* Grew included the highlights of the report in a chapter entitled "Pearl Harbor from the Perspective of Ten Years." He remained convinced to the end that the embassy's recommendations had been right, that President Roosevelt should have met Prince Konoye, that however slim the chance, this last opportunity to save the peace should not have been spurned. Whatever the outcome of such an encounter might have been, it could scarcely have been worse than what really happened.

6

Japanese and Americans in Peru

The Monday morning after Pearl Harbor, officers of the Far Eastern Division of the Department of State suddenly found themselves unemployed. Diplomacy, the nation's first line of defense, had failed, and the military had taken over. The tensions of the secret summer negotiations, which had mounted with the uncertainties of when and where war would break out, vanished overnight. Now we must win the war, and as quickly as possible. But what could the Far Eastern Division of the State Department do? We could worry about the Americans caught in Japan and China and throughout the Far East, but we could do little about them. Communications were cut. One telephone call had reached Ambassador Grew late at night on Sunday, December 7. There was the problem of representation of interests, and it was quickly arranged that the Swiss would handle relations with Japan. But in the first shock of the attack, we felt helpless and, as State Department officers, without a justifiable reason for being.

Americans, stunned and bewildered, found it easy to hate the Japanese enemy. An oriental face was immediately suspect; Chinese labeled themselves as such in self-protection. State Department

Japanese specialists busied themselves in writing articles and speeches to further the Know the Enemy campaign. Most of us would shudder to reread the oversimplified, biased essays we turned out to support the national cause. Even Ambassador Grew, when he was later repatriated, delivered some speeches better characterized as fire than reason.

Galvanized into action, government agencies—all too late—tried to cover their chagrin over the disastrous failure of intelligence before Pearl Harbor by turning in every direction to unearth sources of disloyalty, sabotage, subversion, and espionage. The so-called day of infamy had cast suspicion on every person and everything identifiable as Japanese. There followed the indefensible forced evacuation of one hundred thousand Japanese from California, including thousands of American citizens, and their incarceration for the duration of the war in concentration camps, euphemistically named relocation centers. Then someone's eyes wandered down the map of the Pacific coast, fixing on the startling fact that thirty thousand Japanese were living quietly in the coastal regions of Peru, a vital, strategic area where enemy infiltration, clandestine communication, and all manner of spying could be perpetrated with impunity. Something had to be done about Peru!

The United States immediately proposed to the Latin American republics that they intern Axis nationals and in January 1942, a conference of Pan-American ministers of foreign affairs held in Rio de Janeiro set up an emergency advisory committee for political defense. Among the recommendations made during the course of 1942 were actions to control "potentially dangerous aliens, to intern Axis nationals, to restrict the naturalization of enemy aliens, and to cancel the naturalization of Axis supporters."

Sometime during January 1942, Lawrence Salisbury, one of the most able Far Eastern specialists in the State Department, who had served in both China and Japan and spoke both languages, told me that the embassy in Lima had appealed to the department for a Japanese-speaking foreign service officer. The Peruvian government, which severed relations with Japan that same month, was deeply concerned over the threat to hemisphere security posed by its large Japanese population, as was the United States. It appeared that no one in Peru, except the Japanese themselves, could speak Japanese. Could we help? Larry fixed his twinkling eye on me, "How would you like to go to Lima?" By February we were there.

The nature of my duties in the embassy was supposed to be known only to the appropriate officials of the Peruvian government. The Japanese colony in particular was not to know that an American embassy official spoke Japanese. In the embassy I soon found that my closest collaborators were to be the so-called legal attachés, smart, young FBI agents, and Rolland Welch, a German-speaking foreign service officer who was to look after the Germans.

In June 1940 President Roosevelt had directed that J. Edgar Hoover's Federal Bureau of Investigation would be responsible for nonmilitary intelligence in the Western Hemisphere. The Special Intelligence Service (SIS) was set up in the FBI, and agents skilled in undercover work soon fanned out through South America, to carry on covert activities and, in many cases, to be attached to embassies in order to maintain a liaison with national and local police forces. Their initial purpose was to counter German intelligence operations, but the discovery of the large Japanese colonies in Brazil (three hundred thousand) and in Peru (thirty thousand) led naturally to a closer look at the nation's Pacific enemies. The legal attachés in Lima were difficult to conceal. They were invariably close-cropped, close-shaved, clean-cut, well-pressed, typical American-boy types and, being naturally gregarious, they liked to drink in the bar of the Hotel Bolivar on Plaza San-Martin in the center of the city. Peruvian friends would wink and smile: "FBI!" A few agents spoke Spanish, but unfortunately none knew either German or Japanese.

The FBI was not the only U.S. agency digging up information in Peru. Both the army and navy had sizable staffs and, like the FBI, employed native informants to bring in tidbits about what the Germans and the Japanese were doing—the Italians hardly counted. It is not difficult to imagine how often this network of spies and counterspies got tangled up and how many times agents were tailing each other. But the appetite for intelligence was insatiable, and Washington archives must still bulge with the voluminous reports sent in by all the dedicated, eager gatherers.

In this atmosphere of suspicion and distrust—where every Japanese barber was assumed to be an admiral in disguise and every Japanese tailor a constant recipient of secret orders from Tokyo (suspicious documents and uniforms in at least one instance turned out to be relics of the Russo-Japanese war)—I became fascinated with the story of the Japanese in Peru, how they got there, who they were, and what they were really doing.

Bernardin de Saint-Pierre—a French man of letters, often called an apostle of the return to nature and the champion of innocence and religion—wrote in 1784, " . . . from island to island, the nations of Asia made their way to the New World, where they landed on the shores of Peru. Thither they carried the name of children of that sun whom they were pursuing. This brilliant chimera emboldened them to attempt the passage to America." Not that one should take Saint-Pierre's history too seriously. Gustave Lanson, whose *Histoire de la Littérature Française* we had studied in Paris, wrote that the word *naïve* comes immediately to the lips when considering the words of Saint-Pierre. "The poor man! He wanted to explain nature without being a scholar and in ignorance of science. . . . This pitiable philosopher is a great painter." But some Peruvians and Japanese took Saint-Pierre's fiction as fact. They saw an affiliation between the sun goddess of Japan and the sun god of the Incas.

One Peruvian writer, Francisco A. Loayza, after spending ten years in Japan, published a book in 1926 entitled *Manco Capac, Founder of the Empire of the Incas, Was a Japanese*. Loayza fixes the date of the arrival of the Japanese Inca to Peru in the thirteenth century. He supports his thesis by finding similarities between the Quechua and Japanese languages and between customs and institutions of the two cultures. The International Congress of Americanists invited him to present his hypothesis at a meeting in Rome. The Japanese colony in Peru found it expedient to exploit this legendary affinity and, in 1922, presented to the city of Lima a lifesize statue of Manco Capac, the first chief of the Incas and high priest of their sun god.

The president of Peru, Augusto B. Leguia, attended the ceremonies and lent credence to the theory of common Peruvian and Japanese origins in his remarks:

Our ancestors must indeed have mingled in the remote awakening of the megalithic age. Profound archeological investigations continue to affirm the existence of similar remains in our two continents. Also equal ... are the red and white symbols of our flags. And the sun is likewise inlaid in the throne of the Inca emperors and in the royal emblem of the Mikado.

The good president's knowledge of Japan was a little askew: Japan is hardly a continent, and the emblem of the emperor is the sixteen-petal chrysanthemum and not the sun.

People had long been Peru's lack. In 1845 the Council of State, in a burst of enthusiastic exaggeration, boasted that an abundant and wisely organized immigration would soon transform Peru into an "immense emporium, a colossus of opulence and power." Peru needed workers, *brazos*. The country was like the Venus de Milo, commented a writer in 1891, *"sin brazos"* ("without arms").

Francisco Pizarro, Spanish conquistador, had been Peru's first immigrant. In 1511, along with his soldiers, he had brought fifty black slaves, one-third of them women. More than three hundred years later, in 1849, the Chinese began to arrive. Within thirty years they numbered one hundred thousand, in spite of the fact that, contracted in Macao and packed inhumanly into slave ships, between 10 and 30 percent had died during the four-month voyages.

The Chinese were exotic creatures from another world; Limeños of the 1850s had never seen men of yellow skins in long gowns, pigtails, and queer shoes, who spoke in an unintelligible jargon. The descendants of Pizarro's blacks, emancipated in 1855 and now reveling in their newfound freedom, delighted to inflict upon the new Chinese slaves the sufferings that they themselves had experienced. In 1874 the entry of Chinese into Peru was restricted by treaty, and in 1909 contract immigration ceased. By 1940, a high death rate, the return to China of many, and a gradual process of amalgamation, had reduced Peru's Chinese population to 10,000, of whom only 550 were women.

Exploited by sugar-plantation owners, manhandled by blacks and *cholos* (persons of mixed blood), and cursed by politicians and journalists, the Chinese toiled doggedly and left their sweat in Peru's flourishing coastal agriculture. In 1904 Manuel Gonzales Prada, an incisive and biting critic of Peruvian society, wrote in his essay, "Our Aristocracy," "The sugar-owning nobility should have a coat-of-arms inscribed with an arm brandishing a whip across the buttocks of a Chinese."

Japan encountered Peru in 1872, when the *Maria Luz,* a Peruvian vessel sailing from Macao to Callao with 230 Chinese coolies aboard, sought refuge from a typhoon in Yokohama harbor. Yokohama's authorities, honoring Japan's treaty with China and determining that the *Maria Luz* was indeed a slave ship, released the Chinese and sent the vessel on her way. The Peruvians demanded indemnity, and the two parties submitted the case to the Czar of Russia who, in 1875, ruled against Peru. Captain Garcia y Garcia, the Peruvian emissary in Japan, had meanwhile signed, on August 21, 1873, the first treaty negotiated with Japan by a South American nation. As a result, the Peruvian flag was hoisted at the fort of Kanagawa, near Yokohama, and when the news had crossed the Pacific, the flag of the Rising Sun flew for the first time in the port of Callao.

After abolishing the unequal treaties and winning a war with China, both of which occurred in 1895, Japan was ready for expansion overseas. Her first ship to arrive in Peru, the *Sakura Maru,* docked in Callao on April 3, 1899, with 790 passengers, all from the so-called emigrating prefectures—Niigata, Yamaguchi, Hiroshima, and Okayama—and all destined for the coastal sugar plantations. During the next twenty-three years, nearly seventeen thousand farmers and laborers from the countryside of Japan crossed the Pacific legally to be absorbed into the farms and plantations of the land of the Incas. This human flow continued almost until the outbreak of war, although it had been interrupted and slowed by restrictions and international tensions. After 1931 the tide shifted, due to warfare in China, Japan's policy to settle Manchukuo, and drastic Peruvian restrictions. Every year, from 1931 through 1941, more Japanese left Peru than arrived.

No one knows how many Japanese illegally entered Peru. However, it was common knowledge that Peruvian passports were on sale to both Chinese and Japanese in Yokohama, Macao, and

Hong Kong. (The going rate at one time was one thousand Peruvian soles, which in the early 1940s was equivalent to about fifteen dollars.) A former foreign minister admitted in 1941 that the "administrative corruption" connected with immigration was rife and that certain Peruvian officials had been involved in the traffic.

The census of 1940, the first since 1876, put the number of native Japanese in Peru at 17,598, and that of the nisei, or Peruvian citizens of second generation Japanese descent, at 8,790, making the total "Japanese" population 25,888. The figure of 30,000, accepted by the embassy in 1942, including 10,000 nisei, was probably not far from reality.

While the origins of Peru's Japanese included every one of the forty-seven prefectures, more than a third were from the Ryukyu Islands, popularly known as Okinawa, from the name of the main island. To the outsider, this meant nothing—no one guessed that Okinawa would one day become temporarily an American colony— but to the Japanese residents and their families, the Okinawan element produced a clear-cut division in the community. Surnames immediately identified Okinawans; they spoke a language that was not the emperor's Japanese; by their compatriots from *naichi* (literally, the "inner land"; that is, Japan proper) they were looked upon as the "little people," a step or two down the social scale from the true sons of Yamato. The Ryukyuans maintained their own separate societies and, during the 1930s, trouble had occurred at least once between the Okinawan organization and the Japanese Central Society.

The first Japanese immigrants to Peru were exclusively agricultural laborers. Soon, however, their inherent thrift and propensity for hard work started the migration from farm to town; the recently arrived settlers bettered themselves by utilizing their artisans' skills and tending modest shops. Many plantation workers advanced to the status of *yanacones* ("tenant farmers"). In 1916 the Japanese minister who then resided in Chile requested that the Peruvian government allow, on a reciprocal basis, the practice in Peru of Japanese doctors and dentists. Peru's foreign minister indignantly rejected the proposal, asserting that reciprocity was impossible since no Peruvian doctor or dentist could find a career in Japan. Albert

Ulloa, who related the incident, found the request impertinent, revealing the aggressiveness of the Japanese, their feeling of superiority, their clannishness, and their contempt for Peruvian medical science.

Carleton Beals, an American specialist in Latin American affairs, complained ominously in 1937 that "the whole weight of the imperial Japanese government has been thrown behind the effort to gain a strong foothold in Latin America." He described the Japanese drive to exploit a vast, cheap market for "civilized goods" among low-income Indian consumers, a drive advantaged by cheap labor, depreciated currency, pooled distribution, and the low Japanese living standard, which was close to that of most Latin Americans. Beals was alarmed at the political, cultural, and racial appeal of the Japanese. For instance, they had promised to buy El Salvador's coffee in return for the recognition of their puppet state of Manchukuo. Even more wily was their blatant advertising of the theme that the Incas were really Oriental people. It was the same story, heard so many times in so many decades from so many sources, that unfair competition from cheap goods made in Japan undersold indigenous manufacturers.

The patent success of the Japanese won them enmity. For all to see, they were serious and industrious. Peruvians agreed that they were devoted to the land "by their love of work and their dedication to family life." They utilized to the full every hour of the day and every square meter of ground. They could outproduce and outsell their less energetic Peruvian competitors. They dominated certain classes of small business—the bazaar, the *cafetina,* the barber shop, and the bakery. In the narrow side streets of Lima and in the dusty *barrios* ("districts") of straggling, sun-cooked towns up and down the coast, and even in the huddled villages of the sierra, the bazaar and the *cafetina*—both national institutions—were almost invariably identified by signs reading Yamashiro, Matsuyama, Higa, or Tanaka. The bazaar sold all the cheap goods that the poor Peruvian needed; at the same time, he often resented it. As one foreign observer put it, "He feels instinctively that the Japanese earns his living from the toil of the poor. . . . He is dimly aware that selling cheap goods, which are inferior to good ones, is an indirect form of usury." The Japanese were secure in their monopoly of bazaars; almost no Peruvians and only a few Near Easterners attempted to compete with them. In the little, dark, cramped *cafetinas*, the radio blared popular songs while the paisanos of the neighborhood drank Japanese-produced *chica* (a native drink made from corn) and exchanged the gossip of the day. Not surprisingly, these places became suspect as hotbeds for plots and propaganda.

The first Japanese Barbers Association was organized in Lima in 1907, and within fifteen years there were one hundred shops in Peru. By the time the war broke out and the Japanese were driven from their business, the Peruvians advertised urgently for barbers and opened emergency barber colleges to train replacements for the ousted Japanese. More than 50 percent of Lima's bakeries were Japanese-owned. A crisis situation developed in poultry production in 1943 because of the large numbers of poultry farms operated by Japanese in and around Lima. Japanese workers made the bodies of most of the buses running on the streets of Lima in 1942 and 1943. They were prominent in the manufacture of rubber products and hosiery; one company produced from ten to twelve thousand dozen felt and straw hats and berets annually. In 1938 forty-two out of fifty-two machine shops in Lima were owned by Japanese. Sixteen out of twenty glass dealers listed in the 1942 Lima telephone directory were Japanese. They had earned the reputation as the best plumbers and carpenters; their florist shops and greenhouses were the best known in Lima. Japanese were producing 12.5 percent of Peru's cotton and were growing cinchona and coffee in the interior.

The location of the Japanese disturbed our intelligence services, mobilized to combat enemy subversion. More than 90 percent lived along the coast or in the two cities of Lima and Callao. Callao was totally dependent on the Japanese for its daily supply of green vegetables. Japanese controlled 55 percent of the cotton production of the fertile Chancay valley, fifty miles north of Lima. The most prominent farmer in Chancay was Okada Nikumatsu who operated six haciendas with an acreage of 2,750 hectares, mostly in cotton cultivation. Okada's life was a typical success story. He had come to Peru in the first group of immigrants in 1899. Through his own efforts he rose from common laborer to administrator of the six farms and the leading businessman in the valley. He was decorated by the emperor in 1929, a fact that immediately marked him as a potentially dangerous Japanese. He was deported from Peru in June of 1942.

In early 1940 Peruvian officials were considering additional restrictions to supplement those already effected in 1936 and 1937. The proposed new laws would prohibit Japanese from owning land and would ban further immigration. On Saturday, May 11, the senate met to debate the so-called Japanese problem. No action was taken, but during the same weekend rumors circulated in Lima that arms had been smuggled to Japanese in Callao, that twenty-five thousand rifles had been discovered on a Japanese farm, that eight thousand machine guns had been found concealed in a Japanese florist shop in Lima, that a crate containing an unassembled airplane had been accidentally opened at the port of Chimbote, and that the police had come across caches of arms and ammunition in various towns, intended for use by a fifth column composed of from one to five thousand Japanese ex-soldiers. According to one report, American intelligence officers had been responsible for uncovering the plot.

On Monday, May 13, several hundred youths, assembled in front of the offices of a Japanese steamship company in Lima, began to shout, "Down with the Japanese! *Viva el Perú!*" Stimulated by the growing dimensions of the arms stories, the crowd began to stone windows, smash doors, and loot every Japanese establishment at hand. No one was killed but many were injured, mostly Peruvians, and about six hundred business, farm, school, and private properties were seriously damaged. Both the Peruvian government and the Japanese legation promptly and categorically denied the rumors of hidden arms and Congress voted an indemnity for the riot damage (about half the amount requested by the Japanese). While investigators were still sorting out the results of the riots, a disastrous earthquake shook Lima and Callao on May 24, which may have suggested to the Japanese that the revenge of their gods was swift.

Two months after the May disturbances the government took another step, this time effectively to deprive nisei of their Peruvian citizenship if they returned to Japan for education or other purposes.

Officials explained that this measure was "designed to counteract a maneuver of Japanese subjects who, although born in Peru, were sent to Japan when twelve or fourteen years old, in order to be exposed to the Japanese national spirit, serve in the army, and complete the formation of the Japanese character."

By the time war focused American attention on the Japanese in Peru, the ground had been well prepared by the Peruvians themselves. Rarely has a foreign government cooperated so enthusiastically in actions urged by Washington.

It was in this early, post-Pearl Harbor atmosphere, with the shock still fresh, that we arrived in Lima in February of 1942. Peru, like all Gaul, was divided into three parts: *la costa, la sierra, la montaña* ("the coast," "the mountains"—one went from sea level to sixteen thousand feet in a matter of hours—and the "jungle"). Outside of Lima and a few other cities, the population was largely Indian, descendants of the Incas, and speaking the Quechua language. Only 65 percent of the school-age children spoke Spanish; the remaining 35 percent spoke Quechua or other Indian languages. Of these, 65 percent were listed in the census as "without instruction." Quechua intrigued me, and I took lessons in it for several months. All I can now remember is that it has one unpronounceable guttural sound which was phoneticized by a combination of three *k*'s: *kkk*.

Spanish was essential for anyone living and working in Peru. Learning Spanish was like studying the piano—easy to begin but impossible to finish. The more I became engrossed in the language, the richer and more beautiful I discovered it to be. My two teachers urged me to dip into Peruvian literature and to practice translating English into Spanish. My translations of three articles I had written in Washington about Japanese nationalism were published in *El Comercio* under the pseudonym of Ijin ("Foreigner"). Washington Patiño (his sister was named America, his brother, George) was the enthusiast who guided my Spanish hand in these endeavors. He was a great teacher and a friend who dedicated himself to introducing Peru and Peruvians to me. One day Patiño overheard a conversation in a barber shop in which a Japanese was speculating on who Ijin could possibly be; he was puzzled but convinced that Ijin had lived in Japan.

Manual Gonzales Prada held up to ridicule the Peruvian aristocrats who prided themselves on their pure Spanish blood and direct descent from Pizarro and his conquistadores. "Spanish blood," he wrote, "loses itself in morganatic unions and in the libidinous mysteries of bedrooms, so that the least Africanized of our young aristocrats has his whiteness diluted with 10 percent of pitch. One can discover the Anglo-Saxon in the 'black minstrels' of the United States in spite of the blacking smeared on their faces; in our noblemen, the berber sticks out through the white lining: only the pigment and the kinky hair are lost. The minstrels are white flour in blackened sacks; the others resemble rock coal in ermine sacks." The Japanese, unlike the other races, including the Chinese, did not mix. They sent for picture brides from Japan; more than half of the Japanese population was female in contrast to 5 percent for the Chinese, a fact that contributed to the solidarity of the Japanese colony.

The Indians in Peru drew my sympathy. Illiterate and poor, they eked out their existence in the inhospitable climate of the high mountains and, with no knowledge of Spanish and little beneficence from the government, seemed cut off from the rest of the world. The dominant figure in their villages was the parish priest who more often than not was bigoted and tyrannical. Haya de la Torre's banned Aprista party championed the Indians' welfare and propagated the notion of a democratic society, socialized but not Communist. Except for one designated officer, all of us in the embassy were enjoined from any contact with Apristas. I met one once in the course of my investigation of the Japanese, but I had no chance to further the acquaintance.

I was disturbed by the snobbism of the Limeños, their lack of pride in their country and their lack of civic-mindedness. One Peruvian friend told me that he could scarcely wait until the war was over and he could return to Paris, where he would kneel to kiss the French earth. To the Peruvians, the war was a faraway fire. Not directly involved, although pro-Allies in sentiment, they set about to enjoy the advantages, and these included war on the Axis economic stake. The measures taken against Axis nationals—including the restrictions on location and business, the blacklisting of firms, and the deportations—were welcomed for their destruction of unwanted competition. So-called patriotic Peruvians, inspired by economic motives, vied with each other to give information—for a price—to the various competing American intelligence agencies about suspected acts of sabotage or suspicious persons or incidents that suggested espionage. We were always hearing about strange lights signaling enemies from lonely beaches.

Pressured by American authorities, the Peruvians zealously imposed controls on the movements and activities of Germans and Japanese. The Japanese were restricted in the following ways:

1. All Japanese schools, organizations, and newspapers were closed, and Japanese were frequently arrested for illegal assembly. The colony had maintained twenty-seven schools, where four thousand students were taught in Japanese by 113 Japanese teachers. We compiled a list of 102 Japanese organizations, ranging from the Japanese General Society with a membership of several thousand to something called the Amagusa Social Club. Two Japanese dailies, the *Peru Jihō* and the *Lima Nippō,* were published until December 7, 1941, when the *Nippō* carried these banner headlines: JAPAN AND AMERICA COME TO WAR ... UNITED STATES INSINCERE IN CONVERSATIONS ... STRUGGLE OF THE CENTURY BREAKS ... JAPAN'S PATIENCE SNAPS

2. Japanese were prohibited from traveling outside their home communities without special permission from the local authorities.

3. All licenses for hunting, fishing, and possession of arms were revoked.

4. Responding to an American suggestion, the minister of government ordered the removal of 355 telephones belonging to Japanese.

5. Although no systematic plan of relocation was instituted, as in California, Japanese residents of certain strategic coastal cities were moved to points in the interior.

6. By decree of March 22, 1943, the government canceled the

naturalization papers of Axis subjects "who may engage in subversive activities or in propaganda for systems contrary to democracy."

Although they were severe, we in the embassy doubted that these regulations were being strictly enforced. We learned that travel restrictions were administered haphazardly, and that in some areas Japanese were traveling freely, provided they always carried a few 10-sol bills for emergency purposes. Furthermore, in spite of orders, naturalization continued; to our knowledge, at least two Japanese were naturalized.

To break the economic influence of the Japanese, the Peruvians froze their funds on December 8, 1941, and placed 566 Japanese business concerns on the "proclaimed" or blacklist. Laws designed to implement the resolutions of the Rio conference of January 1942 empowered the government to control Axis firms and to nullify contracts covering rural property. The latter regulation forced Japanese to leave their rented land or to labor as peons at a daily wage. In 1943 the government assumed the right to expropriate the agricultural, industrial, and commercial businesses of Japanese.

This economic warfare, as it was called, crippled but did not destroy the Japanese economic stake in Peru. In a report sent to the State Department on October 9, 1943, I wrote,

> It is agreed by most observers that in spite of inefficiency, delay, graft, and the machinations of the Japanese, economic warfare against them has been in the main successful. The larger enterprises, including farm lands, factories and commercial houses are no longer in Japanese hands. With a few exceptions ... they are out of the business picture for the duration.

Determining that security and economic controls were not enough, the U.S. government urged the deportation and internment in the United States of Axis nationals from Latin America. Twelve nations responded to the American offer and expelled both Japanese and Germans to the United States for custody. More than two thousand of those who left their Latin American homes were

Japanese. From April 4, 1942, until July 9, 1943, during the period I was in Lima, the embassy participated actively in the expulsion from the country and transportation to the United States of 1,024 Japanese, of whom 399 were women and children. They were sent in groups on seven ships and one army transport airplane at irregular intervals during this period.

The first evacuation vessel, the S.S. *Etolin,* left Callao on April 4, 1942, carrying 141 Japanese who had volunteered for transportation to the United States. These were among a total of 978 Japanese who had expressed to the Spanish embassy, in charge of Japanese interests, a desire to leave Peru. On subsequent sailings, no volunteers were accepted. The object of the program was to expel those enemy aliens whose continued presence in the country presented a danger to the hemisphere's security. In December 1942 General Marshall apparently suggested that Japanese brought from Peru might be exchanged for American prisoners of war held by the Japanese. No such exchanges ever took place, and we in the embassy were unaware of the proposal. In selecting the deportees, since no proof of guilt existed, it seemed logical to mark for detention those individuals who by their influence or position in the community, their known or suspected connections in Japan, or by their manifest loyalty to Japan, could be considered *potential* subversives. This selection process, to be reasonable, demanded reliable intelligence based on research into the activities of the Japanese who were then living in Peru. Since no one in the Peruvian government or in the embassy, except myself, spoke or read Japanese, this research task fell largely to me. My friend and colleague, Rolland Welch, performed the same duty with respect to the German nationals.

The Peruvian police, eager to uncover espionage, had for some time fretted over correspondence passing among members of the Japanese community, which no one could read. My presence was greeted enthusiastically as the solution to their dilemma. Regularly, a police officer would appear stealthily at my office laden with mail bearing Japanese names and addresses and wrapped carefully to conceal its identity. Anyone who has studied the Japanese language appreciates the vast difference between handwriting and the printed word. The form of script is called sōsho ("grass writing"). To the uninitiated, much Japanese penmanship, or "brushmanship," suggests that pieces of grass have been dipped in ink and squiggled gracefully down the page.

In our Tokyo language study we had made little effort to learn *sōsho*. It was enough to understand the newspapers; reading handwritten letters was beyond the call of official duty. Fortunately, because of personal interest, I played around with handwriting but never became proficient in reading it. But I could never admit to a Peruvian official, nor even to my own embassy colleagues, that I, as a proclaimed Japanese language officer, could only with difficulty decipher an ordinary Japanese letter. So I made the best of it. Through sheer concentration, the wearing out of a dictionary, and a generous application of imagination, I managed to discover generally what the Japanese were writing to each other about. To the deep disappointment of the Peruvian intelligence officers, I failed to find a single missive which divulged bomb plots, secret trysts, contemplated assassinations, codes, or even plans to signal a Japanese ship from a lonely beach. Nothing emerged to confirm the rumors constantly whispered to our legal, army, and naval attachés by their conscientious paid informants.

One day my police contact came to me triumphantly. He had found what he was sure was the most suspicious document of all, a mysterious printed card, obviously detailing secret instructions to saboteurs. I looked hastily at the card, which, because it was printed, I could read easily. I had to tell a crestfallen policeman that he had brought me a wedding announcement. Later I thought what a mistake I had made. If I had just concocted a secret plot, no one would have known the difference, and how very happy I would have made my friend.

Nonetheless, I did learn some things about the Japanese community. While in Japan I had heard very little about Okinawa. It was the forgotten Forty-seventh Prefecture, the one the emperor had never visited, and since we had no consulate there and no one ever thought of spending an Okinawan holiday, the existence of these islands scarcely penetrated my consciousness. In the letters I was given to read, Okinawa cropped up time and again. One Japanese wrote to another:

... The ones who seem to want to leave Peru are the little ones [Okinawans]. . . . On the next boat the passengers will not all be Okinawans I understand, but most will be from Japan proper.

Another gossiped:

... I have heard rumors that K. M. has married a certain Okinawan by the name of Higa [Higa is the most common Okinawan name: 372 of our 11,000 Japanese registered in Lima–Callao were named Higa]. . . . In the first place, it is a great mistake to marry an Okinawan. I have a feeling of great disappointment at hearing that the daughter of that household has married an Okinawan. I should say that even if by so doing, a girl would get S/30,000, she should never marry an Okinawan.

Some of the Japanese letter writers affirmed their loyalty to their mother country:

... Not only soldiers serve their country. Every Japanese without exception is in this war. We here in this country are in the front lines.

One dangerously referred to *blood* in expressing his patriotic sentiments:

... I listen with the utmost attention to every word and every syllable uttered on the radio. If there is anything we can do in this war, in which 100 million souls are of one heart, then we should be ready to do it even at the sacrifice of our blood.

Still another, in the Japanese tradition, penned a poem:

... We hear the voice of the storm
But our hearts are strong,
We are proud to be sons of men of Yamato!

When I came back home I wrote this poem. . . . When we think of our fighting forces in the bitter cutting cold of the

Aleutians or in the burning heat of the South Pacific fighting and giving their lives, then the persecution which we are receiving here amounts to nothing.

The second-generation Japanese in Peru never faced a challenge to defend the country of their birth, as did the American nisei. Undoubtedly, many did want to prove themselves as Peruvians. One intercepted communication contained notes for a speech on "The Loyalty, Standpoint and Attitude of the Japanese Nisei in Peru." The writer called upon his fellow nisei to make known their unquestionable loyalty as Peruvians. Citing the praise for American nisei expressed by Secretary of the Navy Knox after a visit of inspection to Hawaii, he concluded that to be loyal to Peru was to be loyal to Japan:

> ... The descendents of Japanese are not destined to be used as cat's-paws by Japan's power.
>
> The merit of the Japanese race and the glory of our blood shine throughout the world. Therefore the highest and greatest mission of the sons of Japanese race is to display the spirit of Yamato in the place which gave us birth. To carry out the meaning of loyalty without reservation and to become a part of the country in which we live are the great duties which we owe to our mother country.
>
> If unfortunately Peru and Japan should be forced to war, then Peruvians of Japanese race should fight as Peruvian soldiers against the Japanese forces. In the end, to draw arms against Peru is to draw arms against Japan.

It was natural that we should cooperate with our Chinese allies. Our two embassies were on good terms, and I quickly became acquainted with a bright, young officer on the Chinese embassy staff named George Woo. Although his father had served in the Chinese diplomatic service, George (or Jorgé, as he called himself in Lima) had lived for a number of years in Peru and was trilingual in Spanish, English, and Chinese. We decided that the Chinese in Peru, loyal to the Allied cause, ought to be willing to help in our investigation of Japanese activities in the country. As a consequence, George and I formed a Chinese-American alliance and tirelessly traveled up and down the country, to villages and towns, large and small, both in the coastal region and in the hinterland, seeking information about the Japanese colonies. Invariably, the Chinese and Japanese existed side by side and were engaged in many of the same kinds of small business endeavor. Everywhere we went we were feted by the local Chinese associations; we moved from banquet to banquet. Except for my later experience in Yenan, I have never eaten such delectable Chinese food. I made speeches in broken Spanish and drank innumerable toasts to Allied victory in war and to undying Chinese-American friendship.

We were inescapably conspicuous in these towns; there could be little that was secret about our mission, and the Japanese must have known all about us. Still, we heard a rumor in one village that a mysterious German and a Japanese were traveling together for some unholy Axis purpose. In our travels we gathered masses of information about who the Japanese were and what they were doing and picked up dozens of lurid stories, but we learned nothing reliable or convincing about subversion. George and I became good friends and saw a lot of Peru together. I tried to suppress any awkward thoughts that our lavishly hospitable Chinese hosts might be inspired, not only by patriotic zeal for the Allied cause, but by a back-of-the-mind coveting of their enemies' business. In any case our trips were a triumphant demonstration of Allied solidarity: *Viva el Perú, la China, y los Estados Unidos!*

Lacking incriminating evidence, we established the criteria of leadership and influence in the community to determine those Japanese to be expelled. We prepared lists, which we presented to the Peruvian authorities. These authorities, committed at least personally if not officially, to the expulsion of *all* Japanese, treated our proposed lists rather lightly. As the second and third ships departed, it became clear that the passengers who actually embarked were not the ones so carefully identified by us. The more affluent Japanese were finding that a well-placed monetary contribution would bring immunity from deportation just as it had eased the restrictions against business. Besides, to the Peruvian police who rounded up the deportees, a Japanese face was a Japanese face.

In February 1943 the sixth contingent of Japanese was due to leave from Peru's northern port, Talara, on the S.S. *Frederick Johnson*. Consultation in the embassy and particularly with Raymond L. Ickes of the Department of Justice, who visited Lima in connection with the deportation program, established the consensus that henceforth we must insist that the individuals deported were the ones designated by the embassy. The ambassador sent me to Talara to check the embarking passengers and gave me authority to reject any not on our list. Aboard ship I spoke to the Japanese only in Spanish, to keep our secret. One or two expressed surprise that I was able to pronounce their names with such a good accent.

I looked into the faces of these humble, bewildered people—shopkeepers, farmers, carpenters, barbers, and fishermen—starting out involuntarily on a voyage to an unknown future. These were not spies, saboteurs, bomb throwers, or plotters against the state. One of our picked leaders was Juan Saburō Koide, president of the Japanese Association of Trujillo, who had lived in Peru since 1908. His career was probably similar to that of many of his more successful compatriots. He had progressed through an amazing series of occupations to his position of leadership in the Trujillo colony. He had engaged in the bakery business, the carriage business, in truck gardening, antiques, club management, and wholesale merchandising. In 1929 he had returned to Japan, married, and within five months had come back to Peru with his wife. For six years, he had been a prominent member of the Trujillo Rotary Club. That night in the bare, dark, barrackslike ward room of the *Frederick C. Johnson* I talked at length with Koide about his past and about his present state of mind. He spoke quietly, without evident bitterness or anger. He regretted that he had not returned to Japan with his wife who had left Peru in March of 1941. He insisted—and I was impressed by his earnestness—that the Japanese in Peru were loyal to their adopted country and that he and his fellow countrymen tried to live by the high moral precepts of Bushido. He believed that only a few of the Japanese were interested in political questions or were personally concerned with Japan's war against the United States. Most of them thought only about their personal welfare and their chances of making a decent living in their present homeland, Peru. Juan Saburō Koide was being sent off to internment because he was judged a threat to the security of the Western Hemisphere.

Checking the passengers through a little grilled window in what I suppose must have been the purser's office, I found that many who presented themselves were not identified on any of our lists. Others whom we were expecting had not appeared. Acting on the ambassador's instructions, I refused to accept anyone who was not listed in our rosters. Those so eliminated left the ship with gleeful faces.

A few days later, at a conference in Lima, the chief of police, an energetic, blustering, rolypoly man named Mir y Teran, was livid with rage. Gesturing wildly, he turned to me, *"Pero donde están mis presos?"* ("Where are my prisoners?") Apparently he had emptied Lima's jails of miscellaneous vagrants and petty miscreants with Japanese faces and sent them off to Talara, thinking, Good riddance and money saved to the state. The generous Americans would take this riffraff off his hands. But I had dared to liberate his prisoners. I have often wondered what became of these freed felons who wandered off into the Talara night.

As time went on and the deportations continued, a subtle change began to occur in the attitudes of the beleaguered Japanese in Peru. The letters that started to come back from the camps in Texas and New Mexico may have played some part in this change. The letters said, in effect, "Come on up and join us! It's not so bad here. We see movies twice a week and eat chicken on Sundays." The purpose of the well-placed gift suddenly shifted. Instead of paying to stay off the ships, influential Japanese were now paying to board them.

Just as in Osaka I had turned to Chikamatsu, in Lima I found in music a surcease from the deportation ships and the reading of others' mail. I met a young Hungarian refugee named Alejandro Kossodo, who was preparing to become a concert pianist. We rented a second piano, and I tried to keep up with Kossodo in Mozart's Sonata for Two Pianos and in pieces by Bach, Debussy, and

Shostakovitch. Alejandro was frail and serious and possessed with grandiose ideas for public performances. We did practice enough so that I could concertize for the Sociedad Filharmonica, and just before I left Lima we played a program billed as a *"concierto de despedida al señor* John K. Emmerson." The piano, as always, was an escape from the worries of work and the superficialities of social affairs into concentration on fingers and sounds, which left one exhausted physically but refreshed and elated mentally and emotionally.

Lima was music for us. There we met Erich Kleiber, then a world-famous Austrian conductor who made regular tours throughout South America. His wife, an American, had been a schoolmate of my sister's in Cañon City, Colorado, so we saw much of the Kleibers when they came to Lima. Our children called him Papito, and he unbent when away from the podium. He amazed me by relating how, during the course of long walks, he would rehearse whole orchestral programs in his head. One of his concerts came at the time of the Battle of Stalingrad and he dedicated Stravinsky's *The Fire Bird* to the Russian victors.

We met other musicians in Lima, including Witold Malcuzinski, the impeccable interpreter of Chopin. He practiced in our living room, and our little girl, who was later to become a musician herself, hid behind the door to listen, enraptured. Yehudi Menuhin came and astounded me by saying in all seriousness that he was planning to study Japanese, hoping he might thus contribute to the war effort. We had musical evenings almost every Sunday, inviting Peruvian friends who were more interested in music than in Japanese. Usually we listened to classical recordings; occasionally some of us would play or sing.

Housekeeping was not easy in Lima. The servants were Quechua-speaking Indians whose Spanish was almost as broken as ours. They had a carefree, careless, mañana sort of attitude, which put extraordinary burdens on Dorothy. The children were introduced suddenly, without preparation, into a Spanish-speaking world; our four-year-old shut herself in her room and refused to communicate. Within a couple of months the children were speaking fluently, but the first period of adjustment was a cruel one.

Peru was our only Latin American assignment, and I can speak with no authority on our neighbors to the south. Lima was a pleasant city except for its three months of rainless cloudiness. Its Spanish architecture and Spanish pride separated it from the rest of the Inca-bred country. It was wartime and our countries' policies coincided, allowing us a friendly reception. Nevertheless, Peruvians perceived us—and not without some justification—as wealthy, powerful, and domineering *norte-americanos.*

By the summer of 1943 it became clear that the Japanese colony in Peru was not a threat, if it ever had been, to the defense of the hemisphere. The last ship with which I had anything to do left Callao on July 9, 1943, taking only women and children who wished to join their husbands and fathers already interned in the United States. Shortly after this I told the ambassador that I thought my job was done. No one was any longer worried about the Japanese colony, and he had no further need for a Japanese-speaking foreign service officer on his staff.

Since Parkinson's law is not easily reversed and any diminution in staff is a blow to the prestige of the post, he was reluctant to let me go. Luckily I was saved from a continuing pleasant, though pointless, residence in Lima. My friend Larry Salisbury wrote personally from Washington to ask whether I would be interested in an assignment in the China–Burma–India theater of war. The job might be dangerous, and I would have to be separated from my family for a period of up to two years. He could guarantee, however, that the experience would be interesting. After hesitating only long enough to consult Dorothy, who agreed with qualms but brave understanding, I wrote Larry that I welcomed the assignment.

The ambassador kept me on as long as possible, and it was October before I finally flew to Washington, leaving the family to spend another six months in Peru before settling for the duration in Colorado. Before leaving Peru I had time to write my report on the Japanese, and we took advantage of the opportunity to spend a last quick vacation in Arequipa, Cuzco, Machu Picchu, and La Paz, Bolivia.

As I look back on the Peruvian experience I am not proud to have been part of the Japanese operation. One steeled oneself against the heartbreak being inflicted on hundreds of innocent Japanese caught up in the war-generated hysteria that marked each of them a suspect. It is hard to justify our pulling them from their homes of years and herding them, whether born in Japan or in Peru, onto ships bound for a strange land, where they would live in concentration camps under conditions which at best were difficult, in spite of chicken on Sunday. Of course, we were at the same time interning our own citizens in relocation centers, and the Latin American republics had sanctioned the actions we were taking. Incredible as it may seem, intelligence services reasoned at the time that Japan's war strategy included plans for an attack on the western coast of South America. We knew that Japanese army and naval officers had been unusually active in the Latin American republics during 1941; the Peruvian legation in Tokyo had during that year issued forty-seven diplomatic visas to Japanese, fifteen of them to military officers. We took seriously a letter that the Japanese military attaché in Lima had purportedly written on January 20, 1942, to the chief of the Peruvian General Staff threatening that Japan's fleet would destroy air and naval bases on the Pacific Coast of the American continent, aiming primarily at the Panama Canal and would attack all shipping near the Pacific Coast, especially merchant vessels in service between North and South America. He promised that neutrality would offer Peru, not only immunity for its maritime traffic, but lucrative trade with Japan "when the latter has completely assured control of the Pacific."

During my period of service in the embassy, we found no reliable evidence of planned or contemplated acts of sabotage, subversion, or espionage. Stories that many adult male Japanese in Peru held commissions in the imperial army and navy were never verified.

Much later, I learned something of the problems faced at the end of the war by the Peruvian Japanese who had been forcibly interned in the United States. The Immigration and Naturalization Service found that they were enemy aliens who had entered the United States illegally. In 1945 an inter-American conference in Mexico City recommended that any person who had been deported for reasons of security should be prevented from "further residing in the hemisphere, if such residence would be prejudicial to the future security or welfare of the Americas." On September 12, 1945, the United States, by presidential proclamation, authorized the secretary of state "to remove to destinations outside the limits of the Western Hemisphere . . . all alien enemies brought to the United States from other American republics who are within the territory of the United States without admission under the immigration laws." The Peruvian government had, in the meantime, announced that it would not permit the return of Japanese who had been deported from its territory. Thus, the Japanese could neither return to Peru nor remain in the United States. Their plight can be understood. Many were Peruvian citizens who had never known Japan; to go there would be to start life yet again in an alien land, with little, if any, knowledge of the language and no inkling of the conditions they would face.

What actually happened after some years of bureaucratic delays, legal interventions, and complicated negotiations, was that many returned to Japan, a few finally found their way back to Peru, and some remained in the United States. Some of them found employment on the Pacific coast and in the East, especially at Seabrook Farms in Bridgeton, New Jersey, a large fruit-and vegetable-canning concern. Many became naturalized citizens, married Americans of Japanese ancestry, and served in the U.S. Army.

The forcible detention of Japanese from Peru, arising out of a wartime collaboration among the governments of Peru, the United States, and the American republics, was clearly a violation of human rights and was not justified by any plausible threat to the security of the Western Hemisphere. To understand it, one must return to the atmosphere of the times. The war against Japan was a total war. After the surprise attack on Pearl Harbor, the enemy was deemed capable of any act, no matter how unreasonable or unlikely. As a consequence, the enthusiastic exploitation of prejudice, hatred, emotion, and covetousness became respectable and acceptable.

7

China–Burma–India

Lifted out of the depressing combination of effete, Paris-worshiping Lima society and the sordid herding of miserable Japanese onto gloomy deportation ships, I was suddenly dropped into a theater of war: China–Burma–India.

Brigadier General Frank D. Merrill, who had been a fellow language officer in prewar Tokyo, walked into the office of the political advisers in New Delhi on January 6, 1944. We started to reminisce. He kidded me about my Japanese kabuki impersonations. Suddenly we were singing together the first lines of the Japanese patriotic march, the *Nihon Aikoku Kōshinkyoku,* which everyone who had lived in Tokyo in 1940 and 1941 heard *ad nauseam* from the radio, stage, movies, and every victory lantern parade throughout the China war. *"Miyo! Tōkai no sora akete ..."* ("Look! Dawn breaks over the eastern sea ..."). We stopped suddenly and Frank turned to me: "Come along! I'm leaving for a secret camp in central India. This will be a special operation into the Burma jungle. You'll be great—to talk to the Japanese!"

In a few days I found myself in the middle of India at Merrill's training camp at Deoghar on the Betwa River, the boundary between Gwalior State and the Central Provinces, decked out in green fatigues, jungle boots, campaign hat, cropped hair (Merrill's orders), and GI shoes, mosquito net, leggings, olive-drab underwear, and an M–1 rifle. Later on I acquired a machete for hacking away at the jungle.

The first day I met a lieutenant colonel who was puzzled at my lack of insignia. I explained that I was with the State Department. "The State Department!" he guffawed with incredulity. "What will the State Department do in the Burma jungle? Are you going to make a treaty with the natives?" My lack of military rank and thus a proper niche in the established hierarchy continually perplexed my army companions. The result was usually a simulated rank, in my case, field officer—major or lieutenant colonel—which regulated billeting, PX, mess hall, and all the other privileges of segregated army life.

One day General Merrill said to Jim Shepley, a *Time-Life* journalist, and me, "How about doing a little cross-country reconnaissance to watch a river-crossing exercise?" Jim and I and two officers piled into the jeep with Merrill at the wheel. I never figured out whether he was proving the versatility of a jeep, exhibiting his combined cavalry and tank training, or trying to scare us to death. We struck out, Jim and I and Johnny Jones, the outfit's public relations officer, hanging on for dear life in the back seat. Without bothering about roads or even trails, and using all gears in rapid succession, Frank took us up embankments, in and out of ditches, swerving around trees, rocks, and through little village streets, scattering the villagers, splitting the wind.

Sometime during this hair-raising ride Jim Shepley suggested that the first American combat infantry troops on the mainland of Asia ought to be called something other than their official designation, the impossible, forgettable 5307th Composite Unit (Provisional). The army's code word for the outfit was Galahad but that hardly fit these tough characters who had emerged from jungle training or combat experience in Panama and the Southwest Pacific and who had volunteered for a short, secret, hazardous mission. When Jim suggested Merrill's Marauders, the general snorted and took us over another rump-thumping bump. The name stuck. The mystery was how I, unaggressive by nature, had got myself mixed up with this wild bunch of marauding warriors. I was as surprised as the lieutenant colonel who expected me to make a treaty.

The story had begun in early 1942 in Washington, where I met John Paton Davies, Jr., a foreign service officer born in China, who was brilliant, ingenious, imaginative, and a synthesizer and a doer. John was to be political adviser to General Joseph W. Stilwell, who on February 2 had been appointed commanding general of the U.S. forces in the Chinese theater of operations, Burma and India (CBI). Soon afterward John went to CBI, I went to Peru. Almost a year and a half later, in late May of 1943, Davies proposed that four additional foreign service officers be assigned to CBI to engage in political and economic intelligence and psychological warfare operations. The general agreed, as did the State Department. Of the four selected, two—John Stewart Service and Raymond Ludden—both Chinese-speaking, were already in China. The third was dropped because of ill health. The fourth was to be a Japan specialist, but by the time Larry Salisbury's note trickled down to Lima it was already summer and Ambassador Norweb refused to release me until a replacement arrived. While Dorothy and I were on leave in Bolivia, the news came that John Davies, Eric Sevareid, and the other passengers and crew of a doomed C-46 had parachuted into the Burma jungle. Scenes of fighting my way out of dark, tropical forests infested with enemies and wild animals crowded into my head; I tried to spare Dorothy the worry by not telling her what had happened to John. Fortunately, they all walked out safely. As the delay continued and John heard that I was concertizing for Lima's elite, he was reported to have made caustic remarks about my nonchalant piano playing while Burma burned.

It was December 17, 1943 before I was at last in the hands of the ATC (Air Transport Command) and on my way to India. The route took us to Brazil, to Ascension Island where, as the GIs stationed there described it, "the first ten months you talk to the rocks; the second ten months the rocks talk to you," across Africa, to Aden for Christmas, on to Karachi, and to New Delhi, our final destination.

I met John Davies and found the office of the political advisers in the CBI headquarters building where Peggy Durdin, wife of Tilman Durdin, the *New York Times* correspondent in the theater, was acting as secretary and general adviser to the advisers. Peggy possessed the wit, intuition, judgment, and common sense so cheerfully calming in the charged, confused and crazy atmosphere which characterized the CBI. John's conversation was like a series of lightning flashes, of ideas bounding over each other as he spoke. He had just come from the Cairo Conference, where, with Stilwell, he had seen leading actors in the war at firsthand: Churchill, Roosevelt, Harry Hopkins, and of course, the Generalissimo and Madame Chiang Kai-shek who were not strangers to him. At dinner on my first night in New Delhi I was plunged into the heady aura of crackling talk by John and his friends: Major St. Clair McKelway, the *New Yorker* writer, Air Vice-Marshal Philip Joubert de la Ferté, in charge of British psychological warfare, Frank Merrill, and Sheldon Mills, a foreign service officer assigned to New Delhi. I listened but said nothing. It might be the same war but it was a long way, and not in distance alone, from the simplicity of deporting Japanese from Peru to the mixed-up goings-on in this three-country combination, which was then slated to be the springboard for the defeat of Japan.

During my first two weeks in New Delhi I tried to learn something about the complexities of the China–Burma–India theater. Winston Churchill and Franklin D. Roosevelt had established the Europe-first priority for the war at their meeting in Washington two weeks after Pearl Harbor. At the same time, they decided to set up a China theater of operations under the command of Generalissimo Chiang Kai-shek. Roosevelt believed firmly that China must be treated as a great power and this principle, fiction though it was, guided American policy throughout the war and into the postwar period. Warfare in the area of China had two purposes: to establish a base for operations against Japan and to keep China in the war. An American commander was necessary, to serve as chief of staff to the Generalissimo and to run the American show. General George C. Marshall, then army chief of staff, sounded out Stilwell who wrote in his diary, "So I said, 'What's the job?' and he gave me the paper. Coordinate and smooth out and run the road, and get the various factions together and grab command and in general give 'em the works. Money no object."

Stilwell arrived in India on February 25, 1942. The Japanese were rapidly taking over Southeast Asia; they would capture Rangoon ten days after his arrival. By March 11 the British and Chinese in Burma were being encircled and driven north. Stilwell led the final band of one hundred, which included, in his words, "HQ group, Seagraves surgical unit, and strays," on a 140-mile-long march through the jungles and out to India to escape the victory-bent enemy. At New Delhi on May 25, "Uncle Joe" Stilwell uttered the words that were to adorn his niche in history: "I claim we got a hell of a beating. We got run out of Burma, and it is humiliating as hell. I think we ought to find out what caused it, go back, and retake it."

Retaking Burma proved more difficult than Stilwell had anticipated. Since this British colony now in enemy hands blocked land access to China, it had to be recaptured if China were to play a role in the war. This meant clearing the Japanese out of North Burma, securing airfields so that supplies could be flown to China, hacking out a land route to connect with the British-built southern end of the Burma Road, and laying pipelines to speed the flow of gasoline to thirsty flying machines waiting on the other side. These were staggering enough problems, but they were exacerbated by the human and political intrigues, contradictions, and animosities within the CBI.

You either hated or you worshiped Joe Stilwell. There was no middle ground. His immediate associates were intensely loyal. They understood the fanaticism of his concept of the soldier's duty. If he had been Japanese, he would have been a samurai or a kamikaze pilot. As it was, he spent most of his time in the Burma jungles, away from his numerous headquarters in New Delhi, Chungking, and Ceylon, his battered campaign hat shading his eyes, his carbine in hand, egging on the Chinese and leading a platoon. Scrawny, wiry, half-blind, and consumed by gut energy and determination, "Vinegar Joe" felt only contempt for those who did not, in his opinion, share his single-minded dedication to fighting and killing Japanese. Most of the little admiration he had to spare went to the infantryman slugging it out in the mud, the hero, he believed, of all wars.

He poured out in the little pocket-sized notebooks he kept in his campaign shirt his contempt for those in power. He could be venomous: he called his handicapped commander-in-chief, President

Roosevelt, "Old Rubberlegs." Chiang Kai-shek, for whom he reserved the fury of his frustration, was always "Peanut." The British, the "limeys" in his diary's language, were imperialists out to restore their empire, while Churchill gave lip service to the Atlantic Charter. Stalin, with his hard-as-nails toughness, impressed Stilwell, who wrote, "It was like a blood transfusion to see Stalin put backbone in our gas bags. Churchill wanted to poop around the periphery and take Rhodes. Bah. Stalin said 'No' and that was that." In Stilwell's mind, the Peanut was ready to sit out the rest of the war once the United States had come in: "Coast, boys, the Americans and the British will finish it up." The limeys had no interest in China; Churchill was said to be "quite willing to see China collapse."

Although assigned to the CBI for fourteen months, I met Stilwell only two or three times. He was always considerate, read my reports, and was glad to listen to my account of conversations with Japanese prisoners of war and of my ideas on psychological indoctrination. He usually greeted me with, "How is your Sunday school for the Japs coming along?" As John Davies has written, Stilwell believed "that the only way to beat the enemy was to kill him and that psychological and economic warriors had to prove their worth in body counts." He could be gracious, however. When I congratulated him on receiving his fourth star in August 1944, he wrote in reply, "If, as you say, you are basking in the reflected glory of four stars, I am sure there is no fear that you will suffer from sunburn."

Simply put, Stilwell's mission was to get through to China. One way was the road. By the end of 1943 what later was christened the Stilwell Road stretched 103 miles across the muddy mountains from the starting point at Ledo, Assam, to a spot in Burma called Shinbwiyang, at the head of the Hukawng valley. Colonel Lewis Andrew Pike told his men, when he took over the construction job, "The Ledo Road is going to be built—mud, rain, and malaria be damned." And built it was, doubtless one of the most fantastic engineering accomplishments in history. Jeeping the road, I often came across huddles of black GIs forming impromptu choirs to sing spirituals and popular songs at lunch or rest breaks. The music took on an eerie, vibrant, unreal, echolike quality, an unworldly interlude out of the perpetual rhythm of the background sounds of the road: beat of motors, screech of metal against rock, male profanity, and avalanches of earth.

Another link in the line to China was the Bengal and Assam Railway, running the eight hundred miles from Calcutta to Ledo. By March of 1944, GI locomotive engineers were driving rundown equipment at breakneck speeds over the less than robust tracks, strewing upturned cars along the way, in Charlton Ogburn's words, "like dead giant voles with their paws in the air." Mathematical calculations on the length of the war concluded that equipment, although sacrificed to speed, would still last long enough.

Animal power was not forgotten. Elephants were mobilized to tote logs and railway ties. Mules from Missouri, horses from Australia (seven hundred of them), served Merrill's Marauders to pack equipment on jungle trails.

The direct, rapid path to China was the airway, the Hump trail, from airfields in Assam across the Himalayas to Kunming in Yunnan. In December 1943 a record thirteen thousand tons of supplies went over the Hump. The trip was an experience: you concentrated on your parachute and you wondered what would be down there if you had to jump.

While all this activity was going on, Stilwell and his American-trained and -provisioned Chinese divisions were trying to clear the country ahead of the road. Stilwell had his problems. Not only was he constantly irate at the Peanut and the limeys but he had quarrels with the White House, the Joint Chiefs of Staff, and the War Department; with Captain Milton E. "Mary" Miles and his OSS dirty tricksters in their secret Chinese Happy Valley; and with Major General Claire Chennault and his eager Flying Tigers in Kunming. Only General Marshall's firm support kept Stilwell in command and even that failed in October 1944. Lauchlin Currie, Chennault, Lord Louis Mountbatten, and Vice President Henry Wallace all tried to get Stilwell fired. Chiang Kai-shek succeeded on his second try.

Chennault's extraordinary message of October 8, 1942, delivered to the president by Wendell Willkie, boasted preposterously that he,

Chennault, if he were made American military commander in China, could with 147 combat planes "not only bring about the downfall of Japan" but could "make the Chinese lasting friends with the United States." According to Chennault, his difference with Stilwell was whether the war should be fought in Burma or in China. The leader of the Flying Tigers ridiculed Stilwell's obsession with ground warfare. Writing of the Trident conference held in Washington in May 1943, Chennault commented, "Never once in his presentation did I hear Stilwell mention the word airplane. . . . He was content to fight a strictly ground war with his 'beloved men in the trenches.' " Chennault was not the only one skeptical about fighting a war in Burma. Churchill wrote in his memoirs, "I disliked intensely the prospect of a large-scale campaign in Northern Burma. One could not choose a worse place for fighting the Japanese." The malaria-ridden, footsore Marauders would have agreed with Churchill and Chennault.

By the time I arrived in January 1944, Stilwell's Chinese were about to start down the Hukawng valley—death valley, as the Japanese were to call it; the Marauders were getting ready to enter the jungle; the Ledo Road, the Bengal and Assam Railway, and the Hump airlift, were all in violent motion, and the British, the Generalissimo, Stilwell, and Chennault were all feuding. The Combined Chiefs of Staff had approved the use of B-29s to bomb Japan from Chinese bases and had decided on a major naval advance toward Japan through the islands of the central Pacific. Stilwell had got his long-awaited American ground troops, but only three thousand Merrill's Marauders; and after all the summit conferences (Symbol at Casablanca, Trident at Washington, Quadrant at Quebec, and Sextant at Cairo), he was still, in General Marshall's words, "out at the end of the thinnest supply line of all."

It took only a short time to perceive the confusion that pervaded the CBI. The Chinese, the British, and the Americans, not to speak of the Indians, Gurkhas, Australians, Africans, and other Allied and colonial troops, were fighting to drive the Japanese off the Asian mainland. Yet their quarrels with each other seemed to supersede their determination to beat Japan. Stilwell was caught in this impossible maelstrom in which only a political genius with superior, unconventional military skill could succeed. I joined the Stilwell worshipers because I admired his single-minded devotion to a cause and, under a rough exterior, his human sympathy and respect for the common fighting man. His character was illuminated for me when he so often went out of his way to speak words of encouragement to wounded and dying Chinese soldiers in their native language. But as an administrator, Stilwell was hopeless. Time spent at his headquarters in New Delhi, or in Chungking, where he could seldom be found, quickly revealed the lack of direction, cohesion, and efficiency. And as for the Japanese, Stilwell, like many Americans who had served in China, found nothing but evil in them.

Few responsible Americans in the CBI were worrying about how all of this was going to end. Following Stilwell's cue, only body counts mattered; those on the other side were Nips, Japs, Gooks, subhuman creatures one never saw. Yet the curiosity about the enemy we were fighting was evident among the troops. Since I had lived in Japan before the war, I was frequently invited to talk to units up and down the road on a subject I called, "What Makes the Japanese Tick." My GI audiences listened with rapt attention. They knew little, if anything, of the pre-Pearl Harbor diplomatic history or of the issues involved in our war with Japan.

It was still a military secret that Japanese-Americans were fighting in Asia. As a result they never received the recognition that they deserved, even after the war. In contrast, the 442nd Nisei Regiment sent to Italy became the most decorated and publicized unit in the armed forces. At the camp in central India I met the team of fourteen nisei who had volunteered for combat and were now part of the Marauders. Half from Hawaii and half from the mainland, they had come out of the special Japanese-language training school that had been established at Camp Savage in Minnesota. With grim and steely determination, these Japanese-American boys had volunteered to fight against the country of their ancestors and for a country that had not only interned their families but, immediately after Pearl Harbor, had reclassified them as "aliens not subject to military service." They were Americans, not aliens. Yet, in the paranoiac mood of the times, the general who had recommended and carried out the evacuation would tell a congressional committee in 1943, "A Jap's a Jap.... It makes no difference whether he is an American citizen.... You can't change him by giving him a piece of paper."

The same army which distrusted nisei recruits was searching for nisei who could read Japanese documents and interrogate prisoners of war. Unfortunately, for this purpose, most of these second-generation men were too Americanized; few understood or spoke much Japanese. Interviewers found that only 3 percent of the first 3,700 questioned could meet even a minimum standard of Japanese language. And the best ones were the kibei, those who had lived in Japan and were for that reason tainted with suspicion. Among those chosen, the urge to excel was paramount—they had to prove themselves—and they crammed from dawn to dark, with combat training thrown in.

The Marauders' nisei were not destined to live their war in rear-echelon headquarters, translating captured documents and talking to POWs brought in from the front. When they were given the chance to volunteer for a dangerous mission, they were asked bluntly, "Would you be willing to fight Japanese?" They fought Japanese, in five major and thirty-two minor battles in the course of the Marauders' march through the Burmese wilderness.

One nisei sergeant described his first contact with the enemy, "I had a terrible feeling when the first Jap I shot collapsed and expired with a heartbreaking 'Banzai!' on his lips, but my second shot came easy, the third even easier." At first dubious about these GIs with oriental faces, their comrades in combat became their staunchest defenders. One Caucasian soldier, incensed by the reports of discrimination in the United States, wrote his hometown paper:

> We of the Merrill's Marauders wish to boast of the Japanese-Americans fighting in our outfit and the swell job that they put up.... Many of the boys and myself especially, never knew a Japanese-American or what one was like—now we know and the Marauders want you to know that they are backing the nisei one hundred percent. It makes the boys and myself raging mad to read about movements against Japanese-Americans by those

4-F'ers back home. We would dare them to say things like they have in front of us. . . .

One of the Marauders, Henry Gosho, was to become a lifelong friend. "Hank," a kibei, was born in Seattle. Sent by his parents to Japan in 1933, he went to high school and college at Kansai Gakuin, a Christian institution near Kobe. Gosho remembers seeing an article in the *Osaka Mainichi* about my Chikamatsu studies and talking to me once at the consulate general in Osaka when I apparently advised him to return to America. By August of 1941 he sensed that things were getting too hot and luckily managed to get passage on a ship returning to the United States. If he had missed that ship, he would certainly have had to fight the war for the Japanese, as did many of his compatriots.

Sergeant Gosho first distinguished himself while his platoon was surrounded by a Japanese patrol when the Marauders first clashed with the enemy. So close were they that Hank heard the Japanese orders to make a rear flank attack; he translated them instantaneously, and his buddies took the necessary action. Once when Gosho shouted, "Cease firing!" in military Japanese, the dumbfounded imperial troops obeyed. Later, his outnumbered unit had to flee from their position and, for a while, they lived on bamboo sprouts and rainwater. They went to the rescue of another beleaguered unit and were under fire for thirteen days. Gosho came out of this leveling experience with the name "Horizontal Hank" and the Bronze Star for bravery. Malaria and dysentery hit him, and for a while he was able to continue the march only by hanging on to the tail of a mule.

Once during the campaign Stilwell met Sergeant Gosho and, uninformed as to his identity, asked: "Are you Chinese?"

"No, sir."

"Are you Korean?"

"No, sir."

"Are you Filipino?"

"No, sir."

"Don't tell me you're————!"

"Yes, sir."

The general, solicitous of Hank's welfare, turned to an officer with him, "Transfer that man to division headquarters and keep him there!"

The general's command was ignored and Hank remained in action. His immediate superiors would in no circumstances let him go; he was too valuable to lose to the rear echelon. The same GI who wrote to his hometown paper had this to say about Hank: "One of our platoons owes their lives to Sergeant Henry Gosho. . . . Hank guided the machine-gun fire on our side which killed every Jap on that side. The boys who fought alongside of Hank agree that they have never seen a more calm, cool, and collected man under fire. He was always so eager to be where he could be of the most use and effectiveness and that was most always the hot spot."

My service with the Marauders was brief. I learned how to assemble my gear, carry a pack, and roll and unroll my blankets. I trudged along on night marches and slept in the jungle. I even surprised everybody, including myself, by once hitting five out of eight bull's-eyes in target practice with the M-1. But I was not exactly cut out to be an infantry soldier. It turned out that the Marauders took very few prisoners during the first part of their five-hundred-mile march, and the opportunities for my talking to the Japanese were rare.

While Merrill's troops were crossing India by train, I flew to Assam with Colonel Charles Hunter, the Marauders' second in command—a professional's professional if there ever was one—and several other ranking officers of the unit. The troops arrived at the railway terminus on February 6 and assembled at a staging area near the little town of Margherita. By midnight of the seventh they began their "long penetration" over the Patkai range, into the Hukawng valley, over more mountains, toward a destination on the Irawaddy River called Myitkyina (pronounced Mitchinaw). Their story was a tragic one, lasting until August, and crowded with malaria, typhus, monsoons, mud, exhaustion, enemy fire, ambushes, and human bravery. It ended in near-mutiny, when the siege of Myitkyina bogged down and convalescents, barely able to carry a rifle, were ordered back into combat. One defiant boy tore a dressing from an enormous wound in his chest as he boarded a plane. Stilwell was blamed, and the Marauders' bitterness toward him was deep. Charlton Ogburn wrote that his name was "as a red flag to a bull," and Colonel Hunter began his book *Galahad* with the sentence, "Nuts to you, General Stilwell."

For me, the next few months were a foreign service officer's dream. This was the war—probably our last—about which we had no doubts. However we might question the diplomacy of 1941, *we* had been attacked and *we* had to win. We were spared the gnawing scruples of our successors in Vietnam. It was exciting, exhilarating, with the exuberance heightened by the dark beauty of the Burma jungle and the tensing sense of danger, often sharply, although pleasurably, exaggerated in the imagination. Unchained from a desk, I was in fact my own boss, coordinating my activities with John Davies. Our status was established at the various headquarters in the theater, and we wrote our own travel orders; an obliging adjutant general would always gladly sign a document that began, "The Commanding General directs. . . ." I flew in transports, bombers, hospital planes, and in little one-passenger L-5s, which were fine for getting up and down the Hukawng valley. Once on a trip across the Hump I was a waist gunner on a B-24. Jeeps and trucks were always available, and once I found myself driving a huge weapons carrier over rutted, mud-impacted roads. We four political advisers, scattered as we were, developed our own code for communications that no one else could read. No wonder that Ambassador Clarence Gauss in Chungking, to whom we were all technically assigned as second secretaries of embassy, grumbled about these free-wheeling foreign service officers he could not control.

It developed naturally that my duties in the CBI theater would have to do with the Japanese. John Davies, Jack Service, and Ray Ludden were busily analyzing the fate of China. I was left to speculate about how the war would end and what postwar Japan would be like. I had lived that country's evolution toward militaristic nationalism from the February 26 Incident to the eve of Pearl Harbor, and my studies of Japanese literature and an interest in Japanese theater had given me inklings of the conflicts between obligation and passion, the power of the warrior's code, and the philosophy of fatalism, which still molded the national character.

Suicide, violence in desperation, the unpredictability of impulse, and belief in the karma of retribution—all present in the Japanese psyche—might offer clues to the development of our war with the Yamato nation. Psychological warfare and prisoner interrogation appeared as avenues through which I might try to explore this murky future.

While keeping in touch with Merrill's Marauders at various places along their line of march, I spent a good deal of time with the Office of War Information's (OWI) psychological warfare team located on a tea plantation, Chota Powai, near Margherita and the take-off point for the Ledo Road. The group's functions were to win support and cooperation from the various native peoples in the area of Stilwell's operations and to direct psychological warfare at the Japanese enemy. Unlike the OSS (Office of Strategic Services), OWI's propaganda was "white," or overt, with its origin plainly marked. The OWI team was a remarkable assemblage of colorful personalities. It included Shans, Kachins, and Burmese, who busily wrote leaflets in their own languages, and missionaries with long experience in North Burma. One extraordinary Burmese-born American, Harold Young, was an expert on the Lahu and the headhunting, wild Wa tribes living near the Chinese border. He knew the jungle like the streets of a hometown and lectured to spellbound troops on how to survive there. I went with him to gather plants, which he then identified as those that were poisonous, those that were edible (bamboo shoots, banana buds), and lifesaving (banana leaves for shelter, bamboo stalks for water).

Many of the Americans later became distinguished in a variety of careers as ambassadors, publicists, journalists, scholars, businessmen, and artists: William Roth, as ambassador in the Kennedy Administration and candidate for governor of California in 1974; Porter McKeever as secretary general of the United Nations Association, New York, and special assistant to John D. Rockefeller III; Proctor Mellquist, as editor of *Sunset Magazine*; John Steeves, as ambassador to Afghanistan and director general of the foreign service; Marshall Shulman, as director of Columbia University's Russian Institute and special adviser to the White House on Soviet affairs; David Botsford, as president of his own advertising agency (San Francisco,

New York, and Tokyo); Harry Diamond, as a well-known New York artist; Robert Kleiman of *The New York Times*; and Adolph Suehsdorf, a New York publisher.

Another nisei team had been especially selected for assignment to OWI, a talented group with experience in journalism, labor unions, business, and commercial art; most were kibei with education or experience in Japan and therefore a good knowledge of Japanese.

The team leader was Hawaiian-born Staff Sergeant Koji Ariyoshi, thirty years old and a graduate of the University of Georgia who had worked in Hawaii as a store clerk, coffee plantation overseer, truck driver, road-construction worker, longshoreman, and freight clerk. Koji was stocky, soft-spoken, serious, and already deeply involved in the American labor movement. Although he had never been in Japan, Ariyoshi spoke Japanese fluently and was earnestly conscientious about his responsibilities. A non-nisei sergeant temporarily assigned to the group wrote about him in the *CBI Roundup:* "Our team leader made our unit the best disciplined group at all staging camps we had to pass. We often had to march in formation when it wasn't absolutely necessary. Our carbines were the cleanest, our uniforms the neatest." I was later to take Koji up to China, where he became well acquainted with the Communists in Yenan, staying there until the war ended.

Perhaps the most lively, ebullient, hyperactive nisei psychological warrior was Kenji Yasui. He was short, muscular, loquacious, aggressive, and an inveterate gambler. Yasui had lived almost twenty of his twenty-nine years in Japan, returning to California only in 1938. His colloquial Japanese was probably the best of any team member. Kenny became famous as the CBI's "nisei Sergeant York" when he engineered the capture of thirteen Japanese soldiers on an island in the Irawaddy River at the battle of Myitkyina. Responding to a call for volunteers, Yasui and three Caucasian GIs stripped and swam to the little island where twenty-one Japanese were hiding in the underbrush. When Kenny shouted a command in Japanese, an enemy sergeant peered out cautiously, astounded to see a naked little man announcing he was a Japanese colonel working for the Americans and demanding surrender. After one officer had thrown a grenade, only to kill himself, and after three recalcitrants had been shot and four had escaped, the remaining thirteen lined up shamefacedly and marched in close-order drill to the barked commands of the bogus colonel in the buff. Yasui got the group across the river by ordering the prisoners to swim as they pushed a raft on which sat Kenny, clad only in drawn sword, Japanese colonel to the last. For this exploit, he was decorated with the Silver Star.

In April 1944 I received orders to report to the Northern Combat Area Command, Stilwell's forward echelon for the war in North Burma, directly under the command of Brigadier General Haydon L. Boatner. I was to be "supervisor in charge of all psychological warfare activities in the area and adviser in civil affairs matters."

The civil affairs matters had to do largely with the disorganized state of the civilian population due to the war and with our interest in winning their cooperation and maintaining as much tranquility as possible. The British wanted to reestablish order quickly; the principal problem in the Hukawng valley was the resettlement and rehabilitation of the Kachins who formed the dominant tribe in the area. I worked closely with Major J. A. Liddell, a rugged, old-time colonial service professional who had spent his career in Burma; he was the senior British civil affairs officer but reported to General Boatner.

I spent some days traveling up and down the Ledo Road with Major Liddell, or Jim as I came to call him. I, who had forgotten my razor and toothbrush, was impressed by the major's meticulous planning. His bearer sat ceremoniously in the back of the jeep, holding down the mass of paraphernalia that belonged to Jim—a washbasin with collapsible stand, campstools, stoves, tents, mosquito nets, and rations, including ample supplies of bottled spirits.

On one occasion we stopped by the roadside to investigate a quarrel between Nagas and Kachins in which two Nagas had been killed and one injured. The Nagas were demanding six human heads (two for each Naga casualty), one elephant, two buffalo, and three rifles. The major tried to get them to accept a thousand rupees in lieu of the heads, animals, and arms, but they refused, and he postponed the hearing to another occasion.

Later that evening we had dinner at a British officers' mess. Jim was concerned over the propriety of my dress, a rumpled, muddied jungle suit. He asked whether I did not have some regalia to wear, since he had told his colleagues that his guest was a representative of the U.S. State Department. All I could produce for him in the way of regalia was a pair of khaki pants and a clean shirt. After the mess kit lines and the soup ladling I had been accustomed to with the Marauders, this British mess in the Burma jungle was the Waldorf itself, with the meal amazing—soup, fish, spam (the brutal reminder of war!), a sweet (pudding), and a savory (cheese and toast). My hosts became talkative after the whiskey, gin, and rum had flowed, and their true feelings about Stilwell came out. The Ledo Road was nonsense. They joked about the Naga–Kachin dispute, and the major proclaimed loudly that "America was sitting in; America had seen British justice in action!"

Psychological warfare was tailored to the changing military situation. Since we knew the Japanese had no access to news, we set about to break their morale by informing them in our leaflets about the Allied advances in Burma: Maingkwan falls! Walaw Bum taken! Kamaing falls! Mogaung captured! We tried to play on their isolation and shortages of food, showing photographs of heaping plates of rice and fish awaiting them on the Allied side, and nostalgic reminders of home. Prisoners later told us that one leaflet was well known; many could recite it verbatim. It was called "Burma Night" ("China Night" was then one of the most popular songs in Japan) and had a drawing by Chris Ishii, a young nisei artist who had worked for Walt Disney. All in blue, a lone Japanese soldier stood in a small clearing of the crowding, dark jungle: "The Burma night is long. . . . The war, too, is long. . . . When will the Burma night end?"

The effect of our leaflets was hard to judge. Distribution was a problem; pilots preferred to drop bombs instead of paper: "pieces of bumph," as an air force officer expostulated. Sometimes we had regular leaflet-dropping planes assigned to us. Most captured prisoners had read our leaflets, found them interesting, but denied that they had inspired a desire to surrender.

The climax of the North Burma campaign came with the battle of Myitkyina. On May 17 Colonel Hunter led the limping Marauders onto the airstrip and sent General Stilwell the code message "in the ring." Jubilation was soon replaced by chagrin when crucial supplies failed to arrive, and confused Chinese units started shooting indiscriminately at each other. Meanwhile, the Japanese brought in reinforcements and dug in for a stubborn, last-ditch resistance. They had been ordered, "You will defend Myitkyina to the death." It was only on August 4 that Stilwell could record in his diary, "... Over at last. Thank God!"

Myitkyina, which had a population of seven thousand in peacetime, was pulverized by the fury of the frustrated American army and its Chinese allies. I wrote to the State Department at the time, "Almost every weapon of war which can be transported in an airplane has been used against these Japanese defenders. B-25s have blasted their positions (sometimes not too accurately, as for example, the day they killed six of our own men); dive-bombers have strafed them; artillery and mortar fire has been almost continuous. There is said not to be a house left standing in the city of Myitkyina. Yet the Japanese refuse to budge." It was natural that General Boatner, then in charge of the Myitkyina task force, would call for psychological weapons. More than one hundred twenty-five thousand leaflets announcing defeats, calling for surrender, and promising good treatment to prisoners were dropped during two months of the siege from liaison planes flying low over the city at night.

In June, when the discouraging battle was grinding on, the Allies making little progress, someone picked up a crudely mimeographed letter, written by hand in English and addressed to "General Merrill and His Doomed American Troops." The leaflet read:

The Americans have again used their propaganda organs to the full by stating that they would capture Myitkyina and for 23 days made further attacks against the Imperial Forces who have refused to yield even an inch to the enemy forces.... Poor General Merrill and his so-called fighting forces. Your days are numbered and the tide has now changed its course. The vital hour is fast approaching for the Americans as the Imperial Forces are again display [sic] its [sic] prowess to the world by making a sweeping victory against the enemy. [signed] The Commander, Imperial Japanese Forces.

Ready to try anything, no matter how unlikely, Colonel Hunter asked the OWI team to install a public address system at Myitkyina. Finally, I would get my chance to talk to the Japanese. We set up the microphones in a dugout at the command post of a decimated engineer regiment (drafted into combat to replace Marauder casualties) 150 yards from the front. Two loudspeakers were installed, one on the front line itself (only 50 yards from the Japanese but camouflaged by brush and mosquito nets) and another 100 yards east of the command post facing a paddy field. We devised a thirty-minute program, beginning with a record of the "Washington Post March" to identify us as Americans, followed by news of Japan and the war, interspersed with Japanese music intended to induce nostalgia, and ending with a surrender appeal.

We started July 14 at 7:00 P.M. Hank Gosho, who had been evacuated from combat because of his malaria, dysentery, and a hernia, was commentator. He was well known for his uproarious imitations of Japanese announcers of baseball games, and his elocutionary talent was put to good use at the battle of Myitkyina. We set a schedule for two daily broadcasts at five in the morning and seven in the evening. I described how it was in a letter to my wife: "Five o'clock in the morning is very early, especially when it has been raining steadily all night long and is still raining. You have to get out into that rain and every excuse for not doing it comes roaring into your semi-consciousness. But I always wake up at hours I'm supposed to, so I have to punch Hank and he punches Proc and Proc punches Adie. . . . So you pull on your old shirt soaked with sweat and rain from the day before, and your pants which are stiff with mud and sweat; then you pull on socks that never dried and dig your feet into big shoes with mud all over them." In the jeep we would drive as quietly as possible through the dark, the rain, and the mud, to the command post. Years later, Hank recalled that one morning a lieutenant friend whispered to him as we piled into the jeep, "You're out of your mind!"

I wrote about our first effort: "When the music began, the firing diminished and then ceased. There were a few interruptions during the course of the program but of short duration. When the last record was played, weapons were set off again and the colonel suggested we play another side. Immediately our listeners were silent, only to open up again when the last notes died away."

On July 20 I got my chance. A news bulletin had just come in, and seizing the microphone from Hank, I announced in my best and most stentorian Japanese that General Hideki Tōjō had just resigned as prime minister of Japan, and that this was bad news for the imperial army.

The operation went on until Myitkyina fell. The results were not spectacular. On July 16 following a Japanese withdrawal, the engineers were able to make their first advance in three weeks, a quarter of a mile. The intelligence officer of the unit thought the broadcasts might have contributed to low morale, which made the enemy withdraw rather than stick. During the same night about fifteen natives of the area made their way to our lines, stating that the American martial music had convinced them that the Americans and not Chinese, were in charge. On following nights numerous local inhabitants picked their way across the lines, many able and willing to impart valuable intelligence. On July 24 the first, and so far as I know, the only, Japanese surrendered in response to our appeal. An unexpected result of the broadcasts was its morale-building effect on the American troops; in response to their desires, we began to include brief newcasts in English and to play jive records, both much appreciated on dark nights by soldiers in foxholes half-filled with water.

My second preoccupation, still related to psychological warfare but more rewarding to me personally, was my contact with the Japanese soldier. Our intelligence officers and interpreters were continually amazed at the readiness of the ordinary infantryman to talk freely about whatever he knew. Since the soldier's code contained no provision for capture—death was always to be the way out—prisoners had no guidelines to follow. For them, one life had ended and another had begun. They never expected to return to Japan and the disgrace that would surely await them; consequently, their previous life had no connection with their present existence.

In February and March 1945 I interviewed twelve prisoners of war. All had been interrogated for military information; my questioning was an attempt to learn their general attitudes and feelings about the war, and their hopes for the future. Except for one, these POWs belonged to the Eighteenth *Kiku* ("Chrysanthemum") Division and were from the island of Kyūshū. None was an officer; four had been factory workers and two others, mining engineers; the rest were a farmer, fisherman, policeman, bank clerk, storekeeper, and soldier since 1937. Six of the group had been wounded either before or at the time of capture.

In my interviews I tried always to persuade the Japanese soldier to think about the outcome of the war. Most clung to the certainty of Japan's victory, although some Burma veterans who had experienced prolonged misery and repeated retreats were beginning to harbor doubts. Of these twelve, only one was prepared to return to his homeland after the war. The rest felt disgraced for life and believed it better that their families think them dead. Many prisoners were antagonistic toward the British and Chinese but had a healthy respect for Soviet strength. One pleaded with me earnestly, "If you send us to China or to England, we prefer to die. Our one wish is to go to America."

One day, in talking to an emaciated Japanese GI, lying wounded in his bunk, I discovered that he had lived on Taiwan. I volunteered that I had been vice-consul in Taihoku, two years before the Pacific war had begun, and asked him whether he had seen the American consulate. His eyes brightened. He knew our building and had passed it often. He remembered a foreign baby girl playing in the garden behind the wall. Yes, that was in 1939. When I told him that was my little girl, a human bond suddenly formed between us out of two instants—in 1939 and now—in which our lives had touched.

The prisoners I talked with had been fighting the same war as the Americans, British, Indians, and Chinese, coping with the same dark, entangled jungle and the same mud, disease, insects, and wild animals. The Japanese laughed when you asked them about airplanes; they had never seen one of their own. Progressively cut off from supply lines, they lacked food, clothing, ammunition, medicines, and hospital facilities. Reduced to foraging for food, and debilitated by jungle sicknesses, many died. A Japanese veteran of the campaign entitled one of the chapters in his *Burma War Diary*, "The Graveyard of North Burma."

During the battle of Myitkyina twenty-seven patients from a field hospital were captured as they tried to escape on rafts downstream to the city. I reported: "Racked with beriberi, malaria, and open wounds, they were piled in jeep trailers one on top of the other, caked with mud. Blood was streaming from an abdominal wound in one of them. . . . According to their stories, a temperature of 103 was prerequisite for medicine; bandages had been used over and over until they were bloodsoaked and worn out."

The last days of the defenders of Myitkyina, remnants of the division which had taken Singapore, must indeed have been excruciating. They were surrounded by Allied troops—in the end, "seven hundred men against four divisions," as a Japanese participant described it, with personal weapons rationed to five bullets a day and artillery pieces to three shells—facing the Irrawaddy River as their only escape route. On August 1 further resistance became patently hopeless, and the order was given to build bamboo rafts for escape. The bamboo was green and heavy, and the river swollen by heavy rains. As a consequence, many rafts overturned, and the weak soldiers were drowned while others were swept downriver by the current. It was the belief of some of the POWs in our Ledo camp that the officer in charge, Colonel Maruyama, expected the soldiers to be drowned; such an end would, in his view, avoid their capture and their divulging secret military information to the enemy. One soldier who miraculously survived the combined perils of river, raft, and enemy fire, made it down the Irrawaddy to Bhamo and lived to write his story, *Raft of Death (Shi no Idaka)*.

One day at a hospital situated well behind the lines, one of these emaciated Japanese soldiers died. I wrote in my notes, "Witnessed a funeral today. What would the soul of Sato-san think if he knew about the services today? The *hi-no-maru* [Japanese flag] on the coffin, the firing squad and the service read by the chaplain. The setting was a naturally beautiful one—a garden cemetery near the jungle. War is a strange thing. We devote all our energy to killing and then when faced with one poor soul like Sato, we give him only honors. . . . It was a sunny Sunday afternoon."

With the fall of Myitkyina, the flow of prisoners to Ledo suddenly swelled from a trickle to a torrent. By early August almost two hundred of them crowded newly built wards at the Twentieth General Hospital and a specially constructed stockade. G-2 (Intelligence) and the nisei interrogators, overwhelmed by bookkeeping duties, sought help from the POWs themselves. A Lieutenant Hirata and two enlisted men were chosen to assist in clerical work and the organization of the stockade. Soon, a small group of prisoners, with OWI encouragement, began to hold discussion sessions *(zadankai)* among themselves. Since these proved successful, Hirata was asked whether he would head a committee of six prisoners selected to assist in propaganda activities.

Hirata and his associates stipulated four conditions before they would agree: they would not be asked to do anything showing disrespect for the imperial house; their names would be stricken from the official Allied list of prisoners of war; they would be excluded from any future prisoner exchanges; and they would be permitted to make new lives for themselves in the United States when the war ended. We could assent to the first of these conditions since established policy prohibited derogation of the emperor in American propaganda, but the other three were obviously unacceptable. A promise to refer their requests to a higher authority satisfied the group, however, and, under assumed names, they went to work for OWI.

At first, acting as consultants, they criticized OWI-prepared leaflets and suggested revisions in them, but soon Lieutenant Hirata's volunteers were on their own, writing leaflets and preparing illustrations. Later, they edited a stockade newspaper, written by and for POWs, called *New Life,* which was dropped regularly as reading matter behind enemy lines. OWI's official report on psychological operations in North Burma concluded, "It would be difficult to find anywhere a group more enthusiastic in its application to the job."

The nisei, particularly Kenji Yasui, provided the inspiration and direction for the POW group and won their respect and affection. The principal problems were not with the Japanese but with our military compatriots who could not easily persuade themselves to better the living and working conditions of their enemies, even those who were helping us to defeat Japan. To encourage Hirata's committee, Yasui and the other nisei personnel scrounged cigarettes from the Red Cross, contributed clothes and shoes of their own, and paid for toothbrushes, toothpaste, soap, towels, fresh vegetables, and meat.

No special efforts were made to indoctrinate the Ledo POWs, although they were given access to news files from both Japanese and Allied sources and to antiwar materials prepared in China. The discussion meetings were productive because they offered a friendly, free atmosphere for the prisoners to think and talk about their own experiences, ideas, and perceptions of the future.

I attended several of these sessions, although most of them were held without the presence of Americans, a careful record being kept by one of the participants. A variety of subjects was discussed: Japan before the war, Japan after the war, conditions in the Japanese Army, the position of the emperor, Japanese–American relations and how the two countries came to war, and their own complaints.

These prisoners, in September and October 1944, had not yet accepted the inevitability of Japan's defeat. One of them who had come through battles from South China, Malaya, and Singapore, to North Burma, wrote anonymously that Japan without question would win the great East Asia war. "Defeat is miserable . . . the military is the pillar of the nation." In the *zadankai* the participants were ready to consider the implications of both victory and defeat. They were interested in the antiwar propaganda produced in China—which portrayed defeat as certain—but disagreed with its Marxist orientation. Some of them had qualms of conscience in criticizing the military of which they had been a part. But others pointed out that they must detach themselves and look at things as outsiders, as newly born. Only then could they apply the surgical knife of criticism.

The depth of reverence for the emperor emerged in the discussions, although there was general cynicism regarding the patriotic slogans of holy war, Eight Corners of the Universe Under One Roof, and the Greater East Asia Co-Prosperity Sphere. These infantrymen had seen starving, ill-clad people in China and Southeast Asia and questioned whether the force of arms was the way to win their support. One quoted an old poem: "To compare hunger, love, and the cold: shamefully but true, hunger comes first."

They groped to understand the causes for the war. Japan and America had had close relations in previous decades, but there had been troubles. They remembered the shock of the order freezing Japanese assets in the summer of 1941, but they had also heard that their government had blocked a last-minute message to the emperor, which President Roosevelt had sent on the eve of Pearl Harbor.

They described how their attitude toward Americans had changed since their capture. Hostility engendered by wartime propaganda had been replaced by admiration for unexpected humanity. Those who had undergone hospital treatment praised the American doctor who had become in their eyes a benevolent angel, a "bodhisattva of mercy." One prisoner told how the tears came to his eyes when he awoke at night to find that an American military policeman had pulled a blanket over him and was quietly covering his comrades and lowering the mosquito nets on their beds. This soldier was one of those put on a raft and left to float on the Irrawaddy River. He and others burst out in rage at the civilian and military leaders who had guided Japan to war in "pursuit of a phantom." The "slavery" of a prison camp was better than the slavery of being a "living bullet" for the army or of submission to unscrupulous rulers.

These Japanese were simple men—only the lieutenant had had a university education—but their thoughts and feelings hinted at a state of mind that probably prevailed among many of their countrymen, both in the armed forces overseas and at home. These experiences naturally set them thinking about the major problems of how to end the war and how to plan for the future of Japan.

The announced Allied policy of unconditional surrender was a hindrance not only to psychological warfare but restricted efforts on both sides to bring the war to an end. While the policy had been deliberated within the State Department and confirmed by the British, President Roosevelt's public, unpremeditated call for the unconditional surrender of Germany, Italy, and Japan, at the Casablanca conference, on January 24, 1943, was a surprise, even to Churchill. The demand was not included in the joint statement issued at Casablanca and FDR, when later confronted in a press conference, admitted that "the thought popped into my mind." Unconditional surrender as a war objective was never clearly defined, although Roosevelt and Churchill made general statements, usually with special reference to Germany, that the Allied intent was not to annihilate the enemy peoples. The Japanese leadership claimed, however, that the alternative to resistance to the end was the destruction of the nation, if not of its people. In 1943 a Japanese author warned his readers in a book called *Western Devil America (Yoki Amerika)* that "Roosevelt has threatened to wipe every last Japanese from the face of the earth. . . . Should we be defeated in this war, untold numbers of Japanese people will be brutally slaughtered at the hands of these American fiends."

American military leaders, in turn, expected bitter, last-ditch resistance by Japan and prepared for landings on the main islands with consequent hand-to-hand fighting and enormous casualties. Moreover, it was the accepted belief that resistance would continue on the Asian mainland wherever imperial troops could be found and that they would have to be tracked down and destroyed to the last man.

It was with this horrible prospect in mind that I approached the captured Japanese soldiers for clues to the behavior of their countrymen at the moment of final defeat. It was difficult to persuade these shamed and sickened veterans even to think about losing the war, a consequence for the homeland no loyal subject of the emperor would at first contemplate. Finally, by coaxing them to stretch their imaginations, to conceive the inconceivable, I was able to elicit answers. They came slowly, with hesitation, but their purport was always the same. Soldiers in the field, wherever they might be, fought in obedience to the emperor's command. Should the emperor, in his divine wisdom, order them to lay down their arms, they would of course do so in response to his stated wish. It was that simple.

As early as July 1944, more than a year before the Potsdam Declaration finally brought about the surrender of Japan, I reported to the State Department my conclusion, on the basis of discussions with officer prisoners of war, that capitulation by the government (which would mean the emperor) would assure the cessation of military action. In August, writing from New Delhi, I amplified my ideas in a dispatch called "A Policy Toward Japan," a copy of which I later discovered was sent to the White House and can still be found among the Harry Hopkins papers at Hyde Park. (There is no evidence, however, that it was ever shown to the president.)

I began my memorandum: "We should speak directly to the people of Japan. We should encourage elements in the country opposed to the war." (Not until nine months later did Navy Captain Ellis M. Zacharias begin his broadcasts designed to appeal to just these elements.) I then analyzed the mental change occurring in a Japanese prisoner of war after capture, describing his complete detachment, his feeling that "he no longer belongs to his own country." My dispatch emphasized that we should "say more than unconditional surrender," that we should "offer some hope for the people of Japan in a future changed world." I suggested that we should allow the emperor to remain, that he would be very useful to us in the first days following an armistice, and that proclamation of surrender by imperial rescript would end resistance. The memorandum concluded with a summary of a proposed official statement to Japan demanding the destruction of militarism but assuring the Japanese government that unconditional surrender would not mean the end of the country's existence, that the nation's peace would be guaranteed, that peaceful industries and international trade could be freely developed, and that Japan would be permitted to form her own government with the sole condition that it would not be usurped by a militaristic group.

It was not until May 8, 1945, that President Truman, in a statement paralleling his announcement of the defeat of Germany, proclaimed to Japan that "unconditional surrender does not mean the extermination or enslavement of the Japanese people." And it was not until July 26 that Truman, Churchill, and Chiang Kai-shek, with Stalin concurring, spelled out in the Potsdam Proclamation the Allied terms for Japan's surrender. Even then the status of the emperor was ignored, an omission that unnecessarily prolonged a war that the Japanese civilian leadership was desperately trying to end.

8

Yenan

During the summer of 1944 Stilwell's war moved to China, a country on the verge of collapse, economically, politically, and morally. Although the Japanese had been beaten in Burma, after long and dogged resistance by the emperor's brave Chrysanthemum Division, in China they were aggressively mounting their Operation ICHIGO ("Strawberry"), designed to solidify their position on the mainland and to wipe out Chennault's vaunted air bases in the east. We, in turn, were preparing to bomb Japan from China, using fields carved out of the rock and soil of Chengtu by the muscle power of four hundred thousand workers recruited from surrounding villages during the planting season. On June 15 the first shiny B-29s took off from Chengtu to attack the Yawata steelworks in Kyūshū. On the same day, American forces invaded Saipan Island, an event that was to prove far more significant than the bombing raid. When the enormity of the China-based effort is calculated, the results achieved were picayune. The Kyūshū raid reduced steel supplies by no more than 2 percent, and all bombing flights together produced "no discernible effect on the East China crisis," according to the army's official history. The capture of Saipan, on the other hand, was to lead directly to the defeat of Japan by the navy and the air force.

Victory would not come out of CBI, but China was still

important. Military specialists believed that, even if the Japanese government surrendered, the imperial army would continue resistance on the mainland, determined to preserve its rule over China. War had come largely because of China; we had proclaimed it as a great power, and we had to keep it in the war. Specifically, we needed China for obtaining information on Japan as well as for additional help should coastal landings become necessary.

I made my first trip over the Hump to Chungking on June 17 and called on my chief, Ambassador Clarence Gauss, to whose embassy I was assigned as second secretary. In spite of nearly six months' delay in arriving at my post, the ambassador was cordial and made no references to my tardy arrival, as well he might have done. I was disappointed that he seemed disinterested in my work in Burma and, as a result, I ventured no information. Gauss was a seasoned China hand, respected by those who worked for him. He was frustrated and despondent over the worsening situation in China and over the bickering and lack of coordination among military and civilian representatives of the U.S. government, over whom he had little control. (On June 15 he admitted to the State Department, "I confess there is nothing I can suggest that we might do.")

Three days after my Hump crossing, Vice President Henry A. Wallace paid an official visit to China. He was accompanied by John Carter Vincent of the China Division of the State Department and by Owen Lattimore, a China scholar and specialist on Mongolia, both of whom were later to become victims of the China witch-hunt. (Since this was the only occasion when John Vincent, John Davies, John Service, and John Emmerson were all in Chungking together, the coincidence may have inspired Congressman Walter Judd to refer many years later to the cabal of "the four Johns" who, he testified, were in Chungking, busily undermining the government of Chiang Kai-shek.)

I had met Wallace the previous year when he had made a goodwill visit to Peru. As a junior officer, I had had little to do with him in Lima but remembered his fetish for exercise, long before jogging had become a fad. He eluded his Secret Service guards by rising at dawn to slip out of the embassy residence and walk briskly through the deserted streets of Lima. When at a reception in Chungking he greeted me like a long-lost friend, I was convinced he had confused me with someone else or was doing his politician's act.

Vice President Wallace got Chiang Kai-shek to agree to the stationing of American observers in Communist-held territory. The idea had been discussed among American officials for two years. General Stilwell favored it, and Chou En-lai had told John Davies that the Communists would welcome an official visit. Jack Service, in January 1943, recommended that American representatives, preferably Chinese-speaking foreign service officers, be sent to "combine moderately long-term residence in Yenan or its vicinity with fairly extensive travel in the guerrilla areas." Our knowledge of what the Communists were doing was fragmentary, and yet they formed a growing segment of the Chinese population. The problem was to get the Generalissimo to concur, and he was understandably reluctant to do so. Finally, after numerous memoranda, some of which reached Harry Hopkins in the White House, President Roosevelt, on February 9, 1944, sent a personal telegram to Chiang, making the request. As expected, Chiang's answer was no.

In May, however, a group of journalists obtained permission to visit the Communist region and began to report extensively on what they saw and heard.

Wallace's appearance in Chungking presented a God-sent opportunity. He failed on his first try with the Generalissimo, but in a second interview reassured Chiang, "We are not interested in 'Chinese Communists' but are interested in the prosecution of the war. ... The U.S. Army intelligence group in North China would be able to gather intelligence that would save the lives of American aviators."

To everyone's astonishment, Chiang suddenly reversed himself, announcing, "That can be done."

The U.S. Army Observer Group, dubbed the Dixie Mission, was quickly formed under the command of a capable China hand who spoke florid Chinese, Colonel David ("Dog") Barrett, and left for "rebel" territory on July 22. John Service was a member. Raymond ("Lud") Ludden was to arrive two weeks later.

While in Chungking, I was following my Japanese thread and

learning about the antiwar movements that had been formed among the prisoners of war captured by the Chinese. One Kaji Wataru, a mild-mannered, wisplike Japanese who would fall as a leaf in a breeze, was heading the Anti-War League *(Hansen Dōmei)*, working for the Chungking government, and cooperating with our OWI. Kaji was the pioneer in the antiwar movement. A writer of leftist inclination, if not a Communist party member, he had fled Japan for Shanghai in 1936 along with his wife, a militant in her own right. After war broke out the following year, he started working with Japanese prisoners of war, and by December 1939 had organized, in Kweilin, the first Japanese People's Anti-War League with fifty members. At first welcomed and praised by the Central Government (league headquarters were established in Chungking in 1940), he came under suspicion as a Red and his activities were curtailed. When I met him, he had not recently been in touch with the Peace Village which he had set up in one of the government's prison camps.

More famous than Kaji was Okano Susumu who was with the Chinese Communists in Yenan; his Anti-War League first appeared in May 1940 as the Yenan branch of Kaji's group. Okano was one of the various assumed names of Nosaka Sanzō, who in the postwar period was to lead in the revival of the Japanese Communist party and was to reach the party's highest rank, chairman of the Central Committee. Reports had come back about Okano's Peasants and Workers School and his recently formed (in January 1944) Japanese People's Emancipation League.

The journalists had been most impressed; one, Harrison Forman, included a chapter on the league in the book he published in 1945, *Report from Red China*. Ambassador Gauss disparaged the Japanese antiwarriors as not worth looking into, but John Davies thought Okano's doings might have some relevance for our own psychological warfare and handling of POWs. He suggested that I might therefore be a useful member of the Dixie Mission, but at the time my work in Burma prevented my joining him.

After Myitkyina I manned the desk in New Delhi, while Service poured forth his trenchant reports from the Communists' stronghold, and Davies flew between Washington, New Delhi, Chungking, and Kandy. Lud was usually somewhere in the Chinese Communist bush, slogging it out with the Eighth Route Army.

I summed up the Delhi interlude in notes made at the time:

> But let Delhi be. I shall remember our Political Advisers Office—the mad scramble with codes and superduper stuff about the Kwangsi revolutionaries [who were plotting to depose the Generalissimo] and Pat [Davies] and me decoding, coding, and paraphrasing like mad. A couple of pleasant swims at the Gymkana Club, picnics at the Haus Khan and moonlight on Kutab Minar, talking to prisoners at the Red Fort, our broadcast, writing a few fantasies on Japan, getting acquainted at Headquarters, sleeping on the roof under the bright, white stars, the tum-tum [horse-drawn carriage] and Alim putting "leis" around our necks at Id, music and drinks at Ruth Merrill's, upsetting the equilibrium of FEA [Foreign Economic Administration] by playing Mozart at midnight, buying saris in a hurry for Dorothy, Chinese lessons with Chen Han-seng, steaks at Picadilly, liaising with the OWIers, Thailand's travail, etc., etc.

It was October before I got back to China. During my five days spent in the foggy, muggy, muddy, despondent atmosphere of Chungking, Uncle Joe Stilwell was fired. On October 19 he wrote in his diary, "THE AXE FALLS." On the same day I wrote in mine: "The lightning has struck! Uncle Joe probably leaves tomorrow. Tragedy of China. Horrible mistake of the President. What will become of our effort here?" On October 21 Stilwell left Chungking. The next day John Davies and I were on the plane to Yenan, along with Teddy White, then of *Time-Life,* and Koji Ariyoshi of the OWI nisei team, who had been detailed to the observers mission.

Reports from the Communist areas had been invariably glowing. The correspondents wrote their dispatches in superlatives. Six days after his arrival, Jack Service had expressed determination not to be swept off his feet. Yet, finding nothing to criticize, he concluded that "the spell of the Chinese Communists still seems to work." He had to admit that the atmosphere could be compared to that of a "rather small, sectarian college—or a religious summer conference," with a bit of "smugness, self-righteousness and conscious fellowship." But he agreed with a correspondent who knew China that "we have to come to the mountains of north Shensi, to find the most modern place in China."

Also, succumbing to the spell, I wrote my first impressions: "I am influenced by the cold air and the sunshine and the hills so near. . . . The Chinese food is delectable and we are quite comfortable. Nothing like Burma and C rations! And after the venality of Peru, the somnolence of India, and the chaos of Chungking, this is truly utopian." For me, it was like the revival meetings I had known in my youth, where the converts suddenly got religion. I ended my notes: "This first day in the 'brave new China'! Down the sawdust trail march we!"

At a dinner given for the new arrivals that first evening I sat next to Chou En-lai whom I found animated and intense, with an expressive face. Speaking acceptable English, he also knew some French from his days in Grenoble in the 1920s. After dinner John, Jack, and I were invited to Chou's house, at the top of a little hill, a cave built in the loess. I wrote: "Then Mao enters the room. He is big, with expanse of forehead, crop of hair behind it. He has a young face with bright, intelligent eyes. He reminds one of an artist. He looks like a pianist. He wears a dark blue uniform made of the local woolen cloth."

General Chu Teh, commander of the armed forces, joined us, a gorillalike man (the thick uniform added to his size) with a deeply furrowed, indestructible face. These were the big three of the Communist "state." Unfortunately I remember nothing of the conversation (the food and wine had been good), most of which was interpreted, although John and Jack were both born in China and spoke Chinese fluently. Mao's brand of Hunanese presented peculiar problems to Mandarin-speaking foreigners. What I do recall is the power of Mao's personality, transmitted in this small room in the lamplight, by his musician's hands, his articulate body movements, and his measured pacing of the floor. One of his similes remains in my head: Chiang Kai-shek is like a billiken, the weighted tumble toy, which when pushed in any direction, springs back, but in a different way.

What was crystal clear was that one objective motivated the Communists to extend warm hospitality to us. They wanted help from the United States, to fight Japanese of course, but in the longer run to improve their strength in China. Their ambitions for the future were no secret; they never said, "*if* we control China," but, invariably, "*when* we control China." They sought a coalition government while the war was on, but they were determined to rule China someday.

I spent most of my time in Yenan with the Japanese. But the atmosphere was so electric in this Chinese world that no one could live in it without becoming involved in the problems and prospects of a group working so single-mindedly toward a fixed goal. No foreign service officer, conditioned to analyze the politics of other nations and their implications for American foreign policy, could remain impervious to the ferment of a revolution in the making. Four questions were uppermost in our minds and in the minds of many outside of China, How communistic were the Chinese Communists? How closely were they tied to the Soviet Union? Were they actually fighting Japanese? Was a Kuomintang-Communist (KMT-CCP) coalition possible? The last two questions have been amply and competently discussed by others, and there is no need to discuss them here. For me, the short answers were that the Communists were fighting the Japanese, although the intensity of their struggle may have varied from year to year, and that a KMT-CCP coalition was impossible. The Japanese were the first obstacle to Communist control of China, and the Kuomintang was the second. As for a permanent coalition with Chiang Kai-shek, Mao conceived of a temporary association but demanded an independence of action, which the Generalissimo would never concede.

In later years many of us who had been stationed in Yenan would be accused of blindness toward communism, of having considered Mao and his group to be merely agrarian reformers. It is true that I was no expert in the principles of Marxism–Leninism and Stalinism; my childhood memories included cartoons of bomb-carrying, bearded revolutionaries, labeled Lenin and Trotsky. As an undergraduate in the 1920s, I had been intrigued by the drama and promise of Russia's new experiment. Whatever favorable impressions I gathered were contradicted, however, by Father Edmund A. Walsh at Georgetown University, who earnestly indoctrinated us at the foreign service school in the evils of Russian communism and the dangers of recognizing the Soviet Union. Later Chip Bohlen, during our pleasant months together in Tokyo, put things in perspective through his wisdom grown out of experience in Moscow: mordant criticism of the regime coupled with deep sympathy and attraction to the Russian people. I had not, however, served in a Communist country, nor had I made a special study of Communist literature. Associating with live Communists in Yenan, in an open, friendly way with substantive communication encouraged, was a novel, exciting experience, like enjoying forbidden fruit.

The emphasis in Yenan was on democracy and the peasant revolution. Only a few years before Mao had written "On New Democracy," and we heard much about the three–three–three principle for representation in assemblies: one-third Communist, one-third Kuomintang, and one-third nonparty elements. It was easy to understand that the power of the Chinese Communists rested in the peasants; they controlled no cities. And no evidence turned up to dispute the contention that agrarian reforms had been carried out and that relations between the peasantry and the military were amicable, something that could not be said for the rest of China. We took the Communists too seriously on democracy; it was too easy to fall into the vocabulary we heard in daily use. Mao's democracy and Jefferson's democracy were not quite the same.

Occasionally, we would ask our Yenan friends why, if they were indeed pursuing democratic policies, they did not change the name of their party when the word *Communist* frightened capitalistic Westerners. They replied with astonishment that they could not deny their heritage. The correspondent, Harrison Forman, who stated as fact that the Chinese Communists were "no more communistic than we Americans," asked Mao why he didn't change the party's name. Mao replied that while his communism might not fit the Russian definition of the word, a change of name would arouse suspicions that they were "trying to cover up something."

Chou En-lai was more precise, "Our ultimate ideal is the socialist collectivism of communism—which, however, I don't believe can be achieved in China for a long, long time to come." My own belief was that a change of name was unthinkable. These people were Communists and would always be Communists, but democracy and agrarian reform were steps on the way to power.

A key question was the nature and degree of Soviet influence on the Yenan leadership. These were the pre-Tito days, when the conventional wisdom perceived a monolithic Communist empire ruled from the Kremlin. We knew there were Russians in Yenan. One was a doctor, Orlov, whom I met. A craggy, dark, imposing figure, he practiced surgery at the Yenan hospital. We also knew that there was at least one Tass correspondent in Yenan, a man known, at least by sight, to some of the Americans. Jack Service, in a dispatch to the department on March 23, 1945, identified three Russians, Orlov and two representatives of the Tass News Agency, known by their Chinese names as Kuo Li and Shen P'ing. Service wrote that these three had been in the Communist area since 1942 and that the correspondents were said "to have no radio equipment except a receiver" and to send all their news dispatches through Chungking, thus submitting to Chungking censorship. Jack was nevertheless skeptical and believed it most likely that the Soviet and Chinese parties were in communication with each other.

In 1974 a remarkable book appeared in Moscow, *Osob'i Raion Kitaya 1942–1945 (China's Special Area)*, purporting to be the diary of Pyotr Parfenovich Vladimirov, Tass correspondent and official representative of the Communist International in Yenan during the period 1942–45. The publication of these diaries a quarter of a century after the years concerned, neatly coinciding with the nadir of Sino–Soviet relations, can only have been a calculated act, since the book demonstrates that Mao was an enemy of the Soviet Union from the Yenan days. Vladimirov's writings cannot be authenticated nor their accuracy determined. He himself is long since dead, and his manuscript was abridged and prepared for publication by others. His denunciation of Mao is extreme, but he suggests what we suspected, that Yenan, although in touch with Moscow, did not take orders from the Kremlin. In many ways, this record, the only published Russian account we have, rings true.

Vladimirov's diary confirms Service's report that there were three

Russians in Yenan in 1944 and states that until October 1943, there had been six. Not only were they in constant radio contact with Moscow but were frequently asked by Mao to transmit messages for him. Vladimirov notes that "Mao Tse-tung has personal communications with Moscow [powerful radio station, personal codes] but he stubbornly keeps on sending telegrams through me." The extent of the communications traffic with Moscow is indicated throughout the diary: "Candles are burning, the telegraph key is tapping in Kolya's radio room in these last moments before dawn. . . . I write my reports in a hurry. Kolya transmits while I am sleeping." In his diaries Vladimirov proves himself an alert and enterprising reporter, sending long messages to Moscow, even as we were sending long messages to Washington. It is intriguing today to compare his diary with our reports. On August 27, 1944, Service wrote the State Department after an interview with Mao Tse-tung that Chinese Communist "orientation towards the United States is clear. The Communists do not, for very practical reasons, expect that Soviet Russia will be able to play a large part in China. And they believe . . . that this Russian participation should be secondary to that of the United States."

Three days later, on August 30, Vladimirov recorded in his diary: "Mao believes that the USSR has been weakened by the war. This prejudice makes him abstain from following a policy to protect interests of the USSR but instead to rely upon the United States. . . . He prefers a gamble to the honest cooperation with Moscow based on the affinity of ideas."

Vladimirov knew much more about us than we knew about him and his group. He was at the airfield with his Leica when the observers mission first arrived, and reported accurately the goings and comings of American officials and correspondents. He wrote descriptions of Service ("young, full of bounce, and has a good, retentive memory . . . the most important member of the American group"), Davies ("lean, long face . . . little too broad mouth . . . very energetic . . . perfect command of Chinese"), and Barrett ("baldish, thick-set . . . amiable despite the sullen expression of his face"), and summarized in detail conversations purportedly held between the Americans and Communist officials. Obviously having no love for

Americans and no desire to cultivate our acquaintance, he wrote, "My earlier contacts with American servicemen convinced me that they have deep-rooted anti-Soviet feelings which in many cases grew into frank Russophobia."

Vladimirov's hostility to Mao Tse-tung is intense. Mao is seen as a Menshevik, a betrayer of socialism, a destroyer of the Communist party, even ready to change its name, a coward, a liar, a deceiver, and deeply anti-Soviet. Mao is pictured as trying to build with the United States a political counterweight to the USSR in Asia. The United States, in turn, is observed as trying to prevent Russian domination in Asia through cooperation with the Chinese Communists.

With the hindsight of history, the first statement may well have been true and the second statement could be a quotation from reports of Davies and Service. As early as January 1944 Vladimirov finds Mao saying, "For China, United States policy is a question of paramount importance." Consistently running through the diary is the theme that the Chinese Communist Party under Mao is looking to the United States, not the Soviet Union, for help in obtaining arms to establish its power in China.

Power, according to Vladimirov, is Mao's obsession. He must, however, at the same time keep the Russians friendly; if American assistance fails, he must be able to turn to Moscow. Mao's diligence in sending messages through Vladimirov's channels is interpreted as a method of currying favor with the Soviet Union and making it embarrassing for Vladimirov to send contradictory reports. The Russian also suspects Mao of flattery and of attempting to conceal from the Soviet government the true meaning of his political intrigues. Mao tries to reassure him, for example, by telling him (with great honesty, as later history was to prove) that "no matter what form the contacts with the Americans will take, our revolution will eventually turn against the imperialists."

The Chinese Communists never slandered the Russians but consistently emphasized their independence from them. Just before leaving China, I wrote in a dispatch to the State Department: "There is no doubt that a strong sentimental attachment holds for Mother Russia, the home of their [the Chinese Communists'] ideology. At a recent showing of newsreels in Yenan, loud applause greeted Stalin's appearance; there was none for Roosevelt, Churchill, or Chiang Kai-shek. Stalin's speeches receive prominent space in the newspapers. But the Communists point out that the Kuomintang has received Russian aid while they have not, that they are engaged in building a society peculiarly Chinese, and that they are independent in their policies and in their actions."

In the course of a six-hour interview, held on August 23, 1944, Mao told Jack Service that he looked to the United States and not to the Russians for help, but he saw no conflict between Russian and American interests in China. In my own interviews with Communist officials, I found them calm about the Russians but confident in their own independence.

I was the only member of our group to meet K'ang Sheng, then known to be the head of Mao's secret police, who is described in *China's Special Area* as an arch enemy of the Soviets, so much so that Vladimirov fears for his life at the hands of K'ang Sheng's operatives. The Tass correspondent was not alone in his estimate of K'ang Sheng. Nikita Khrushchev, in the second volume of his dictated memoirs, refers to K'ang as Mao's "butcher" and "hatchet man," performing for Mao the same functions assigned to Beria by Stalin.

Russian hostility toward K'ang Sheng was apparently reciprocated. K'ang, who had worked in Moscow with the Comintern from 1933 to 1937, had, according to at least one writer, "grave doubts about Russian loyalty to the Chinese cause." He is described as believing that a devious Soviet Union practiced imperialistic power while pretending to protect other nations living under the threat of imperialism.

Because of a letter from Chen Han-seng, my Chinese teacher in New Delhi, K'ang Sheng received me in early December in a meeting that went on for several hours, including drinks, dinner, and a Chinese opera at the end. His moustache and the contours of his face suggested Tōjō; his eyes twinkled, more with sharpness than with humor. Huang Hua, who in the 1970s was to become Chinese ambassador to the United Nations and later foreign minister, interpreted for me. On Russia, K'ang Sheng took with me the line of Marxist realism which so irritated Vladimirov: "Marxism must be adapted to local, individual circumstances . . . what will work in one place cannot be transplanted bodily to another place. The Chinese Communists have always worked independently, have worked out their own policies and programs. If they were independent before the dissolution of the Comintern, certainly they have been more so since that took place. . . . Mao says it would be impossible to impose communism on Yenan. The circumstances are not suitable to it."

K'ang talked at length about his clandestine operatives, who were smuggling published and unpublished Japanese materials across enemy lines. These were data which were made available to us and were valuable to our intelligence and psychological warfare officers. He remarked that the enterprise was dangerous, that five of his men carrying on this activity had been killed during the past year.

He pumped me for criticism of the Communist society I was witnessing in Yenan. I told him that my experience was too brief to make valid judgments. It had, however, occurred to me to question the ability of the Chinese Communists to govern cities. Theirs had been an agrarian revolution, and their experience was limited largely to the countryside. Would they be able effectively to administer urban areas? K'ang Sheng replied that this was a problem which concerned the leadership deeply; they realized they would face great difficulties but three points were in their favor: (1) they recognized the gravity of the problem; (2) they were now training cadres in municipal administration; and (3) many Chinese in the *liberated* areas—as they called the Communist-controlled regions—had originally come from cities and were conversant with urban problems. He cited a book by Kuo Mo-jo, a well-known Communist writer, which described the failure of a revolutionary hero who had tried to adapt to cities the tactics which had been successful in villages.

K'ang was pessimistic about an agreement with the Kuomintang, because he believed Chiang Kai-shek would never give up his one-party dictatorship. Still, no one wanted civil war, neither the Communist party, the Chinese people, nor China's foreign allies. He feared that Americans would not understand why his party refused to accept posts in the Nationalist government. Chiang's policy is one of "waiting" until America defeats Japan; in the meantime he clings to his one-party dictatorship. Communists entering *his* government would be giving victory to Chiang and would lose their own objective, which was a democratic China. His attitude told me that there was little hope for a coalition government, which Major General Patrick J. Hurley, who had recently been appointed ambassador, was so optimistic about achieving.

It was light in the room when the interview started. We sat at a round table covered with a white cloth, having a china teapot and teacups on it. It grew dark and a boy brought candles. K'ang sat in shadows, but I could discern in the constant play of expressions on his face a keen, intelligent alertness.

Although those of us in Yenan in 1944 knew neither the extent of communication between Yenan and Moscow nor the true nature of the interparty relationship, we felt that Mao meant it when he talked about looking to the United States for cooperation, not only during the war but in the postwar period as well. We realized that much of his motivation was selfish—to arm his troops—but we were convinced that a Chinese alliance with the Soviet Union was far from inevitable and that goodwill between a Communist China (which we saw as an almost certain eventuality) and the United States would be in our own national interest.

My purpose in going to Yenan had been to investigate Japanese, not Chinese or Russians, but I necessarily became caught up in the problems and prospects of a new nation in formation and in contemplating its future relations with the United States, Russia, and Japan. The presence of Japanese there created the opportunity to follow my Japanese thread.

I met Okano on my third day in Yenan. For someone who had spent much of his life in the Communist underground, a change of name (from Nosaka to Okano) was to be expected. He used a number of aliases during his career. He was a small man, then fifty-two years old, neatly dressed in his homespun Yenan uniform, kindly and softspoken, with clear, penetrating eyes. We conversed only in Japanese, although his English was good. He lived with his "wife," a lively Chinese girl fluent in Japanese, in a modest, newly built stone house, surrounded by a spacious vegetable garden. His true wife, Ryū, had remained in Moscow when Okano left for China. Theirs was a close partnership, begun in early youth. She had been used to long separations in a life dedicated to the Communist party. When he came to write his memoirs many years later, he devoted a chapter to a touching eulogy of Ryū, who had played her own important political role but had obviously been a source of personal strength to him. He likened her death (in 1971) to the crumbling of a pillar that had always sustained him.

Okano led me to his study-library, built in a cave above and behind his own house. Members of his Japanese research group lived in adjoining caves. The library shelves were stacked with Japanese books, newspapers, and magazines. Some of the newspapers from Tokyo were less than two months old, testimony to a remarkable delivery across a sea and hundreds of miles of enemy territory. The library's card index was kept on crude scraps of cardboard in drawers that hardly opened or closed.

In a society without clocks—I never saw one in Yenan—conversations began early and ended late. Koji Ariyoshi and I would talk to Okano for hours at a stretch, interrupted only by the appearance of bowls of steaming food—lunch or dinner as the case might be—and a continuous filling of teacups. Some nights in a reminiscent mood, Okano would talk late about his experiences in the underground, especially his travels under assumed names and with false passports. The flickering lamplight and the moving shadows on the walls provided appropriate atmospherics for tales of his life as a fugitive.

Nosaka, to use his rightful name, was born in Yamaguchi prefecture, the old Chōshū, home of many Meiji founding fathers. The youngest of six children and orphaned at fourteen, the young Nosaka was lucky to have been supported by his eldest brother who paid for his education at the Kobe Commercial School and Tokyo's Keiō University. He early became conscious of the inequalities of wealth (his father had become bankrupt) and remembered vividly the trial and execution of the American-educated anarchist, Kōtoku Shūsui, who in 1910 was accused of plotting the assassination of the emperor. He startled his high school teacher and classmates by writing a paper on socialism, and at Keiō his thesis was "Revolutionary Trade Unionism." He graduated second in his university class, but instead of accepting an offer to enter Japan's biggest textile company, Nosaka went to work for the *Yūai Kai* (Friendship Society), a labor-oriented study group. In 1919 he enrolled in the London School of Economics and, in 1920, joined the British Communist party as a founding member. He was deported from England for leftwing activities and traveled to Paris, Geneva, Berlin, and Moscow before returning, via Marseilles and Shanghai, to Tokyo, where he immediately became a leading member of the Japanese Communist party. From then on, he was dodging the police; he served prison terms of seven months in 1923 (experiencing the Tokyo earthquake from his cell) and of eight months in 1925. Three years later he was caught in a mass arrest of three thousand suspected Communists. In 1930 he petitioned the prison authorities for leave to have an eye operation; surprisingly, a month's parole was granted but with residence prohibited in Tokyo. He lived with his brother in Kobe and, obtaining monthly extensions by submitting letters from his doctor, managed to stay out of prison for eight months, although he remained under police surveillance. His temporary parolee status did not deter him from Communist activity and, to get him out of the country and free him from the police, the Comintern ordered him to Moscow to serve as its Japanese representative. His departure from Japan was skillfully and successfully arranged, and he was in the Soviet capital by March of 1931.

During the war and for some years afterward, Nosaka revealed little of what he had done during his assignment to the Comintern. He told us that he had spent much of the nine years outside Moscow, that he had been illegally in and out of Japan numerous times. He joked that the technique was easy: party sympathizers in the railroad and seamen's unions, alerted by the grapevine, were ready at the right time and the right place to help him travel. He did not then admit that he had spent three years in the United States—source of his English—between 1934 and the end of 1938 interrupting his stay there in 1935 to attend the Comintern Congress in Moscow. At that time it was too dangerous to risk printing Communist materials in Japan. Since Japanese type was available in New York, Communist literature was printed there and shipped to sympathizers in Los Angeles. Nosaka was there and worked with American and Japanese comrades to get the literature in the hands of seamen who carried the materials to Japanese ports and mailed them in plain envelopes with Japanese postage. Their operation remained undetected. (Nosaka smiled, as he recalled these exploits in a conversation with me in 1975.)

In 1944 Nosaka told us, and Mao himself had so announced, that he had arrived in Yenan from Moscow in 1943. After the war he corrected this statement, admitting that he had traveled from Moscow to Yenan in 1940, accompanied by Chou En-lai and an Indonesian Communist, whom he now remembers as Amin, on the order of the secretary general of the Comintern, Georgi Dimitrov. Incognito in Yenan from 1940 to 1943, he had begun to reeducate prisoners of war and had written extensively, but anonymously, for Chinese Communist publications.

Yenan's landmark is the nine-storied pagoda on a hill overlooking the Yen River. When we asked our hosts about the ancient history of the area, they replied that they were making history, not studying it, and that archaeology would come later. A little distance up the valley, in the side of the cliff below the pagoda were the dug-out cave quarters of the Japanese Peasants and Workers School. Our first visit was made on ponyback, since the distance was three or four miles from the observers mission compound. The ponies were small Mongolian characters with minds of their own. I described our homeward journey thusly:

> Koji's got excited and did a bucking bronco act all of his own for about five minutes. Mine seemed peaceful until I got on him. He then refused to go the way I wanted to. Finally, he broke out of control and started a dash across the landscape toward the river. Not relishing the ride, I decided off was better than on, so relaxed and fell off. The horse went on across the river where he pranced and bucked in fury. A Chinese boy brought him back. Koji and I led our steeds home—and by this time it was dark so we got lost and didn't get there until 7—too late for supper. But a word and all was arranged—hot bath and a good meal. Retired early. Slightly sore.

At the school the prisoner-students were waiting at the gate to greet us. Enthusiastically, they explained the organization of their school, their curriculum, and their antiwar activities, carried on in the name of the Japanese People's Emancipation League. Enrollment in the school was one hundred and thirty-five; all were prisoners of war except one, Sawada (all used assumed names), who, like Nosaka, was a civilian and long-standing party member, with experience in and out of jails, in the underground, and in northern China for more than a year. The educational background of the POWs was not high; only five had progressed beyond middle school; 85 percent were privates, and there were only two officers—lieutenants—among them. About 70 percent of the prisoners had been captured in battle; the rest were deserters or stragglers. A number of spies had been discovered during the existence of the school, soldiers sent by the Japanese Army to infiltrate and disrupt the antiwar movement. We were told that, after good treatment and indoctrination, these agents confessed and worked hard for the group. One had held out for nearly two years before finally succumbing to the congenial atmosphere among his fellow students.

The Eighth Route Army in 1938 established a policy of good treatment for Japanese prisoners. It apparently took some time to convince Chinese soldiers that they should not kill or mistreat their captives and, understandably, it took even longer to convince Japanese troops in the field that falling into the hands of Communists would not mean death. According to information obtained in Yenan, about twenty-five hundred Japanese soldiers were captured by Red Army troops between July 1937 and December 1944; most of these were returned to their own lines, where they presumably became living testimonials of good treatment. Retribution at the hands of their officers was so cruel, however, that during 1944, captured POWs were usually not returned. In that year some three hundred were said to be participating in antiwar propaganda, both in Yenan and at outposts in the Communist-controlled region. The competition never ended between the Japanese discipline applied to Japanese troops and the Eighth Route Army's tireless attempts to lure the disgruntled soldier over to its side. Communist methods were ingenious, with the terrain and closeness of battle lines facilitating their actions; telephone taps, loudspeaker operations, dispatch of letters and comfort kits by obliging Chinese peasants, and actual infiltration into the Japanese lines by Emancipation League volunteers.

Telephone communications across enemy lines established a strange, momentary bond between the soldier still fighting for his emperor and the Emancipation Leaguer urging his erstwhile comrades to surrender. Some recognized each other's voices: "I'm Kamada, who used to be with you guys. . . . Remember my voice?" The Yenan students believed such incidents were disturbing to morale among the Japanese troops, especially as conditions on the North China front deteriorated for them. Telephone chats weren't always successful, however. An American observer reported that an Eighth Route Army group tried "to talk a blockhouse full of Japs into surrender one night without success; the next night they blew them to hell."

The stated purposes of the Workers and Peasants School were to "educate the students politically, develop strength, ability, and unity to stop the war, and to participate in postwar Japan." The school's motto was Justice, Peace, Comradeship, Work, and Application. Instruction included a course in political common sense, which appeared to be an elementary exposition of economics and politics from a Marxist viewpoint, using such texts as Mao Tse-tung's *On Protracted War* and Okano's 1943 *Appeal to the Japanese People*. After attending a class on our first visit, I wrote: "There was ample opportunity to refer to the inordinate profits of militarists and capitalists in Japan and to point out that the poor worked but always remained poor. At the beginning of the lecture Umeda (a prisoner, of course) told the class that he had big news—the Jap fleet had just been defeated in the Philippines!" One day as we walked unexpectedly into one of Okano's lectures, he looked flustered and quickly switched his subject from Marxism–Leninism to democratic principles.

Just as there was no question about the Communists being Communist, the orientation of the Peasants and Workers School was evident. But in 1944 the greatest Communist country in the world was our ally, and the Japanese in Yenan were opposing the same regime that we were determined to defeat. When they called for the overthrow of the militarists and the construction of a new, democratic Japan, they were echoing our own propaganda; more accurately, we were echoing theirs because they had been at it for two years longer than we. Our observations convinced us that these prisoners in Yenan had, in truth, died once and were genuine in their enthusiasm for a cause they now believed in. There were no intellectuals among them, but otherwise they were probably representative of the Japanese common people. In my words:

> These were country boys, without much education. The rugged faces, stocky physiques! And the language—the miner who sat at my right—he had a rectangular face, mouthed his words, enjoyed talking. He earned 185 yen a month but over half of it went to the government. A young kid, also a miner, earned 80 yen a month and, after his compulsory contributions—bonds, etc.—had only 20 yen left. The fisherman, the *"zū-zū ben"* [northeastern dialect] boy, the rough, hard-faced one—what types ... these are the Japanese Mr. Grew should have known.

Whether a busy ambassador should have cultivated workers and peasants is a moot point, but we in an embassy, which in the 1930s had no labor attaché, should have been more conscious of the complaints and conditions of the kinds of people I was meeting in Yenan.

We took a poll to probe the attitudes of Okano's schoolboys. Ninety-eight responded. Not surprisingly, they were almost unanimous in believing that Japan was wrong both in the China Affair (ninety-six to two) and in the war against the United States (ninety-two to six), and that Japan would lose the war (ninety-four to four). Only eleven were willing to return to a victorious Japan, whereas all but four would go back if Japan were defeated. They were divided on the emperor's responsibility: seventy-five thought he had favored the war; seventeen thought not; and six had no answer. Ninety-four favored abolishing the emperor system. All but two were willing to help the Eighth Route Army and the American Army end the war more quickly.

These answers reflected the conditioning of Yenan, but more than brainwashing was involved. The students ascribed the change in their minds to several factors. First was the discovery that the Eighth Route Army did not kill or torture prisoners. Second was the psychological shock of meeting Japanese on the other side. Relief at being able to speak and be understood was followed by a flash of feeling that the enemy could not be wholly wrong if Japanese had joined him. Third, good treatment became a continuing object lesson. Fourth, the first contact with outside news suggested the probability of Japanese defeat and a changed government at the end of the war. Finally, the instruction at the Workers and Peasants School achieved the ultimate metamorphosis. The successes of Okano and his cohorts reinforced the conclusions I had begun to draw in Burma: once the consciousness of defeat came to the Japanese nation, a mental change, like that experienced by the captured POW, would occur.

The workers and peasants in the school belonged to the *Nihon Jinmin Kaihō Renmei* (Japanese People's Emancipation League), which claimed branches throughout Communist-held territory and was the stated source of propaganda to the Japanese troops. Propaganda themes were designed to offer a way out for the miserable, harried soldier in the field: good treatment, food, clothing, shelter, freedom from officer cruelty (the Japanese Army was famous for slapping and brutalizing the privates), and a chance to win freedom from the militarists and big industrialists responsible for the war. Nothing was said about communism. We asked the more experienced league propagandists to criticize our leaflets, and they did so with gusto and in detail. We exchanged materials; they read ours and we read theirs. In the name of the league and the school, the students produced plays, variety shows, exhibitions, and the inevitable *zadankai* or "discussion sessions." The latter, some arranged on our behalf, took up such subjects as the education of newcomers, suicide, preparation of propaganda leaflets, and the problems of postwar Japan. Most of the students believed that the concept of suicide was ingrained from primary school and reinforced by army indoctrination, but they believed the urge to kill oneself to avoid capture came not from any idealistic love of emperor but because the soldier expected death or torture at the hands of the enemy or disgrace and shame should he ever return home. Talking about their own experiences in a warm, group atmosphere, as in Ledo and in Yenan, gave the prisoners a welcome release.

Much friendship for the United States was exuded by the Emancipation Leaguers, possibly for our benefit, but on the whole, I believe, it was sincere. At a special celebration on Pearl Harbor day, Koji Ariyoshi and I were asked to make speeches. For forty-five minutes I talked in Japanese about prewar Japanese–American relations and the glories of American democracy. I displayed a recent issue of *Life* magazine, which fortunately had portrayed some of the positive elements in Japanese culture, acclaiming this as an example of freedom of speech in a democracy, even in wartime. Koji told them about the nisei fighting for their country in spite of their Japanese ancestry. The audience was boisterously responsive, clapping uproariously whenever we mentioned annihilating the militarists or building a new Japan. I gave a similar speech to Chinese students of English one evening, extolling the freedoms for all varieties of thought and action guaranteed by the American Constitution. One day Sawada came to me to ask that we teach the school the American national anthem—at the request of several students. We agreed but, without a piano, without vocal expertise, and considering the difficulties of singing "The Star-Spangled Banner," we somehow never got a chorus going.

My most interesting conversations with Nosaka concerned the future of the Japanese Communist party and the nature of postwar Japan. At that time he was the party's most authoritative spokesman; all other prewar leaders were in prison, had died, or had recanted, either from conviction or under police pressure. His long service to the Comintern in Moscow and his successful clandestine operations in the Communist underground had given him the prestige and stature which would assure him a position of leadership in the postwar party. His opinions therefore carried weight.

The Japanese Communist party had been born in an upstairs room of a founding member's home in the Shibuya district of Tokyo on July 15, 1922. The organizers were a furtive band of dedicated Bolsheviks who risked their freedom to promote an outlawed cause. Their first program called for the abolition of the emperor system, Privy Council, House of Peers, General Staff, and military conscription, and it advocated guarantees of the freedoms of speech, press, assembly, and organization, as well as the institution of the eight-hour work day. From the beginning, the Japanese party operated under the tight direction of the Communist International. Nosaka wrote, in 1959, that "without the leadership and help of the Comintern, the Japanese Communist party would not have been organized. Its later growth and expansion would have been impossible."

Katayama Sen, considered to be the father of Japan's proletarian movement, was a member of the Presidium of the Comintern in 1921 and is the only Japanese to be buried in the Kremlin wall. Nosaka, who replaced Katayama upon the latter's death in 1933, had already played a prominent role in drafting the 1932 theses approved by the Comintern, which in 1944 were still the bible for Japanese Communists. This platform attacked the emperor system, the landlord system, monopolistic capitalism, and proclaimed a struggle for a soviet republic of workers and peasants. It condemned the "imperialistic, antirevolutionary war," which had begun in Manchuria, demanded the freedom of Japan's colonies—Korea, Manchuria, and Taiwan—and appealed for support of the Soviet Union and the Chinese revolution. The theses also called for the abolition of the Diet, Japan's legislative institution.

In Yenan Nosaka produced a party platform which differed in important respects from the 1932 theses. While opposing a hereditary House of Peers, he placed great emphasis on a Diet which should have "full government power," be totally free from the threat of "arbitrary dissolution by other constitutional organs," and have a cabinet responsible to it. He rejected confiscation of property as impractical, instead proposing the purchase by the government of the holdings of absentee landlords as a first step toward liquidating the traditional landlord system. Nosaka said nothing about supporting the Soviet Union. In 1943 he had welcomed the dissolution of the Comintern as releasing the Japanese party from certain restrictions and as encouraging supporters who might otherwise have been frightened by the Moscow connection. He endorsed whole-heartedly the pronouncements of Mao Tse-tung.

In fact, Nosaka's program, as described to us in 1944, sounded like a paraphrase of the American Bill of Rights: unrestricted universal suffrage (only men could vote in prewar Japan); full legislative power in an elected Diet (the prewar Diet was impotent); freedom for all political parties (leftist parties were outlawed); guarantees of the freedoms of speech, thought, expression, person, and assembly (freedoms were abridged by law); land reform (much land was owned by absentee landlords); freedom for trade unions and the institution of collective bargaining, and an eight-hour work day. Japan should be stripped of its overseas possessions, its war criminals and responsible leaders should be punished or purged, and the emperor system reformed.

The Comintern theses had called for the destruction of the emperor system as the starting point for the Communist program, but Nosaka modified this position to permit the existence of an emperor should the Japanese people so desire. He believed that most Japanese held affection and reverence for the emperor, which would not easily be swept away. He therefore deliberately avoided the old prewar Communist slogan Down with the Emperor! and favored a cautious approach to decisions relating to the imperial household once peace was restored. He did contend, however, that Hirohito should share responsibility for the war and should be replaced. Nosaka's ideas were later spelled out in a report that he delivered to the Seventh National Congress of the Chinese Communist party, held in Yenan in May 1945. In that speech he stated, "If the majority of our people fervently demand the perpetuation of the emperor, we must concede to them."

What smacked of communism in Nosaka's postwar policy planning was his advocacy of "voluntary collective farming," government control of "monopoly capital" with confiscation of "excess" profits, and inclusion of Communists in the postwar government. He foresaw a three-stage revolution—a "bourgeois democratic revolution" in two stages, culminating finally in socialism. Only at the end of the second stage did Nosaka hope for the liquidation of the "remnants of feudalism"—the emperor system, nobility, Privy Council and House of Peers—the "democratization" of the army and navy (he did not call for their abolition), and the end of discrimination against the Eta, or "outcasts." Nosaka told us that he did not expect to see the third stage, socialism, realized in his lifetime. In this he was no doubt right (he was eighty-five in 1977), but certainly his wildest imagination could not have perceived the lightning-swift reforms, in some cases exceeding his aspirations, later to be accomplished by the MacArthur revolution.

Fascinated by Nosaka's recitals of party life and programs, I decided to write a brief history of the Japanese Communist party, especially when I discovered that no foreign service officer had reported on it since the early 1930s. No doubt influenced by the crisp air and the contagious zeal of Yenan, I used language that might not have found its way into a dispatch composed in the more disciplined atmosphere of a State Department or embassy office. Still, my conclusions do not seem horrendous, even in the light of passing years. I transferred our worries about Soviet predominance over China (which Vladimirov had suspected) to Japan and thought we should try to keep Japan, including the Japanese Communists, out of Russian control. My final paragraph read:

> The Communists will not be strong enough to seize control in Japan. Realistically they will be content to receive legal recognition for the first time in their history. We may expect them to seek power in the future and Japan may be fertile ground for their growth. We can, however, best prevent Japan's political system from again becoming a danger to us by adopting and activating a positive policy. In spite of war-whipped hate, the Japanese fundamentally like us more than they do the Russians. It is for us to make the most of our opportunity.

The longer I stayed in Yenan and the more I associated with Nosaka and his students, the more I became convinced that the United States should take some political action—first, to end the war quickly, and second, to prepare the Japanese psychologically for the occupation of their country. Intelligence proved that conditions were becoming desperate in the Japanese home islands; couriers secretly traveling back and forth confirmed that a country cut off from its sources of food and materials, with its navy and air force all but annihilated, could not hold out long.

How to get through to those leaders who we knew were seeking a way out? I wrote repeated dispatches, from August 1944 until I left the theater in February 1945, proposing "statements" to Japan. I recommended that we set up our own indoctrination program, based on the principles of American democracy, for the Japanese prisoners of war in our hands, and that we establish an organization of "free Japanese," which could issue manifestos and propaganda materials in the name of the Japanese rather than Americans. The fact that prisoners of war were in a mentally malleable state had been demonstrated by our own work in Ledo, by Kaji's Anti-War League in Chungking, and by the Yenan Workers and Peasants School and the Emancipation League. It seemed important that we, as Americans, use the opportunity to introduce to Japanese the ideas on which our own institutions of government were based. These, we believed, would present an alternative to the system that militarist-dominated rule had imposed on Japan. My ideas were not revolutionary; I later learned that POWs were working for us in the Pacific theater and free movements among nationals of various enemy countries had become a pattern. My reports to the State Department stipulated that there would be no communism in the content of the programs I proposed, nor Communists in the direction of those projects. But I had my premonitions: even then I feared that my sojourn in Yenan might engender suspicions of procommunism on my part. As I wrote in Yenan, I contemplated my schemes would sound "impractical to powers that be at home, and they will certainly flinch at the sight of Red!"

The stimulation of Yenan focused in two directions: on the new China which was in gestation in these hills and loess caves and on a new Japan which would emerge from certain defeat. This was heady stuff—contemplating two revolutions within the two greatest nations of Asia. Although we wasted little time in philosophizing, what a moment in history! Communist control of China seemed foreordained, and since we could do nothing to prevent it (short of a massive military intervention in a civil war), the wisest course seemed to be to lay foundations for friendly coexistence. Japan was different. The Communists were not going to take over Japan, and Nosaka himself knew it. He looked forward to a legal existence for his party for the first time in history and to the release from prison of his erstwhile comrades. He hoped for an energetic, aggressive political life and some successes in his lifetime. Basic requirements for a future Japanese Communist party were the freedoms for activity previously denied him. In the recommendations that he described to us, Nosaka's ideas were mainly consistent with the postsurrender directives already being hammered out in the State Department.

His and our ultimate objectives were, however, far apart. We were looking to the democratization of Japan, not its communization. Our vocabulary did not include such phrases as "monopoly capitalists," "bourgeois democratic revolution," or "people's democracy." But the punishment of war criminals, purges, the break-up of the *zaibatsu* ("monopolies"), the guarantee of civil rights, changes in the status of the emperor, land reform, educational reform—all of these reforms were elements of both Nosaka's and the American programs. We also knew that our interests would not remain compatible, that a parting of the ways would come sooner or later. The United States could never support communism, and Mao and Nosaka were committed, respectively, to a Communist China and a Communist Japan. For Japan, we assumed that our Occupation would permit the Japanese to choose their own form of government. The premise would be political freedom in which the Communists would have to take their chances. For the immediate future, however, and from the perspective of Yenan, what concerned us was the defeat of Japan and the subsequent fundamental changes in that country's regime on which we and the Communists then happened to agree.

In Yenan, General Albert Wedemeyer had taken over Stilwell's command of the China theater and Major General Patrick J. Hurley had arrived in Chungking as the president's personal representative for bringing the Communists and the Kuomintang together. Hurley flew to Yenan unexpectedly on November 7, the anniversary of the Russian Revolution. I remember *Time* correspondent Theodore

White stomping on his hat in rage, believing that he had missed Hurley's arrival, and the chance for an important story. The general's exit from his plane was indeed a mixture of pomp and circumstance: first, his Choctaw war whoop; then David Barrett rounding up workers on the airfield to form an impromptu welcoming committee; and finally, the frenzied last-minute arrival of Mao Tse-tung, Chu Teh, and Chou En-lai in their battered, coughing, old Red Cross truck. On that day I wrote, "Oklahoma comes to Yenan!" Hurley's stars shone; he was erect, ruddy, with a trim mustache and handsome face—confidence and exuberance personified. Dave Barrett is supposed to have made an immortal remark, "You've got every medal there except one for Shay's Rebellion." Hurley held us spellbound in our quarters with his tales of Indian days, when he spoke Choctaw and not English, and when, with a group of fellow tribesmen, he had surrendered to U.S. forces and been led through the streets of Indian territory, dragging ball and chain behind him. He recited "Oh What A Beautiful Morning," "The Chisholm Trail" and proclaimed his three best friends to be Will Rogers, Admiral Byrd, and an Indian chief. He was serious about his mission, which he described to us over lunch in our mess hall, "I'm going to explain to these Communists that I'm a Republican working for a Democratic president. They're the Republicans of China but their president happens to be a 'Democrat.' Two parties can cooperate here just as they do in the United States!"

That night the Communists hosted a banquet in their great hall (usually used for dances) to commemorate the Russian Revolution, in the presence of the whole Communist hierarchy and their commanders who had been called from the field for a military conference. The toasts in *mao tai, baigar,* and *hu-ku* ("tiger bone wine") followed, one after the other: Mao to Roosevelt, Hurley to Mao, and then both to Churchill, Stalin, and even Chiang Kai-shek. This was probably the climax of Chinese Communist–American friendship, not to be seen again until Richard M. Nixon toasted Mao in 1972. After Hurley left Yenan, carrying with him his "treaty," solemnly signed by Mao and him, and containing a rich mix of the Magna Charta, Bill of Rights, and Declaration of

Independence, everything went downhill. Even the bracing air of Yenan lost some of its zing as word filtered back that the Generalissimo was not about to shake hands with his bitter rival Mao Tse-tung.

December came and the snows fell, and the sunshine—which had lured us out of doors to read and write while stripped to the waist—faded. "These people," I wrote on December 10, "are on their high horse and will not climb down." K'ang Sheng, in his conversation with me on December 14, said that a settlement with the Kuomintang looked very difficult. K'ang asserted that the Communists would never accept posts in the central government; no true coalition could result, since Chiang would never relinquish his one-party dictatorship.

On December 12 a radio message came from John Davies: "Finish up work in Yenan and take next plane for here prepared to go immediately to Washington for consultation." I hoped to get home for Christmas, but the next plane didn't come until the seventeenth, and complications in Chungking dashed my hopes. I prepared to leave this Shensi stronghold with its Japanese revival meetings, where, as I recorded, "the reclaimed sinners testified how they were saved."

Yenan, now the holy city for the masters of China, will always evoke vivid impressions for me. All was not unremitting work for the founders of a new nation. The Saturday night dances were the relaxing time for the party leaders. Several hundred people shuffled solemnly over the floor, the girls indistinguishable from the men in their thick, drab blue cotton trousers and coats. The conscientious orchestra consisted of eight instruments—harmonicas, drums, and Chinese violins. They played "Red Wing" and "Anchors Aweigh." The commanding general, Chu Teh, and his wife usually attended, as did Yeh Chien-ying and Chou En-lai. It seemed to be their one recreation.

A pastime among us observers was poker, into which capitalist vice we managed to lure "Doc" Ma (Ma Hai-teh, or George Hatem), an American physician who had been with the Communists for years and has in recent years appeared as a greeter of foreign visitors to Peking. We must have lent Doc the chips for his poker because Yenan society was hardly a money economy. Doc Ma, whose name means "Horse," ran an efficient hospital in the caves, dependent on native herbs from which to concoct his pills. He had a charming wife and a beguiling baby whom they called Yu-ma or "Little Horse." My claim to fame among the poker players came one night when, nine dollars in debt and with only fifteen cents left in my pockets, I played one more hand, to finish with fifty dollars, the only time in my life that I ever won at poker.

Politics and propaganda colored almost everything in Yenan but some byways were worth pursuing. We visited the art and music school (Yenan woodblock prints are treasures now), special cultural exhibitions, and the foreign-language school, not to speak of arms factories and rural communities. We heard how illiteracy was to be wiped out, through concentrated learning of Chinese ideographs and reduction of the vocabulary to a thousand characters. A poster depicted comically a furious husband protesting to his wife that he wanted to go to bed without learning his character for the day.

I held lengthy conversations (arranged by Huang Hua or Ch'en Chia-kang, another interpreter assigned to our mission) about the educational reforms proposed for China and visited the Korean Workers and Peasants School, where cadres were being prepared to take over an independent Korea. I was not overly impressed, commenting, "These people are not of the caliber to run a country— but of course who is?" We heard that Yenan harbored many Communists from Southeast Asian countries who were preparing for their postwar opportunities, as were the Japanese and Koreans, but we were never invited to meet these groups. There were too many things to investigate, too much to read, and too many people to talk to.

Two days before I left Yenan I was invited to call on Generals Chu Teh and Yeh Chien-ying who persisted in asking the question, Was it possible to deal directly with the United States without going through the Kuomintang? I did not then suspect that Mao Tse-tung and Chou En-lai would, in January, propose a trip to Washington to talk personally to President Roosevelt. After a farewell session with Nosaka, I was informed on the day before my departure that Mao would send a car at five in the afternoon for us (John Davies had flown up with the plane and was returning to Chungking with me). The next day, with my irrepressible tendency to dramatize, I wrote:

> It was dark when we drove into the gateway—guards above, below, around. The Chairman had come outside to greet us; he is always warm, cordial. He accompanied us into another courtyard and into what seemed to be one of many rooms. The furniture was very simple. Last night his features seemed stronger than had been my impression before. He has an intelligent, alert face but last night I thought there was more force—perhaps a relentless will behind his eyes and high forehead. I decided I would not like to cross him.
>
> He lashed out at Chiang. There is no more reluctance, no more holding back on that score. No one can deal with him—the Japanese—the United States—the Communists. He plays all games—against soft and hard treatment. He will ever negotiate but never settle. Mao stood up and spoke—in the shadows his frame loomed up and his own shadow against the wall was tremendous. How far, I wonder, will that shadow be cast over future China?

Knowing that I had worked for Ambassador Grew, who in 1944 had become undersecretary of state, Mao asked that I deliver a special oral message from him when I met Mr. Grew in Washington: that he sent his best personal wishes, that the Chinese Communists had only goodwill for the United States, and that he looked forward to cooperation in the future. When I later reported to the State Department, I told Mr. Grew of this conversation.

On December 17 we arrived in Chungking, along muddy roads, with the weapons carrier that met us slipping on the curves. The mud seemed to symbolize the deep gloom that weighted Chungking. Stilwell's recall and the lack of progress in Communist-Kuomintang negotiations had combined to produce despair among the Americans.

Hurley had replaced Gauss as ambassador, the "Gambassador" as we called him in deference to his general's two stars combined with his new diplomatic status, and relations between him and his embassy staff were strained, to put it mildly. He had ordered them to send no reports to Washington critical of the central government, a government whose sovereignty, as Barbara Tuchman was to put it so cogently many years later, "was a husk, just as its democracy was an illusion." Hurley was frustrated at his inability to reconcile the so-called Chinese Democrats and Republicans and was looking for people to blame. He became erratic, emotional, and suspicious. John Davies particularly aroused his ire by flying to Yenan without his permission; Hurley accused John of trying to break up the negotiations and threatened to break him, telling me that he would recommend to Washington that Davies never be assigned to China again nor be allowed ever to have anything to do with Chinese affairs. Ironically, this was to happen, not solely because of Hurley and not only to John, but to many others of us as well.

My immediate return to Washington stretched out to five weeks. The projects I intended to discuss and about which I had already written were the statement to Japan, a prisoner indoctrination program, and a Japanese organization to carry on psychological warfare. I needed approval for these projects from both Ambassador Hurley and General Wedemeyer, and I hoped to receive orders to return to China via the Pacific, permitting me to discuss anti-Japanese political warfare with officials engaged in such activities in those war theaters. Wedemeyer would be away from Chungking for several weeks so I had to await his return.

Davies and I called on Hurley together. I had just launched into my presentation with verve and conviction when the general suddenly pointed to my shoes, a non-GI pair bought at home, and bellowed, "Where did you get those shoes?" This abrupt non sequitur flustered and deflated me; I stammered, "Washington," and went on weakly. Finally John, in a moment of inspiration, suggested that if my ideas could come from the ambassador, their success would be assured. Hurley's pride touched, he at once gave his approval and asked no further questions.

Christmas and New Year's came and went. During a lone walk on Christmas Day, an unknown foreigner, whom I thought to be a missionary, wished me Merry Christmas and, as the saying goes, made my day. At a New Year's party, no one could think of an appropriate toast for 1945. Someone suggested, "the inevitability of historical process," and another, "that we have something to drink to for 1946." Harold Isaacs, author of the classic *Tragedy of the Chinese Revolution,* was particularly despondent that we did not toast 1945. He was the deepest pessimist in the crowd. He questioned whether the Chinese man in the street would be better off under communism than under the Kuomintang.

On January 10 I put on my long underwear, my Communist suit (a Yenan tailor had made homespun wool uniforms for all of us in the observers mission), my flight jacket, and boots, and flew up to Yenan with several colonels and order of battle intelligence specialists. I noted how different the country was, powdery white under snow. I marveled again how Champ (Captain Jack Champion, Stilwell's pilot) could find Yenan, beyond the complex and seemingly interminable system of similarly spaced valleys and ridges. Huang Hua and Ch'en Chia-kang were there to meet us. It was stiffening cold.

The mood had changed. The Communists were grim. On the ninth, the mission had transmitted a message to Chungking ("eyes only for Wedemeyer"), reporting that Mao Tse-tung and Chou En-lai were immediately available to go to Washington to interpret and explain the present situation and problems of China to President Roosevelt and American officials. On the eleventh, Captain W. K. Evans, intelligence officer with the Dixie Mission, showed me a message he had sent to headquarters (also "eyes only for Wedemeyer"), which specified that the Communists had positive, top-secret proof that the Kuomintang government was secretly negotiating an agreement with the Japanese. The Communists did not want either message to be shown to Ambassador Hurley. As Evans told me, the Yenan leaders did not trust Hurley's discretion and demanded that he be kept ignorant of their communications.

Evans was much excited about the Communist revelations, contained in documents that he said would take four hours to examine. He urged me to postpone my return to Chungking, scheduled for that same day, in order to investigate these charges. Knowing that Hurley would be furious, I told Evans I could not involve myself in such a matter without instructions from head-quarters. I remembered his tirade against John Davies. I assured Evans that I would personally discuss the problem with General Wedemeyer and urge that a thorough investigation be instituted. The next morning after my return to Chungking, on January 12, I saw the commanding general and reported on my conversations in Yenan. He had shown both telegrams to Hurley whom he described as low, both physically and mentally. He suggested that I talk to the ambassador.

I saw Hurley at 5:30 that same afternoon. At first he appeared to be somewhat chastened but soon got off the track and bellowed to me about John Davies again. Then, suddenly he turned on the Jews, naming some of the correspondents in the theater. In his usual, disjointed conversation, he quoted John as saying that "Chiang must go sooner or later."

"Of course he must go sooner or later," he shouted. "We all do; we don't live forever. Of course Chiang will die. I will die." Then he confided that he would now try a different tack in the negotiations. He had been leaning toward the Kuomintang; now he would turn the other way and lean toward the Communists. On the Yenan report, I told Hurley that the evidence was serious enough to require investigation. We could not ignore it. He agreed, but, in an apparent effort to rebut the Communist charges, he suddenly switched: "Foreign Minister T. V. Soong is coming in a few minutes with proof that Mao and company have been dealing for years with the Japanese; they have a plan to unite all Asiatics against the whites." T. V. was announced. I met him in the hall on my way out.

In a memorandum written on the thirteenth, I tried to sort out Communist motivations in presenting their revelations to us. Perhaps, in view of increasing U.S. aid to the Kuomintang, they felt they must act quickly to discredit the Chungking government. Convincing the United States that the Generalissimo was courting the Japanese might bring American help to the Communists. Mao's and Chou's willingness to meet the president might lend credence to their report of a Kuomintang–Japanese agreement. In a separate column, I listed the "elements supporting credibility," including Communist confidence, the feeling that they were "on the make," the unlikelihood that they would suggest a trip to Washington if their report were false, and plausibility based on our knowledge of Mao's intelligence and underground organization.

I felt that the depth of feeling expressed by the Communists in presenting the report to us was more significant than the truth or falsity of the charges themselves. The Communists were on the point of making important decisions and were impatient to discover whether the United States intended to help them. I wrote:

> The Communists are openly talking of civil war. Civil war would negate our war effort in the China theater. It may not be possible to delay fundamental decisions of American policy much longer— if such decisions are to be made. In any case we must weigh the consequences of such decisions—or lack of decisions—since it is possible that we may have arrived at a turning point in Chinese history and in Chinese-American relations.

Hurley's first report of Mao's offer to go to Washington was buried in a telegram sent January 14 to the president. It was again mentioned incidentally in a long message of February 7, advising Roosevelt on the general situation in China. It was never treated seriously. As for the secret documents, they were transmitted to Chungking and forwarded to Washington. Hurley dismissed them as unconvincing.

According to Edgar Snow, who saw the president in March 1945, Roosevelt, busy with other more pressing duties, seemed "baffled yet acutely fascinated" with what was happening in China. Snow's report of the conversation reveals how confused and unrealistic the president's view of China seemed to be. Snow asked, "We can't support two governments in China, can we?" He reported FDR's answer, " 'Well, I've been working with two governments there.' The president threw back his head decisively, 'I intend to go on doing so until I can get them together.' " But it was already too late to get them together.

On January 15 I visited a Japanese prison with Kaji Wataru. The prisoners shuffled in to meet us, their ankle chains fastened together with huge padlocks. Kaji and I tried to draw them out, but there was little response. The contrast with the happy workers and peasants in Yenan could hardly have been more striking.

On the nineteenth, the embassy burned to the ground and my report on the Koreans in Yenan with it.

On the twenty-second I met bouncing, breathless General ("Wild Bill") Donovan, chief of the Office of Strategic Services (OSS), who swept me off my feet by inviting me to return to the United States on his plane, leaving in two days, and by proposing that I join OSS. I delightedly accepted the ride to Washington but said that I hoped to continue to be assigned to General Wedemeyer, although I would be glad to cooperate with OSS activities. Wedemeyer had approved round-the-world travel orders for me.

On my last day in Chungking I had interviews with four generals—Wedemeyer, Hurley, Donovan, and McClure (chief of staff to Wedemeyer). Wedemeyer was exceptionally genial, con-firming that he wanted me to continue on his staff. He was sorry that John Davies had been hurt by Hurley's remarks. Hurley had his heart in the right place, but he talked too much and was becoming senile. Wedemeyer would no longer provide the ambassador with copies of our reports.

The ambassador gave me a harangue on his mission and importuned me to give Under Secretary Grew and the State Department my own opinions of him and what he was doing. This day he felt hopeful; things had been fouled up before, but the Chinese government was now ready to make greater concessions than the Communists had demanded in the beginning (nothing about leaning toward the Communists). Chou En-lai would be in Chungking the next day, and they would resume their talks. Hurley would try to bring all the armed forces of China under one control. I thought, not easy, remembering the futile attempts to put the Chinese armies under Stilwell. The ambassador wanted me especially to understand that he had not been taken in by T.V. Soong, who was "as slippery as an eel." T.V. had said that whoever prevents civil war in China would get the Nobel Peace Prize. T.V. wanted the credit and would get it if Hurley succeeded. People, including Al

Wedemeyer, were saying that Hurley was taken in by T.V. "This is not true," and he told me I could tell the Department so.

We left China on January 24 in Donovan's plush C-54, which could fly at the breathtaking speed of 210 miles per hour. The general had business along the way, however, and it was two weeks before we touched down in Washington, having meandered to Calcutta where I noted "the spindly-legged squatting forms." I wrote my impressions of the journey: "I shall always think of India in a squatting position"; Colombo and Kandy, Ceylon: "fighting the war in the lush botanical gardens of Kandy, politics crackle in every exotic bush: we *love* political warfare"; Calcutta: "the burning ghats, the itching palmists"; Delhi: "home in a few days"; Karachi: "the cycle of India–Burma–China completed"; Cairo: "the pyramids: all that work for what?"; Casablanca: "the casbah without 'As Time Goes By' "; Terceira Island in the Azores: "pink-and-blue plaster houses, like a bad Hollywood set"; Stephenville, Newfoundland— and home!

It had been a year, three months, and two weeks since I had flown into the Peruvian skies to begin my own journey among warriors. Loudspeakers at Myitkyina; brass, British, and bureaucrats in New Delhi; flying the Hump, the Hukawng valley, and the Delhi–Chabua run; Kaji's chained prisoners in Chungking, Nosaka's students in Yenan; Chiang, Mao, Stilwell, Hurley, Wedemeyer—all that was behind me, or so I thought! Back to the desk, nine to five, in a Washington swollen with uniforms and civil servants, backbiting, competing, duplicating, stumbling over each other with zeal and good intentions, in what we called the war effort. My fling was over.

9

Washington 1945

Some of the rare air of North China must have remained lodged in my lungs and since jet lag had yet to be invented, I charged eagerly into the State Department the very morning after our snowy night arrival at Washington's military airport. The old, pillared, layer-cake of a building next to the White House was familiar: the high ceilings, wide corridors, and the swinging latticed gates in front of tall oaken doors before which Negro messengers had traditionally nodded in their chairs. I was heartily welcomed by Eugene Dooman, my old boss at the embassy in 1941, who promptly ushered me into a meeting of Japan and China officers, most of them old friends.

Dooman went directly to the point, "We've been much interested in your reports. They coincide with the thinking we have been doing in the department." I reported on my proposals for a statement to Japan, on Yenan, on Okano and his prisoner-students, on psychological warfare, on my ideas of indoctrinating our Japanese POWs, and of setting up an organization to work for the ending of the war. The audience was receptive and urged me to develop the ideas that I had outlined.

Few guessed in February 1945 that war in East Asia would be over in six months. Yet, in retrospect, peace should have come before it did.

As I arrived in Washington, Stalin was promising at Yalta to attack Japan "two or three months" after Germany's defeat, and President Roosevelt was agreeing to hand over the Kurile Islands to the Soviet Union. So secretly held were the results of the Yalta conference that no one in the State Department except Secretary of State Stettinius, Averell Harriman, and Chip Bohlen knew about the agreements. No Far Eastern expert was a member of the U.S. delegation, nor were the comprehensive papers that had been prepared by the State Department consulted, yet major decisions on Asian policy were made. The senior officers responsible for Far Eastern affairs, still in the dark, urged me to lunch with Bohlen, in view of our prewar friendship in Tokyo, to find out if I could what Yalta decisions pertained to the Far East. Chip was frank; he had been sworn to secrecy by the White House and could divulge nothing to his colleagues in the State Department. Joseph Ballantine, a senior Japan specialist, wrote later that he first learned of the Yalta accords six months after the conference and that his closest colleagues—especially Stanley K. Hornbeck and Nelson T. Johnson, former ambassador to China—were shocked since they saw no reason why the Russians should have been paid to enter the war against Japan when their staying out would have suited our interests better. More than thirty years later, President Roosevelt's offhand gift to Stalin of the Kurile Islands was still obstructing a peace treaty between Japan and the Soviet Union.

It was also at Yalta that the British and American Combined Chiefs of Staff estimated, for planning purposes, that Japan's defeat would come eighteen months after the capitulation of Germany, which they forecast for sometime after July 1. To force unconditional surrender on Japan, the Combined Chiefs of Staff projected an invasion of Kyūshū for December 1, and of the Tokyo plain for March 1946. As an army chronicler put it, "The American planners did not think there was any urgency to prepare for Japan's surrender."

My experiences in the China–Burma–India theater had convinced me that it was urgent to make such plans. I felt that Japan's situation was approaching desperation, and that we could take actions which would speed surrender. In a memorandum addressed to General

Wedemeyer, I had, before leaving Chungking, again recommended sending an official statement to Japan. But my friends in the State Department needed no persuasion of this. As Dooman had said, my ideas did coincide with their thinking.

I had written of the typical Japanese prisoner of war encountered in Burma and China: "There seems to be no feeling that he is a traitor to his own country, but rather that he no longer belongs to his own country." I wanted to test this conclusion among POWs captured by American forces and to see what could be done to induce them to think about the new Japan which we envisaged at the end of the war. A practical objective would be to smooth the way for Occupation. Admittedly, there was a missionary zeal in these motives, the kind of zeal which later inspired many well-meaning occupationaires when they came to rule Japan.

My enthusiasm, sparked in Yenan and still alive in Washington, was quickly dampened by the frustrations of hidebound bureaucracy. Everyone endorsed my proposals; the State Department was on record as having been "impressed by the thoroughness and initiative" of my work; and my colleagues were sympathetic and encouraging. I soon discovered that planning for postwar Japan had been in progress in the State Department since the fall of 1942. At the end of 1944 the State-War-Navy Coordinating Committee (SWNCC), known inevitably as SWINK, had come into being and, in January 1945, a subcommittee was formed, cumbersomely designated as the Inter-Divisional Area Committee for the Far East. Another organ, the Postwar Program Committee, was also functioning. It was into this maze of committees and subcommittees that I must plunge if my proposals were to be activated. It was a one-man effort, since all other officials in the Office of Far Eastern Affairs were too busy writing papers, attending meetings, and fulfilling the requirements of their respective job descriptions. I was a loner, an outsider on temporary duty, a free-wheeler; able to float but still expected to work through channels if I wished to get anything done.

Yenan was a glamorous word in the Washington of 1945. Those of us who had been there were sought after to tell our stories. The journalists who had entered Communist-held areas were lecturing and writing books. Harrison Forman's *Report from Red China* and

Gunther Stein's *Challenge of Red China* were both published in 1945. For the first time, Americans were discovering who Mao Tse-tung was and how he and his group could threaten the continued domination over China of the "great power" leader, Chiang Kai-shek, and the beguiling Madame Chiang. Yet Edgar Snow had published his *Red Star Over China* in 1937, eight years before. Accounts of the isolated cave town nestled among the barren hills of Northwest China, where serious Chinese in dark, padded garments were methodically planning a new democracy fired the public imagination. As Harrison Forman wrote, "The Communists claimed to wield influence over something like ninety million people in north and central China—equivalent to nearly three-fourths of the population of America. This alone made them news."

Numerous audiences were eager to hear my tales of Red Yenan and Okano's brainwashed prisoners. I was invited to address groups in the War Department, Commerce Department, Office of Strategic Services (OSS), Office of War Information, and even the later-to-be-maligned Institute of Pacific Relations. Okano had presented me with a set of colorful wall posters, describing in pictures and charts the activities of the Japanese People's Emancipation League and the Workers and Peasants School. Japanese soldier-artists had vividly portrayed pillboxes being assailed by loudspeakers, comfort kits being smuggled across enemy lines, and the happy converts damning their former military masters and praising democracy and the Allied cause. At each lecture I displayed these charts and startled my hearers by advancing what was for them a new thought, that even fanatical, hardened, modern samurai could be metamorphosed into ardent collaborators in our war to defeat their country.

The so-called Yenan reports, which included my own as well as those of other officers from the State Department and OWI who had visited Yenan, received broadside distribution within the government and were apparently avidly read. I was young enough to be flattered when an intelligence officer, Douglas Fairbanks, Jr., in uniform, greeted me at an official meeting, "Yes, I know you. I've read your reports." Although we automatically classified our own dispatches, their scatteration across Washington made it inevitable that some would turn up in odd places, such as the offices of

Amerasia magazine, a left-of-liberal periodical, and thus produce the sensationalized Amerasia case, reported by a Senate subcommittee publication in 1970 as "the clue to the catastrophe of China."

Educating prisoners of war seemed to be a good idea. Kaji had tried it in nationalist China. We had tried it on a small scale in Ledo. Even the British had made a stab at it with POWs assembled in India. Nosaka had done it, successfully I thought, in Yenan. Why shouldn't we try it in the United States? Of course, Nosaka's communism provided readymade answers. He could convince peasants and workers in uniform that life would be better, not only without officers who slapped them and militarists who ruled them, but without fat capitalists who would grind them down for profits. The Communist practice of teaching POWs to repeat slogans like parrots resembled in form the spiritual mobilization that they had experienced in the imperial army. The Communist appeal was strong because of the promises of a better life for the common man. Our education would have to be more subtle. Representative democracy could not be painted as utopia. Still, setting up a program while the war was on would provide a laboratory for discussing the reforms that we assumed we would institute in a vanquished Japan. Also, it might produce a few cooperative Japanese who would help us when the time for landings came.

The problem was how to do it. Bureaucratic red tape, far from vanishing in wartime, became more entangled as agencies and personnel proliferated. Writing papers to be forwarded through channels, gathering initials and comments during a slow course through a labyrinth of offices seemed an interminable process. Chance intervened. One day at lunch I mentioned my project to a friend from prewar embassy days in Tokyo, who was then private secretary to the Roosevelt Cabinet's maverick fighting liberal, Harold L. Ickes. Ellen Downes (who was later to marry a foreign service colleague, Brewster Morris) reacted instantaneously, "Why not see the boss?"

Within a few days, to the astonishment of my State Department associates, for whom an interview with the secretary of the interior, arranged outside channels, would have been unthinkable, I was ushered into the presence of the redoubtable, self-styled curmudgeon. Ickes had an interest in the Japanese; the Office of Indian Affairs in his own department had shared responsibilities in the administration of the relocation centers into which West Coast Japanese had been summarily evacuated at the beginning of the war. After listening attentively and sympathetically, he reached for the telephone, and within minutes I had an appointment to see John J. McCloy, assistant secretary of war, who was responsible, through the provost marshal general, for prisoners of war held in the United States.

McCloy, with whom I became better acquainted in later years, was cordial and endorsed my project without hesitation. With his introduction, I met the provost marshal general who, assuming McCloy's favorable judgment to be decisive, set about at once to put the operation into motion. He suggested that I first visit prison camps in the United States, interview Japanese prisoners of war, and present detailed recommendations to him. The War Department was also interested in my experiences in China and scheduled talks at several of the civil affairs training schools which had been set up to prepare officers for the expected military government of Japan. By this time it was early April. Three of us set out, a Major Gemill from the provost marshal general's office, Dr. C. W. Hepner, a former missionary to Japan then attached to the OWI, and myself. We visited Camp McCoy, Wisconsin, the largest camp for Japanese in the United States, which housed several hundred POWs captured in the Pacific war theater, and a detention facility an hour and a half's drive from Francisco. In the course of the trip, which lasted from April 4 to 30, I delivered lectures at civil affairs schools at Northwestern University, the University of Chicago, Stanford University, and the Presidio in Monterey, California.

At Camp McCoy, talks with prisoners and their GI guards at once revealed that the camp's organization had been taken over by the Japanese. A navy captain was the senior inmate, and he ruled his subordinates with firm authority. The American military supervisors, knowing no Japanese and nothing about Japanese society, were happy to keep their hands off management so long as order and discipline were observed. They had only praise for the cleanliness, respect for rules, and self-sufficiency of the Japanese. They wanted no interference nor disruption in the way things were. As military men with a clearly defined, fixed purpose, they looked upon psychological warriors with some suspicion and distrust.

Junior officers and enlisted men were reluctant to speak in front of their superiors. Captain Saito obviously had intimidated them. They were very different from Okano's students. They had not accepted Japan's inevitable defeat and said they were not prepared to return in disgrace to a Japan they expected to be victorious. They were curious about Japanese soldiers captured in Burma and China and pumped me with questions about them. They had heard about Okano and dismissed his liberation leaguers: "But they're Communists!" It was clear that if we were to establish an educational program, the cooperative prisoners would have to be identified and segregated as early as possible after capture. Otherwise they would be cowed and controlled by the self-appointed leaders of the group.

I was in San Francisco while the founding meeting of the United Nations was taking place. The Chungking government had been persuaded to include a Communist in the Chinese delegation. Consequently, Tung Pi-wu, one of the founders of the party and a member of the Politburo, was at the conference with Ch'en Chia-kang as his interpreter. I called on them in their hotel suite and found them somewhat incongruous in these luxurious Western surroundings, away from their loess caves and homespun uniforms of Yenan.

At lunch with Ch'en Chia-kang, we talked about the Russians. He was confident that no *fundamental* conflict would arise between the Chinese Communists and the Soviet Union but felt there would be differences over minor issues and the application of policies. On one point he was adamant: all lost territory must be returned to China. This would include, not only Manchuria, but Outer Mongolia as well. He obviously did not know that Stalin at the Yalta conference in February had insisted that Outer Mongolia would be "independent." Ch'en stressed the fact that none of the three top leaders of the Chinese Communist party—Mao Tse-tung, Chu Teh, or Chou En-lai—had been educated in Moscow and that the Chinese Nationalist Government had received far more aid from the Russians than had the Yenan regime. He knew none of the

Soviet delegates at the San Francisco conference, and the Chinese Communist group had had no contacts with them.

Our recommendations for the establishment of a special indoctrination camp for Japanese prisoners of war were submitted to the provost marshal general and to the Department of State on April 12. Our objectives proposed to create in the selected Japanese a favorable attitude toward the United States and an understanding of American life and institutions; to provide a laboratory for the study of the psychology, temperament, character, beliefs, and reactions of Japanese; to train Japanese personnel who might assist in psychological warfare operations, cooperate at the time of landings in Japan in order to reduce civilian resistance, and participate in programs of reeducation and rehabilitation in the occupation period. A supervisory committee, consisting of representatives of the State, War, and Navy departments, and OWI was to be set up; the camp director was to be an army officer with the rank of major or above, having a knowledge of Japan and the Japanese language; the director of education was to be a civilian with longtime experience in Japan; and the instructors were to include Japanese living in the United States or Americans of Japanese ancestry. The report included a suggestion that "several of the indoctrinated POWs now working for us in China might be brought to the United States to assist in the indoctrination program, if deemed advisable." In the revision process, this sentence was amended to require such POWs to have been OWI-trained and to have expressed concern over the suitability of indoctrination conducted in China. Because of this suggestion I was later to be accused of advocating the Communist indoctrination of Japanese prisoners of war.

Our proposed curriculum included elementary instruction in current events, American history and institutions, the English language, international relations, problems relating to postwar Japan, and Japanese institutions and culture.

In late June the provost marshal general ordered that a special camp be established under the command of a friend from the prewar period, Lieut. Col. Baude C. Moore, a former missionary in Japan who was fluent in Japanese, and Dr. Hepner was appointed as the educational director. The camp, built at Huntsville, Texas, some seventy miles north of Houston, functioned for several months. But the war ended, and the influence of its members on the democratization of Japan could never be judged.

In 1947 the ranking Japanese officer in the Texas facility published a book in English called *American Democracy and Its Ways,* which included transcripts of lectures on democracy delivered at Huntsville and, in an appendix, the texts of the Articles of Confederation, the Declaration of Independence, and the Constitution of the United States. Instead of participating in landings on Japan, these "democratized" prisoners had an opportunity to prepare themselves in some degree for the momentous changes that were already taking place by the time they returned to their home country. Two years after the end of the war, the stigma of capture by the enemy had not entirely disappeared. Captain Yamaga Moriji confessed in his book his reluctance to reveal his POW status by publishing the collection. He wrote the preface in his own English:

I returned suddenly in January [1946] after having been away from my country for four years and four months and I could not help but be amazed at the present conditions in Japan.... I wondered when I read a Japanese newspaper which we had waited so long to read; it seemed to me at first glance to be like a Communist's propaganda sheet. Such a great change had come over my mother country!

Although we were in the United States, we were able to understand some of the new conditions in Japan, in which various changes of thought, such as the rights of people, liberty and democracy, were spreading all over Japan ... because we could read the American papers and magazines and also talk with some American authorities.

... During the last three months of 1945 in the special PW camp at Huntsville, Texas, I, along with thirty other Japanese officers, had an opportunity to study, discuss, and attend lectures on American Democracy and its ways, which were delivered by American professors.

... As the Commanding Officer repeatedly emphasized, the object was to educate us and not necessarily to change our ideas, but they insisted that we should know the true meaning of

American democracy and its strong points and weaknesses, stressing that if the former were thought to be applicable to Japanese life, we should adopt them, though at the same time warning us not to adopt carelessly and at random an imitation of the latter. . . .

It is certain I think, that there are many good points adoptable at once in Japan and there are other points which shall be modified to Japanese needs after due consideration, and that there are other points which are weaknesses even in America, and Japan should not follow in their wake.

The comment of this Japanese officer suggests that our American brainwashing did not extinguish the critical faculties of the prisoners in our charge, nor did it produce the automatic responses and clichés of the comrades in Yenan. Perhaps the idea had not been such a bad one after all.

The idea of an international association made up of Japanese who would call for the surrender of Japan and cooperate in its occupation sounded fine in Yenan and Chungking. Kaji and Nosaka endorsed the project enthusiastically. The Australian chargé d'affaires in Chungking expressed interest and officials of the British Ministry of Information in New Delhi offered their cooperation. Although we knew the noose on Japan was tightening, we took seriously the estimate of the Combined Chiefs of Staff that a long struggle lay ahead and that landings on the Japanese mainland would be required to end the war. The rationale for the organization that I proposed seemed persuasive in the atmosphere of February 1945:

We may expect the resistance of the Japanese to an invading enemy to be violent in the extreme. For this reason, it is worth our while to consider any act whatsoever which might in the least degree temper that resistance. An organized *Japanese* force, known to the Japanese, working on our side and prepared to offer an attractive alternative to a disillusioned, disorganized, demoralized populace, is the best means to achieve that end.

It was clear from the start that the organization would never assume the character of a government in exile, nor would its leaders have political ambitions. The group was to be apolitical, dedicated to simple principles understandable to all—"The quick defeat of Japan, the destruction of the militarists, and the encouragement of a democratic postwar Japan."

In this memorandum submitted on February 9, immediately after my return from Chungking, I faced the expected objection that the association would have a Communist taint:

> It should be emphasized that no suggestion is here made that such an organization be Communist-inspired or Communist-controlled. . . . The headquarters of the organization should be in the United States, and there must be meticulous avoidance of acts or statements which might permit its being labeled "leftist" or "Red." At the same time the affiliation of the organization in China should be accepted and their experience and cooperation utilized to the fullest extent.

Two problems faced us. One was obtaining the approval of the U.S. government. The other was the discovery of appropriate Japanese in the United States who would be willing to take leadership roles. The bureaucratic road was long. My proposal was first considered by the Inter-Divisional Area Committee (IDAC) for the Far East, on February 23, and, after discussions at four subsequent meetings, was approved for transmission to the next-higher organ, the Coordinating Committee, on March 14. The chairman of the IDAC was George H. Blakeslee, who for forty years had been a distinguished professor at Clark University and who had come to the Department of State in 1943 to participate in postwar planning for Japan. The already venerable Blakeslee was calm, quiet, steady, able to smooth ruffled feathers but firm and confident in his opinions. Others who worked over my paper in these sessions were the Japan experts in the department at the time, including the two most senior, Eugene Dooman and Joseph Ballantine. At the first meeting, the committee members favored the plan in principle but, according to the minutes, many of them realized that its practical operation would be difficult. It was recorded that Mr. Grew supported the project.

By the time my proposal reached the Coordinating Committee, it had lost its international character. The cautious bureaucrats in the State Department, shying at communism, rejected any connection with the Japanese in China and restricted membership in the organization to Japanese nationals in the United States and in American-controlled territory, including prisoners of war, if they so desired. Also at this stage, to my surprise, one of the committee members, arguing for flexibility, won a reversal of the previous taboo against a political coloration, with the acceptance of a proviso that the organization *could,* if conditions justified, become a "free Japanese movement."

Time went on. The Coordinating Committee passed the project to the secretary's Staff Committee which referred it to the Joint Chiefs of Staff which sent it to the State–War–Navy Coordinating Committee. At long last, on June 5, the "Plan to Permit Overseas Japanese to Organize for Political Warfare Against Japanese Militarism" received SWNCC approval and thereby became U.S. policy. According to Blakeslee, some sixteen officers of the State Department, representing six different divisions, participated in the discussions of my paper. Counting other agencies of government, from thirty-five to forty officials considered the project. By the time responsibility for action had been assigned, on July 30, the climactic battle of Okinawa was over and the Potsdam Proclamation had called for Japan's surrender.

While the committees were grinding out papers, I was encouraged to talk about my ideas with representative Japanese in the country. This experience was less encouraging than I had anticipated. The Japanese whom I met were, without exception, opposed to Japanese militarism and ready to support the Allied cause. But the problem was to find a leader with prestige, one whose name would be known in Japan. The obvious choice was Ōyama Ikuo, a longtime professor, opponent of militarism, leader of the Labor-Farmer party, and former member of the Diet. Ōyama had studied at the Universities of Chicago and of Munich; and as a professor at Waseda University and later as an editorial writer for the *Mainichi* newspaper, he had become involved in student movements and proletarian causes in the 1920s. A *Who's Who* of proletarian leaders, published in 1931, noted that Ōyama had "severed all connection" with the Communist party when he founded the new Labor-Farmer party in 1928. His election to the Diet occurred in 1930, but he had gone to the United States two years later. In 1945 Ōyama was doing research and teaching at Northwestern University under the patronage of the well-known American Japanese specialist Kenneth Colegrove. Both Nosaka and Kaji had given me letters to Ōyama, urging him to assume leadership in an international organization of Japanese.

My visit to Chicago, to speak to the military government school at Northwestern, provided me an opportunity to interview Professor Ōyama. We talked over lunch at the faculty club, with Professor Colegrove present, and later Ōyama and I conversed at length in his quarters. He had recently withstood a serious stomach operation and, while now recovering, remained frail. He was then sixty-five years old and was looking forward to his return to Japan, where he hoped he might play a role in the transitional postwar period. He was intensely interested in the activities of the antiwar Japanese in China, but he did not wish to make statements or to affiliate with a Japanese group of the kind that I outlined. He feared that such action by him might jeopardize the lives and security of his many followers in Japan but, more important, he preferred to await a clearer definition of UN policy before taking a public stand. Ōyama had faith in Japan's democratic traditions, which he believed had remained strong in spite of militarist dominance. He assumed that the constitution of Japan would be revised in order to establish genuine party government and to guarantee the freedoms of speech and of press. He emphasized his differences with the Communists who advocated a one-party state and would never permit free speech or a free press. He recalled that the Communist International had, at its sixth congress in 1928, denounced him as a social democrat and a handmaiden of the capitalist imperialists. He was sure the Communists would not prevail in the early postwar period, although he speculated that within forty or fifty years Japan might have a Communist government. Ōyama opposed the removal of the emperor by the Allied powers but was confident that the Japanese themselves, if given the opportunity, would reform the imperial institution. He expressed some anxieties over the future, Would Japan be permitted to develop industries to maintain the livelihood of her citizens and would the peoples of Southeast Asia be allowed to develop self-government? He worried that Japanese imperialism might be replaced by Anglo–French–Dutch–American imperialism. As Ōyama spoke, I remembered the dark warnings against resurgent European imperialism that I had so recently heard expressed in Chungking by that stalwart anti-Communist, Patrick J. Hurley.

I could understand Ōyama's qualms, given his background in political movements in his home country and his uncertainty over Allied policy toward Japan. This was April, three months away from the Potsdam Proclamation.

Ōyama did not return to Japan until 1947. He reentered politics, was elected to the House of Councillors as a candidate of a short-lived, revived Labor-Farmer party, was awarded the Stalin Peace Prize, and died in 1955.

I peddled my organization to a great many Japanese. Among them was K. K. Kawakami, a journalist of many years' residence in Washington, D.C. I had worked with his son, Clarke, a member of our OWI psychological warfare team in Assam. Kawakami, who received me warmly, was well along in years and, although he subscribed fully to its aims, did not feel up to leading an organization of antiwar Japanese. Eugene Dooman, who at that time was enthusiastic about my schemes (he was to change his mind in later years), introduced me to a group of OSS psychological warriors in Washington. He also took me to New York where I met the members of a highly secret operation, preparing to carry on "black" propaganda in the China–Burma–India theater. These included both Japanese–Americans and Japanese; it later turned out that several were Communists. They were planning to take Japanese type to China and to print newspapers with disguised origins for circulation in Japan. These supersecret propagandists, working behind double sets of locked doors in a Manhattan skyscraper, were fascinated by my reports of the Japanese in China. One of them, Fujii Shūji, later revealed to me as a Communist, was known to Nosaka and Kaji, and I brought introductions from them. No one questioned their Communist affiliations since the Soviet Union was our ally, and

Communists were then people on our side. Dooman, who later was to become obsessed with the menace of communism, intervened personally with the formidable "Ma" Shipley, chief of the State Department's Passport Division, to persuade her to provide passports so that the Communists in this secret group could travel to the CBI theater as American government employees. Through the members of the New York unit, I learned the names of other Japanese who might be inclined to join our freedom for Japan organization. They included professors, businessmen, and quite a number of Protestant Christian ministers.

I met Eitarō and Ayako Ishigaki in New York. He was an artist, she a writer. We had lunch together at the Miyako restaurant, perhaps the only Japanese restaurant that functioned prosperously on Fifty-fifth Street throughout the war. The Ishigakis were anxious to cooperate. He was serious and dogmatic; she was lively and alert, with intense, flashing eyes. They had lived in the United States since 1926; they were at home among the liberal-leftists of the Japanese colony in New York; Mrs. Ishigaki had been co-editor of a labor publication. I did not know whether they were Communist party members, although a cryptic remark dropped by Mr. Ishigaki at one point led me to suspect that this might have been the case. My meeting with them occurred before I had gone to Chicago and before I had talked with Professor Ōyama. Mrs. Ishigaki had been one of his students and offered to write to him. In a book published in 1967 she described this episode and quoted Ōyama's reply which paraphrased the comments he made to me: "I am in favor of the organization of a democratic group of Japanese in the United States but I must positively refuse to join a triumphant American occupation army entering a defeated Japan. How could one bring a democratic revolution into Japan under the umbrella of the authority of the victors? I fully intend to step again on the soil of Japan and to exert my efforts for the construction of a new homeland but as, and only as, an individual."

Those of us who in 1945 still clung to our idealism felt that an American Occupation could bring to the Japanese a new *opportunity* for representative democracy, but how it would evolve would be up to the people of Japan. As I talked to more of the Japanese in

America, I began to understand how difficult it would be to assemble a group of them who, although convinced that the war was wrong and should be stopped, would agree to work together to propagandize their home country. The weakness of our policy in the spring of 1945 was that we had not yet defined *unconditional surrender.* Japanese voices, speaking to their compatriots at home, could hardly go beyond official policy. And that was as yet uncertain.

Mrs. Ishigaki looked back on our lunch at the Miyako from the atmosphere of 1967, during the height of the Vietnam war. She wrote in her book:

> From the beginning of 1945, the year of Japan's defeat, the problem of what to do with Japan after the war took priority over the question of how to end the war, and the Japan section within the State Department was concretely formulating this policy. In March of that year we met John Emmerson. . . . I had the impression of a youthful, sincere diplomat trying to promote and advance the democratization of Japan. However, as later reality revealed, my eyes were mistaken. Emmerson until a few months ago held the important post of minister to Japan, next after the ambassador. Needless to say, he was a top-level official who supported and vigorously promoted America's policy of aggression, beginning with the Vietnam war. When I think of the two faces of Emmerson, the present one and the one we knew before, I cannot help seeing him as the symbol, in an extreme form, of the radical sudden turn in America's policy toward the world. From the bottom of my heart I realize how the wheel of history grinds down individual after individual and applies its frightening pressure.

Ishigaki's phrase, the "two faces of Emmerson" went to the core of postwar history. In 1945 we could agree on democracy as a goal for China, Japan, and for other countries. We and the Communists were fighting the same war against fascism. Only later did it become evident that all along we had been putting different meanings to the same word. *Our* democracy was different from *their* democracy, and the cold war, regardless of the responsibility for its origins, brought it all out in the open. So that the democracy we said we were fighting to save for Vietnam was not different, in our minds, from the democracy we had sponsored in Japan.

As the summer wore on, I lost interest in my project for an association of free Japanese. There was no outstanding leader whose name would carry weight in the homeland, and the most zealous Japanese seemed to be Communists or liberal-leftists. Chip Bohlen, over lunch in February after his return from the Yalta Conference, had reminded me of the character of Communist "front" organizations and the pitfalls of starting something which could be captured by forces we could not control. Moreover, by July the project had turned into a "black" operation to be conducted by the OSS and had lost the genuine, popular character that I had idealistically envisaged for it in the beginning. The war's end wrote finis to the idea.

Few periods in history can have been so climactic as the spring and summer of 1945. Hitler's end, the nuclear destruction of Hiroshima and Nagasaki, Japan's surrender, and the beginning of an Occupation which would indelibly stamp Japan: events crashing one upon the other in a telescoping of time. Even as war had begun in a cloud of mistakes and misunderstandings, so we stumbled out of it, after unnecessary delays, inaccurate estimates, and failures of communication. While the carnage went on, in Okinawa, in Japan's flaming cities, and in the twin victims of man's newfound atomic monsters, sincere men in Tokyo and Washington groped blindly for a way out.

Even in 1944 it was clear that Japan was approaching defeat. American military strength gained daily, while Japan's declined. The battle of Leyte Gulf, fought in late October, ended, in the estimation of a Japanese diplomat, the "glorious history" of the empire's navy, which no longer could muster a fleet capable of offensive operations. The problem for American policymakers was determining how long the imperial forces would continue to fight. Would they surrender, or would they fight to the death of the last defender? The prisoners in Burma and China had the clue, it seemed to me: they would fight until the emperor told them to stop. The conclusions seemed obvious: the Allies must define unconditional surrender and must guarantee the survival of the emperor.

Secretary of State Hull called the disposition of the emperor "one of our most difficult questions to answer." Shortly after my arrival in New Delhi, in January 1944, I wrote a memorandum on the emperor, in the course of which I stated: "It is only very recently that the [emperor] institution has been made to serve Japan's expansionist urge. If destroyed by act of the Allies, the resulting violent reaction in the country might impede for a long time the formation of any stable government. On the other hand, if reduced to the position of an impotent symbol, the emperor might actually facilitate the organization of an ordered administration." A memorandum produced in the State Department, on May 9, 1944, took the same position but recommended that the emperor be kept in seclusion and that his official functions might have to be suspended. Opinion was far from unanimous on the question of the continuance of the imperial institution. Robert Sherrod, then a war correspondent, complained that we were "deluding ourselves with our spare-the-emperor appeasement," which inspired Under Secretary Grew to write, on January 3, 1945, "He [the emperor] might be found to be an important, if not an essential, asset, both in bringing Japan to unconditional surrender and in avoiding chaos and guerrilla warfare after our eventual occupation of Tokyo. In other words, the presence of the Emperor may conceivably be the source of saving thousands of American lives. At least, the Emperor's voice is the only voice which the Japanese people, and probably the Japanese military forces, are likely to obey."

The only conversation I recall having with Alger Hiss is one that occurred when he stopped me in the corridors of the State Department in the spring of 1945 to ask, "What shall we do about the emperor?" I emphasized to him the importance of preserving the imperial institution for the stability of postwar Japan. Hiss disagreed, arguing the insidious effects of maintaining a totalitarian influence. Dean Acheson was another who opposed the retention of the emperor. In his *Present at the Creation,* he confessed: "I was soon engaged in a sharp difference of opinion with Joe Grew regarding the future of the Emperor of Japan. Grew argued for his retention as the main stabilizing factor in Japan; I argued that he should be removed because he was a weak leader who had yielded to the military demand for war and who could not be relied upon. Grew's view fortunately prevailed. I very shortly came to see that I was quite wrong." Drew Pearson expressed a popular view when he attacked the emperor; but, like Acheson, he later admitted that his criticism of Grew had been wrong.

A 1945 public opinion poll showed that one-third of the respondents favored Hirohito's execution; one-fifth, his imprisonment or exile; and one-sixth, his trial by judicial process. Only 3 percent supported his survival on the throne and his use by the Allies.

Some Japanese had begun to think about how to end the war almost as soon as it had begun. In February 1942, Marquis Kido Kōichi, lord keeper of the privy seal, advised the emperor to seek a way to stop hostilities. General Koiso Kuniaki secretly feared that the war was lost when he took office as prime minister in July 1944. He later testified that Japan could have sued for peace at that moment, after the fall of Saipan, had not she faced "merciless terms" from the Allies. An officer of the Navy General Staff, Rear Admiral Takagi Sōkichi, who six months earlier had studied the "war's lessons," began research in September 1944 on how to get the army to agree to an imperial decision for ending the war. By February 1945 Prince Konoye was memorializing the throne to the effect that "Japan has already lost the war" and that "we should seek to end the war as speedily as possible."

In April General Koiso was replaced as prime minister by Admiral Suzuki Kantarō, whose purpose in taking office was assumed to be termination of the war. In the usual Japanese fashion, few confidences were exchanged among those responsible for Japan's fate. Expression and understanding were expected to develop nonverbally, through the "art of the stomach" *(haragei)*. In 1941 Japanese leaders had advanced toward war like blind men pulled by an irresistible force, unable to consider objectively the consequences of their actions. Now, in this noh drama of 1945, the principal actors appeared transfixed, telling each other that they must fight to the end but knowing in their hearts that their cause was lost.

Those with courage and the clearest minds turned out to be Marquis Kido, Tōgō Shigenori (who became foreign minister in the Suzuki Cabinet), and the emperor himself. Tōgō refused to take the post until he felt assured the government would strive to end the war. Suzuki could not bring himself to say so openly at the time, although at the war crimes trials he testified that he "understood" that the emperor sought an end to war. Tōgō, after assuming office in April, confirmed directly with the emperor the latter's desire to make peace as soon as possible.

The missing element was the lack of an Allied definition of unconditional surrender. Quite apart from my own efforts to promote the issuance of a statement to Japan, there was general agreement within the U.S. government that such a clarification would be desirable. On April 18, 1945, a Pentagon Joint Intelligence Committee paper concluded that "a clarification of Allied intentions with regard to the Japanese nation might bring nearer the possibility of unconditional surrender." On May 8 President Truman included one sentence in his proclamation of the end of war in Europe, "Unconditional surrender does not mean the extermination or enslavement of the Japanese people." But this was not enough. The Japanese would not respond until assured of the preservation of their "national polity," or, in plainer language, the continuation of their unique line of emperors who had reigned from "ages eternal." On May 28, Grew, who was then acting secretary of state, made an eloquent case to President Truman on behalf of retaining the emperor and defining unconditional surrender in a public statement:

> The greatest obstacle to unconditional surrender by the Japanese is their belief that this would entail the destruction or permanent removal of the Emperor and the institution of the Throne. If some indication can now be given the Japanese that they themselves, when once thoroughly defeated and rendered impotent to wage war in future, will be permitted to determine their own future political structure, they will be afforded a method of saving face without which surrender will be highly unlikely. . . . such a statement would have maximum effect if issued immediately following the great devastation of Tokyo which occurred

two days ago. . . . The institution of the throne can . . . become a cornerstone for building a peaceful future for the country once the militarists have learned in the hard way that they have nothing to hope for in the future.

On the following day the question of Grew's proposed presidential statement was discussed by the secretaries of war and navy, Stimson and Forrestal, General Marshall, Elmer Davis of OWI, Judge Samuel I. Rosenman, Eugene Dooman, and Acting Secretary Grew. Grew, in a May 29 memorandum on the meeting, reported that Stimson, Forrestal, and Marshall "were all in accord with the principle but for certain military reasons, not divulged, it was considered inadvisable for the President to make such a statement just now." No one mentioned the atomic weapon, the use of which on Japan was decided three days later, on June 1.

In early June, at an imperial conference in Tokyo, the government reaffirmed its policy to continue the war. Tōgō opposed the decision and was dismayed that his friend and colleague Navy Minister Yonai did not support him. When Tōgō told Yonai, "I expected help from the navy minister but I got none," the navy minister responded with typical *haragei,* "Well, at this point a thing like that can't be helped, can it?" Kido set about immediately to reverse the conference decision and presented to the emperor on June 9 a "tentative plan to cope with the situation." He recommended that Japan move resolutely to the restoration of peace on the basis of minimum demands: the security of the imperial family and the preservation of the national polity. He considered opening direct talks with the United States and the United Kingdom but concluded that Soviet mediation would offer more "flexibility."

If only the Japanese had known that Stalin had, in February, promised at Yalta to enter the war against them three months after V-E day, Kido probably would have proposed an approach to Washington. But, blindly confident in Stalin's neutrality, the Supreme Council decided, on June 18, to enter into peace negotiations with the USSR. At the same meeting, according to Tōgō, "There was general agreement that we must inevitably continue resistance so long as the United States and Great Britain persist in expecting from us an unconditional surrender."

It proved impossible for Washington to define Allied terms. Grew tried again on June 18, suggesting a statement to coincide with the victory on Okinawa. However, the Joint Chiefs of Staff wished, in Harry Truman's words, to "wait until we were ready to follow a Japanese refusal with the actual assault of our invasion forces." Truman decided that the proclamation should be issued by the chiefs of state already scheduled to meet at Potsdam, by which time the participation in the war by the Soviet Union and the results of the atomic bomb would have become known.

Throughout these months American officials had been reading the secret messages exchanged between Tokyo and Moscow. We knew that the Japanese were desperately trying to get out of the war; we knew of their futile efforts to dispatch Prince Konoye as a special peace emissary to the Kremlin. We must have read the despairing telegram sent by Ambassador Satō Naotake from Moscow on July 20. It took supreme courage for this gentle diplomat to cable his foreign minister: "There is no hope of achieving our aims. We must put a stop to continued resistance; the lives of hundreds of thousands are caught in a hopeless death trap. We are only a step away from the total annihilation of our country. I pray that we may act now to save our 70 million compatriots, preserving at the least our national existence."

At the Potsdam Conference (July 17–August 2) Stalin asked President Truman's advice on a Japanese request to send Prince Konoye to Moscow to discuss peace terms. Stalin wanted to brush off the proposal and Truman agreed with him. It is strange how little attention was paid by the Big Three (Stalin, Truman, and Churchill, and later, Attlee) to the problem of Japan's surrender. Most of the discussions dealt with European problems, principally the administration of defeated Germany. One of Truman's principal objectives, according to Charles Bohlen, who was there, was to confirm that Stalin would join the war against Japan. The text of the Potsdam Proclamation was not shown to Stalin before it was released. In his memoirs Bohlen does not even mention the Potsdam Proclamation to Japan, which seems to have been issued without serious expectation of its acceptance.

I talked with Chip Bohlen shortly after his return from Potsdam, and he gave me some of the flavor of the conference. Truman, who was trying to establish his authority with Stalin, casually sat down at the piano one evening after dinner and began to play. "And," said Chip, "to my amazement, he played *your* piece—Paderewski's Minuet in G." Chip, having heard me play the minuet so many times during our life together in Tokyo, thought of it as my piece. Truman told an interviewer many years later that he played Paderewski's piece for "old Stalin" but that, as for Churchill, "I don't think he was listening. Churchill was a man who didn't listen very often."

The text of the Potsdam Proclamation was written largely by Eugene Dooman, and its preamble by Douglas Fairbanks, Jr. Communicated to the Japanese government on July 26, it differed in only one major respect from the draft Grew handed President Truman on May 28; one crucial sentence had been omitted.

This sentence in the original State Department draft stipulated that a peacefully inclined, responsible, and representative government in postwar Japan might include a "constitutional monarchy under the present dynasty." This was the essence of the national polity which the Japanese were determined to preserve at all costs. Former Secretary of State Cordell Hull has described in his memoirs what happened. Before leaving for Potsdam, James F. Byrnes, who had only recently succeeded Stettinius as secretary of state, telephoned Hull at his Washington apartment to give him the gist of the proposed proclamation to Japan. Hull at once bridled at the mention of the Japanese emperor, insisting that it sounded like appeasement and a catering to the feudal privileges of a ruling imperial caste. He followed up his telephone remarks by a telegram to Byrnes at Potsdam on July 16, reiterating his objections to mention of the emperor and advising postponement of an Allied declaration "to await the climax of Allied bombing and Russia's entry into the war." Byrnes replied on the following day, assuring Hull that the statement would be delayed and that any commitment to preserving the emperor would be stricken from the text.

As we now know, receipt in Tokyo of the Potsdam Proclamation ten days later threw the Japanese leaders into near panic. Foreign Minister Tōgō jumped at the phrase "following are our terms" and concluded at once that the Allies were no longer demanding *unconditional* surrender. The Supreme Council and the Cabinet agreed not to answer the Allied demands for the time being while continuing to pursue Soviet mediation. Tōgō told the emperor that the proclamation must be treated with utmost circumspection, that he feared the consequences if Japan should appear to reject it. Meanwhile, Prime Minister Suzuki, either inadvertently or influenced by military hardliners, failed to follow explicitly the government decision and told a press conference that Japan would "ignore" the Potsdam Proclamation. His use of the word *mokusatsu*, meaning literally "to kill with silence," but with a nuance of uncertainty, became another historical example of the failure of communication. Played up sensationally, *mokusatsu* instantaneously and incorrectly became the English word "reject," and American nuclear retaliation followed relentlessly. The cabinet secretary recalled many years later that "no comment" would have accurately expressed Suzuki's true meaning. Tōgō was desolate, recognizing how much Suzuki had set back Japan's move for peace.

Hiroshima was destroyed August 6. Even then, Japan's leaders could not bring themselves to accept without condition the Potsdam demands. At six o'clock in the evening of the eighth, Molotov received Satō in Moscow and instead of responding to Japan's entreaties to mediate peace, read aloud to him in Russian a declaration of war. In the car on his return from the Foreign Ministry, Satō remarked to the embassy secretary who had accompanied him, "What had to come has come!" In Tokyo, on the ninth, the Supreme Council went into session. The army was still holding out for impossible conditions: no Allied occupation, self-disarmament, and war criminals to be tried by Japanese themselves. Tōgō insisted that the inviolability of the imperial house must realistically be the sole condition. In the early morning hours of August 10 the emperor took his unprecedented decision—he supported Tōgō. Japan's reply was sent. Meanwhile, Nagasaki had been A-bombed.

Joe Ballantine learned at 7:00 A.M. on August 10 that the Japanese would accept the Potsdam terms so long as the "prerogatives of the emperor as a sovereign ruler" would not be prejudiced. Ballantine reacted immediately. Since the emperor's prerogatives were all-embracing, to grant this concession would be to undermine Allied authority at the time of occupation.

At the White House, President Truman met with the secretaries of state, war, and navy (Byrnes, Stimson, Forrestal) and with his chief of staff, Admiral Leahy. There was a difference of opinion on how to respond to the Japanese note. Byrnes was uncertain about acceptance because of bitter public statements, especially by Roosevelt and Truman, which had been made about the emperor. Admiral Leahy, in Stimson's words, "took a good plain horse-sense position that the question of the emperor was a minor matter compared with delaying a victory in the war which was now in our hands." Stimson was forthright, "We would have to continue the emperor ourselves under our command and supervision. . . . He was the only source of authority in Japan under the Japanese theory of the state." Stimson had approved the original draft with the provision for continuance of the emperor and was disappointed that it had been struck out. Forrestal thought that Byrnes's objections could be met by "an affirmative statement on our part in which we could see to it that the language of surrender accorded fully with our intent and view."

The president asked Byrnes to draft a reply. Back at the State Department Ballantine and Dooman persuaded Grew to intercede with Byrnes to modify the provision regarding prerogatives. According to Ballantine, who presumably had not been informed of the content of the conversations at the White House, Grew reported that both Truman and Stimson were ready to accede to the Japanese condition. Ballantine and Dooman then asked permission to present their case directly to the secretary; they enlisted the cooperation of Benjamin Cohen, then counselor of the department, who, according to Ballantine, saw the point "in three minutes." Within a few minutes more, Cohen had drafted the stipulation that the "authority of the Emperor and the Japanese Government to rule the state shall be subject to the Supreme Commander of the Allied Powers."

This phraseology acknowledged the possibility that the emperor would continue but did not guarantee his prerogatives. Ballantine, Dooman, and Cohen then together successfully persuaded Byrnes to accept their revised language. In his book *Speaking Frankly,* Byrnes takes credit for drafting the sentence pertaining to the emperor. Ballantine noted this in his diary-memoirs, commenting ruefully that since Byrnes mentioned neither Grew, Dooman, nor Ballantine, all of whom had been referred to in the press as "emperor worshipers," he had "probably forgotten" what really happened.

The drama was still not over. It took another meeting in the palace bomb shelter, after further objections to the American reply by the military and further vacillation by Suzuki, before the emperor again silenced dissension by taking the decision to "endure the unendurable," to acknowledge the defeat of the Great Japanese Empire. And in the last hours, during the night of August 14–15, impulsive members of the imperial guard tried to seize the record of the emperor's voice before it could be delivered to the broadcasting station for replay to the nation at noon of the following day.

Reduced to its essentials, the story of the spring and summer months of 1945 is that the Japanese knew they were defeated, that their civilian leaders were desperately trying to end the war, that their minimum demand was the preservation of the emperor, and that the Americans failed, until the last minute, to define unconditional surrender in those terms. Japanese intelligence, amazingly, never discerned that Stalin had promised to attack. American intelligence disclosed that the Japanese were beseeching the Russians to mediate an end to the war, yet American policymakers failed to draw the obvious conclusions from that knowledge. We were mesmerized by the vaunted fanaticism of the Japanese soldier and were convinced that only force would stop resistance. We did not listen to the voice of the foot soldier in Burma who had said quite simply that if the emperor told him to lay down his arms, he would obey. Those who knew about the atomic weapon had determined that we should use it against Japan. Mr. Grew's repeated appeals for a statement to Japan were rejected; the president and his military advisers wanted to wait until a Japan that refused our terms would face nuclear destruction and Russian attack. Certain revisionist historians have contended that the atomic bombs were used as political weapons to threaten the Russians, but the evidence does not support this hypothesis. While the bombs' potential effect on Stalin was not ignored, our all-consuming objective at that time was to spare American lives by avoiding an invasion of Japan's main islands. Thus American leaders justified the dropping of bombs on Hiroshima and Nagasaki as well as Russia's joining the war. The loss of Japanese lives and the political consequences of these events did not enter into the calculation.

Had Mr. Grew's May draft, including its assurances regarding the emperor, been communicated to Japan, conceivably Tōgō and Kido, working with the emperor, who needed no convincing, could have induced an imperial rescript to end the war, even before the Allied chiefs of state assembled at Potsdam. Even if this had failed, the dispatch on July 26 of the original, unexpurgated version of the Potsdam Proclamation would certainly have speeded acceptance. And finally, the dropping of the second bomb on Nagasaki was senseless. The drama enacted in Tokyo between August 6 and 9 would have moved to its inexorable conclusion, without reference to the destruction of Nagasaki or to the Soviet declaration of war.

It is a credit to the diplomat's profession that two of the heroes of this drama, one on each side, were Joseph Grew and Tōgō Shigenori. Ironically, both had been in official positions in Tokyo in 1941; it was Tōgō who at midnight on December 8 had received from Grew the president's message to the emperor—only a few hours before Japanese planes bombed Pearl Harbor. Tōgō worked untiringly and with supreme courage during the tense summer of 1945 to bring an end to the war, taking risks outside the ken of most foreign service bureaucrats. Grew, as acting secretary and as under secretary of state, incurred public scorn in Washington by doggedly preaching the unpopular theme that the Japanese right to keep their emperor was the key to peace.

Many of us in the State Department dared not believe that Japan would accept the Potsdam terms. When the first messages came through, the thought was too alien to grasp. War had become a way of life. One could scarcely imagine peace. It was time to uncork the bottle of champagne left undrunk on Pearl Harbor day. On the warm night of August 14, the four of us in our family joined the crowds walking up and down Connecticut Avenue. You hugged and kissed total strangers.

Father, Sister, Mother, and Toots in Cañon City, Colorado, 1917

The Delaware Group (JKE first on left, third row), 1927

*Mme. Mathis-Schouller
and Mlle. Laure, Nancy,
France, 1927*

Beppo Johansen, Dorothy, and JKE, Nikkō, Japan, 1937

JKE in white tie and tails at the emperor's New Year's reception, 1937

Elisa Vaccari, ca. 1936–37

Countess Watanabe
Tomeko, ca. 1936–37

The embassy staff (JKE sixth from right, second row), with the ambassador's residence in background, 1941

Kossodo-Emmerson, "Two Pianos," cartoon-drawing, Lima, Peru, 1943

JKE in fatigues, China-Burma-India, 1944

JKE interrogating Japanese prisoner of war, Burma, 1944

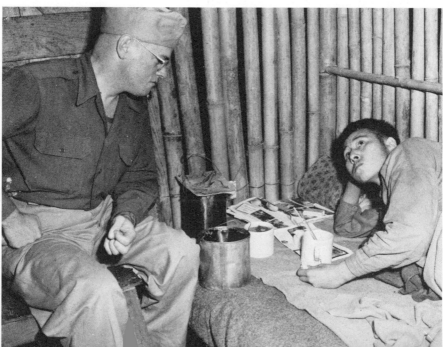

Chou En-lai, Chu Teh, JKE, Mao Tse-tung, and Yeh Chien Ying, Yenan, 1944

Nosaka Sanzo, Yenan, 1944

Mao Tse-tung (back to camera) with JKE and U.S. officers, Yenan, 1944

JKE during the Occupation, with Mt. Fuji in background, 1945

Presentation of credentials by Ambassador Kirk (JKE sixth from left), Moscow, 1949

Sir Zafrullah Khan and JKE signing the U.S.–Pakistan Military Aid Agreement, 1954

JKE with prime minister of Nigeria, Sir Abubakar Tafawa Balewa, Lagos, 1960

Dorothy, Sir Roy Welensky, prime minister of the Federation of Rhodesia and Nyasaland, and JKE, 1961

JKE, Haru Reischauer, Ambassador Reischauer, and Dorothy at the American embassy residence, Tokyo, August 1966

JKE and Dorothy at the Sacred Bridge, Nikkō, Japan, 1966

10

Occupation

On V-J Day, September 2, 1945, while MacArthur and the Japanese were signing the surrender documents on the battleship *Missouri* in Tokyo Bay, I was in the air between Washington and San Francisco. In those horse-and-buggy days of aviation, my United Air Lines plane stopped at Chicago, Omaha, Cheyenne, Rock Springs, Elko, and Sacramento, during a trip of a day and a night. Some weeks before, I had been named political adviser to Fleet Admiral Chester W. Nimitz, Commander in Chief, U.S. Pacific Fleet and Pacific Ocean Areas, and was to report to him on the island of Guam. But with the end of the war, the navy's role receded. Upon my arrival in Guam, I was handed a telegram from the State Department, transferring me to the Office of the Political Adviser to the Supreme Commander for the Allied Powers in Japan. Admiral Nimitz received me, expressed his regret that I would not be serving him, and sent me on my way with cordial best wishes. Navy men, who thought *they* had won the Pacific war, were disappointed that their chief was not awarded command of the Occupation of Japan. One wonders what the difference would have been had this genial, warm-hearted seafarer ruled the island empire instead of the imperious MacArthur.

By the end of my one day's assignment to the admiral, I was

airborne and headed west. After a midnight touch-down at Iwō Jima, powdered eggs and stewed prunes at 2:00 A.M., and a few hours' try for sleep while stretched out on bucket seats, we resumed our flight. Our navy plane was directed to land at Kisarazu, a small airfield in Chiba prefecture across the bay from the Yokosuka naval base and from Yokohama, where MacArthur's headquarters had been temporarily established. Ours was the sixth American aircraft to land at this field; the two surrender planes, white with green crosses, which had flown Japanese conferees to Manila, were parked nearby. A puzzled lieutenant telephoned for instructions, "I have a State Department man here. What shall I do with him?"

In the end I and my three bags rode a violently bouncing landing craft in drenching spray, boarded a destroyer where the hospitable officers gave me coffee and let me dry my shirt, before I was transferred to a launch that hunted a place to offload me. Finally on shore, I mounted an old brown, unsteady bus with blue upholstery, which convulsed to naval headquarters at Yokosuka. After a night at the officers' club and twenty-four hours without food, I still had to get to Yokohama. I wrote to Dorothy:

> It is 6:00 A.M. but the *semi* (locusts) have been singing themselves hoarse for hours. There are the sounds of birds—the natural atmosphere of Japan—but no Japanese. The houses and streets are vacant. It is as though from a moving picture all the characters had suddenly been lifted. There should be boys on bicycles, *tōfu* ("bean curd") vendors, women sweeping, a whole world of sounds and people. Instead a couple of G.I.'s are laughing up there on the hill—a sentry is pacing back and forth beneath me. Bugles on ships are sounding. A few minutes ago a fleet of planes droned over us.

An understanding officer arranged for a jeep and a driver, suitably armed, to take me to the supreme commander's headquarters at Yokohama's Grand Hotel. I wrote:

> The ride was fascinating. I saw the people again. Every woman wears *mompei,* or "pants," and they were out, doing their many

chores. Long lines at the rice and seaweed stores. The people looked indifferent; a few smiled; a few looked glum and bitter. Children and a few grownups waved to us. Not much devastation until we got to Yokohama. Then blocks of rubble and rusted iron. Yokohama was destroyed in one raid of two hours, they tell us. A few patched up tin huts and people poking around the rubble.

I was the first member of the State Department's Political Adviser's Office and the second foreign service officer to reach Japan. U. Alexis Johnson, who, with his wife Pat, had greeted us on our first arrival at Tokyo in 1936, was again waiting to welcome me to Occupied Japan. He had been sent out to assist in the repatriation of civilian Americans from the Far East; we shared a room at the Grand Hotel.

My first conversation with a Japanese was with the room boy. He exulted at the ending of the war, and his eyes flashed as he spoke angrily of Tōjō and his military associates who had led the nation to catastrophe. "They brought it on us! How could we have beaten a country as strong as yours?" These first words were the essence of the Japanese people's reaction: no deploring the surrender; no castigating the American enemy; no contrition. As I lived through the first five months of occupation, these sentiments were confirmed over and over again. Even Admiral Nomura, who had delivered Japan's final note to Cordell Hull on Pearl Harbor day, is supposed to have said (in colloquial translation), "If I were to have a hand in choosing someone to fight, I'd make sure it was someone I could lick." This attitude explained the popular cooperation with the American reformers, which was to come; it explained the lack of hatred over the destruction we had wrought. Democracy, whatever it was, had won out; it had been too strong to resist. In the vacuum of defeat the Japanese people, like the so-called reborn prisoners of war in China and Burma, were ready to reject the past and clutch the straw held out by the former enemy.

While I was in Guam, the appointment of George Atcheson, Jr., as political adviser to General MacArthur had been announced. Ambassador Grew had first been offered the job by Secretary of State

Byrnes but had declined, he later wrote, for three reasons: first, General MacArthur "would not want much advice"; second, he did not want to face his old friends in Japan as a conqueror; and third, he had gallstones. Grew, in turn, recommended to Byrnes that one of the department's senior Japanese specialists—either Eugene Dooman or Joseph Ballantine—be named political adviser.

A few days after V-J Day, Dean Acheson, who had replaced Grew as under secretary, asked Ballantine's opinion of appointing George Atcheson as MacArthur's political adviser. Ballantine, according to his own account, asserted that although Atcheson was an able foreign service officer, he was a China specialist without experience in Japan. Dean Acheson responded with enthusiasm, "Fine. That's what we want, an able officer familiar with State Department policy but unfamiliar with Japan."

War's end brought an exit from the State Department of the old Japan crowd (Grew, Dooman, and Ballantine). Grew, irked at being ignored by Secretary Byrnes, resigned on August 16. Dooman retired August 31. Ballantine, who got neither the assignment to Tokyo nor an ambassadorship, was succeeded as director of the Office of Far Eastern Affairs by John Carter Vincent, a China hand. Both Acheson and Vincent, as well as George Atcheson, supported a more vigorous pursuit of far-reaching reforms for Japan than suited Grew, Dooman, and Ballantine. The last deplored the coming into ascendancy of new people who were getting their hands on Japanese affairs, "New Deal economists, political scientists, and law graduates with little experience in the world of practical affairs and none in Japan."

My first visit to Tokyo, on September 14, left me in deep depression. Much of the downtown area, except for the stone-and-concrete constructions for business and finance, was a wasteland, sparsely forested with rusty iron safes, spectral symbols of vanished commerce. The Ginza was a country lane. At the embassy, the roof of the chancery had been burned, and rain had entered freely. The great chandelier in the upper hall had crashed to the floor; desks were scorched; and mud was everywhere. Such scenes present details one never forgets. In the drawer of a fragile Louis XVI end table in the chancery library reposed the ultimate insult—dried human excrement. And on the marble balustrade in the upper hallway, amidst the debris left by rain and fire, a silk hat sat defiantly, as if to say, Diplomacy Forever!

The institution, nominally Allied, but actually American, which ran the Occupation, immediately became known as GHQ or SCAP (Supreme Commander for the Allied Powers). On September 17 MacArthur and his retinue officially moved to Tokyo, where they set themselves up in the Dai-Ichi (Number One) building, the former—and later—home of the Dai Ichi Mutual Life Insurance Company. It was the sturdiest and most imposing edifice left intact by the bombing. For himself, MacArthur took over the magnificent American Embassy residence, where from 1931 to 1941 Ambassador Grew had presided over the turbulent course of Japanese–American relations.

During the first few weeks no one knew what to do with the State Department, so we fended for ourselves. SCAP officers, most of whom knew nothing about Japan, asked us questions, and Japanese citizens, both old friends and people with problems, sought us out, thinking mistakenly that we might be a sort of embassy. Our own duties and responsibilities were unclear. We were not a staff section and therefore not in the chain of command. We had no separate communications facilities; telegrams between the State Department and ourselves were often delayed or even acted upon by officers in GHQ without our knowledge or consultation. George Atcheson resented the fact that he was never accorded the same status as Robert Murphy who had served as political adviser to General Eisenhower in Europe. Fortunately, Atcheson developed a good personal relationship with General MacArthur, and as time went on, we began to be consulted more frequently. It was not until April 1946, however, that the Political Adviser's Office became integrated into headquarters as the Diplomatic Section, and not until May 1950 was Atcheson's successor, William J. Sebald, able to use his own codes.

One of MacArthur's first acts was to arrest war criminal suspects. The Japanese press was calling for blood. Brigadier General Elliott R. Thorpe, chief of the Counter Intelligence Section (CIS), relates that on his first night in Japan MacArthur ordered, "Thorpe, have your people arrest General Tōjō and lock him up." Tōjō tried to commit suicide but failed and lived to be hanged. The UN War Crimes Commission in London had, on August 29, issued recommendations about Japanese war crimes and atrocities, but the State–War–Navy Coordinating Committee did not formulate a U.S. policy until September 12. Arrests could not await directives. I wrote out the names of Tōjō's Cabinet colleagues to start the CIS's first major war criminal list. *Who's Who in Japan* was the basic source book for additions, and by September 11, thirty-nine military and civilian leaders were in jail. Later, the selection of suspects became more organized. By the end of November, the Political Adviser's Office, at MacArthur's request, had submitted four lists, totaling forty-eight names.

One day a CIS officer came to me in great secrecy. The army had been experimenting with a machine called a wire recorder, and they wanted us to test it out on one of the incarcerated "criminals." Would I be willing to interview Admiral Shimada Shigetarō, who had been navy minister in the Tōjō Cabinet? This was long before the International Military Tribunal for the Far East had been established and before any war crimes experts had arrived in Japan. I was escorted to a private house near Yokohama, where a room had been especially arranged for the interview. I sat behind a desk with Admiral Shimada facing me, a telephone containing the microphone ostentatiously placed between us, while the CIS boys listened in from an adjoining room.

The stocky admiral, then sixty-two, wore prison garb. He was balding and his remaining hair was closely cropped. He bowed and sat down. Neither he nor I knew what we were expected to talk about, but when he discovered I spoke Japanese, his reserve broke down and he began to respond with interest and animation to my questions. I asked him about the philosophy of Japan's prewar military men and, particularly, about the influence of such nationalistic writers as Yoshida Shōin, who in 1854 had tried to stow away on one of Commodore Perry's "black ships" but later had been executed for trying to stop the opening of the country to foreign trade. Shimada, doubtless pleased that one American had at least heard of Yoshida Shōin, tried to explain the latter's ideas to me, reminding me that he had not necessarily preached aggression but rather selfless leadership to revitalize and modernize Japan. The admiral took pains to tell me that he had known nothing about the plans to attack Pearl Harbor when he joined the Tōjō Cabinet in October 1941. What could he then do but follow a policy already decided?

Admiral Shimada impressed me as being a loyal professional; he had not conspired to wage aggressive war. Instead, his crime was that the nation he served had lost a war. I had no heart for the lengthy Tokyo war crimes trials and found absurd the studied formulation of an artificially rationalized theory in which the acts of the suspects from 1928 to 1941 were arbitrarily fitted together to produce a calculated, evil conspiracy to dominate the whole world. Admiral Shimada was later sentenced to life imprisonment. As for my interview with him, the first, I am convinced, conducted by an American with a war criminal suspect, the wire recorder failed to function properly, and the result was gibberish that no one could transcribe.

Another punitive action of the Occupation was the so-called purge, which ousted more than two hundred thousand military officers, civilian officials, businessmen, teachers, and holders of other responsible positions. Politicians and bureaucrats were particularly affected; chosen more because of the categories of offices held rather than for individual misdeeds, many suffered injustices. The immediate effect was widespread disruption in administration and temporary obstacles for more conservative politicians. Over the longer term, the new, younger blood suddenly introduced into the political and economic bloodstream produced in many cases healthy results.

With the arrival on September 22 of George Atcheson and Jack Service, both China hands, our office began to assume some order. Although a Japan hand, I had been tainted by China—how seriously I was to learn much later. I liked George Atcheson, whom I had come to know in Chungking. It was he, who in February 1945 during Ambassador Hurley's absence, had courageously sent a telegram—later to become famous—in which he recommended cooperation, solely on grounds of military necessity, "with the Communists and other suitable groups who can assist the war against Japan." Assuming his new post in Tokyo, Atcheson recognized his lack of Japanese experience and was ready to consult fully and freely with his staff. He had a sweet disposition, but worried a lot and as a consequence was often frustrated. He had a curious way of speaking with a slight twisting of the lip, but his honest decency came through. He always made you feel that he really wanted to know what you thought. Although Jack Service had been arrested on June 6 by the FBI and charged with leaking government documents, the grand jury refused to indict him by a vote of 20 to 0, and this clearance made him available for assignment overseas. Atcheson was delighted to have him with us in Tokyo.

On October 1 the Political Adviser's Office moved out of headquarters to the Mitsui Bank building at Nihonbashi, about a fifteen-minute jeep ride away. General MacArthur tolerated the State Department within his realm but wanted us at arm's length and clearly outside of his staff complement. I walked into our new offices just as a Mitsui junior executive was clearing the last items from his desk. Before turning to go out the door, he hesitated, pointing to a map on the wall depicting Japan's Co-Prosperity Sphere in East Asia. "There it is," he said, smiling. "We tried. See what you can do with it!" Somehow at that moment the whole burden of American foreign policy in Asia hit me in the stomach. What *were* we going to do with it? If I could have foreseen the future: China, Korea, Vietnam! Fortunately, the powers of prescience were not mine. It was enough to think about Japan, which in the words of another author, we were "forcing to be free."

Both the Potsdam Proclamation and the initial postsurrender policy for Japan had stipulated that basic civil rights should be guaranteed to the Japanese people. Consequently, one of the early major acts of SCAP was the issuance, on October 4, of the civil rights directive, which ordered the abrogation of all prewar laws and decrees restricting the freedoms of thought, religion, assembly, speech, and discussion of the emperor, as well as those controlling the collection and dissemination of information and those that were discriminatory on grounds of race, nationality, creed, or political opinion. One of the stipulations of the order was the release from detention of all persons charged with the violation of these restrictive laws.

Harold Isaacs, the *Newsweek* correspondent with whom I had solemnly toasted the 1945 New Year in Chungking, had interviewed several Communists in Fuchū prison, near Tokyo. Over drinks at the Dai-Ichi Hotel, our field-grade officers' quarters, he suggested that someone from GHQ might profitably talk with these future political activists. I discussed the idea with Herbert Norman, the Canadian friend whom I had known in Tokyo in 1941. Norman was now representing Canada's Department of External Affairs and simultaneously functioning as chief of the Research and Analysis Section in SCAP's Office of Counter Intelligence.

Herb was enthusiastic and, with the blessing of our respective chiefs, we set off in a driving rain for Fuchū on the morning of October 5, the day after the directive freeing political prisoners had been announced. Fuchū officials were glum but reluctantly respected the authority of our GHQ credentials. The warden, I wrote to my wife, "looks like a pig—literally. Thick neck with wrinkles in the back, shaved, bullet-shaped head, small eyes, sadistic face!" A prison minion in striped trousers and black coat took us briskly through long corridors and through the iron gates into the cell blocks. We found sixteen political prisoners—two Koreans, two members of the Tenrikyō religious sect, and twelve Communists. Among the latter were two who were to become leaders of the postwar Japanese Communist party, Tokuda Kyūichi and Shiga Yoshio.

Asking the prison official to leave the room, we assembled the sixteen in a hall which had been used for Buddhist services. The senior member and spokesman for the group was Tokuda, born in Okinawa, a Labor-Farmer candidate for the Diet in 1928, and for eighteen years a prisoner of the state. He and the others spoke volubly, with the pent-up flood of nearly two decades of isolation. He showed us a hard knob on the back of his hand, sustained from police torture, which he said had nearly lost him the use of his fingers and hand. Shiga, less flamboyant and more intellectual, had graduated from Tokyo Imperial University in sociology and spoke English fairly well.

Tokuda and his associates had already drawn up a manifesto to be published upon their release. After promising support to Allied peace policies, it denounced fascism, militarism, the emperor system, the imperial household, the Japanese police administration, and capitalist monopolies. It proposed a program of social and electoral reform and castigated pseudo liberals and socialists who might condone the emperor system.

The Communists had hoarded documents describing the activities of the secret police and identifying political prisoners. They had a copy of a book by Kodama Yoshio, notorious in the prewar period as being a henchman for the military, and a right-wing activist, smuggler, and black market operator. (His notoriety was to be revived in 1976, when he was revealed as a go-between for Lockheed bribes to Japanese officials.)

Two years later Tokuda and Shiga were to write a book, which included a description of our visit to Fuchū: "Emmerson and Dr. Norman of the Supreme Commander's Headquarters came to see us, asking: 'What do you intend to do after your release?' and at the same time telling us about the policies of SCAP." Still later, this sentence was to be held against me. What was I doing revealing to Communists the policies of SCAP? The only policies we had mentioned were contained in the civil rights directive, which had become public knowledge on October 4.

Since these prisoners were about to enter the political life of Japan, it would be useful to size them up. We therefore recommended that three or four of them be interrogated at headquarters. Thus, on Sunday, October 7, Norman and I, in the company of several military officers from CIS, drove to Fuchū in staff sedans and brought Tokuda, Shiga, and a Korean Communist to the Dai-Ichi building. The interviews lasted all day. For lunch, we served GI rations on trays. On the way back to the prison, Tokuda became ill. The strange food had been too much for him.

I interviewed Tokuda, a rough, fiery, dynamic spellbinder, the direct opposite of the quiet Nosaka, who had not yet returned from China. Tokuda eagerly told me his life story. A founding member of the Japanese Communist party, he had attended meetings in Russia in 1921 and 1922, was imprisoned in Japan for a year in 1923, and by

1926 he was back in Moscow as party representative. After another year in jail, he made a third trip to Moscow and returned to run for a Diet seat in 1928. Six days after the elections on February 22 he was arrested. He had been in various prisons ever since but had continuously maintained contact with the outside world, writing propaganda with pieces of lead removed from pencils and smuggled into him. He and his comrades had composed broadsides attacking Japan's war in China, nazism, fascism, and the Axis Pact. Tokuda recited in detail the history of Japan's oppressive legislation and the identity and nature of its secret societies and political parties. He singled out the socialists for particular contempt, calling them the "Socialist Emperor Party." The Communists, he said, would demand the overthrow of the emperor who was responsible for the war. They would not seek help from the Soviet Communist party. "One of the objectives of the Japanese Communist party," Tokuda insisted ingenuously, "will be to satisfy the United States that we have no connection with Soviet Russia. ... Communism may not come to Japan for a hundred years." Nosaka had modestly predicted, "not in my lifetime." On one point, Tokuda was categorical, "The Communists will support completely the policy of Great Britain and the United States."

I commented to the State Department that, like Nosaka in Yenan, Tokuda was "a professional revolutionary who had never wavered throughout a lifetime in his support of a cause which must always have looked hopeless." It was noteworthy that his attitude toward the emperor differed from that of Nosaka. I wondered whether the two would agree or compromise upon Nosaka's return from China.

Our routine interrogation of the Communists spawned rumors that have had a hardy life. In the later atmosphere of McCarthyism I was charged with having paraded top Communists through the streets of Tokyo to the plaudits of admiring well-wishers, thus adding one hundred thousand members to the Japanese Communist party. A book published in 1954 (*Typhoon in Tokyo* by Harry Emerson Wildes) reported that our "transfer of the Reds to Tokyo in an official car" had confirmed Communist propaganda that "MacArthur was their friend." According to an account published in

1965 (Walt Sheldon's *The Honorable Conquerors*), the Communists had pointed to the interrogation incident "for years afterward to prove how the United States accorded special privilege to Communists." The most recent and most sensational version appeared in a volume of a Japanese journalist's *Secret Postwar History*, entitled *Red Flag and GHQ*, published in Tokyo in 1975:

> In the latter part of the war, John Emmerson, a United States government official who spoke fluent Japanese, trod the path of a secret agent, following the course: Washington–Chungking–Yenan–Chungking. After the war ended, John Emmerson came to Japan as a member of the Political Adviser's Office in MacArthur's headquarters and visited Tokuda Kyūichi and Shiga Yoshio before they were released from confinement. It can be said that by his action Emmerson helped to bring about and hastened the release of Tokuda, Shiga, et al.

There was no need for me to bring about or to hasten the freeing of political prisoners, even had I so desired, since the decision had been made, without consultation with the political adviser, before Norman and I ever went to Fuchū. Our so-called parade through Tokyo could scarcely have excited much attention. Khaki-colored staff sedans were common, and few Japanese pedestrians would have been astute enough to recognize Tokuda and Shiga, who had been imprisoned for more than eighteen years, sitting in the back seats. As for party membership: on November 24, more than a month after our so-called joyride, Shiga estimated that six hundred people had joined the Japanese Communist party. Three months later, as I prepared to leave Japan, the Communists optimistically placed their membership at five thousand. My own zigzag course as a "secret agent" in China, Japan, and Washington, was only too well documented by the constantly flowing stream of reports that, in my exaggerated enthusiasm, I dispatched to the Department of State.

My interest in the Japanese Communists, as in the other political parties blossoming like dandelions after a spring rain, was strictly in the line of duty. On October 3 General MacArthur, in a gesture intended, I am sure, to keep us State Department types busy and out of his hair, sent a directive to George Atcheson requesting our office to submit a weekly report on the activities of political parties in Japan. George turned to me, "You're it." For the next few months I met my weekly deadline and, like a cub reporter sniffing out the news, went to party meetings, interviewed politicians of all ilk, and read masses of propaganda. Never before did my Japanese get such exercise!

The Communists were solid, determined, and had a program. They could claim, with justification, that they had been the only organized political group that had consistently opposed Japan's militarists and overseas adventures. They were the martyrs who had suffered imprisonment, torture, and death. They were immune to charges of war crimes and to being labeled "exponents of militant nationalism." The manifesto which Tokuda and Shiga had shown us in prison, a ringing acclamation of the policies of the Allies, was published in the first issue of the party organ *Akahata (Red Flag)*. Captioned "Appeal to the People," it began: "We express our deepest gratitude that the occupation of Japan by the Allied forces, dedicated to liberating the world from fascism and militarism, has opened the way for the democratic revolution. We positively support the peace policies of the United States, Great Britain, and the Allied Powers." The manifesto went on to call for the abolition of the emperor system and the establishment of a people's republic based on the will of the people.

The first postwar issue of the Communist party newspaper, *Akahata,* a small pamphlet of eighteen pages, was presented to me by Tokuda and Shiga. The last line of the introduction "Greetings on Republication" had been blacked out, but beneath the ink one could just decipher a warning: "Readers, we appeal to you to make every effort to see that this magazine does not fall into enemy hands." The prewar conspiratorial aura of communism could not easily be shed.

I was to see more of the Communists. Tokuda and Shiga called at our office from time to time to keep us posted on party developments and to make sure that we had copies of their evolving plans and platforms. Shiga talked to me about many subjects, including Japanese literature. His favorite author was Shiga Naoya, whose prose was clear, direct, and beautifully honed. Liberal but not

Communist, Shiga Naoya, who died only in 1972 at the age of eighty-nine, had been a leader of the *Shirakaba,* or White Birch, school of literature, which had reacted against naturalism in favor of humanism. Shiga Yoshio recommended highly his namesake and urged me to read his stories.

Some conservative Japanese leaders became alarmed at the freedom suddenly extended to Japan's Communists. Yoshida Shigeru, first foreign minister and later prime minister, referred in his memoirs with obvious disapproval to the "leniency" of the Occupation toward "native Communists." Prince Konoye, in an interview with General MacArthur on October 4, spent the greater part of his time explaining how the Americans had misjudged the responsibility of the *zaibatsu* and "feudal elements" in bringing Japan to disaster. The facts, he insisted, were just the opposite: these elements had been a brake on militarist expansion. It was the Marxists who had bolstered the forces of militarism and ultranationalism and had, since the Manchurian incident, played a sinister, behind-the-scenes role.

Opinions on how to deal with Communists differed within headquarters. Reform-minded officers of the Government Section scarcely saw eye to eye with the right wing, Prussian-principled General Willoughby and his G-2 staff. General MacArthur, in the early phase of the Occupation, was willing to give the reformers a free hand. It was only later, when blasts from the cold war began to penetrate the Japanese islands and the inching toward a "reverse course" began to set in, that SCAP's attitudes toward Communists changed.

I supported fully the civil rights directive and the democratic principles that became the rationale of the Occupation. As for politics, it seemed to me that we had to trust the good judgment of the Japanese people. The "freely expressed will of the people," embedded in the Potsdam Proclamation and to be restated in the new constitution, was an article of faith. We could not deny freedom to Communists because they were Communists. If we believed in the system we preached, we would have to take the risks.

Sometime in December a message came through from U.S. Army Headquarters in Korea that a certain Japanese, Nosaka Sanzo, was seeking repatriation to Japan. He claimed to know two foreign service officers named Emmerson and Service. Did SCAP object to his return? Service and I confirmed that we had known Nosaka in Yenan and that he was a well-known Communist leader. Thousands of Japanese, civilian and military, were coming back from all parts of Asia and the Pacific area. No Japanese was being denied the right to return to his homeland. GHQ must have confirmed Nosaka's identity and eligibility for repatriation.

Many years later Nosaka related the saga of his progress from Yenan to Tokyo, which took from September 10, 1945, to January 13, 1946. Accompanied by three comrades from the Japanese Peasants and Workers School, he managed to join twenty high-ranking Chinese Communist officials on an American transport plane headed for North China. Thence the trip proceeded by stages—on foot, horseback, by truck, ox-cart, plane, train, ship, and train again—through Manchuria, North and South Korea, across the straits, and from Kyūshū to Tokyo. In Soviet-held territory, Nosaka learned that Soviet soldiers were harassing Japanese residents. He appealed to General Malinovsky, who promised to shoot malefactors on the spot. For a time, the four Japanese disguised themselves in outsize Soviet uniforms to assure themselves protection from the Russians. Acclaimed in other towns with welcome signs and receptions from Soviet and Chinese comrades, the party by turn rode Soviet planes and trekked through uninhabited regions without food. At one point Nosaka fainted from exhaustion. They arrived in Pyongyang, North Korea, in late December. Introduced by a Russian officer, Nosaka for the first time met the Korean Communist leader, Kim Il-sung, who, he was amazed to find, was only thirty. They decided to cooperate closely in the future.

I later learned that Nosaka had written from Pyongyang to the U.S. commander in Seoul, Lieutenant General John R. Hodge, asking permission for his party to proceed through South Korea to Japan. The group crossed the thirty-eighth parallel on New Year's Eve and entered the American zone, where they were inspected by sentries. Nosaka had to give up a small fruit knife, which he had bought in the United States. In Seoul the next day, the Japanese were taken to a military police dormitory, assigned canvas cots in a large room, surrounded, as Nosaka tells it, by empty beds by day and by large, slumbering American soldiers by night. Held for a week, they were suddenly released and sent by train to Pusan, where, with hordes of repatriating Japanese, they embarked on a ship for Hakata, a port in Kyūshū. Enterprising Tokyo reporters, alerted to the arrival from China of Japan's leading Communist, dispatched news bulletins from every whistlestop during the train trip from Hakata to the capital. Nosaka spoke to crowds assembled at stations along the way and in his beguiling manner pronounced for the first time the words *aisareru tō* ("Lovable Party"), which were to become the watchword for the first years of the legal, reborn Japanese Communist party.

His first official act in Tokyo was to pay formal respects at MacArthur's headquarters, to express gratitude for the liberation of Japan. His most urgent task, however, was to bring unity to his renascent party. Tokuda and Shiga had emerged from prison shouting, "Down with the Emperor!" (exactly the tactic that Nosaka had told me would be a mistake). After a hurried conference of the new triumvirate, they issued a joint statement in the name of Nosaka and the Communist party which clarified their position on the emperor:

> The Communist Party and Nosaka agree on the abolition of the Emperor system because the maintenance of this system may be taken advantage of by reactionary forces. The abolition of the Emperor system means the abolition of the system as a State institution. The maintenance of the Imperial Family is a different question which should be decided by the people in the future, when a democratic country is established.

Reminiscing to the author in 1975, the still-serene and soft-spoken Nosaka, at the age of eighty-three, affirmed that Lovable Party had been a useful slogan. It had helped to break down the popular image of Communists as "frightening" and "dark." He denied, however, that he had tried to change the party's position on the emperor; Edgar Snow had embarrassed him in 1945 by reporting from Korea that "Nosaka supports the emperor system." Conversations with the Emancipation Leaguers in Yenan had convinced him that the Japanese people's sentimental attachment to a god-emperor was too ingrained to be quickly dissipated; his proposal that the emperor be separated from the emperor system was a tactical move, and history had proved him to be right.

When Prince Konoye called on General MacArthur on October 4, he requested the supreme commander's guidance regarding the organization of the Japanese government and its parliament. MacArthur replied, "in a determined tone of voice" (according to the Japanese record of conversation), that the constitution must be revised and suffrage expanded. Konoye regretted that in the past he had been unable to accomplish his desires but assured MacArthur that he was now ready, with the supreme commander's encouragement and advice, to do his utmost to serve his country. The general responded, "That is splendid. Although you are from a so-called feudalistic background, you are a 'cosmopolitan' and know the world. You are still young, and you should dare to take leadership. If you should gather together people of liberal persuasion and produce for publication a proposal for revision of the constitution, the Diet would accept it, I believe."

Prince Konoye took MacArthur's words as a mandate to revise the constitution. On October 20 I wrote a memorandum to the supreme commander for Atcheson's signature, noting that Konoye had assembled a commission to prepare draft revisions and that, at the same time, the Cabinet had designated Matsumoto Jōji, a minister without portfolio, to conduct parallel research. My memorandum made the point that, in carrying out constitutional reform, it would be essential to guarantee the right of full discussion and amendment, that a constitution seen as a "gift from a benevolent emperor" would not promote democratic aims.

At the request of MacArthur, our suggestions were amplified in a second memorandum, submitted October 23, in which we urged that, pending constitutional revision, pertinent laws and regulations should be suitably altered and that, following full public examination and criticism, the Diet should make its final decision. In the meantime, Konoye had talked to Atcheson, and Professor Takagi Yasaka of Tokyo Imperial University, whom I had known before the war, had called on me on behalf of Prince Konoye. The State Department obliged by sending us a list of principles to be incorporated in any revised Japanese constitution, the most important of which was a government fully responsible to an electorate based upon wide representative suffrage. I handed a copy of these principles to Professor Takagi for the Konoye group.

Adverse comments regarding Konoye's credentials to revise the constitution began to appear in Japanese and American newspapers. On November 1, SCAP issued a press release disclaiming sponsorship of the prince's activities. MacArthur then enjoined Atcheson to cease official relations with the Konoye enterprise, and I was instructed to inform Professor Takagi of this decision. For me, this was a most painful task. Takagi had logically thought that the revision of the constitution would be of primary concern to the State Department, and he and Konoye had turned to us in good faith. We were now forced to reject this spontaneous effort by a Japanese group who wished to cooperate closely with the principal occupying powers in working out a new and mutually acceptable national charter for Japan. As Takagi later wrote, "... Konoye was fighting against fearful odds, against the criticism of our jurists and scholars, to say nothing of his political opponents, and against the most unexpected cut of all, the withdrawal of support of the General Head Quarters [sic]."

Early in November the question of the possible indictment of Konoye as a war criminal began to be discussed. Herbert Norman wrote a devastating memorandum to General MacArthur, affirming that Konoye's decisions as prime minister, made at critical turns in Japan's prewar history, had "invariably favored aggression and the tightening of the vise in which the army and its civilian aides held the country." Norman argued that if Tōjō were to be blamed for Pearl Harbor, Konoye was responsible for Japan's aggression against China. Concluding that "a strong prima facie case can be made against Konoye as a war criminal," Norman's memorandum ended dramatically: "One thing is sure, as long as he [Konoye] is allowed to occupy any position of importance, he will retard and frustrate any potential liberal and democratic movement. As long as he dominates the Constitutional Drafting Committee, he will stultify any serious attempt to write a democratic constitution. Whatever his hand touches turns to dust and ashes."

Atcheson forwarded the Norman memorandum to the State Department with his endorsement and included Konoye's name in a list of suspected major war criminals. On December 15, the night before he was to be arrested on SCAP orders, Prince Konoye, of long and noble lineage and three times prime minister of Japan, drank poison and died. He left a note to his son, which contained the sentence: "The winner is too boastful and the loser too servile."

Konoye's death ended the first Japanese effort to amend the constitution and eliminated the State Department from any participation in the constitution-making process. Japan's new charter was written by uniformed Americans closeted in the Government Section of GHQ in February 1946, after I had left Japan. In the end, the Japanese and English texts were hammered out in a continuous thirty-two-hour session behind locked doors, which ended in the late afternoon of March 4. After some revisions and approval by the Diet, the constitution went into effect on May 3, 1947.

Had Konoye prepared a constitution, it might have been undemocratic in nature, but if close and continuous collaboration between responsible Japanese and Americans, which we had recommended, had taken place, the fundamental principles of free, representative government would probably have been incorporated, resulting in a Japanese document rather than, as is charged, a Japanese translation. The miracle is, of course, that the "made in U.S.A." constitution, which finally became the law of the Japanese land, has survived its first thirty years without any serious attempt having been made to amend it.

Living through the first few months of the MacArthur revolution was a once-in-a-lifetime experience. We were indeed transforming a country. Looking back now, we occupationaires were a confident and patronizing lot. Obligated to democratize Japan, we knew only too little of the country we were trying to remold. Soon after my arrival, I wrote to my wife: "It is pathetic how few people here know Japan or have had any experience here. I am appalled and astounded at the problems and the lack of qualified people. Wish I had the power and means to put this idea across to people who count in Washington." Language was a formidable barrier. Outside of the handful of prewar Japanese-language officers and some truly competent, trained nisei, interpreting was a hit-or-miss process. Hundreds of loyal, conscientious nisei soldiers struggled with their Hawaiian and Californian Japanese learned after school and were too proud to admit the breakdowns that frustrated and distorted communication.

For me, communication with Japanese was possible in a way never known in the constrained conditions of the 1930s. Everyone wanted to talk, and, minus interpreters, thoughts and feelings cascaded in torrents. My assignment to investigate political parties took me to party meetings and to interviews with politicians from farthest left to farthest right. I talked with editors, writers, historians, educators, labor union leaders, former Diet members, actors, and students; in the provinces, I met mayors, governors, local trade unionists, teachers, businessmen, and farmers.

At a Foreign Office party I encountered an intelligent, talented geisha, Nagano-san, forty-three years old, who knew more about Japanese public personalities and politics than most officials. She welcomed a few of us who spoke Japanese to her plain but undamaged little wooden house in the Shimbashi district. We supplied canned C rations and chocolate, in return for which would magically appear sukiyaki, tempura, raw fish, delectable delicacies unknown in a GI mess. Together, the soft tatami floor, the glowing charcoal brazier, warm sake, and warm conversation engendered rare communication with our Japanese friends. Nagano-san herself contributed flashes of insight into the war, Japan, and herself. Tragedy mixed with humor and irony. She amazed us by describing, in the style of a haiku poet, the combined "beauty and death" of raiding B-29s: great silver birds swooping through the sky. In the best tradition of the professional geisha, Nagano-san knew when to be silent and how to encourage us to talk among ourselves. Her place became a refreshing oasis in a world of khaki and rank.

I attended the founding meeting of the Socialist party at Hibiya Hall on November 2. This was the first postwar political party to be organized; 2,600 people filled the auditorium. Much argument ensued over the name of the party, which was to be Nippon Shakai-tō (Japan Socialist party) in Japanese and Social Democratic Party of Japan in English. Some members shouted objections to this contradiction, but amidst the general uproar, the chairman called for applause to settle the question, and the names were approved. While the inclusion of *democratic* in the English name was probably done to please the Americans, the discrepancy in nomenclature intimated a deep division, which was to plague the party for many years and was to cause it later to split, reunite, and split again.

The inauguration of the Liberal party (Jiyū-tō) was held a week later in the same Hibiya Hall with a capacity attendance. The meeting was better organized than that of the Socialists, and no speeches from the floor were permitted. In introductory remarks, a prewar politician, who had been a member of the Diet since 1920, described Japan's status as that of a "naked person seeking a new kimono." After he had demanded the punishment of war criminals, someone from the audience cried out, "What about yourself? You're guilty too!" Hatoyama Ichirō, who had been a member of the House of Representatives since 1915, a minister in two prewar cabinets, and a leader of the old Seiyukai party, was elected president by acclamation. Delivering the principal address, he attacked the Communists and defended the emperor, who was "of our flesh, our blood, our bones." Hatoyama proclaimed a "free economy" to be the policy of the Liberal party, explaining that the word *jiyū* ("free") which forms the party name should be taken as synonymous to the word *jinkaku* ("personality," or "individual"), meaning that the politics and economy of the nation should be conducted by individuals for individuals. In my report of the meeting I noted that applause had been most vociferous at the mention of war responsibility and the punishment of war criminals. "Laughter," I wrote, "greeted the remark of one speaker that, although Americans had expected thousands of public suicides following Japan's surrender, not one has taken place."

On November 16 Japan's third postwar political party (the Communists had not yet been formally organized) announced itself: the Nippon Shinpo-tō (Japan Progressive party). More than two hundred of its members had been elected to the wartime Diet in 1942 and represented the Tōjō-sponsored Political Association of

Great Japan (Dai Nippon Seiji-kai). Distinctively conservative in coloration, the Progressives' platform differed substantially from that of the Liberals only in a readiness to institute a limited planned economy. Its handicap was vulnerability to the purge, since its predecessor, the Political Association, had been outlawed by SCAP directive. Politicians returning to active political life worked under constant threat of the purge. They used every ingratiating device to fend off the uncertain axe. Tsurumi Yūsuke, a Progressive leader who might have expected to become prime minister, assured us that the party was cleansing itself by banning members of wartime cabinets and "Tōjō henchmen." Tsurumi himself was "excluded from public office" soon thereafter. Hatoyama, president of the Liberal party, was permitted to run for a Diet seat in April 1946 and was promptly purged after his election. Fortunately for him, he resumed political activity after the Occupation and served three terms as prime minister in the 1950s.

By December, thirty-nine political parties had declared their existence, including the four that were to provide the political basis for Japan's postwar parliamentary system: Liberals, Progressives, Socialists, and Communists. The Liberals and Progressives, after successive realignments and name changes, were finally to emerge in 1955 as the Liberal Democratic Party. The Socialists, unable to decide whether they were Socialists or Social Democrats, became the contemporary Japan Socialist Party (JSP) and the Democratic Socialist Party (DSP), respectively. Other groups fell by the wayside, and it was not until the 1960s that the Buddhists of the Sōka Gakkai organized the fifth party in Japan's present political spectrum—the Clean Government Party of Kōmei-tō.

I found stimulation in Japanese who were not politicians. One of my most enlightening evenings was a four-hour session in my room at the Dai-Ichi Hotel with four Japanese university students. Slim, pale, wearing ill-fitting navy blue school uniforms, they were from three institutions—Tokyo Imperial University, Tōhoku University, and the Japan Conservatory of Music—studying law, architecture, agriculture, and music. I provided Kirin beer and a box of crackers from home, which they consumed ravenously. I could believe them when they recounted that most students got along on two meals a day and conserved strength by staying in bed on Sundays. The piano student described his acute need for the physical energy required for practice. They laughed about how hard it was to study when all they could think about was food. But they were not asking for pity or handouts. They were eager to talk about themselves, their random thoughts, and their feelings to a foreigner who would listen. SCAP was power and should be more strict. Only SCAP could stop the black market. The Japanese would welcome complete control by the Americans; a long occupation—ten or twenty years—that would be fine. Farmers, factory owners, and businessmen were well off; farmers could eat, and the others could afford the black market. Dissatisfied, demobilized officers were dangerous; their extremist ideas might lead them to cooperate with Communists, who were also extremists. The emperor was like the tokonoma (ceremonial alcove) in a Japanese room—decorative, useless, but indispensable. Nobody worried about his sanctity nor about State Shinto, which had been abolished by MacArthur's directive. No one worried about war criminals; the Japanese ought to submit lists themselves. The Social Democratic Party was popular among intellectuals but didn't state clearly what it wanted. Progressives and Liberals would win the election because they had money. Giving women suffrage was like putting a dog in a tree: he can't climb. Women have no political conscience and no desire to exercise their rights. A jar of cold cream would buy the vote of any one of them. Democracy? Who knew what it was? Japanese were always friendly to the United States, looked down on China, and either knew nothing about Great Britain or thought of it as a third-rate power. Nobody liked Soviet Russia. The Communists denied connections with the Russians to curry favor with the Americans and so lost the respect of the Japanese. Militarism might come back. After all, a man could separate from his wife, but if he met her again after ten years, his affection was likely to revive. Who could imagine a country totally without arms? World disarmament was fine, but until it came about, Japan would need weapons for self-defense.

In retrospect, the students' ideas were probably widely shared and, except for their exuberantly expressed male chauvinism and their eagerness for a twenty-year Occupation, they would continue to characterize Japanese society in a later postwar period.

My association with Herbert Norman became one of the more pleasurable aspects of occupied Tokyo. We had common interests in the Japanese language, history, and politics, and compatible personalities. Our respective official duties led us to share interviews and visits. He had opened the spacious Canadian embassy, and lived in heatless grandeur in one of the bedrooms upstairs. Eating our warmed-over C rations, we found in the embassy another retreat where the atmosphere was conducive to frank talks with our Japanese friends. It was there that we met Ushiba Tomohiko, who in the summer of 1941 had told me about reading our codes. Ushiba had come under suspicion in connection with the conviction and execution of Richard Sorge as a Soviet spy during the war. Then Prime Minister Konoye's private secretary, Ushiba had attended breakfast sessions with Sorge's principal Japanese accomplice, a respected and trusted scholar and official in the Research Department of the South Manchurian Railway. Tomo, as we called him, related the torment he had suffered during the investigation of the case.

Norman was a sensitive scholar, a "classical humanist and ardent libertarian," as a biographer later described him. He was dedicated to the defense of human rights and loathed totalitarianism. He searched for the indigenous democratic elements in Japanese history on which he believed the Japanese could construct their postwar society. Many zealous toilers in the reforming sections of SCAP headquarters smugly thought that we Americans were the first harbingers of democracy for Japan. Yet the strivings for equality, human rights, and representative government had long been an integral part of Japanese life. Such strivings, smothered by the nationalism and expansionism of the 1930s, were forgotten by the outside world. Norman was then planning to write a biography of Andō Shōeki, a lesser-known advocate of an egalitarian society and an opponent of shogunate policy in the Tokugawa period. His book, *Andō Shōeki and the Anatomy of Japanese Feudalism,* was published in 1949. In our more imaginative moments, we dreamed of collaborating in research and writing on the democratic traditions of Japanese history.

I did not share the degree of Norman's moral indignation over Konoye, expressed in his emotional memorandum recommending that the prince be tried as a war criminal. I remembered the summer of 1941 when Konoye, in spite of his vacillations and weaknesses of character, had, with Ambassador Grew, tried to prevent war. We also know that he, together with Marquis Kido and Foreign Minister Tōgō, had sought a way out of the war in 1945. In my opinion, these should have been mitigating circumstances.

In mid-January 1946 the department transferred me to Washington. I reacted with joy and regret. I wanted to go home. Two separations from my family were enough. But the job was exciting. The era was like the Meiji restoration. Everybody was trying everything. Then it was modernization, westernization, now it was democratization, Americanization. It was like the school teacher in Yamanashi prefecture when we asked him what he was teaching now that the war had ended: he replied instantly, "Democracy."

"But," we asked, "what do you mean by democracy?"

"Oh," he shot back, "we are waiting to be told by the Ministry of Education."

Every GI was interpreting democracy. Two young soldiers, hearing sounds of plucked strings coming from an upstairs window, banged on the door of a house. A terrified housewife peered out at the soldiers whose sign language indicated a desire to hear the music. Finally invited inside, the boys sat quietly listening to the daughter of the family play the *koto* with her trembling fingers. Entranced by the music, the GIs came back often, just to listen to the *koto*. Of course, brawls and escapades and ugly incidents occurred as well. But no Japanese attacked an American in revenge. Democracy worked, after a fashion.

There are certain moments from the five-month period that I wanted to remember. One was the return to Kyoto, the ancient capital, saved from atomic-bombing because Henry Stimson knew it was a cultural center. I took nostalgic walks through the city, to the Heian shrine, to Kiyomizu temple, and to find my prewar Japanese teacher, Kuroha-sensei. She had taught all the Americans who lived in Kyoto in the 1930s, many of whom—including Edwin Reischauer—became well-known Japanese specialists. The born teacher, Kuroha-san was both frail and vigorous, sparkling, interested, and as always, correcting my Japanese mistakes. Another experience was a visit to Yamanashi prefecture, west of Tokyo. We talked to everyone: the governor, mayors, local officials and farmers. Their problem was obtaining fertilizers in order to boost rice production. The farmers were indifferent to politics. One said, "All Japanese hate Tōjō. But too many people have been purged just because of the jobs they held." Among my brighter moments were night visits to deserted studios in Tokyo's Radio JOAK, where I found a kindred soul in Mac McClatchey, an air force major who flew planes by day and played the piano by night. We discovered two beautiful Steinway grands and played Mozart's two-piano sonata, which I had learned in Peru.

The time for my departure came. The Far Eastern Advisory Commission, an eleven-nation body established to formulate policies for the Occupation, was paying an official visit to Tokyo before undertaking deliberations in Washington. Their departure for the United States was scheduled for January 31 aboard a special navy communications ship, the S. S. *Mount McKinley*. I was attached to the commission for the duration of the trip and thus profited from conversations and conferences among the distinguished representatives onboard. Among them were General Frank McCoy, the American member and chairman of the commission; Sir George Sansom, the British representative; George Blakeslee, who had directed much of the presurrender planning in the State Department; and Herbert Norman, who was the Canadian delegate.

In my leisure time I wrote my impressions of the situation in Japan, calling my report, "Political Factors in the Present Japanese Situation." I began my dispatch by stating the obvious, that the struggle for livelihood was uppermost in the mind of every subject of the Japanese nation, that political parties, elections, democracy, the emperor, were all of academic importance when the rice bowl was empty. Political factors could therefore be understood only against this economic background.

I concluded that, after five months of the Occupation, the Japanese respected, admired, and liked Americans. Certain of their attitudes were worthy of note. The first I called "gravitation toward strength," illustrated by the Japanese proverb, *nagai mono ni wa makarero* (to be taken in by the strong). With Buddhist resignation, the Japanese accepted MacArthur's supreme authority as inevitable. So complete was this acceptance that the initial dependence and subservience could be disconcerting, if not nauseating. One therefore admired Ozaki Yukio, the grand old man of parliament, staunch democrat through war and oppression, who had remarked at the December session of the Diet, with a twinkle in his eye, "We are grateful for our new freedom and our new liberty, even though they are rationed by MacArthur's headquarters."

A second element was a desire for a long Occupation. Many Japanese believed that an extended period of guidance and pressure from the outside would be necessary if democracy were to flower. Few went so far as my student friends, who had talked of ten to twenty years.

Third, some Japanese anticipated a war between the United States and the Soviet Union, a war they regarded as not only inevitable but of great advantage to Japan. Because American strategy would require the use of the Japanese islands as staging areas for military operations against the Soviets, the buildup of Japan's industrial potential would be encouraged. General Hata Shunroku, before entering Sugamo Prison as a war criminal, had remarked that the time would come when his talents would again be needed. This prognosis regarding Soviet–American military hostilities was mistaken, but the cold war lay dead ahead. However, such forebodings were rare in those early days. Most Japanese wanted to contemplate only perpetual peace.

Finally, the Japanese were conditioned to an American Occupation. In a strange way they felt some pride in defeat by the most powerful nation in the world and saw no reason for other countries to share in this "American Interlude." Enmity toward the Soviet Union was profound. Curiously, in the minds of many Japanese, the stab in the back at the end of the war overshadowed the atomic destruction of Hiroshima and Nagasaki.

Occupation reforms, the civil rights directive, arrests of war criminals, the purges, and the abolition of State Shintō were taken in stride. Even country folk, presumably the tenacious guardians of superstition and conservatism, were unperturbed that gods had been unseated. One remarked to me wryly, "Who believes in gods who failed so miserably?" Many Japanese were grateful that General MacArthur, with a few strokes of his pen, had achieved a revolution that they could never hope to have accomplished. They looked upon SCAP directives not as punishment but liberation. I found little popular interest in constitutional reform; most Japanese were unfamiliar with the terms of the Meiji constitution and seemed unconcerned over fundamental changes in the nation's basic charter.

According to public opinion polls, a large majority of Japanese wanted to retain the emperor. But even without his New Year's renunciation of divinity, Hirohito, for most people, was no longer sacred. The Japanese I talked to laughed irreverently about *"maketa papa-san"* ("beaten papa"). They lost whatever awe or trepidation they might have retained, when morning editions of Japanese newspapers on September 27 carried front-page photographs of General MacArthur, towering in shirt sleeves over a stiff, solemn, diminutive figure in morning coat, who had proved where sovereignty rested by coming to call on the supreme commander at his American embassy residence.

As I left Japan, the political parties were preparing for the first postwar elections, scheduled for January but later postponed until April. The Socialists and Communists were least affected by the purge; the Socialists were expected to do well, but the Communists still labored under the handicap of long-ingrained distrust and dislike. The conservative vote would be divided between the Liberals and the Progressives, the latter at a disadvantage because of the inroads of the purge.

My predictions, made two months before elections were held, exaggerated the strength of the Social Democrats, whom I expected to become the leading party. Instead, the Liberals led, with the Progressives and the Social Democrats capturing almost the same number of seats each. I had estimated that three or four Communists would win; the number was actually five. The elections of 1946 set the pattern for the years ahead; except for the succeeding election, in 1947, when my predictions for a Socialist plurality came true, the conservatives were to rule Japan.

By February 1946 it was clear that the emphasis in the Occupation should shift from the *destructive* to the *constructive* phase. The political tasks ahead, in my view, consisted primarily in the establishment of a new structure of government, a new educational system, and the development of new national leadership. At that time, it seemed likely that the emperor would abdicate following revision of the constitution. I felt strongly that we should neither arrest the emperor as a war criminal nor abolish the imperial institution, which even the Communists were willing to tolerate temporarily. I felt that we should, however, continue to guide and encourage the political regeneration of Japan.

The British agreed with my analysis of Japan under the Occupation. A copy of my dispatch of February 1946 was shown in strict confidence to their embassy in Moscow, which in turn transmitted it to London with the comment that "it may be interesting to see the sort of advice which is being tendered by State Department experts on Japan, and the sort of spectacles through which they see the Japanese scene." A specialist on Japan in the British Foreign Office wrote a covering memorandum to his superiors:

> Mr. Emmerson is a member of the U.S. Foreign Service and is an expert on Japan. On the whole his views appear to be extremely sound. We can heartily agree with his statement ... that the present striving for democracy is based on a respect for success and not on any understanding of moral issues. Our only hope of establishing democracy in Japan is to show the Japanese that it pays in their country and elsewhere. If we can make them democrats by self-interest, there is a chance that after a number of years they may become democrats by conviction.

As time has passed, memories of the Occupation have dimmed for both Japanese and Americans. MacArthur himself lived in such austere isolation that few Japanese, except for the emperor and the prime ministers, Shidehara and Yoshida, ever met or talked with him. He was imperious and aloof. So far as I know, he left Tokyo only once, before the Korean war, for a brief visit to Taiwan, and his route in the capital city never deviated from the shortest distance between his American embassy residence and his headquarters at the Dai-Ichi Mutual Life Insurance building. Herbert Norman described a conversation with him, "The General's words steam along like warships with no great cargo of meaning."

When the General died in 1964, Japanese journalists, searching for an interview with someone who knew him, pounced upon Muragi Tamotsu, the barber who had cut the supreme commander's hair regularly and had seen him in intimate surroundings. Muragi described the bedroom which he had visited every month, MacArthur's blue bathrobe, wet with toothpaste, his "thinning hair, as soft and fine as silk thread," and the case of corncob pipes next to the bed. "My hand holding the scissors shook with nervousness, so conscious I was of serving the Supreme Commander for the Allied Powers." MacArthur tried to put him at ease but talked little. After the last haircut, he said to Muragi very simply, "It's been a long time, hasn't it?" The Japanese barber won prestige from his association with the supreme commander: he cut the hair of MacArthur's successor, General Matthew Ridgway, and so far has been barber to every succeeding American ambassador to Japan.

A few years ago I had occasion to take a taxi in Tokyo to an office near the old Dai-Ichi building. The youthful driver knew neither the building I wanted nor the Dai-Ichi. I remonstrated, "You mean to say you don't know where General MacArthur had his headquarters?"

The young man turned to me in disgust, "General MacArthur? Who's he?"

I persevered, "You have never read about General MacArthur in your history books?"

Exasperated, the young cabbie replied, "There may be two Chinese characters about MacArthur in our schoolbooks, but if so, that is all." At his reply, I felt my age.

Today's Japanese youth, in the words of a recent popular song, are "children who do not know the war" (*"sensō wo shiranai kodomo-*

tachi"). They do not know the war or the Occupation or General MacArthur. For them, it is as though it all never happened. Yet the Occupation was a revolution, a revolution whose history remains to be written. A short-time witness to it can convey merely a subjective glimpse of a minuscule segment of a mammoth canvas. An army of American civilians followed the GIs into Japan with the goal of transforming a nation in the American image. The first five months of this effort (from September 1945 through January 1946), which I experienced, were characterized by surprises, floods of unexpected goodwill, and confusion confounded. Imbued with the Buddhist philosophy of the transiency of all things, the Japanese accepted defeat, recovered rapidly from the humiliation of surrender, and, applying the innate energy which had propelled them through history from ancient times, set about clearing the rubble and reestablishing their livelihood.

The tone was set in these early months. MacArthur became the father figure, the emperor renounced his divinity, and the Americans launched democratization with a zeal that often exceeded sensitivity. The ordinary Japanese did not, at first, comprehend his unaccustomed freedom so intent was he on scrounging for food and repairing his shelter. To his relief, he discovered goodwill among the Americans and he reciprocated. To be sure, the black market flourished; venal Americans consorted with venal Japanese; fortunes were built; and foundation stones for future political power were adeptly laid. Purged Japanese politicians plotted for the times ahead, and those who escaped the purge found ways to deal with the occupationaires skillfully and to their own advantage.

Fortunately, in the first phase of the Occupation, we were able to concentrate on the democratic freedoms for Japan without the strictures of a cold war mentality. During these months, we strengthened the Japanese hatred for war and militarism born out of defeat. Freedom, even for Communists, signaled in my view our faith in the durability of democracy and in the common sense of the Japanese people. We nurtured the seeds of pacifism and neutrality in Japan, and we should not have been surprised when the Japanese, in succeeding years, resisted remilitarization. True, the later, so-called reverse course reflected changes in the international situation over which the Japanese had no control. Security became a concept which the pragmatic Japanese had to face. But, in my view, the principle symbolized by the constitution's no-war clause became so deeply imbedded in the Japanese consciousness during the first months of the Occupation that Japanese militarism will not rise again.

The Occupation was a success, a unique undertaking in history. It represented a rare confluence in time of American ideals, Japanese character, adaptability, and energy, and goodwill on both sides.

11

Moscow 1947–49

The United States effectively kept the Russians out of the Occupation of Japan. The day after the emperor surrendered, Stalin proposed taking over the northern half of Hokkaido Island. President Truman rejected his plea forthwith, offering instead Soviet participation in "Allied token forces" under the command of General MacArthur. Stalin, who had stated that Russian public opinion would be seriously offended if Soviet troops were not accorded an Occupation zone in Japan proper, replied curtly, "I have to say that I and my colleagues did not expect such an answer from you." Nevertheless, the Soviet dictator, recognizing power where power lay, did not pursue his demand.

The Occupation was to be Allied—and the Russians were Allies—and control machinery had to be devised. During the fall of 1945 an acrimonious exchange of messages ensued between Washington and Moscow. Ambassador Averell Harriman advised the State Department that the Soviets would be uncooperative in Europe if snubbed in Japan. He was patient but firm in dealing with Stalin, whose respect and personal friendship he managed to earn. The Russians were incensed that the United States was deliberately excluding them from the administration of postwar Japan. Stalin railed to Harriman in October, "The Soviet Union had become an American satellite in the Pacific. This was a role it could not accept. The Soviet Union would not be a satellite of the United States in the Far East or elsewhere. . . . It would be more honest if the Soviet Union were to quit Japan than to remain as a 'piece of furniture.' "

In 1977 Averell Harriman recalled his role in keeping the Russians out of the Occupation of Japan. In a press interview, he reminisced, "The most important job I got involved with was when Stalin wanted the island of Hokkaido as a base. . . . I was determined he shouldn't get it because he had been in the war [against Japan] such a short time and had contributed nothing to it. I had something to do with preventing it. Can you imagine what would have happened to Japan if it had a Russian occupation in Hokkaido?"

By December the plans for an Allied Council for Japan (ACJ) and a Far Eastern Commission (FEC) had been worked out and were accepted by Molotov, Ernest Bevin, and James F. Byrnes at a foreign ministers' meeting in Moscow. Neither the four-power Allied Council, which was to meet in Tokyo, nor the eleven-nation FEC, established in Washington, was to possess any real authority over the supreme commander. In case of a failure to reach agreement on policy decisions within the commission, General MacArthur was empowered to issue "interim directives," which left him unhampered in his dominance over the Occupation. The council became in essence little more than a debating society. Both the FEC and the ACJ provided forums for Russian obstructionist tactics and for criticism of American policy, not only by the Soviet representatives, but also by our other Allies who often thought we were being too soft on the Japanese or were too much obsessed by "reform-mindedness." We in the State Department who worked with the FEC during this period found ourselves busy defending American interests before our Allies and trying to impress the supreme commander that by international agreement he was presiding over an allied administration.

The early months of 1946 brought a change of atmosphere, the onset of the cold war. The Russians had emerged in 1945 as the occupiers of half of Europe—Poland, Hungary, Rumania, Bulgaria, and parts of Germany and Austria. Regimes friendly to Moscow were in place in Finland, Albania, Yugoslavia, and Czechoslovakia.

The Communist conquest of China was under way. The wartime alliance between East and West had disintegrated. The heroics of the Russian defenders of Leningrad were transmuted into Red threats. The West perceived a compound menace—expansionism which was both Soviet and Communist. Three events, occurring within a span of twenty-four days in 1946, symbolized the transformation which was taking place in the world situation. The first was an election speech delivered on February 9 by Generalissimo Stalin, in which he exhorted his war-weary countrymen to rebuild a war machine in preparation for a coming crisis. U.S. Supreme Court Justice William O. Douglas dubbed the statement a "declaration of World War III," and Secretary of the Navy James Forrestal concluded from it that "there was no way . . . in which democracy and communism could live together." The second event, a signal read and reread in high U.S. government circles, was George Kennan's so-called red-light telegram of February 22 from Moscow (see chapter 4, pages 90–91) in which he analyzed in depth the ideology and political force of the Soviet Union and prescribed courses of action for the United States. A third alarm, sounded publicly, was Winston Churchill's speech at Fulton, Missouri, on March 5, in which he said, "A shadow has fallen upon the scenes so lately lighted by the Allied victory. . . . From Stettin in the Baltic to Trieste in the Adriatic, an iron curtain has descended across the Continent."

In Japan, not only the Japanese talked about a coming war between the United States and the Soviet Union, but journalists were quoting American military officers on Japan's potential as a staging area for future hostilities. The journalist Mark Gayn was describing Tokyo's atmosphere as one of "frontline trenches," "We're at war with the Russkys. Whose side are you on?"

In commenting on a Tokyo dispatch, which posed the unlikely prospect that Japan might in the future reverse its pro-American policies and align itself with the Soviet Union, I deplored tendencies to think of a Soviet–American war as inevitable and that Japan would be a battleground. "If, as Walter Lippmann suggests," I wrote, "Germany is profiting from a Soviet–British rivalry over her, it would be most unfortunate if the spectacle arose of Soviet–American rivalry over Japan."

In August, John Davies, who by this time had been assigned to the embassy in Moscow, analyzed Soviet policy toward Japan as one based on the fear that Japan would be converted into a "place of arms" for the United States. He warned that the Soviets would utilize the Japanese Communist party to disrupt Japan's development as an ally of America. Davies called it "a delusion to assume that Japan can be reconstructed as a neutral, self-sufficient nation, enjoying friendly relations with both the United States and [the] Soviet Union.... If we withdraw from Japan without having assured ourselves of a favored position there, Japan may in all probability sooner or later be captured by the Soviet Union. The tables will have been turned and we shall be confronted with Japan as a *'place d'armes'* of the only other first-class power."

After my experience in Yenan and occupied Tokyo, I had come to the conclusion that communism was not the wave of the future for Japan, that the inherent hostility of the Japanese toward the Russians and their built-in suspicions of communism would prevent them from succumbing to a Red lure. I believed that we need not fear to be consistent with our principles and that we should give the Communists the same freedom of action that we were extending to any other political party. We should direct our efforts during the Occupation to the construction of strong, Communist-resistant, democratic institutions. In a memorandum, written in the State Department on October 9, 1946, I objected to Davies's assumption that Japan could not enjoy friendly relations with both the Soviet Union and the United States. American security requirements, I felt, would be adequately fulfilled by our naval power and strategic bases and would not require the rearming of Japan, which would be contradictory to enunciated policy as well as being of dubious long-term validity and effectiveness. The Soviet Union, in my view, would have great difficulty in securing control over Japan. The Japanese liked neither Russians nor Communists and, except for Nosaka, Communist party leadership was inept.

I concluded, "Our acts in Japan should not be conditioned by a fear of communism so strong that we lean toward the very elements we have set out to destroy. We shall assure ourselves of a 'favored position' in Japan if we succeed in effecting lasting reforms, in giving impetus to a genuine liberal movement, and in starting the process of democratization in Japanese education. Then, perhaps, will Japan become neither a *place d'armes* for the Soviet Union nor a *place d'armes* for the United States."

Anxious to test my reactions with others in the department, I asked my chief, John Carter Vincent, then director of the Office of Far Eastern Affairs, to "intimate to me whether I am all wet in my comments on John Davies's memo." Notes came back to me from Vincent, "You are not—you are crisp, crystal clear, and right," and from Major General John H. Hilldring, who was then director of the Office of Occupied Areas, "Emmerson is absolutely right. I recommend that we disregard the Moscow memorandum."

Whether I was right or not, the issue that Davies and I addressed became a central one for Occupation policy. In 1946 and early 1947 State Department officials were overly concerned that Japan might again revert to militarism. Secretary of State Byrnes proposed a forty-year disarmament and demilitarization treaty with provisions for swift punishment for violation of its terms. By March of 1947 a small working group in the State Department, of which I was a member, had begun to draft a peace treaty for Japan in which control mechanisms—in the spirit of the Byrnes pact—would place Japan indefinitely under the supervision of a Council of Ambassadors, representing nine nations, including the Soviet Union.

General MacArthur, after reading these proposals, exploded. In a memorandum dated March 21, 1947, he called the text "imperialistic in concept, in purpose, and in form." The supreme commander at that time envisaged an unarmed, neutral Japan, free to chart a course toward economic revival under the protection of the United Nations. Even he, however, still admitted the need for "minimum future inspection and control, for at least a generation, by the United Nations." In retrospect, it seems incredible now that policymakers could have conceived of a Japan so restricted by outside powers for forty years or for a generation.

Meanwhile, events in China and Europe were stimulating fears of an expanding communism, and visions of a helpless Japan open to Communist aggression appeared. I believed that the time for punishment was over and that the economic recovery of Japan was essential, but I did not see the necessity for rearmament. Outside events had their impact, and a shift in Occupation policy turned into the reverse course of 1948 and 1949. Thenceforward, emphasis was to be on recovery rather than reform, that is, Japan was to be strengthened rather than to be kept weak. The period of phenomenal economic development began. Fortunately, the MacArthur peace constitution and the good sense of the Japanese leaders themselves made it possible to resist pressures to rearm. Even the self-defense forces, created in response to the Korean war, never reached the scale of remilitarization. As for communism, it became part of Japan's free political scene but never threatened the stability of the state nor eroded Japanese democratic institutions.

The Soviet Union, in 1947, was looming so large on the international horizon that I thought I should see the Red Giant at firsthand. Chip Bohlen had preached to me since our days together in Tokyo in 1941 that my career would be incomplete without the Moscow experience. By early 1947 John Davies's time in the Moscow embassy was nearing its end, and the policy of including an officer with Far Eastern experience on the embassy staff had been established. John, who had entered my life once before when he had asked me to join him in the China–Burma–India theater, again stepped in to act on Chip's suggestion. A telegram arrived from Moscow, drafted, I am sure, by Davies, who laid it on thick: "Embassy wishes express strong feelings that officer should be ... widely familiar with Communist activities in Far East ... also have firsthand knowledge of prewar and postwar Japan. Only man who fits this bill is Emmerson. ..."

By summer we were off to Moscow, with two children, by then seven and nine, and eighteen pieces of assorted baggage, including several old trunks. For the last leg of our journey, from Stockholm to Leningrad, we had reservations on the Russian ship, S.S. *Sestroretsk*. An accommodating Swedish employee of our embassy in Stockholm accompanied us to dockside and saw that we, children, baggage, and all, were safely aboard and in our staterooms. I walked out on deck to watch our departure. As we inched away from land and moved down the long Stockholm estuary, I noticed a ship still tied up at the pier. My few lessons in Russian had barely taught me the alphabet, but I thought I could spell out its name—*Sestroretsk*. Our ship! But no—the Russians couldn't be wrong. They had checked our tickets and assigned us cabins. I hunted the sailing schedule displayed on the bulletin board: the *Byeloostrov* sailed for London at 4:00 and the *Sestroretsk* for Leningrad at 4:30. We were on the *Byeloostrov* headed for London. Bellboys and pursers disbelieved my fragmentary Russian but each rushed to find a person of higher rank. Finally, the captain himself verified the mistake. Officers barked orders, bells rang, and engines ground to a halt. We gathered our bags and waited for the chugging tug to take us off. The four of us, one by one, drenched by a driving rain, climbed down rope ladders to the deck of the tugboat; our enormous trunks were hoisted up from the hold and over the side, with the scene being witnessed by open-mouthed passengers lining the railings.

The more I thought about our experience, the more astonished I became. Onboard the *Byeloostrov* we were on Russian territory; we had tickets for Leningrad and neither tickets nor reservations for London. Where was the reputedly meticulous surveillance by which the movements of foreigners, especially diplomats, would be checked and rechecked? The crestfallen countenance of the captain betrayed his chagrin. Every Russian who had handled our boarding had made the same mistake. It was our first lesson in Soviet inefficiency, to be repeated often during our time in Moscow. As for the children, "The Wrong Boat" became the title of class compositions for years thereafter.

Not long after our arrival in the Soviet capital, the Muscovites celebrated their eight-hundredth anniversary, bringing momentary color and gaiety to the otherwise uninterrupted grayness of the city and its people. The embassy, then housed in Mokhavaya, a building facing the great plaza leading to Red Square, looked out on the dancing, singing, and parading which made up the celebration. A thirty-foot-tall portrait of Stalin glared at us from the entrance to Red Square across the way; amidst the fireworks at night, and picked out by searchlights, were huge balloons, each bearing the mustachioed face of the great leader, scowling from the sky.

We learned that while most embassy personnel lived and worked in Mokhavaya, we were to inhabit a dacha (a tumbledown log cabin, it turned out to be) in the suburbs, near the Sheremeteev Palace in Ostankino. I paraphrase from a description that my wife and I wrote in 1952:

We bumped over cobblestones surrounding streetcar tracks and someone shouted, "That's it." The car veered sharply to the left, leapt through a sagging gate and there before our eyes it stood: "our" house. Built of logs, it had a glassed-in porch that hung tipsily from one side to another, and windows which also drooped and which, at some time or another, must have been painted blue. To our left we glimpsed a jumble of bushes, plants, and a few trees. There was a garage (the door was rotting but was to hold together for a few months) and a coal shed, and in a spot near the hanging front gate, a "potato house." The Russian name for it— *kartofelny dom*—reminds one of a cathedral, and it did have a sharp little spire sticking straight up out of the tip of a pointed roof. . . .

To the Russians, we lived in luxury; we were the only family to occupy our house. Most Russians lived in crowded apartments, several people in one room. A Russian friend of our son's came to the house but didn't want to play. Donald explained: "He says he just wants to sit and look at our beautiful house!"

There were always crises at the dacha. One happened whenever the axe handle broke. . . . The furnace, when it worked, ate up wood like a starved thing. No one could coax it to try coal. So when there was no axe handle, and therefore no axe, the fire went out and we all put on our coats and overloaded the power lines by turning on electric heaters and hot plates. This blew the fuses and blew out the heaters. By the time the carpenter, in his artisan-like way, had fashioned a new axe handle, we were almost, but not quite, getting accustomed to continuing, pervading chill. . . .

The night the kitchen caught fire we had been to a late party. We awakened to a peculiar, acrid odor. Little puffs of smoke hugged the ceiling above our beds and curled out between the wall boards separating us from the kitchen stove. We wrenched out the boards and poured water behind them. Russian houses are insulated with dried grass and Russian dried grass apparently catches fire like other dried grass. We thought about calling the fire department, which was just a few doors down the street, but the servants, aroused, were adamant: the firemen would tear down the house!

All services for foreign diplomats in Moscow were handled by a bureau in the Foreign Office called, for short, Burobin (pronounced like "Ciri, Ciri Bin"). When we wanted our cesspool emptied we called Burobin just as one would call Burobin for a cook, a dance orchestra for an Embassy party, tickets to the theater, or roof repair. A hefty, drably bundled woman was usually in charge of the cesspool operation. We were charged 27 rubles for each "load" carted away in a dirty green truck with a big tank and a long hose. Noting an absence of scrupulosity in calculating the amount due, Dorothy started counting the loads. One day, one of the employees engaged in this particular bit of foreign affairs asked if Dorothy wouldn't just sign for "three or four extra loads"—it would help her out a lot personally and why should the *Amerikanski posoltsvo* [embassy] mind?

One mixed protocol and makeshift. Because the dirt road to our house got a little uncertain during wintry parts of the year the agriculture attaché graciously lent us his shiny green jeep with red wheels which he could not get permission to use in the countryside. The jeep was more practical than our low-hung Studebaker. Dorothy discovered that she had to step high to get into the jeep and a long evening dress was hardly made for that exercise. Ever alert, our imaginative chauffeur (no American was ever allowed to pass a Russian driver's test so we had to hire a driver) produced a gasoline can and carefully painted it green. Whenever Dorothy was ready to mount or to alight, Leonya nimbly leapt out of the jeep, took the can from its resting place between the two front seats, swept around the front of the car, ceremoniously deposited the can in the proper place, and Dorothy made her entrance, or exit, as the case might be. The red-wheeled, curtained jeep and the green gasoline can became well known at the foreign embassies in Moscow!

The scarcity of embassy housing required the working-wives rule. No wife could accompany her husband to the post unless she agreed to take a full-time clerical position in the embassy. One or two wives were unavoidably declared "unemployable" but everyone else worked. Dorothy was assigned the commissary and as a special exception, because of the dacha, the distances, and the children, was permitted to serve half-time.

Russians employed by embassy families, supplied by the omnipotent Burobin, always had at least one strike against them, which made them vulnerable to state pressure. Two sisters, Maria and Hilda, worked for us, Volga Germans from families uprooted at the time of the war because no Germans were trusted. Leonya, the chauffeur, was of Polish ancestry and was a Roman Catholic; his father, an army officer, had been arrested in the purges of 1937 and had never been heard from again. No news was good news, according to Leonya, because he would have been notified if his father had died. Leonya was eighteen, a kid like our own, who enjoyed playing cops and robbers with the plainclothes police who followed us when we drove on the few country roads open for diplomats. One day, watching the little car in our rear-view mirror and getting ready to whisk off the road to fool our escorts, Leonya suddenly became serious: "The MVD is no joke!" Ded ("grandfather") Misch', the gardener-furnace man and fourth member of our entourage, was a Tatar, amiable, carefree, who disappeared to drink vodka for four days after every payday. When I left Moscow, I presented Ded Misch' with the scratchy, khaki, homespun suit that the Chinese Communists had presented to me in Yenan. He never knew that he had benefited from Mao Tse-tung's largesse.

After the children had learned enough Russian to get along, we decided to enroll them in Russian schools. I made a diplomatic demarche to the Soviet Foreign Office, requesting admission to the Bolshoi Ballet School for Dotty (one of George Kennan's daughters had studied ballet, setting a precedent) and applied to an appropriate primary school for Donald. In due course an official Foreign Office note to the embassy rejected the application to the Bolshoi for lack of openings but approved enrollment for both children in two ordinary schools within walking distance of the dacha. The student experience provided an entry into Russian society, which no one else in the embassy enjoyed.

The children adapted quickly to the Russian educational environment. They tried to look like Russians, act like Russians, and soon were speaking like Russians. Their teachers and classmates had never seen real American children. They were among the non-Russians, who were openly identified in their classes as "Ukrainian," "Byelo-Russian," "Kafkazki" (from the Caucasus), "Jewish," and "American." Instruction centered on the three *R*'s, with few frills. Working in the Russian alphabet influenced our children's handwriting for years afterward. Arithmetic was sound, more advanced than in a comparable American school. Poems and stories about "Papa Lenin" and "dear Stalin" were interspersed with traditional Russian fairy tales.

Don suffered more teasing from his classmates than did his sister, although he said little to us about it. We did hear about the opposing snow forts and the snowball fight. Members of the "enemy" force were shouting insults about "Amerikanski!"

We asked our son, "Did you shout back?"

He looked at us in consternation, "Of course not! Everybody else on *my* side was a Russian!"

My only personal association with Russians was at parent-teacher meetings, which I was allowed to attend. I found that I was not only the sole foreigner but also the only papa in a sea of mammas. The teacher at our daughter's school, Olga Nikolaevna, began the meeting by saying, "Now we will discuss the pupils." She started down the list, beginning with the child who was receiving the lowest marks, and continuing to discuss in detail the weaknesses and strengths of each pupil in ascending order of merit. One problem child lived in a home without a *babushka* ("grandmother"), in which both father and mother worked. Unsupervised after school, she ran wild. To my paternal pride, Olga Nikolaevna praised the little American girl, Dari, who had mothered her Russian classmate and helped to keep her out of mischief.

I was proud to accompany my son to his school and to confer with his teacher in Russian without an interpreter. We discussed, in his presence, his progress and his tendencies to look bored and seemingly to fall asleep in class. His teacher was a heavyset, determined woman and, after some conversation, looked me straight in the eye, "You know, of course, that your son speaks better Russian than you do!"

Life was never dull at the dacha. Our house and extensive yard became a playground for the neighbors' children and Don's and Dotty's classmates. I would push my way through them when I came home from the office. Leonya, entering into the fun, built a *shalash,* or lean-to playhouse, and a boxlike sled. We had animals: two cats—aristocratic, Siberian long-haired Vladimir from Vladivostok and plebeian, wayward Gravel Gertie, who turned up regularly with litters of kittens. Then there was our black Scottie, Tovarisch, a guinea pig, and assorted chickens. The children and their Russian friends would put on plays for us in the big attic. The climax of one production was little Lushka being borne in the air on the hands of Don and several of his stalwart boyfriends, waving an American flag, while everybody shouted: *"Da zdravstvuyet Kommunicheski Parti Lenina Stalina!"* ("Hail to the Communist Party of Lenin and Stalin!").

In the summer of 1973, twenty-four years after we had left the Soviet Union, my daughter and I made a trip to Moscow. Outside of Intourist control, we decided one Sunday afternoon to revisit the dacha at Ostankino. We found the street, paved and without streetcar tracks, and on the site of our house an ugly, barrackslike, government building now stood. The rest of the neighborhood was familiar. The same rundown, slightly leaning, unpainted, old wooden houses were there. Dotty, whose Russian had survived better than mine (reinforced by a summer at the 1959 U.S. Exhibition), approached a young man tinkering with an old car, to ask the whereabouts of her classmate Luisa. The youth was puzzled but suggested she ask the "old grandmother" next door. A few knocks on backdoors and an old lady, startled and squinting, peered out. Luisa? Very slowly recognition dawned. "But you are Dari! The American girl!" Smiles and tears burst out spontaneously. A young man appeared. One by one, others came out of neighboring houses. "Of course we remember you. We children all played together. But those were difficult times. Now, we can talk with you because there is détente. How is Don? He was my classmate!" The young man's eyes glistened; his words toppled over each other.

We asked, "How are Leonya and Hilda [we had heard they were married]? How is Lushka?" Questions and answers gushed out. One youngish woman said to my daughter, "But you're a singer. We heard you on the Voice of America!" Dotty had forgotten that years before she had been asked to sing and speak in Russian on a VOA program beamed to the Soviet Union. They promised Dotty to help track down other school friends; we pledged undying friendship all around, shook hands, and swore to keep in touch. Luisa's telephone number was produced, and the young man accompanied us to a public telephone booth to call her. But there was no answer. "She's out," he explained. "Try her tomorrow."

Dotty dialed Luisa's number many times, but the line was busy, or there was no answer. To inquire further, she returned alone to Ostankino the next day. Sunday's spontaneity, warmth, and good feeling were gone. The old woman appeared nervous and frightened; she hesitated to invite Dotty into the house. Perhaps Don's pal had been wrong about détente. Twenty-four years had made less difference than he thought.

Our assignment to Moscow coincided with a toughening of Soviet control over every aspect of life, which was designed to inculcate vigilance against foreign influence and to produce the pure Soviet man, uncontaminated by bourgeois culture. By a special decree of 1947 the most innocuous information had been declared secret, with penalties reaching twenty years in corrective labor camps being specified for unintentional revelation. Contacts between foreign and Russian officials were severely limited in early 1948, and travel by diplomats to most parts of the Soviet Union became impossible. However, Leningrad, Stalingrad, and Tiflis (Stalin was a Georgian) were accessible. The cultural purges, which gained momentum in 1948, affected biologists, economists, novelists, playwrights, composers, painters, and sculptors. Composers Shostakovitch and Khachaturian confessed their lapses into "formalism"; Prokofiev was more stubborn. Irreverent foreigners decided that for music to pass the test, Stalin had to be able to whistle it on his way home from the theater.

Foreigners in Moscow, isolated from the Russians, developed a siege mentality and in compensation, compulsively consorted with each other. Even a middle-ranking second secretary like myself found the mileage building up on the Studebaker—or the jeep—as we circulated to diplomatic luncheons, cocktail parties, and dinners. The American colony in Moscow consisted of the embassy personnel, a few journalists, and three fur buyers. Many others had valid claims to American citizenship but possessed dual nationality, were married to Russians, or for some other reason, could not leave the Soviet Union. The embassy would get heartrending letters from Americans in Armenia, Siberia, or other distant places, pleading for help to return to the United States. The Soviet bureaucracy was impervious to representations in such cases.

Our reaction to the oppressive, brooding Stalinism, which enveloped us, was to find an escape through our own forms of merriment and satire. Movies and dances in the great ballroom at Spaso House were a release for ourselves and our friends among the journalists and diplomats. Who among the Moscow-stationed foreigners of that period will ever forget Walter Cronkite, then a United Press correspondent, and Elbridge Durbrow, counselor of the embassy, dancing the "Skater's Waltz," hilariously choreographed in a series of slipping slides, pratfalls, and rolling tumbles? Or Nellie Stevens, wife of the naval attaché, singing about "rubies and diamonds and pearls" and pounding out piano ragtime? Even I got in on the act with my rendition of "When You and I Were Young, Maggie." Dick Service, Jack's younger brother, later became the embassy's balladeer-laureate, and his biting verses to familiar tunes became choruses at late-night parties or at the crowded ritual send-offs for departing embassy families at Leningrad station.

Another satire, which circulated among the foreign community like a premature underground *samizdat*, was written by Robert Magidoff, an able American correspondent who later was accused of espionage and expelled from the Soviet Union. In a period when "cosmopolitanism" was a synonym for "bourgeois decadence," he became intrigued with a poem our son had written called "The

Monkey Wrench" and wrote his piece as an "excerpt from a six-column editorial in *Literary Culture and Life,*" titling it "The Spiritual Tragedy of Donald Kenneth Emmerson." Part of it read:

The Monkey Wrench

I speak in German, I speak in French
   But to tell you the truth, I'm just a monkey wrench.

All I have for lunch is a bottle of punch
   But to tell you the truth, I'm just a monkey wrench.

I live in China, my cat's named Dinah,
   But to tell you the truth, I'm just a monkey wrench. . . .

Commentary:

The American poet, Donald Kenneth Emmerson, is a typical product of his age—the age of the decline of monopolistic capital in the United States, that last obstacle in humanity's march toward its crowning achievement: world communism. Just as a droplet of water reflects the entire sun, so does Emmerson's poem, "The Monkey Wrench," reflect the depraved psychology of the poet and his Muse. It is the psychology of an Imperialist. Influenced by the Marshall Plan which is seeking to catch in its net all of suffering, post-war Europe, the poem roams the world. "I speak German, I speak French," he says significantly, and "I live in China."
   Here is cosmopolitanism. . . .

Both Magidoff and Walter Bedell Smith, the ambassador, included the piece in their books, making "The Monkey Wrench" Don's first published work.

For me, one escape was the language, that Russian tongue that Turgenev eulogized: "In the days of doubts, in the days of oppressive reflections concerning the destinies of my native land, thou art my stay and my staff. O great, mighty, true and free Russian tongue: Wert thou not, how could one do ought but fall into depths at the sight of all that is taking place at home? But it is past all belief that such a tongue is given to any but a great people."

Senta introduced me to Russian. She was an Armenian girl who was permitted to teach a few embassy officers. She was svelte, had black eyes and black, bobbed hair and was possessed with wit, enthusiasm, and a dedication to defend and explain her country. We assumed that, like all Russians permitted to work for us, she reported to the police. Yet, in unguarded moments, a trace of cynicism showed through and at other times a revealing sadness, which she could not suppress, suggested Turgenev's lament. For instance, she once described to me, almost, but not quite, with a straight face, how a Soviet university professor would present *Hamlet* to his class in English literature as a tragedy growing out of the class struggle. Another time she spoke with ill-concealed pain about the crisis for Russia of the 1934 assassination of Sergei Kirov in Leningrad, a deed which, she dared not admit, had set off the long agony of Stalin's revenge.

The State Department taught us Russian so that we could read *Pravda* and *Izvestia,* a less than shining reward. For me, Russian became a key to the theater, to the glorious dramas of Gogol, Chekhov, and Ostrovsky, played to perfection by the great actors of the Moscow Art Theater (MXAT) and the Maliy. This vicarious participation in Russian life became a substitute for the realities of association and friendship with Russians. Our seats were invariably on the front row, where we could look directly into the faces of the players at a distance of a few feet. Our children were with us once for a performance of Gogol's *Dead Souls.* At moments in the play two of the leading actors became so fascinated with the rapt attention from two American youngsters that eye communication was established. On another occasion, at a performance of *Revizor (The Inspector General),* a uniformed, bemedaled Russian officer struck up a conversation with Donald and asked permission to hold him on his lap through an entire act.

Life in the embassy was punctuated by defections and disappearances. During the time of my service in Moscow, two American employees deserted: Annabelle Bucar, a tall, sinewy girl, born near Pittsburgh into a large, Czech immigrant family, and Sergeant James

M. McMillin, a twenty-one-year-old army code clerk and the son of an army officer known to Ambassador Smith. Both were lured by infatuation, rather than by ideology, but both wrote letters, duly published in the Soviet press, denouncing American warmongers and exploiters and professing their intentions to remain in the Soviet Union to struggle for peace and world prosperity. Annabelle, who married a light opera singer, wrote a book *The Truth About American Diplomats,* in which she identified the "anti-Soviet clique in the State Department" and the spying activities of Americans in the embassy. She wrote detailed, unflattering sketches of senior officers; Foy Kohler, counselor and later ambassador to Moscow, and I were chagrined to find ourselves omitted from Annabelle's thumbnail biographies.

More chilling were the disappearances of employees. One was our Russian telephone operator who received a warning and knew that once she left the embassy premises she would never return. She mustered courage and walked out through the iron gates. We never saw her again. Another was Alexander Dolgun, a handsome young man of twenty-two. He was a citizen of the United States but was claimed as Russian by Soviet authority. Alex had been brought to the USSR by his family at the age of nine. Caught by the war, his father, a Polish-born American technician, was drafted into the Red Army. Later Alex, a clean-faced, happy-go-lucky fellow, succeeded in getting a job with the American embassy and was a file clerk when I knew him in Moscow. On December 13, 1948, he went out to lunch and disappeared. I never heard of him again until I read his name in 1973 in Solzhenitsyn's *Gulag Archipelago.*

Alex luckily survived to reveal in a book his torture and suffering in prison from 1948 to 1956 and his detention in the Soviet Union until 1971. He writes bitterly about the lack of effectiveness of the American embassy in securing his release, ". . . All that was done for me by the U.S. Embassy then was a couple of letters of protest, one of which Sidorov [his inquisitor] had shaken maliciously in my face." In the atmosphere of 1948, the ambassador and senior officers believed that vigorous and repeated demands on behalf of an embassy employee would, in the eyes of the Soviet police, confirm his guilt, establish his status as an important agent, and intensify his punishment. The blood-curdling details of Dolgun's experience, read even at this distance in time, bring shudders of self-reproach to one who was a member of the embassy. Although I had no decision-making responsibility, was there anything that I could have done? Probably not, but a personal inquiry by the ambassador to Stalin or to Molotov conceivably might have helped. Certainly after Stalin's death in 1953, someone should have remembered Alex. Finally, it was a private word passed by Secretary of State William Rogers to Foreign Minister Gromyko in 1971, twenty-three years after Dolgun's arrest, which released him to return to the United States. While we were in Moscow, several Russian employees were arrested, never to be heard of again, and several Americans were expelled (Magidoff and an assistant naval attaché among them). Dolgun was the rare American who endured the gulag system for eight excruciating years.

Annabelle Bucar was not overly exaggerating when she called us all spies. She wrote that we in the embassy were ordered to use "every possible opportunity to obtain prejudiced information on the standard of living and morale of the Soviet people, data on industry and agriculture in the USSR, and so on." She was wrong to use the word *prejudiced.* We reported what we saw. In a country where reliable statistics were withheld and information routinely published in the United States was kept top secret, every scrap was grist for the intelligence mill. Finding a telephone directory was like discovering an original copy of the Gutenberg Bible. Most of us were amateurs; the CIA had been founded only in 1947 and was not yet in operation. We assumed that our houses were bugged, although it was several years later that a microphone was discovered, hidden in the great seal of the United States, in Ambassador George Kennan's office.

The longest trip I made in the Soviet Union was one of two weeks, covering more than four thousand miles by rail and by air, to Tiflis in the Georgian republic and to Stalingrad, with a two-day stopover at Saratov on the Volga. A younger, Russian-speaking embassy officer went with me, and together we collected enough information to make a thirty-page report. From the train windows we observed the height of grain plantings, crop conditions, draft animals (including camels near Stalingrad), soldiers repairing embankments, guns being loaded on flatcars, and counted planes on airfields. We meticulously recorded prices, finding that in Tiflis a man's cap cost $14, a motorcycle $420, and two cucumbers in a restaurant, $5.

The farther we got from Moscow, the easier it was to strike up casual conversations. The young factory foreman sharing our train compartment to Tiflis was warm and voluble, although he parroted what he read in *Pravda*. He protested that American military bases in nearby Turkey threatened his country, whereas the Soviets had no bases so close to the United States. His conversation touched on U.S. responsibility for deterioration of the good Soviet–American relations prevailing at the end of the war; Roosevelt's virtues versus Truman's vices; the Negro question; Bucar's book; and a theme we heard many times, "Who wants war?" He asked this question as he pointed to the still-visible signs of devastation outside the car window.

We encountered the only criticism of the regime, and at the same time gained a sense of the friction between Georgians and Russians, in a conversation with a Russian woman we met in the confined quarters of a gondola car on an aerial funicular near Tiflis. Since the three of us were literally for a time suspended in air, she could talk freely. She was disgruntled in Georgia; she thought things must be better in the United States under a system based on the individual instead of on communism. She wanted to move from Tiflis, she said, because "here we are aliens."

We concluded from our trip, made in May 1949, that "the present state of the Soviet economy is still so weak and disorganized that it is difficult to see how any realistic policy would favor war at this time" and that "there is general popular support of the present regime and little dissatisfaction with government policies."

My embassy job was to watch the Far East. There was nothing I could do or say about China, although I was later, with others, to be accused of "losing" it. The news reported one Communist advance after another until, by October 1949, the victors were able to proclaim the founding of the People's Republic of China.

As for Japan, we had been, as I have said, discussing a peace treaty since early 1947. The United States proposed a peace conference and set the date for August 19. The Soviet Union objected, insisting on a prior meeting of the Council of Foreign Ministers of the United States, USSR, China (then still under the Kuomintang), and Great Britain. The Soviet press denounced the unilateral action of the United States in initiating peace treaty negotiations and revived its accusations that the "American protectors of Japanese imperialists are planning to use Japan as a barrier against Soviet influence." My newly acquired Moscow view of the world had made me skeptical of the advantages of an early peace treaty. In December 1947 I drafted a telegram which sequentially listed Soviet objectives in East Asia (Communist domination of Korea, China, Southeast Asia, and eventually Japan) and concluded that either an early end to Occupation or a peace treaty boycotted by the Soviet Union would be dangerous. Three months later, in March of 1948, George Kennan was recommending the same thing to the secretary of state: "We should not press for a peace treaty." Negotiations were indeed postponed, due to objections by both the Chinese and Russians, and when the treaty was concluded, five years later, representatives not only of Moscow, but of the two Chinese regimes, in Peking and in Taipei, were absent from the peace table.

More than a quarter of a century later, it is difficult to comprehend how seriously we took the threat of a Russian–American conflict. Those years (1947–49) were the years of the Truman Doctrine, the Marshall Plan, Kennan's "containment" proposal, the establishment of the Cominform, the Communist seizure of Czechoslovakia, the Berlin blockade and the Allied airlift, the expulsion of Yugoslavia from the Cominform, the signing of the North Atlantic Treaty, the explosion of the Soviet atomic bomb, and the Communist victory in China.

On March 5, 1948, General Lucius Clay, U.S. commander in Berlin, sent a telegram, which in Defense Secretary Forrestal's words, had the "force of a blockbuster bomb." Using Ambassador Grew's phrase of 1941, Clay warned that war "may come with dramatic suddenness." Tension begat tension, and action provoked response. Marshall Shulman, an outstanding American Soviet specialist and one of my wartime associates in the China–Burma–India theater, later wrote, "There is an element of tragic irony in the way in which Soviet superiority in armed forces and Western superiority in nuclear weapons and long-range aircraft, instead of creating a military equilibrium in this period, led to an interacting spiral of mutual anxiety and rearmament."

In this atmosphere, a joint intelligence committee, of which I was made chairman, was set up in the embassy in early 1948 to study Soviet intentions for war or for peace. The committee included members from the political, economic, and information sections of the embassy as well as representatives of the offices of the army, navy, and air attachés. We produced a fifty-five page, top-secret report, which was sent to Washington on April 1, concluding that "the Soviet Union will not deliberately resort to military action in the immediate future but will continue to attempt to secure its objectives by other means." We went on to state that conditions impelling a decision for war "might arise this year but they are far more likely to develop between one and two years from now." In trying to analyze what might force the Soviets to initiate war, we became caught up in the contradiction of cause and effect. On the one hand, the prospect of a future disadvantageous increase in the military strength of the United States and Western Europe could lead to a Soviet judgment that *immediate* war would serve Moscow's interest. On the other hand, we estimated, the Kremlin might *defer* military action "if confronted by such a rapid and positive growth of United States and Western Europe strength, particularly during 1948, as to convince the Soviet government that the outcome of war would be doubtful." In other words, a *rapid and positive* buildup *particularly during 1948* might deter the Soviets *but* its prospect might impel them to immediate action. A desk officer in the State Department, commenting on our dispatch, wrote with some justification: "The conclusions ... are not clear cut."

We estimated that Soviet military forces, in 1948, totaled 4.1 million men (Khrushchev, in 1960, put the figure at 2.87 million), that they could take continental Europe, the Middle East, and key areas of Asia "within a few months," and could hold Europe for at least two years before the United States and her Allies could attempt a continental invasion. Neither the Soviet Union nor the United States had the capacity to launch extended strategic air operations against the territory of the other, although the United States could deliver the atomic weapon, of which it still had a monopoly, to Russian targets from bases in England. The army's prediction that the Soviets would have the bomb by 1952 was off by three years; they produced their first explosion in July 1949. Soviet naval strength was far inferior to that of either the United States or England; Stalin is supposed to have said in February 1948: "We have no navy." Our report concluded that, in spite of the inefficiency and weakness of the Soviet economy, it could be controlled to support a war, although at an enormous cost in living standards. In assessing morale, we tried to balance the power of the state's propaganda machine against the war-weariness of the Russian people and their vulnerability to discontent. We decided that one should never underestimate Russian morale when the country was under attack nor overestimate it when internal problems were the focus of national attention.

In trying to assess the chances of war, we in the embassy faced a classic dilemma of forecasters. The Japanese in 1941, in spite of their patent inferiority in war potential, decided to attack, before their enemy further outdistanced them and their position became untenable. Would the Soviets do likewise? By 1948 we and our Russian adversaries had already entered an escalating competition. The burning question was whether Stalin, observing an alerted America, reviving political and economic stability in Europe, and a strengthening Atlantic military alliance, would resort to war against a perceived threat or would look to his own defenses. I could never believe Stalin would initiate war. The trip to Georgia had convinced me that the secret that he had to hide was Soviet weakness, not strength. In the end Stalin took, for him, the sensible course: his genuine fear of the bomb led him toward furiously intensive concentration on research and development and to an all-out arms buildup. On our side, the course of ascending military budgets began and the race was on.

In the course of preparing our report, an event occurred which was to beset me in later years. We held our committee meetings in a small library on the third floor of the chancery. I kept pertinent classified documents in a black binder, used for reference purposes at the time we foregathered but otherwise stored in a combination safe. One day in early March, when I went to get the binder from the safe, it was not there. We searched every office in the chancery but failed to find the papers.

Responsibility for guarding secret documents is a cross a foreign service officer must bear, and absent-mindedness is one of my congenital defects. I could not remember what I had done with this document, which ordinarily and invariably I placed in the safe after use. I had probably left it in the library after one of our meetings. In those days we had no Marine security guards in the embassy; senior officers took turns making inspection rounds after hours, and one of us slept in the code room at night (where we often took telephone calls from heavy-breathing females). A Russian cleaning woman swept and dusted the offices in the morning before the embassy opened for business, and I am convinced that this janitress—an ample, friendly, grandmotherly, accommodating lady—purloined my book and turned it over to a grateful KGB, deep in whose files it reposes today.

I can never forget the torment which gripped me when I discovered the document was missing. I walked downstairs, out the front gates, and slowly around the long block, trying to contemplate what I had done. Very fleetingly the thought passed through my mind that I could say nothing to anyone at all. Originals of the documents were all in the embassy files; the ones lost were my own and for use in the committee. If I said nothing, the loss would never be known. Immediately, however, the thought of a life-long turmoil of conscience made this unthinkable. I returned to tell Foy Kohler, the officer who shared my safe, and we instituted the search which was to prove fruitless. The ambassador was stern, but, in lecturing the staff on security vigilance, recalled an instance in which, as secretary of the Combined Chiefs of Staff, he had misplaced a document that was so secret only one copy existed. He had drawn a total blank and only after three days' search was it discovered that he had given the top-secret paper to a fellow officer who had it safely in his possession.

The contents of the folder were committee minutes and a 1946 embassy report on Soviet strengths and weaknesses, including no so-called hard intelligence, of which we possessed practically none. Since George Kennan had already (in July 1947) published his "Mr. X" article, on "The Sources of Soviet Conduct," the 1946 report could have revealed little new to the Russians on the trend of policy thinking among official Americans. Bedell Smith was later to write that "there were few messages which we exchanged with the Department of State that I would not willingly have shown on request to the Soviet Foreign Minister." All of this however, did not mitigate for me my sense of professional dereliction over the security breach for which I had been responsible.

In September 1948 I was assigned to the U.S. delegation to the General Assembly of the United Nations, then meeting in Paris. The department's motives for the appointment were twofold: first, to give me a breather from the stifling atmosphere of Moscow; and second, to fill a delegation slot reserved for a Soviet expert. Not that my expertise was remarkable, but more than a year's exposure to life in the Communist capital had given me a certain feel for Soviet behavior. Dorothy joined me later, and together we luxuriated in the freedom and spine-tingling wonderment of Paris. Our good friends, Brewster and Ellen Morris, took care of our children at the dacha, and we returned in time for Christmas.

The night before I left Moscow we saw *The Cherry Orchard* at the MXAT. In the last act, the grand lady who has lost her orchard is emotionally preparing to return to Paris, while the sound of axes cutting down the cherry trees reverberates in the background. Her servant says with glee, "In six days I'll be in Paris."

I whispered to Dorothy, "Tomorrow I'll be in Paris!" For me, it was the first return to that great city of my boyhood dreams since I had left in 1928 as a youth of twenty. Even though Paris was but three years removed from war and was partially paralyzed by strikes, the sight of the streets and the taxis and the Place de la Concorde brought all my sentimentality welling up, and there were tears in my eyes.

Andrei Vyshinsky was the evil star of the 1948 General Assembly. His white mane bobbed to the eloquent invective he spat out at imperialists, capitalists, and warmongers. World events were crowding each other: the Palestine question; the future of the new Israel; the crisis of the Berlin blockade; and the infant monster—the atomic weapon. Free world delegates were seriously questioning whether Europe could stand up to the menace of militant communism. It was the time that the French Communist party was exhorting its members to join the enemy and fight against their own country if France should be attacked by the Soviet Union.

Fresh from Moscow, I was full of facts and figures. I agreed with those who felt that Soviet intentions were not well understood. Drawing on material we had collected in the embassy, I wrote a speech for Senator Warren Austin, chief of the U.S. delegation, and another for Frederick Osborn, deputy U.S. representative to the UN Atomic Energy Commission. Austin's speech, delivered October 12, has been called by some the first cold war speech made to the United Nations by an American delegate. If so, I hold the dubious honor for its inspiration. Both speeches described the nature of the iron curtain, detailed the extent of Soviet war preparations, and outlined the principles which guided Marxist–Leninist policy. The issue was an arms control resolution proposed by the United States; in those days of our "automatic majority," as charged by the Russians, we won the vote 46 to 6.

Another agenda item with which I was involved was the problem of the Soviet wives of foreigners who were prevented from leaving the Soviet Union. The foreign husbands of Soviet citizens faced a choice: to abandon their wives in Moscow or to stick it out with them. Most of them elected to remain and joined an unhappy little colony. We introduced this question in the Human Rights Committee, and Eleanor Roosevelt argued eloquently against Vyshinsky and Jacob Malik, demanding compassionate consideration for these Soviet women. Eventually, all were permitted to accompany or to join their husbands abroad.

Outside of the long hours spent in committee and plenary sessions, in our own delegation meetings, in drafting speeches and memoranda, and in floor-walking activities to cultivate and persuade our friends, I found time to become reacquainted with the Paris of my student days. I found Monsieur and Madame Couderc, who twenty years before had taken me into their home on rue de Babylone. They had aged: their lameness was more pronounced, and Madame, as ever, corrected my French. I met their sons, now grown and married, who talked much about their wartime suffering and about France's continuing tribulations.

By the summer of 1949 our two years in Moscow were up. The tight, closed society in which we were forced to live made us eager for our transfers when they came. Dorothy, especially, suffered in Moscow. Depressed by the atmosphere of fear and suspicion around us, she was yet responsible for maintaining a tumbledown house, caring for two active, developing children, dealing with inefficient and untrustworthy servants, meeting the obligations of a frantic social, diplomatic life, and at the same time carrying on her job at the embassy commissary. The requirements, it could be said with understatement, went beyond the call of official duty.

Finally, our day came to leave and the clan gathered at Leningrad station. Only this time *we* were the departing travelers. Russian passengers and railway guards looked on disapprovingly as we sang lustily and defiantly. There were lumps in our throats, though. We had made fast, life-long friends in Moscow; we would ever feel the closeness of the Moscow crowd. Also within me was an affection for Russians, for these deep-feeling, spiritual, boisterous, exuberant, poetic, and sly Slavs, whom I had read about, seen on the stage, passed in the streets, but had never known. The four of us stood in the corridor of the old *wagon-lit* railroad car, our faces pressed against the windows, waving to our friends whose transfers were yet to come and hearing the fading strains of the singing as the train gathered momentum:

> *We will serenade our transfers*
> *While life and voice shall last;*
> *Then we'll pass and be forgotten*
> *With the rest.*

12

McCarthyism—The Aftermath

The time was December 30, 1951, and the place, New York. I had been assigned by the State Department to join our delegation to the UN General Assembly then meeting in Paris. The Korean question was up, and I was to be an adviser during its discussion. The family was with me to enjoy holiday festivities in the great city before I flew to Paris. This evening, we had studio tickets to watch one of the popular audience participation television shows of the day, "Beat the Clock," in which couples would be induced to come on stage to perform ridiculous antics within time limits set by a ticking clock. Just before we were to leave the hotel to go to the theater, the telephone rang, and Alex Johnson, then assigned to the State Department, was calling from Washington. "It's your old friend Gene Dooman. He's after you. You'd better cancel your flight to Paris and come back here." I was jolted but decided to say nothing to spoil the evening. I tried outwardly to respond to the hilarity produced by the self-conscious participants and the clowning of the master of ceremonies, Bud Collyer. When I later told the children that I was not going to Paris after all, they were gleeful, and we drove back to Washington to celebrate New Year's Eve.

In the department on January 2, I was presented with a letter dated December 29, which, citing various laws and regulations, informed me that I was being charged with violating the established standards of loyalty and security. Failure to rebut the charges would cause my removal from employment by the Department of State. The letter specified eight allegations (additional ones were added later). Principally, I was accused of having been sympathetic to communism in China and Japan, of having associated with Communists in those countries, of having written reports "slanted" in favor of Chinese Communists and "colored" in sympathy with Japanese Communists, and of basically possessing "a close affinity for the Communist cause."

Much water had flowed over dams since we had left Moscow in the summer of 1949. I had been assigned to return to Washington to spend a year at the National War College. Graduation, which took place in late June 1950, coincided with the North Korean march across the thirty-eighth parallel. I went immediately to work in the State Department as planning adviser in the Bureau of Far Eastern Affairs, then under Assistant Secretary Dean Rusk.

At the War College we had the privilege of listening to a parade of distinguished military and civilian leaders, including cabinet secretaries, scientists who had made atomic bombs, academics of varying ideological views, journalists, officials, and Margaret Mead. We had time to read and to write. From my freshly absorbed Moscow viewpoint, I wrote a paper on Stalin looks east and west, analyzing "Comparative Communist Policies in Europe and the Far East." Research enabled me to read Lenin and Stalin as I had not done before, and to evaluate the power of Stalin's dual thrusts toward "socialism in one country" and "world revolution." Revolutions had failed in both Germany (1923) and China (1927), but communism's problems in Asia and Europe were perceptibly different. Mao Tse-tung had said that the Chinese revolution would develop "under the sole leadership of the Communist party of China."

"To the Kremlin," I wrote, "China is an epic, Eastern Europe, a colonial report." I conceded that the Chinese Communists had, up until October 1949, supported faithfully and without exception the Soviet line in foreign policy. Still, remembering our doubts of

Russian control over Yenan in 1944, I believed that continued Chinese acceptance of the dictates of Moscow was doubtful. If the Soviets should exhibit heavy-handedness in their policies toward China, "there would develop a party split which could eventuate only in a Soviet-dictated purge or in successful defiance of the Kremlin by a Chinese Tito."

In the fall and winter of 1949–50, the recognition of a Communist government in China was still an arguable question. Acting in our irresponsible status as War College students, we staged a formal debate—Resolved: That the United States Should Recognize Communist China. Two military colleagues and I presented the affirmative case. Since we expected Taiwan to fall momentarily, we were not worrying about the existence of two Chinas. I had learned at Georgetown that, to be recognized, a state should possess and control its territory. Whether you liked the government or not was immaterial. This view was not, however, universally shared, especially among members of the U.S. Congress. Recognition would probably have been politically impossible, even if the State Department had recommended it, which it had not. Furthermore, the Chinese were not particularly cooperative. Their mistreatment of Angus Ward, the American consul general in Mukden, received widespread publicity. He related his experiences to us at the War College with passion born out of bruises. Recognition of Communist China was not to be, and the long twenty-three years of noncommunication, war (both hot and cold), and attempted containment began.

Our preoccupation at the War College was with the Soviet Union and the struggle against communism. While we were contemplating the world from our cloistered halls, the Soviet Union set off its first nuclear device, the debate over our development of the H-bomb began, China became Communist, and war in Korea climaxed our graduation. Would the Russians attempt the war we had considered in Moscow? George Kennan talked to us about the changes which were inherent and inevitable in the Soviet system.

Secretary of State Dean Acheson, in a memorable address to us, on December 21, 1949, emphasized the limitations of power, a truth that impressed me more the longer I followed my foreign service career. He said, "The proper search is for limited ends. . . . to get ourselves away from the absolute, to find out what is within our powers." Acheson went on to preach the doctrine of coexistence with our opponents, although he did not call it that, "We must understand that for a long, long period of time they will continue to believe as they do, and that for a long, long period of time we will both inhabit this spinning ball in the great void of the universe." In the words of Acheson's biographer, the secretary meant that he "did not agree that the conflict could be resolved by a resort to war."

From June 1950 on the Bureau of Far Eastern Affairs was seized with Korea. I found myself attending the constant meetings endemic to bureaucrats and drafting innumerable papers, some of which in revised and re-revised form became part of National Security Council (NSC) documents. I worked closely with friends in the Pentagon, and we frequently collaborated on top-secret papers, which our respective departments would receive for review and approval. General MacArthur was a constant irritant, acting repeatedly on his own, without consulting or even informing Washington. He assured President Truman at Wake Island on October 15 that the Chinese would not come into the war. Yet Chou En-lai had told the Indian ambassador in Peking, K. M. Pannikar, at a midnight meeting on October 2, that if United States forces crossed the thirty-eighth parallel and advanced toward the Yalu River, China would enter the war. Pannikar, like Krishna Menon, the long-time Indian representative at the United Nations, was so thoroughly disliked by American government officials who had had to deal with him officially, that no one had confidence in his word. As a result, we disregarded Chou's clear warning.

As a planning adviser, I made one or two unsuccessful attempts to divert some attention from Korea to Indochina. In 1950 and 1951 the French were obdurate in refusing to set a date for independence. I proposed that we urge the French to prepare Indochina for a peaceful transition to independence in order to avert an otherwise certain catastrophe. When my memorandum reached the Bureau of European Affairs (EUR), it raised the roof. Put pressure on our French allies? Impossible. "We cannot rock the boat and jeopardize the solidarity of NATO." Thus, the paper died a quick death. Seeds of the Vietnam war were already beginning to germinate, and actions taken then might have forestalled the tragedy that was to come.

While I was absorbed in Korea, other things were happening that would seriously affect my future. The cold war was turning the national spotlight on communism. President Truman, in March 1947, had by executive order established standards and procedures for the investigation of the loyalty of government employees. On February 9, 1950, Senator Joseph R. McCarthy of Wisconsin made his famous speech to a women's Republican club in Wheeling, West Virginia, during which he "held in his hand" a list of Communists in the State Department. Whether he said there were 205, 81, 57, or a lot became a matter of dispute since no text of his remarks ever became available. Ironically, the idea of communism as a profitable political issue was suggested to the senator by my old Georgetown mentor, Father Edmund A. Walsh. At dinner at the Colony Club in Washington, McCarthy was searching for a dramatic issue for the 1952 election campaign. Father Walsh suggested communism, its power in the world, and its capacity for subversion. McCarthy jumped at the idea, "The government is full of Communists. We can hammer away at them."

In the four short years of the senator's activity, "McCarthyism" swept the country as no "ism" had done before. Joseph and Stewart Alsop were probably right in calling it a "by-product of the Cold War." While McCarthy's attacks became random and wide-ranging, the State Department, particularly its China hands, were central targets of his assaults. The loss of China was fresh in the popular mind and was a concept that the man in the street could understand. The revelation of the names of guilty Americans offered the satisfaction of revenge. The secretary of state himself, Dean Acheson, was labeled Communist; thus, a department whose head was under fire could hardly protect its employees with confident vigor. The department reacted by a fierce determination, expressed in mixed metaphors, to oust the "bad apples" and to assure that its employees were "as clean as a hound's tooth."

By August of 1950 Congress had enacted a law, authorizing heads of government agencies to suspend or dismiss employees on security grounds. During 1951 more detailed regulations were promulgated by the Department of State to provide for the issuance of charges, hearings before a Loyalty Security Board, and review by a Loyalty Review Board. Two standards were established, one for loyalty and another for security. Under the first, an employee could be dismissed on grounds that "a reasonable doubt" existed as to his loyalty to the government of the United States. Under the security standard, the secretary of state could fire an employee by finding that his removal was "necessary or advisable in the interest of national security."

From documents in my security file (made available under the Privacy Act of 1974), I discovered that the FBI had, on October 20, 1950, initiated a full field loyalty investigation of me and that evaluations of me and of my activities had been solicited from friends and associates by the FBI, the State Department's Security Division, and the Department of the Army. My name had, of course, already been publicly linked with China-specialist colleagues, particularly John Davies and John Service, and had been included in hostile testimony given by General Patrick J. Hurley in 1945. I had, however, received little attention in the press, and, so far as I knew, Senator McCarthy never discovered me as a candidate for his list. As a result of the FBI investigation, the department's Loyalty Security Board decided, on April 19, 1951, to hold hearings and the result was the letter to me of December 29.

Of the reports amassed by the FBI at that time, with names of informants obliterated, most were favorable. One critical communication from Major General Charles A. Willoughby, General MacArthur's chief of intelligence (G-2), dated March 3, 1951, contained twenty-seven enclosures, and was fifty-five pages in length. The general's covering letter reported that there was little to be gained from investigations in his theater (Japan) since "the persons who know or knew Emmerson are the same persons who defended his friend and colleague, John Stewart Service, when we ran a similar investigation last year." Willoughby wrote that the enclosures would "paint a picture" of one of Emmerson's main activities while in Japan, namely, that of expediting the return to Japan of such well-known Communists as Nosaka Sanzō and Kaji Wataru. The enclosures included copies of my reports, long descriptions of Japanese antiwar activities in China (not written by me), correspondence relating to Nosaka and Kaji, and documents dated as late as April 1946, two months after my departure from Japan, and with which I had no connection. Willoughby's letter expressed the belief that I was the one who "fit into the larger picture" (obviously a shady one), which included such associates as John Service, Herbert Norman, John K. Fairbank (the present dean of Chinese studies at Harvard), and Tsuru Shigetō, a Japanese scholar–diplomat I had known during the Occupation.

Meanwhile, my China friends, one by one, were being called for hearings before loyalty and security boards in the department. I was inspired in the summer of 1951 to write an editorial for the *Foreign Service Journal,* anonymously of course, which I called "Career vs. Conscience." It attracted some attention and was featured by the *Providence* (R.I.) *Journal* which reprinted the text in toto and wrote a supportive editorial called "McCarthyism's Fruit." My point was the dilemma facing the foreign service officer: should he report fearlessly "as he sees it," or should he resign from the service to seek fields where his talents would be less circumscribed and his future less in peril? I declared bluntly:

> Courage is needed, on the part of the Department and of the Government. If there are disloyal members among us, no one will resist their removal forthwith. But if the rest of us are loyal, let the Department have the courage to defend our loyalty and to reaffirm a creed of the Foreign Service—to serve to best of ability, to observe keenly, to report what is seen and heard and felt, without inhibition, fear, or mental reservation—to know our enemies as well as to cultivate our friends, and to pursue as best we can the honorable profession we have chosen, in the constant and undeterred conviction that ours is the first line of defense of our country.

At about the same time Herblock, the famous *Washington Post* cartoonist, published a caricature of a foreign service officer writing a report while an unshaven, burly character labeled "Smear Threat" sits with his feet on the officer's desk, holding a long stick with which he prepares to dump a hanging bucket of mud on the perspiring head of the officer. The caption read: "Feel Free to Write Whatever You Want."

Washington's morning papers of September 15 carried the headline: DOOMAN SAYS LEFT-WINGERS RAN JAP POLICY. Among the left-wingers named were Dean Acheson, Owen Lattimore, John Carter Vincent, John K. Fairbank, and John K. Emerson (misspelled as usual). Eugene Dooman, my boss from prewar Tokyo days and superior in the department in 1945, had testified the day before in a session of the McCarran Committee, then investigating the Institute of Pacific Relations. Much of his testimony was a denunciation of American policy toward Japan in the period following his own resignation in August 1945. Encouraged and abetted by Senator James Eastland of Mississippi, Dooman described the Acheson-Vincent policies for postwar Japan as being identical to those imposed by Russia on the satellite nations of Eastern Europe. The purges, the dissolution of the *zaibatsu* ("industrial combines"), and the land reform—all elements in American occupation policy—were directed, in Dooman's opinion, to the destruction of the capitalist class in Japan.

Later in the hearing Dooman got around to me. Supposedly, in 1945 I had returned to Washington from China to recommend that Japanese prisoners of war held in the United States should be "turned over to Japanese Communists in the United States for indoctrination along methods used by the Japanese Communists in Yenan." Furthermore, I had brought back posters and other materials from Yenan, including letters, which I had shown Dooman, addressed to certain Japanese employed by the Office of Strategic Services (OSS), who, according to Dooman, were Communists. His most dramatic revelation was the story, admitted by him to be hearsay, that, on October 10, 1945, in Tokyo, Herbert Norman and I had driven the released Communist leaders to their homes, so enhancing their prestige that one hundred thousand new members joined the Japanese Communist party.

I wrote to Mr. Dooman, recalling our previous friendly relations and expressing surprise at his charges. I explained that Norman and I had met the Communist political prisoners at Fuchū Prison before their release by MacArthur's order and that we and other SCAP officers had interrogated them at headquarters, the official reports of which meeting were on record. Dooman replied, confirming that he had supported my POW indoctrination and psychological warfare proposals made in the department in the spring and summer of 1945 and that he "at that time" had had no anxieties about me. He added that, subsequent to retirement, "information kept coming to me from firsthand sources, which required me to take a different view of your wartime and postwar activities." After including the secretary of state among those whose policies he disapproved, Dooman ended his letter, "I can only recommend that you who share in varying degrees responsibility for the present dangerous posture of affairs in the Far East manifest your sense of responsibility in a manner that would be appreciated with respect by decent people." I sent a copy of the correspondence to Ambassador Grew, then in retirement, who had been very close to Dooman in the prewar period and in 1945. My first chief in the foreign service replied graciously; "I myself never lacked confidence in you and I am glad that you have set forth the facts with regard to Mr. Dooman's charges."

Five days after Dooman's appearance, General Wedemeyer testified before the McCarran Committee. During his comments on American policy in China, Wedemeyer responded to questions by Robert Morris, special counsel to the committee, on his four political advisers—John Davies, John Service, Raymond Ludden, and John Emmerson. After expressing disagreement with our reports, as commendatory to communism, the general was asked bluntly by Senator Ferguson whether his political advisers were "disloyal to the government and the policy that we had there?"

Wedemeyer replied: "I cannot answer that question sir. Honestly, I cannot answer it. But I can say this: if I had followed their advice, communism would have run rampant over China much more rapidly than it did."

My relations with General Wedemeyer had been cordial and warm; he had sent me a very flattering letter of commendation after my service with him. I wrote to him, expressing dismay at the implications of his testimony and reminding him that my concern in his theater had been with Japanese affairs and that I had not made recommendations with respect to China. The general replied in a friendly tone, "You may be certain, John, that I have never maliciously harmed any individual much less men who served me faithfully and loyally." He enclosed a letter to the McCarran Committee which, in his words, attempted to clarify some discrepancies in his previous testimony. The letter stated that my responsibilities had been confined to political reporting, intelligence, and psychological warfare, with respect to Japan. "Therefore, remarks that I have made or testimony submitted pertaining to reports on China from political advisers on my staff do not pertain to him [Emmerson]." Nevertheless, when his book *Wedemeyer Reports* was published, the old charge was left intact.

By December 1951 the Loyalty Security Board was ready to schedule hearings. Foreign service friends advised me to obtain legal counsel. It would be expensive, but the experience of others who had tried to defend themselves alone had been less than satisfactory. I hired a Washington attorney, Bennett Boskey, who was sympathetic but entirely businesslike and thorough to the point of exasperation. We decided that I must lay my entire life before the board. If my reports were alleged to be slanted and colored toward communism, then every report I had written during my seventeen years of service had to be dug out of the files and submitted to my judges' scrutiny. As I delved into the archives, my amazement rose at how prolific a reporter I had been.

By the charges I was assumed to be guilty, and it was my job to prove innocence. At Boskey's insistence, we sought testimony, by personal appearance or by affidavit, from every individual I could think of who had associated with me and knew something of my activities during my foreign service career. It was an unpleasant experience to have to ask colleagues and former superiors to respond to a long list of charges which questioned my loyalty to the United States. In the end, twenty-three witnesses testified personally in my favor, and more than 150 exhibits were submitted, including 57 affidavits and statements. The hearings, before a board composed of three State Department officers, occupied eleven days, spread over the period from February 26 to April 18, 1952.

The allegations related to my service in China and Japan between 1943 and 1946 and centered on the accusation that I had possessed a "close affinity" for communism, which had inspired me to acts and writings directed to the furtherance of the Communist cause. In addition to questions concerning my so-called leftist attitudes, pro-communist reports, and my numerous contacts with Japanese and Chinese Communists, the board alleged that I had clandestinely transmitted letters from Japanese to American Communists, that I had recommended that Japanese Communists democratize Japanese POWs in American hands, that I had aided and sponsored the release of Japanese political prisoners at the end of the war, that I had personally arranged the return of Nosaka Sanzō, the Japanese Communist leader, from China to Japan by military aircraft of the Air Transport Command, and that I had been responsible for a security breach in Moscow.

The hearings, closed and confidential, opened in a room in the building then known as New State. I was in the prisoner's dock, accompanied by Bennett Boskey, facing the three-man board and its counsel, an officer of the Department's Division of Security. This court would admit into evidence rumors, hearsay, and anonymous reports. My feelings were strange. This was a new experience; I was on trial—for my job and, in reality, for my life up to that point. Yet, at the same time I could not suppress a kind of perverted pleasure that all these man-hours were being expended by busy officials on me and what I had done. How could I be that important?

Eugene Dooman appeared initially on February 26, and his testimony and questioning occupied the entire day, from 10:00 A.M. until 3:45 P.M., with a short break for lunch. He was the only adverse witness to testify at the hearings, and because his charges were based on hearsay and because his bitterness and his bias against postwar State Department policy were so transparent, his agreement to come in person proved of great benefit to me. He conceded at the beginning that he had had no suspicion of my personal philosophy until a year or more after his retirement when an army officer friend who had been assigned to General MacArthur's headquarters told him that there were "a number of queer birds" in the State Department section of SCAP, one of whom was Emmerson.

Dooman was a brilliant foreign service officer, with a solid knowledge of Japan and Japanese. The role he played with Ambassador Grew in the months before Pearl Harbor was impressive, as I have noted in earlier chapters. I consistently supported the Grew–Dooman thesis that the emperor should be retained in postwar Japan. My reports from China and India in 1944 and 1945, calling for a "statement to Japan," fit exactly into Dooman's thinking, which belatedly produced the Potsdam Proclamation. Although in the hearings, he dismissed my efforts as inconsequential and professed to forget our meeting upon my return from CBI in February 1945, he recalled that he had supported my projects for indoctrinating Japanese prisoners of war and for establishing a free Japanese organization. He characterized me as an impulsive young man, who had been aroused by the conditions he had found in Yenan and by the enthusiasm and success of the Japanese Communists.

My counsel asked Dooman whether it was important for the State Department to know that the Communists had succeeded in changing Japanese attitudes:

> Dooman: Yes.
> Boskey: In view of the very widespread belief that it is almost impossible to change the attitude of the Japanese?
> Dooman: Yes.
> Boskey: And it was a proper thing for Mr. Emmerson to report that to the department?
> Dooman: Quite.
> Boskey: And because you thought that there was some possibility of the method of indoctrination being put to good use, you supported the project?
> Dooman: That is right.
> Boskey: And you joined with Mr. Emmerson in supporting the project?
> Dooman: That is right.
> Boskey: You never had any doubts about the project at the time?
> Dooman: At the time, no.

Boskey: Did you ever have any doubts about your free
            Japanese project?
Dooman: No, not at the time.

Dooman's change of mind must have begun at the time of his resignation from the department on August 31, 1945. His antagonism toward Dean Acheson and John Carter Vincent already had been building up. At a State-War-Navy Coordinating Committee (SWNCC) meeting, after a report by Dooman on Occupation policy, Acheson is reported to have sneered, "... These Far Eastern experts are a penny a dozen...." Sometime in 1950 I met Dooman at a dinner meeting of the Council on Foreign Relations in New York. He launched into a tirade against Dean Acheson; U.S. policy in Japan during the previous six years had been a complete failure; "Dean Acheson more than anyone else was responsible for the mistakes and failures of this government in the Far East."

In another part of his testimony, Dooman said of me, "... All I know, he [Emmerson] was in Tokyo ... sometime after the surrender, and so far as I know, so far as I recall from what was told me, he threw himself body and soul in support of these directives coming from Washington, which I thought were destructive of the interest of the United States." Mr. Dooman also testified that I had a special affinity for communism, and as an officer of the U.S. government, had been "actively supporting" the Communist program for the take-over of Japan. Questioned about my motives, Dooman replied,

> Now, Mr. Chairman, you have the choice between two alternatives. Either he knew consciously that he was promoting the interests of the Communist party or that he was stupid. Now, I know Mr. Emmerson: he is not stupid. The State Department doesn't believe he is stupid. He has had a very rapid career. He is now, after only fifteen or sixteen years, fairly well at the top of the service.

Probing as to who might share my affinity for Communists, my attorney introduced the following dialogue:

Boskey: Did you feel that the persons who were responsible for carrying out these policies [toward Japan] had an affinity for communism?

Dooman: Quite.

Boskey: Did you feel that the present secretary of state [Dean Acheson] was one of those persons?

Dooman: Certainly. . . .

Boskey: Did you feel that General MacArthur during this period had an affinity for communism?

Dooman: General MacArthur was acting under directives from Washington, prepared in large part by people in the State Department of the second and third level.

Boskey: And did you feel that the president had such an affinity for communism?

Dooman: The president I don't think was conscious that there was a place called Japan out there. . . .

Boskey: Did you feel that Secretary of State Byrnes had an affinity for communism?

Dooman: Mr. Byrnes to my knowledge had no interest whatever in the Far East. You must remember that I was a member of his entourage taken to Potsdam to advise him on Far Eastern matters, and so far as I know, Mr. Byrnes never paid the slightest attention to the Far Eastern field.

It must have been a sour and embittered Gene Dooman who submitted his resignation in August 1945. He denied in my hearings that he had told me during our visit to the OSS unit in New York that he had expected to be named political adviser to MacArthur: "I certainly did not." A few days later he wrote to the Loyalty Security Board that his conscience had been "a trifle uneasy" over his reply to this question, since, in fact, Acting Secretary Grew had asked him to become political adviser and had recommended him to General MacArthur. Dooman declared in his letter that he would never have accepted the job under the circumstances then prevailing.

Dooman's despair over American policy toward Japan was not justified in the end. The Occupation did not depose the emperor whom he had defended against Dean Acheson and Archibald MacLeish. Capitalism was not destroyed—far from it, as witnessed by the enormous accomplishments of free enterprise in postwar Japan. The land reform did not eliminate the capitalist class in the agrarian field as he had predicted. In fact, the land reform has been hailed as the most successful act of the Occupation. Communism did not take over Japan. The reforms of the American-run Occupation denied credit to the Communists for many proposals that Nosaka had long advocated in his propaganda: reform of the emperor system, universal suffrage, land reform, and a parliamentary system with power concentrated in the Diet. The stories brought to Dooman about my associations with Communists and his reinterpretation of my dispatches fit his gloomy view of Japanese policy in which he was no longer to play a part. I therefore became an outlet for his bitterness and frustration, a symbol of the policies he felt he had to fight.

We tried to handle each of the charges as comprehensively as possible. All of my reports that we could find were laid before the board; in addition, a senior officer of the department was asked to read them for evidence of Communist coloration. The report which drew most attention was the one on "The Japanese Communist Party," which I had written in Yenan and submitted from Chungking on January 5, 1945. Material for this report was obtained exclusively from interviews with Nosaka, which fact I assumed would be clear to the reader. My writing was not precise enough, however, and critics read statements of Communist policies and programs as my own opinions. I also made certain recommendations that looked suspicious in the McCarthyist atmosphere of 1952. Imbued with the need to mobilize every force, including Churchill's "devil," in the war against Japan, I suggested that the Japanese Communists were "people on our side," that the Communist underground in Japan might be useful to the Allies (as the Communists in the Resistance were in France), and that the Communist party—as the only political force which had consistently opposed Japan's war policies—might collaborate in a postwar Japanese government. In my testimony before the board, I declared that I had learned much from my later assignment to Moscow and that I had come to realize more clearly the dangers inherent in a popular front government which included Communists.

Chip Bohlen, who was then counselor of the department, testified in my behalf. Asked about the Communist party report, he replied:

> I think my judgment concerning the writer of it would be that, I should say it is a perfectly honest report, but I would say it reflects the fact that the writer had not had the opportunity to go very deeply into the manner in which the Communist parties operate. I do not detect in it any attempt to "plug a line" that was favorable to the Communists. . . .

Chip delivered a brilliant analysis of Communist strategy and tactics and recalled the luncheon we had had in 1945, during which he had expressed some skepticism about Communist participation in a free Japanese organization; he remembered also that I had not argued against his opinion. Bohlen referred to the atmosphere of 1945 and to the fact that General de Gaulle, "than whom there is no more bitter enemy of communism in the world," had during the war called to London a French Communist leader to make a cooperative arrangement with him. Bohlen quoted a sentence from my report, "If we fail to adopt a positive attitude, some other country, such as the USSR, may take the lead and boldly carry out a policy in the long run inimical to our interests." Commenting on this, he said, "In my experience, you would not find statements like that in a report of this kind, if the writer was consciously plugging some line."

The episode of the letters failed to excite the board since Dooman testified that I had shown them to him, that he knew their origin and their destination, and that he had made no comment or remonstrance to me at the time. The text of two letters, from Nosaka and Kaji to Professor Ōyama at Northwestern University, had been included as enclosures to one of my dispatches to the department. The letter to Fujii Shūji had been delivered to him at the OSS meeting in New York, in Mr. Dooman's presence. It was a letter of introduction from Nosaka, including some comments about mutual interests in defeating the Japanese militarists. I met Fujii as an employee of the U.S. government and knew nothing about his Communist affiliations which later were alleged.

Association with Communists in China and Japan had been a part of my assigned duties; this fact was verified by numerous colleagues who had been with me in Yenan and Tokyo and knew of my activities. My voluminous reporting provided the reasons for and the results of my contacts.

The prisoner-of-war indoctrination project and the plan for a free association of Japanese were fully documented by numerous memoranda, reports, minutes of meetings, and written and oral testimony of persons involved. The director of the POW project in Texas wrote heatedly that no Communist would ever have dared to influence his curriculum or to come near his installation.

How Nosaka returned to Japan from China puzzled the board in light of reports that I had arranged the trip. I managed to track down an army captain who had been in Yenan at the end of the war. He wrote that he remembered vividly Nosaka's departure from Yenan on a U.S. Army C-47 transport plane within a fortnight after the Japanese surrender. The plane had been destined to fly to an airfield near Kalgan in the Communist border region to pick up rescued or detained American military personnel. The Chinese Communist military headquarters asked U.S. authorities in Yenan whether a number of Chinese and Japanese personnel might ride the plane, since on its way north it would be empty except for the crew. The Americans approved the passenger list, which included Nosaka and three Communist comrades. My friend witnessed the plane's departure with the Communists aboard and its return to Yenan later with the rescued American soldiers.

Nosaka had, on December 19, 1945, written to Lieutenant General John R. Hodge, commanding general of the U.S. Army in Korea, stating that he was a former member of the Central Committee of the Japanese Communist party and that he and three other members of the Yenan Japanese People's Emancipation League had arrived in Heijo (now Pyongyang, North Korea) on the thirteenth and were anxious to proceed through South Korea on their way to Japan. He stated that he had worked closely with the

U.S. observers section in Yenan and was well known to John Emmerson. Tokyo headquarters, apprised of the letter to Hodge, sent a young sergeant to interview John Service and me about Nosaka, who was still using the name Okano. We related Nosaka's cooperation with our section in Yenan and expressed the opinion that he might be a moderating influence on the Communist movement in Japan. In response to a question, we stated that it would be difficult to prove that the Russians were then aiding the Chinese Communists and that we had found no overt evidence of Soviet help to the Japanese Communists. Army headquarters in Korea later notified Tokyo that Nosaka and his party arrived in Seoul on January 2 and, after interrogation, were sent under protective custody to the port of Pusan, where they were released for return to Japan. As I have written earlier, the Japanese press reported extensively on Nosaka's arrival in Korea and on his journey from Pusan to Hakata by boat and to Tokyo by train.

The board, still concerned about Dooman's charge that I had arranged a military flight for Nosaka from Korea to Japan, asked the Air Transport Command (ATC) to check the manifests of all planes flying from Korea to Japan during the period 1945–46. Searches were apparently made of all ATC records, then in Kansas City, but, understandably, to no avail.*

We were able to document convincingly the episode of the Communist political prisoners in postwar Tokyo. Affidavits and personal testimony by the interrogators substantiated the facts in the case and disposed of the fanciful reports of parading Japanese Communist leaders through the streets of Tokyo. General Thorpe, chief of the Counter Intelligence Section, who had authorized the project, took advantage of his affidavit to get in a swipe at his arch-enemy in general headquarters, Major General Willoughby, chief of G-2:

---

* *The communications regarding Nosaka's return, including his letter to General Hodge and the correspondence between Tokyo and Seoul, were not made available to me at the time of hearings and came to my attention only when I received the documents in the summer of 1976.*

It is further declared that disgruntled persons, including Major General Charles Willoughby, have made statements seeking to discredit John K. Emmerson and others for acts performed during the period described above. Further, such disgruntled persons had no direct contact or concern with the work during this period and any statements made by them must in fact be other than firsthand knowledge.

Since the missing document in Moscow was included among the charges, we decided to approach General Walter Bedell Smith, who had been ambassador to the Soviet Union at the time. Now in 1952, the director of the Central Intelligence Agency, he was a gruff, severe, unrelenting military man, and his illness and surgery following his tour in Moscow had probably not improved his disposition. I trembled at the thought of his response to our request for a testimonial. He received my lawyer and me in his office and immediately refused to submit an affidavit or a written statement. "But," he frowned, "I will come in person to testify at your hearing."

On the morning set for his appearance, one of the members of the board was late in arriving and the general was kept waiting for fifteen or twenty minutes. I could see the anger in his face mount at this cavalier treatment, as he fidgeted impatiently in his chair. When the hearing began and he was asked his opinion of me, he replied curtly that my performance had been eminently satisfactory, except on one occasion when I had lost a secret document. Prefacing his remarks with the statement, "There is a possibility that I myself am unduly sympathetic for anyone who, for a moment through mental aberration, may lose a paper." General Smith repeated the story he had related to the embassy staff in Moscow, about how he had drawn a mental blank regarding a document in his custody. "Now, it is possible for a man to do such a thing when he becomes so completely absorbed in his work, so I can understand a man drawing a blank on a thing of that kind, because I have done it."

The general testified that during my service with him, "There was nothing which would in any way lead me to think that he at that time or previously had had any affinity for or sympathy for communism or the Communists' cause or Asiatic communism per se, or for communism generally—quite the contrary." He went so far as to state that he would employ me in the CIA "which is probably as sensitive an agency as we have in government," but he would give me an efficient secretary to take care of my secret documents!

In the course of his testimony, General Smith made a statement which was pertinent to the charge that I had brought Nosaka back from China at the end of the war. Noting that he knew nothing of my China service, he expressed the opinion that if he had been in the Asian theater during the war, he would have "been in the same bed with General Stilwell" in respect to attitudes toward Communists. On his own actions, he testified:

> You will shake hands with anybody. I myself approved assistance to the Communists in Yugoslavia and in Italy and in France; and, even after the surrender of the Germans, I approved and assisted in the arrangements for the return of the Communist leader Togliatti to Italy because, then, we military and diplomatic alike were laboring under the illusion that we could establish in Italy a coalition of parties, and the Communists of Italy were primarily Italian first and Communist second. I have learned a great deal since then; that was a mistake, but there were a lot of other people making mistakes also.

On the afternoon of April 18, after eleven days of testimony, 1,412 pages of transcripts, and 150 exhibits, the hearings came to an end. My entire foreign service career had been laid out for scrutiny. It was a rare experience—even fascinating if it had been less serious—to hear what unidentified informers had told FBI agents about me. No one, except Dooman perhaps, questioned my loyalty. I was astonished by the contradictory, distorted, and garbled versions of the indoctrination project, the political prisoners episode, and my relation to Nosaka's postwar return to Japan. Other comments on my personality must have been more confusing than enlightening to my judges. A few quotes from the testimony:

Emmerson would always be in demand for parties because of his joviality.

John is a very reserved individual, even in relations with his closest friends.

He may have read *Das Kapital* and other such books as, in discussions, he expressed favorable opinions of parts thereof; however, he also weighed the good with the bad. [I had never read *Das Kapital*.]

The only lead with regard to his outside activities is that he and one Alejandro Kossodo performed concert pieces for two pianos. There is nothing to indicate that Mr. Emmerson was associated with Kossodo for any purpose other than the concert. [Testimony from the security officer in Lima, Peru.]

... Tactful, level-headed, hard working, cooperative person who studied constantly and was never known to have hurt anyone.

"... Naïve, odd and careless individual who could easily be persuaded." Informant felt this was due to the many years Emmerson had spent in oriental countries as a result of which he had become somewhat dreamy and careless and rather weak-willed.

Asked to comment on this last characterization, General Walter Bedell Smith replied, "I do not consider Mr. Emmerson weak-willed or easily persuaded—rather on the contrary. I thought he was a bit on the stubborn side."

By the end of the hearings the board had probably become convinced that I was neither a Communist nor a security risk. General Smith had offered to hire me in CIA; Dean Rusk had testified that I had worked on the most highly classified project in the Bureau of Far Eastern Affairs and that he would not hesitate to ask me to do so again; and Major General Frederick Osborn, with whom I had cooperated at the Paris UN General Assembly in 1948, had sworn in an affidavit, "Mr. Emmerson's loyalty is unimpeachable and his hatred of Communists and of the government of the Soviet Union is deep-seated and implacable." It was clear, however, that the board members were still worried about my dispatch of January 5, 1945, which dealt with the Japanese Communist party, in which I had stated, "Our political responsibility for Japan which we cannot evade makes it imperative that we begin to evaluate the forces on our side. One of these forces is the Communist party." Again, they asked me to explain my attitude toward communism in the light of this statement.

I replied that in 1945 I had had no illusions about the ultimate aims of Communist parties. As an enclosure to the January report I had included Nosaka's own outline of the "Program of the Japanese Communist party," in which he set forth the concept of the three-stage revolution, in which socialism would replace capitalism only at the third stage, which Nosaka expected would not come for fifty years or more. I expressed my conviction—still held in 1952, and in 1978 for that matter—that Japan would not go Communist, that the suspicion of communism was deep-seated in the country, that an American Occupation could control it, and that the conservative strength would never permit a Communist take-over. I was thinking, in my report, of the immediate Japanese situation to be faced at the end of the war, which many thought might be chaotic. We would need every force on our side, and the Communists at that time would be one. I confessed that I had underestimated the dangers of Communist participation in a coalition government, of which Chip Bohlen had warned after my return from China to Washington. But in the early stages, as I had written in one of my reports, "We should not let the Communists use us; we must use them."

On May 19 the Loyalty Security Board rendered judgment, finding that "no reasonable doubt exists as to his loyalty to the Government of the United States" and that "he does not constitute a security risk to the Department of State," recommending that the case be closed. In a separate seventeen-page "Rationale," the board discussed the case in detail, expressing its rejection of sixteen separate charges. On August 1 the Loyalty Review Board postaudited the case and confirmed my clearance. It was not until August 20 that the State Department notified me by letter that my loyalty and security had been established.

The period between January and August was a strained and painful one. Unlike certain of the other officers under investigation, I had not been suspended from my duties in the department. Thus I carried on my regular work, while spending hours reliving and analyzing the experiences of seven and eight years previously and soliciting evidence from friends and former associates. The hearings were closed and kept confidential so that I was fortunately spared publicity. I did not want to burden the family with the details of my ordeal; the children were too young to understand its meaning, and when I returned from the office in the evening, I wanted only to forget my troubles.

My clearance made me again eligible for assignment overseas, but I soon learned that the Far East would be a prohibited area, as it was for my friends who had served in China. Our then-ambassador to Indochina talked to me glowingly about becoming his deputy to Saigon. "Where else in the world," he said tantalizingly, "can you be accredited to one emperor [Bao Dai of Vietnam] and two kings [of Cambodia and Laos]?" My yearning to go to Saigon was not unquenchable, but if it had been, the post clearly would not be available to me. I did not know then that the taint would be so strong that it would be sixteen years before I saw Asia again.

The position of deputy chief of mission at Karachi, Pakistan, was open and I accepted. This would be a new part of the world for me; I had spent only a night or two in Karachi on my way to the CBI theater. The country was a developing one, just five years independent from Great Britain, and the problems would be challenging, and the climate likewise. I arrived before the departure of the ambassador and took charge of the embassy for an extended period of nine months before a new chief of mission arrived. The embassy was expanding, largely due to a rapidly developing economic aid program. The personnel grew with every plane's arrival. It was one of Pakistan's pro-American periods. Government leaders were anxious for military assistance (thinking of India but speaking of communism), and the U.S. agreed to send it. As chargé d'affaires I signed with Sir Zafrullah Khan, the foreign minister, the military agreement that became the foundation stone for the Baghdad Pact, later to become CENTO. These were the Eisenhower years, and Secretary of State John Foster Dulles was later to be accused of "pactomania" for the pacts he fathered—SEATO, CENTO, ANZUS. Dulles came to Karachi during the course of an extended tour. He had just fired John Davies and, at an intimate dinner at our house one evening, complained that he had had to devote an entire weekend to reading Davies's file in order to come to a judgment.

I did not know at the time that in 1954 my entire security file was again reviewed by the Department of State, which checked the records of all intelligence agencies in Washington, including the investigative files of the Civil Service Commission and the FBI. The reason was a recommendation that I be given a meritorious service award. A five page, single-spaced report of January 29, 1955, stated that no new information had been received since 1952 but proceeded to repeat all the charges and conclusions of the Loyalty Board hearings and to recommend ponderously at the end that the case be "favorably readjusted." I got the award.

In the same year, 1955, after nearly twenty years in the foreign service, I was promoted to Class 1, the highest numerical rank, topped only by career minister and career ambassador. With this double expression of the State Department's satisfaction with my performance, I thought, with relief, that my troubles were over and that my professional future would be bright. Luckily, I had no way of discerning what was to come.

In 1955 I was transferred to Beirut, Lebanon, again as deputy chief of mission. Lebanon is a beautiful country, where one can swim in the Mediterranean in the morning and ski at the Cedars of Lebanon in the afternoon. Members of the Lebanese elite were charming and sophisticated, but the socialites were shallow and pretentious. The country's French heritage was still strong, but the American University had educated many of the country's leaders; for that matter, not only those of Lebanon but prime and foreign ministers of many other countries in the Middle East. The overriding importance of religion was immediately apparent. The mathematical formula for apportioning government offices among the Christians and Moslems was so meticulously devised and so ironclad that one knew that an infinitesimal deviation would bring disaster. The fact that the formula worked then seemed a miracle, but no one believed that it would last forever.

In the fall of 1956 I was again assigned to the UN General Assembly, this time in the guise of a Middle Eastern expert. I left Beirut in late October as the Suez crisis was breaking. Stopping for a few days in Paris and London, I found that an eerie silence had fallen upon our embassies' normal daily contacts with the foreign offices of France and Great Britain. Communication had ceased. In London I sat in the House of Commons with a colleague from our embassy, hearing Anthony Eden electrify his auditors with the ultimatum of a British–French attack on Suez, to be coordinated with an Israeli invasion.

The General Assembly's Hungary–Suez session was unique in UN history. Few governments can successfully face two crises at the same time; yet, in New York, delegates from many nations were performing under the double shadow of the Soviet repression of the Hungarian rebellion and a combined British–French–Israeli action, which both the United States and the Soviet Union denounced.

I was a liaison officer, a floorwalker, always with the job of "getting out the vote." We worked particularly hard to get Wellington Koo, the venerable diplomat from Nationalist China, elected to the World Court. Defections toward the People's Republic in Peking were growing, and it took all of America's influence plus the oratory of one of the congressional members of our delegation, Senator William Knowland of California, known as the "senator from Formosa," to get Koo elected. Henry Cabot Lodge was the U.S. representative at the United Nations and presided over us with aloof arrogance. Arranging meetings between him and foreign ministers or chiefs of state of newly admitted member nations, which was one of my tasks, was like negotiating a treaty. Lodge liked to conduct conversations in the delegates' lounge and to get him and the visiting chief of state or foreign minister to sit in the same corner at the same time was not an easy task.

I had to maintain relations with both Arabs and Israelis. Fortunately, the foreign minister of Iraq, Mohammed Jamali, had been a fellow student at International House in 1930 (he was later narrowly to miss assassination in Baghdad), and Golda Meir, then Israel's foreign minister, had been her country's first ambassador to Moscow and had therefore been among those diplomats we had known well in that closed setting.

In the latter part of February 1957, with my duties in New York completed, I left for consultation in Washington. While in the department, I was asked to go to Paris as political counselor. Before returning to Beirut to say my farewells and help my wife pack, I planned a few days' visit with my father in Colorado. The evening before I was to fly West, a press officer from the department telephoned to tell me that some derogatory statements had been made about me that day in the Senate. The next morning at National Airport, I picked up a newspaper with headlines: STATE DEPARTMENT AIDES ACCUSED OF BEING PRO-RED. The article quoted a March 1 speech made by Senator William E. Jenner of Indiana. I immediately called the assistant secretary for Near Eastern Affairs and asked whether I should cancel my flight. He said, "No, but keep in touch." From my old hometown, Cañon City, I again telephoned the department to learn that Senator Eastland, chairman of the Subcommittee on Internal Security, would like me to appear before the subcommittee.

Senator Jenner's statement was directed at two of us then serving in the Middle East—Robert Strong, counselor of embassy in Damascus, and myself, in Beirut. Strong had also been tarred by China. The Senate was then debating the Eisenhower Doctrine for the Middle East. Senator Jenner began his statement by quoting a report that four Arab governments were eager for American aid but refused to commit themselves to "the West against the East." He then recalled "the story of the American State Department officers in China who spread false information and propaganda helpful to the Communists," and went on to say, "Let me refer to the record of one of these men, John K. Emmerson." He launched into the well-worn statement of General Wedemeyer about the four political advisers and into the old charges about my reports from Yenan, association with Nosaka, and proposals for indoctrinating Japanese prisoners of war. Then he dropped his bombshell, "Now hear this, Mr. President: John K. Emmerson is today counselor of [our] embassy at Beirut, Lebanon." He followed with a brief attack on Strong, revealing that he was counselor in Damascus. Jenner continued:

> I do not know how many of this group of State Department officials in China may be in the outlying parts of the area vaguely called the Middle East. . . . We can be sure, Mr. President, that the termites are hard at work today, as they were in the 1940s. Now we know they are hard at work right in the center of things, in the Middle East. Is the President of the United States relying on the reports of such officials in making plans for the defense of the vast Middle East area with the lives of our sons?

I returned to Washington on Sunday, March 10, and went to the department the following morning. Scott McLeod, then in charge of security, advised me to go up on the Hill to clear myself, again, "once and for all" of the charges. Bob Strong was in Damascus; fortunately for him, the department found it inconvenient to call him home. But I was there.

Loy Henderson, then deputy undersecretary, told me that Judge Robert Morris, chief counsel to the congressional committee, had mentioned in a telephone conversation that one of the interests in the hearing, which was scheduled for March 12, would be my relations with Herbert Norman. Henderson had replied that it would not be appropriate for a foreign service officer to testify about a diplomatic colleague in open hearings. Morris then assured Henderson that the hearing would be held in executive session; that is, it would be closed and confidential.

My first meeting with Morris on the afternoon of March 11 was not a comfortable one. I expressed my complete willingness to testify but remarked that the events in which the committee was presumably interested had taken place twelve to fourteen years previously, and I had not thought about them since my State Department hearings in 1952. Would it not be possible to postpone the session to give me more than one day to refresh my memory? Morris cut me short; the schedule had been set and no change was possible. He went on to say that, as a naval officer during the war, he had been shocked by my reports. He then abruptly pulled out a document and, after reading two or three sentences, demanded, "Why did you say this?" From the two sentences I could not at once identify the report and asked for more information about it. He shoved it at me, and I saw immediately that it was one of my China reports about Japanese psychological warfare activities. I started to explain it, but he interrupted, "We will talk about that at the hearing."

After this unsatisfactory interview, my only clue as to the interests of the committee was my wartime and immediate postwar activities in China and Japan and my relationship with Herbert Norman. During the morning of the twelfth, before my Senate appearance, which was set for 2:15, I leafed through the thirteen volumes of transcripts of the 1952 hearings. Since the episode had been so distasteful, I had deliberately tried to shut it out of my mind and had taken at face value the final words of the Loyalty Security Board that "the case is closed." I thought again about my association with Norman, but in my conversation with my lawyer that morning, oddly enough—and perhaps I am, as charged, of a dreamy nature—I neglected to mention that Norman was then Canadian ambassador to Cairo and that at the time he presented his credentials as concurrently minister to Lebanon, he and his wife had lunched with us at our apartment in Beirut. Since the meeting had been entirely a social one, with no professional intent or purpose, it did not impress me as being especially significant to the matter at hand.

Senator Jenner presided at the hearing; also present were Senator Arthur V. Watkins and four staff members, including Robert Morris. The line of questioning, directed by Judge Morris, began with my experiences in Yenan, my reports, the letter incident, my relation to Nosaka's return to Japan, and the "releasing" of Japanese Communists after the war. The latter incident brought in the name of Herbert Norman and, from then on, the committee's (or rather, Morris's) focus was on Norman. Did I know he was a Communist? I replied, "I had no reason to think he was a Communist either then or now. He is presently Canadian ambassador to Egypt." The statement was like a shock wave: the sharp investigators had not known where Norman was and what he was doing. Both senators asked me to repeat it. Morris asked the senators if they would like to see the evidence in the security files that Norman was a Communist. He proceeded to read into the record reports about Norman's communism, laying stress on statements by a former Communist, Karl August Wittfogel, that Norman had been a member of a summer Communist study group in 1938 and that he had been identified as a member of the Communist party in 1940. In response I could only say, "In searching my memory I simply cannot recall any statements, any conversations of his [Norman's] which would lead me to the conclusion that he was a member of the Communist party."

Then, instead of allaying the committee's suspicions, I succeeded in creating new ones. I mentioned that Norman and his wife had been with my wife and me for about two hours on the day he arrived in Beirut by ship from Cairo. Due to some kind of mental block, I could not remember how we got in touch with each other, stating that we had never corresponded. (Later it came to me in a flash that Norman, who previously had been Canadian High Commissioner to New Zealand, had heard from the Brewster Morrises that we were stationed in Beirut and had written me, in April 1956, that he was being transferred to Cairo, with accreditation to Lebanon, and looked forward to meeting us. I replied that we would be delighted to see them. This was my only correspondence with Norman in the ten years since we had both served in Washington.)

Pressed to relate the substance of my conversation with Norman in Beirut, I could not recall details but knew that we had discussed the Middle East situation, which was then on the eve of crisis. I testified that nothing in Norman's conversation struck me as being strange or being pro-Communist. At the end of the hearing, Senator Jenner stated, "I will admonish everyone here that this is an executive session."

Over a cup of coffee in the Senate Office building after the hearing, one of the State Department security officers who had been present remarked that my testimony had been excellent, but that I had seemed to be less than forthcoming during the questioning relating to the Beirut meeting. Then I realized that I should have recalled details of the sequence of events and testified at length regarding the circumstances of the luncheon. The next morning in the department I racked my memory and wrote out in memorandum form the most minute account of the circumstances which I could bring to my consciousness. We got in touch with Judge Morris and asked to elaborate on my testimony. He scheduled another hearing for March 21.

Contrary to the firm agreement that the session would be an executive one and to Senator Jenner's specific admonition, the full text of the testimony was released to the press at 4:30 P.M. on March 14, two days after the hearing. The headlines, as could be expected, had nothing to do with Emmerson, but blared: SENATORS PROBE CANADIAN ENVOY, and CANADA TO PROTEST SENATE GROUP'S RELEASE OF "SLANDEROUS" TRANSCRIPT. Canada reacted violently. Lester Pearson, minister for external affairs, announced that his government would make a strong protest to the United States, that Norman, after the same charges had been made in 1951, had been given a "clean bill of health" and that nothing he had done had affected "the confidence we have in him as a devoted, efficient, and loyal official of the government, who is doing extremely important work at a very difficult post in a way which commands my wholehearted admiration and deserves my full support." The State Department issued a statement that allegations about Norman made in the committee "do not represent opinions of the United States Government." *The Washington Post,* in an editorial headed SMEAR, INC., asked, "When is the Senate going to put a bridle on this sort of rampaging irresponsibility?"

At the hearing on March 21, again in executive session, in the presence of only one member, Senator Watkins, and the staff, I explained the circumstances of the meeting with the Normans in Beirut, including the steps leading up to it. I was urged again and again to dredge from my memory every moment of the conversation with Norman during the luncheon. Since it was a purely social occasion (I had neglected to inform the committee that my sister and her husband, Mr. and Mrs. Alfred D. Sinden of Aurora, Illinois, were our houseguests at the time and were also present during the luncheon), I had made no serious mental notes of what we talked about. I assumed that we discussed the Middle East crisis, in which we were both professionally concerned, and our respective experiences with investigations. Norman had furnished me an affidavit regarding our interrogation of Japanese political prisoners, and I am sure we told each other that we had been respectively cleared by our governments.

Senator Watkins, Judge Morris, and J. G. Sourwine, another counsel to the committee, took advantage of my presence to go over again the subjects of the first hearing: Yenan, the prisoner interrogation, my attitudes toward China, every association I had had with Norman, and the charges that Norman was a Communist. At the end, Morris announced that there were further questions they would like to ask me at another date. On March 28 the transcript of the second closed hearing was released to the press.

I was subjected to a third inquisition on March 23, lasting three hours and taking up eighty-three pages of printed transcript. This time, J. G. Sourwine was the principal interrogator; he again went over my reports in detail, had copies of several inserted in the record, and asked me to identify a list of 115 names, to specify whether each was or was not a Communist. For some reason, the pledge of executive secrecy was honored in this case, and a Senate staff member told a department security officer that my testimony on the twenty-third had "cleared the air" for the subcommittee. Undoubtedly, they found nothing in it that would make headlines. The text appeared six years later in one of two volumes published by the committee, *The Amerasia Papers: A Clue to the Catastrophe of China.*

After being informed that I was no longer needed by the committee, I returned to Beirut, preparatory to my transfer to Paris. On the afternoon of April 4, I paid my farewell call on Charles Malik, then foreign minister of Lebanon. He told me that he had just received what he knew would be sad news for me. The Lebanese ambassador in Egypt had telephoned to inform him that Herbert

Norman, Canadian ambassador in Cairo, had that morning committed suicide by jumping from the roof of a nine-story apartment building.

I was stunned. I knew the Jenners and Morrises would call his death a confession of guilt. Guilty of what? I thought again of my friendship with Herb, of our many quiet talks, when his sharp, probing intellect had shown through an all-enveloping compassion. He could never have been a conspirator secretly concocting Communist plots against his government and mine. Intellectually he had, indeed, seen some good in left-leaning causes and some of his writings showed influences of Marxism. He enthusiastically supported and worked for the reforms put forth in the early stages of the Occupation but hoped that the indigenous democratic roots in Japan's own history could be nurtured and permitted to flower. I still could not remember an utterance that would have suggested to me that Herb was a member of the Communist party. Yet it was my fate to give testimony which provided the setting for his persecution. If only I had not been on the Hill those days . . .

A wave of indignation swept over Canada after Norman's suicide. Students at the University of Toronto burned Robert Morris in effigy. The Norman case became the subject of brisk debate in the Canadian Parliament. An election was approaching, and Lester Pearson, the foreign minister, was under attack from the opposition. There were rumors that Pearson was the real target of Morris and company. An article in the *Toronto Star* of April 5 began, "Hon. Lester B. Pearson may be next on the list of persons the United States Internal Security Subcommittee can do without." Pressed repeatedly for elaboration on Norman's investigation and clearance in 1951, and asked by the opposition leader, J. G. Diefenbaker, to deny categorically the truth of the charges brought before the Senate subcommittee, Pearson revealed on April 12 that "Mr. Norman, as a university student many years ago, was known to have associated quite openly in university circles with persons who were thought to be Communists or who appeared to behave like Communists. He made no secret of those university associations." After describing the security investigations and resulting clearance in 1951, Pearson affirmed categorically: "I was convinced of his loyalty and decency as a Canadian from the first day he entered the Department of External Affairs until the day of his tragic death."

Reaction in the United States was antagonistic to Morris and the subcommittee. Senator Jacob Javits of New York declared that the subcommittee's statements indicated it was operating "as if it were a body independent of the Senate." Canadian–American relations, he surmised, "seem to be blowing up into a situation as acute as any since the pre-Civil War dispute involving the Northwest frontier." The American press expressed abhorrence; sample editorials were headed: RECKLESS AND UNFAIR *(The New York Times)*, SUICIDE AND SLANDER *(The Washington Post)*, TRAGEDY IN CAIRO *(Evening Star, Washington)*, LICENSE TO DESTROY *(The Washington Post)*, and DISGRACEFUL HARASSMENT! *(New York Herald Tribune)*. *The New York Times* judged that, "the suicide of E. Herbert Norman, Canadian Ambassador to Egypt, has brought shame to the government and people of the United States." *U.S. News and World Report* featured the Norman case in its issue of April 26. With great red headlines on the cover: THE STRANGE CASE OF MR. NORMAN, the magazine published a thirty-five-page article, including, among other material, long excerpts from Dooman's testimony before the McCarran committee, my testimony in the hearings of March 12 and 21, numerous press reports, both Canadian and American, and parts of discussions in the Canadian House of Commons. On two facing pages, my photograph stared across at one of Karl Wittfogel, whose testimony had directed the subcommittee's attention to Norman.

The press outside the United States was equally outraged. The *Times* of London, in an editorial entitled RECKLESS PERSECUTION, pronounced, "Mr. Norman's death emphasizes again the nastiest aspect of the Committee's investigating technique. It is bounded neither by the forms of law nor by the abstract principles of justice."

The uppermost question in the minds of the press and public was why the Senate subcommittee had released transcripts of closed hearings to the press. The committee's rejoinder was that the State Department had approved their publication. Spokesmen for the department weakly argued that the release of Emmerson's testimony *only* had been authorized, pointing out that it had been favorable to Norman. Just how my statements could have been separated from the rest of the hearing and make sense was not explained. The State Department had ignored the admonition of its own deputy under secretary, who had warned me and Morris about testimony by a foreign service officer regarding a diplomatic colleague in an open hearing. The State Department had cowered before the self-righteous zeal of Jenner, Morris, and company.

On March 18, before Norman's suicide, the Canadian government protested the subcommittee's actions "in the strongest terms." Secretary of State Christian Herter responded on April 10, only *after* the suicide, that "derogatory information ... was introduced into the record by the subcommittee on its own responsibility." The delay in the U.S. reply from March 18 to April 10 led a Canadian member of parliament to remark in the House of Commons that "if the United States administration had answered the protest of the Canadian government promptly and generously, the life of Mr. Norman would have been saved."

On April 10 Lester Pearson, in a second note, asked for assurances that security information regarding Canadian citizens not be passed to committees or organizations over which the United States government had no executive control. Until such assurances were given, Canada reserved the right to withhold security information on Canadians to any U.S. government agency.

The fact was, as I was to learn only many years later, that Norman had joined the Communist party while a student at Cambridge University in March 1935. In those years radicalism was rampant on university campuses. A fellow student of Norman's is reported to have commented: "The only people who didn't lean left were the dull ones—the muscle boys, the drunks, and the hunters." Fascism was on the rise in Germany and Italy; militarism was growing in Japan. The Civil War in Spain, breaking out in 1936, caught the imagination of young radicals; Norman himself considered joining up with the Loyalists. In 1939, after completing his Ph.D. requirements at Harvard, Norman, after considerable wrestling of conscience, decided on a diplomatic instead of an academic career. He entered the foreign service and was sent to Tokyo early in

1940 as a third secretary and language officer. It was during this period that we first became acquainted.

When accusations were brought against him in 1950, Norman was summoned to Ottawa from Tokyo, where he was then Canadian diplomatic representative. Norman's interrogation in his own ministry was so thorough that it lasted six or seven weeks and was a traumatic experience for him. Nothing was found to challenge Norman's loyalty, as Foreign Minister Pearson repeatedly stated in public. Norman, according to a later attestation by Pearson, acknowledged that "he had had mistaken beliefs and had been following a false ideology." Pearson affirmed emphatically that from the time of Norman's entrance into the Canadian Foreign Service in July 1939, none of his contacts or his actions "could in any way be questioned from a security point of view."

When I saw him in October 1956, Norman had been exalted over his new double assignment to Egypt and Lebanon. He had already become a scholar on the Middle East and looked forward to thorny but demanding problems—a contrast to his previous, quiet post in New Zealand. In Cairo, the pressure of work due to the Suez crisis was unrelenting. Pearson had proposed the stationing of a UN peacekeeping force in the Middle East, and Norman bore the brunt of negotiating with Nasser, with whom he had established an amazingly good working relationship. The publication of the committee hearings probably affected Norman more deeply because of the state of his fatigue and nervous exhaustion. He was a sensitive, introspective person, and a gentle man; the previous accusations against him and the extended investigations in 1950 must have caused him deep inner turmoil. Now he would face more charges, more frustrations, more publicity, and the fact of his past membership in the Communist party would be confirmed.

Norman was Japanese in some respects: in his intensity and his bottling up of emotions, and probably in his conception of suicide. The night before he committed suicide, he and his wife Irene were guests of the Japanese embassy at a showing of a Japanese movie *Mask of Destiny,* which portrayed suicide as one answer to man's problems. Herb was a complex character; probably no one really understood him. He combined in one person his Christian upbringing (his father had been a missionary in Japan), his insatiable thirst for knowledge, his genuine concern for the weak and under-privileged of this world, his immersion in Japanese history and culture, his deep studies in classical and world literature, his grasping at Marxism as one explanation of history, and his later disillusion-ment and return to his first religious faith. He was a superior scholar and writer (his books are still read today, especially in Japan, where he is highly honored), a competent diplomat—a true renaissance man.

In notes left to his brother and to his brother and wife, Norman put down some of his last thoughts: "I am overwhelmed by circumstances and have lived under illusions too long. I realize that Christianity is the only true way.... I have never betrayed my oath of secrecy—but guilt by association as now developed has crushed me.... You must have faith in my complete innocence—despite the filter of slander and speculation that will appear."

13

The Thread Winds Back

On April 7, 1957, I flew to Paris from Beirut. Paris! The very air brought back my youth, the time I became twenty. It would seem I could forget the torment of the past months upon reentry into my first loved city. And at last we were to *live* in Paris. I remembered my naïve expectations when I entered the foreign service that, because of my French, a kind and discerning Department of State would rush me to Paris. Now, after a delay of twenty-two years, I had made it!

France, by 1957, had let go of Indochina, Tunisia, and Morocco but was still clinging desperately to Algeria. Passions were high, and the generals, with powerful support, were determined not to relinquish this last North African territory. The French shouted intervention, when John F. Kennedy, then an up-and-coming Democratic senator from Massachusetts, made a speech in the Senate calling for the independence of Algeria. But his was a minority voice speaking during a Republican administration.

The American ambassador was Amory Houghton, former president and chairman of the board of the Corning Glass Works, a capable, wealthy businessman who took his job conscientiously and with true dedication. He called some of us into his office one day and asked with some supplication, "Does anyone have any ideas about Algeria?" We could think of no easy way out for our host country. To say, "Give it up," was too bold and too injudicious. Kennedy could say it, but the State Department would not. *Le grand général,* Charles de Gaulle, was then sulking at his country place in Colombey-Les-Deux-Églises, waiting for the moment to save his country, which he knew would surely come. From time to time, just to keep in touch, he would quietly visit a modest, sparsely furnished little office in the rue Solferino, on the Left Bank. It was there that Ambassador Houghton called one day, to pay his respects. During the conversation, de Gaulle asked, with some asperity, "Why is Algeria of concern to the United States?" The ambassador replied that he did not believe Americans were especially agitated over Algeria; for the French, however, it was clearly their most important problem.

The Political Section, of which I was chief, had to keep in touch with the numerous parties then contending for power, analyzing for Washington the shifting shades of the political spectrum and the prospects for solutions or chaos. The section was an unusual gathering of bright experts, all of whom spoke fluent French and most of whom were later to become ambassadors. One, Frank Meloy, a keen, lively bachelor, was to become a martyr by assassination in Beirut in 1976. Another, Walter Stoessel, sound, steady, and serene, was to serve as ambassador to the Soviet Union and West Germany. A third, Dean Brown, fiery and imaginative, was called back from retirement after a succession of tough, well-executed assignments, to be a trouble-shooter in the Middle East.

The presence of many political parties meant many politicians to talk to. The French Assembly was often in session until late at night, and it was difficult to meet members at evening functions. But the Frenchman's lunch is sacred and lunch diplomacy became our best entrée to the mind of a *deputé*. For us, it meant three-hour repasts at Michelin-starred restaurants, starting with apéritifs and followed by nonstop political talk (I never met a reticent French politico) until the cognac. One would stagger back to the embassy between three and four in the afternoon, logy with lunch and tongue-tired from speaking French, to write the usual memorandum of conversation.

But we kept in touch. Dean Brown, who handled internal affairs, would, at a time of parlimentary crisis, spend late hours at the Assembly, listening to debates when they were interesting, buttonholing legislators in the corridors, and reporting instantly by telephone and later by telegram.

The telephone was a nuisance in Paris. Now it has become a primary tool of diplomacy, but twenty-five years ago Washington officials seldom picked up the telephone to call Karachi, Beirut, or Tokyo. The psychology of distance was such that Paris seemed next door and our friends in the State Department thought nothing of telephoning, usually at midnight or after because of the time difference, to ask for information or to instruct us to take some immediate action.

We became involved in the good-offices mission to solve a dispute between France and newly independent Tunisia, arising over the bombing of a Tunisian village near the Algerian border by the French Air Force. Robert Murphy, veteran foreign service officer with previous extended service in Paris, and Harold Bealey, senior official of the British Foreign Office, were the conductors of the *bons offices*, as they shuttled between Paris, London, and Tunis, trying to bring the two sides together. I became the note-taker for the meetings in Paris and made one trip to Tunis.

One morning at about two o'clock, several of us were sitting in the ambassador's office during a tense moment in the Tunisian crisis. The French government seemed about to fall. Houghton was on the telephone every half-hour or so with Secretary of State Dulles in Washington, and he or others of us were talking to French ministers or Foreign Office officials in between times. During a lull in the activity, when most of us were glassy-eyed, the ambassador turned to us and smiled, "And to think I don't *have* to do this for a living!"

The dispute was settled, as most disputes are, eventually, but the government did fall; the prime minister, Pierre Gaillard, young and energetic, faded into obscurity, and the carriers of the *bons offices* returned quietly to their respective chanceries.

The Algerian war ground on. I was in Paris on the famous May 13, 1958, when the *paras* ("army parachutists") were expected to drop out of the sky into the Place de la Concorde, immediately in front of the embassy, to take over France. Then de Gaulle stirred at Colombey-Les-Deux-Églises, and France was never the same again. Two French journalists wrote a book about it, which they called *The 13 Plots of the 13th of May or The Release of Gulliver*.

I was transferred from Paris just as the general took over. The Political Section must have lost a lot of its verve and frenzy since it no longer mattered what the socialists or the radicals, or any of the other political clusters thought. The politics of France were concentrated in the head of Charles de Gaulle, and access to that was limited indeed. I was glad to have served in Paris during the immediate, hectic, pre-de Gaulle period. One witnessed from the French side the slow, bloody amputation from the mother country of her last important colony, and the failure of the multiparty system. Only the general could stop the carnage, and for the moment, in truth, de Gaulle and France became synonymous. Louis XIV's *"L'etat c'est moi"* became de Gaulle's *"Je suis la France."*

My absorption in French politics and the sentimental joy of living in Paris were not untouched. The Senate Subcommittee on Internal Security was still alive and busy in Washington. Its annual report for 1957 contained a section called "The Norman Case," which vigorously defended the publication of the record of my two hearings on March 12 and 21, 1957. Noting the difference in my testimony in the two appearances with regard to the details of arrangements for the Beirut lunch with the Normans, the subcommittee inserted a footnote: "In the context of the questions which had been asked Mr. Emmerson, this seems incredible." This statement was directly contradictory to the press release issued on April 6, 1957, by Senator Arthur V. Watkins, who had been present at both hearings: Watkins said "... The testimony at the second hearing was very favorable to the witness [Emmerson] and to Dr. Norman." This footnote, to the State Department, was a red flag which raised the old doubts all over again, and was probably principally responsible for the troubles I suffered during the rest of my foreign service career.

Additionally, unfavorable press reports and letters to congressmen began to appear. Sometime in the spring of 1958, I was waiting in a doctor's office in Paris, idly leafing through the magazines on the coffee table. An article in the *American Legion Magazine* caught my eye: "How We Have Been Losing Japan." The story of my "freeing" the Communist political prisoners was there with a new twist: "Emmerson ... released two notorious Communists, Shiga and Tokuda, taking them away in a staff car flying the American flag." Now a flag had been added to the scene! The author commented blackly, "John Emmerson, we might add in passing, is still with the State Department." *U.S. News and World Report* again took up the Norman case on May 23, inspiring an irate citizen to write to Secretary Dulles: "Prominently mentioned in this report is John K. Emmerson, whom I wouldn't trust as far as I could throw Alger Hiss."

In the spring of 1958 I was asked to go to Lagos, Nigeria, as consul general. Nigeria, one of the most important countries in Africa, was on the road to independence from Great Britain and the United States needed good relations with the coming leaders of the country. I would be given the personal rank of minister, a White House designation, but an appointment that would not require Senate confirmation. We dreaded to leave the sights and sounds and smells and tastes of Paris after so short a time, since it takes a year to become effective in any new post. But in those days foreign service officers rarely argued over assignments. And the more I thought about Africa (after finding Lagos on the map) the more appealing I found a potentially exotic experience on a new continent. Furthermore, I would be my own boss and the consulate general, with its broadening functions and responsibilities, would be a small embassy in all but name. We opted for the Dark Continent.

Lagos was hot and humid, situated on the old Slave Coast, a post known in the British colonial service for producing "one dead consul every year." Its climate had saved it from colonization by whites, and it therefore was spared the fate of Rhodesia and South Africa. The consulate general, when I arrived, was located in an upstairs suite of rooms in a business block. We erected a new office building, a beautiful, glass-enclosed box in the downtown government section. State Department planners in those days were not thinking of student riots and invitations to rock-throwing. Indeed, in due course, long after I had left Nigeria, the great glass windows were systematically smashed. Now, State Department architecture around the world—like university architecture—imitates fortresses rather than glass castles.

It was a stimulating experience to witness the preparations for independence of a huge, ambitious country, teeming with people (fifty-five million then and seventy-nine million in 1976) and rich in resources (peanuts, cocoa, palm oil and kernels, and oil). Indirect rule in Nigeria had been one of Britain's colonial successes. The prime minister at the time of independence, Sir Abubakar Tafawa Balewa, a London-educated Hausa schoolteacher from the northern region, had served fourteen years in local, regional, and national assemblies, restricted in power but still offering experience in the methods of representative government. The Nigerians liked to remind us that Balewa had served longer as a parliamentarian than had the then-candidate for the presidency of the United States, John F. Kennedy. The British had drawn lines on a map, and so long as Britain's power was supreme and the district officers were on the spot to guide the administration, the system worked. Muslim Hausas from the North, Christian and animist Yorubas from the West, and Ibos from the East coexisted with each other and with dozens of other tribes, although their divisions were deep, in language, religion, geographical situation, and cultural heritage.

Americans and British alike were bullish about Nigeria. This would be the biggest, most powerful, and most successful country in Africa. The leaders were Oxford, Cambridge, and London University graduates, urbane and talented, capable of running a country on democratic principles inculcated by their British mentors. Although there were only 880 lawyers and fewer than 1,000 doctors in the federation, these numbers were far beyond the handful of college graduates who were suddenly entrusted with responsibility in newly independent Congo. We saw the tribal fissures, the preponderance in population and area of the Northern Region over the rest of the country and the contempt of its leaders for the South. The northern premier, the Sardauna of Sokoto, had referred to those "irresponsible southerners whom circumstances forced us to join." At the same time, the southerners resented the authority of the North, expressed in regimes of "feudal and reactionary northern aristocrats." Sir Abubakar, the federal prime minister, was the only leader who had won sufficient prestige to be accepted throughout the new nation; he had become the only true Nigerian leader at a time when the very term *Nigerian* had hardly supplanted the tribal loyalties of vast numbers of the population.

In the infectious jubilation over independence, symbolized by the tumultuous shouts as the green-and-white flag ascended its pole at the Lagos racetrack at midnight on October 1, 1960, we overestimated the chances for future unity. A little more than five years later, in January 1966, Balewa, along with other ministers, was brutally assassinated in the first of a series of coups. His removal destroyed the federation as originally conceived, and the Biafran war and military rule became inevitable consequences.

It was stimulating to be in Nigeria. Not only was the most populous nation in Africa important to American foreign policy, but the Nigerians were captivating people—active, extroversive, and with a boisterous sense of humor. The Muslim Hausas from the North were more reserved: tall and sedate in their flowing white robes and serenely confident in their feelings of superiority, despite the lower standards of education of their people. The many-colored, flamboyant costumes of the Ibos and Yorubas gave the wearers a mien of dignity and identity which was absent from the drably pants-and-shirt-clad East Africans whom I later met. Festus Okotie-Eboh, finance minister while I served in Lagos, adopted a distinctive dress of his own, his trademark being a stiff straw hat with a long feather sweeping upward from it. At the formal opening of parliament, in a hall constructed as an exact model of the British House of Commons, Okotie-Eboh inspired cheers, applause, and gales of friendly laughter when he made his grand entrance, dressed in a robe with a long train, designed from cloth manufactured especially for the occasion in a pattern of repeating medallions of his own photograph. The finance minister waved and smiled majestically as he proceeded up the aisle, while obliging, laughing fellow members of the House jumped to hold his train and march behind him. Even the Supreme Court justices, on the raised dais at the front, perspiring in their black robes and long wigs, could not restrain smiles at the rollicking scene.

Official duty required my traveling to all parts of the country, to pay respects to premiers of the regions and to local rulers, such as the Emir of Kano in the north, the Alake of Abeokuta in the west, the Oba of Benin and the Oni of Ife in the east, the Chief of Big Bamanki, and the fons in the British Cameroons. The word *fon* is reputed to be a vestige of German colonial rule, derived from the German word *von* and thus denoting nobility. Near Bamenda we met the Fon of Bafut, already immortalized in Gerald M. Durrell's *Bafut Beagles,* who though aged, remembered a few words of German, danced for his guests, and liked nothing more than a bottle of gin. Another lesser Cameroonian chief exhibited in his courtyard his proudest possession, a vintage Ford on concrete blocks, which would never run but stood as a monument to prestige. Asked about his desires in this world, the chief, who was sitting in a broken-down, canvas camp chair, replied hesitantly through the district officer's interpretation, "A medal and a new chair!"

The primitive, symbolized by occult rites and gory ceremonies, which still persisted in the remote bush and in other areas not so remote, was being eroded by the extension of education and the inevitable creep of modernization. A brilliant Nigerian writer, Chinua Achebe, painted the turmoil of transition in an auto-biographical novel called *Things Fall Apart.* The title encapsulates the process. Things fall apart as the youths of a native village encounter the sudden outside shocks that brutally destroy their inheritance.

The thirst for development was unquenchable, and we responded with escalating aid programs in agriculture, education, technology, industry, and home economics, until they became the largest for all Africa. We cooperated with the British in an educational mission that recommended five universities for Nigeria, all of which now function. Some of us felt that as independence approached, a seminar on the constitutional problems of federalism might be useful. Government officials and Nigerian barristers and judges, of whom a number were British, welcomed the idea, and the seminar took place in August 1960 with internationally known jurists and legal specialists from the United States, England, Australia, Canada, and Ghana, discussing federalism for five days with all the leading members of the Nigerian bar and bench. The papers presented dealt with the problems of taxation, credit, trade and commerce, and international agreements. The solicitor general of the Western Region wrote on "Fundamental Human Rights in a Federal Constitution." All participants entered enthusiastically into the exercise of considering together the application of the rule of law in a new federation; few could contemplate that under a future military-dominated regime, many of the constitutional legalities they were then debating might lose their relevance.

As an independence gift to Nigeria, I recommended to the State Department that we offer a grant for the foundation of an institute of international affairs. By some miracle, the United States government was able to find one hundred thousand dollars, which I duly presented to the prime minister. Some years later I was gratified to learn that the institute had indeed been established in Lagos in a suitable building and was performing the service of a center for the study of international relations.

Our aid programs may have become too large and unmanageable, and waste and corruption interfered with our efforts. Coups and war later removed, or drove, from the country most of the leaders I had known. Africa receded from the center stage of America's interest. Nigeria cooled toward the United States. Some may judge that our efforts were in vain, but only the longer run of history and future developments in Africa can decide the question.

To the protocol-minded British and Nigerians, rank was impressive. To enhance the prestige of the U.S. presence in the country I was to be accorded the title of minister. The accreditation did not coincide with my arrival in Lagos, but the delay could be attributed to the usual bureaucratic procedures. Months passed, however, and I began to realize that the old charges were still cluttering the files of the department's Office of Security and were blocking my White House designation. I did not know that the request for the designation had been sent in early spring and had activated yet another full field investigation by the FBI. Again, my former colleagues in various posts were asked their opinions of my loyalty and security, and particularly, for details of any *singular* relationships with Herbert Norman. Most of my associates, except those who had testified long ago in 1952, had never met Herbert Norman nor had any firsthand knowledge of my acquaintance with him, let alone of any singular facets of the relationship. Still, the security boys were worried about that footnote in the committee's report. So long as that remained unexplained and on the record, they could not clear me.

By December 1958 the department decided that I would have to come back to Washington to defend myself once again. The letter inviting me to appear in the department described the purpose of the consultation as including "possible technical interrogation." For a while I was baffled but it gradually dawned on me that *technical interrogation* was a polite reference to a lie detector test.

In February 1959 I left for Washington for the ostensible purpose of discussing Nigerian–American relations. The British and Nigerians were pleased that Nigeria had become important enough for the State Department to summon its consul general home for consultation.

On February 18 I submitted to a day-long interrogation by two staff members of the Office of Security in the department. The questioning covered every aspect of my case, including the inevitable driving of Communists through the streets of Tokyo, but concentrated on Herbert Norman and the discrepancies in my testimony in the two Senate hearings. How could I have forgotten the circumstances surrounding the lunch in Beirut? How could I have forgotten the exchange of letters with Norman before he came to Beirut? I answered to the best of my ability:

> Now, to try to explain why I testified the way I did [at the first hearing], I can say sometimes it's as hard to analyze one's own motivations and actions as those of another person. There was this subconscious reticence. [Henderson had warned me about testifying about a diplomatic colleague in open hearing.] There was, secondly, the shock at hearing these various reports about Norman, which probably put me somewhat on the defensive. And, thirdly, I was concentrating on the substance of the discussion, thinking *that* was what was important about it as far as the committee was concerned. I forgot this exchange of correspondence and these details about arranging the meeting. It simply

didn't appear to me as of importance at the time. I have had experience at other times with some mental blocks occurring. . . .

My interrogators again read into the record reports of Norman's Communist activities and again pressed me for my opinion regarding Norman's communism. I repeated my previous statement that nothing in our association had led me to such a conclusion adding:

> I felt, perhaps wrongly—and I know I can be wrong because the Communist conspiracy is such that Communist members will make every effort to conceal that fact—but I had felt that he had perhaps become involved in Communist organizations in his Harvard days, but that he had not carried on those activities in later years during his service in the Canadian diplomatic service.

If we are to believe the Canadian government, my statement was correct.

The next procedure was the so-called technical interrogation. I later learned that the State Department had requested the CIA to perform the operation, but that Allen Dulles, then director, had refused on the grounds of (1) my rank and (2) the possibility of unfavorable publicity. The Security Office then turned to the Army's Counter Intelligence Group Headquarters in Washington, which promptly agreed to do the necessary testing. The experience was a unique one. I was asked to sign a document, affirming that "of my own free will and volition, without any duress, promises or influence, I hereby volunteer for a polygraph examination." The statement went on to specify that a refusal to take the test would in no way be held against me! I contemplated, however, the reaction of my examiners should I refuse to let my truth be tested.

On February 27 I was driven by a departmental security officer to one of the numerous wooden temporary buildings in Southwest Washington, at Second and Eye streets. In the lie detector room the major in charge explained that the machine, a Stoelting Deceptograph, would indicate and record changes in blood pressure, pulse rate, breathing pattern, and skin resistance on a continuous chart. I was duly connected to the apparatus by wires attached to the tip of each finger, to my forehead, and to my chest, feeling that I was being prepared for an electrocardiogram if not for electrocution! I was told to be calm and relaxed. (The report of the interrogation states that the "subject was slightly nervous and apprehensive when he reported for the test.") My inquisitor instructed me to answer questions with yes or no, and I was to keep my voice, as would he, low, slow and deliberate. The thirty-seven brief questions dealt with my sympathy for communism and participation in Communist activities, but most were focused on the relationship with Norman. One question produced a slight reaction, Was I withholding any information about my association with Norman? For a split second, I wondered whether there was some detail I had forgotten to relate. Then I recalled that, in addition to the multiple interrogations and interviews, I had, while in Paris, searched the obscure corners of my memory again to write out in memoranda form the tiniest detail of my relationship with Herbert Norman. The interrogator asked the question three times, and at the end of the interview, after he had told me that the ordeal was over and I might relax, he suddenly, without warning, put the same question to me again, under, as he was to say, *shock* conditions.

The results were favorable, even to the so-called shock question, which apparently produced no speeded pulse, jumping blood pressure, or sweating fingers. The official report concluded, "subject did not attempt to deceive on any of the questions asked."

In spite of hours-long interrogations and the lie detector test, the guardians of security were still not appeased. Although the under secretary of state on May 18 recommended that my security clearance be approved, someone had second thoughts, and it was decided to start the sleuthing all over again. Another supplemental full field investigation by the FBI was carried out in July 1959. It was not until November 25 that the notification of security clearance was signed with the statement; "Mr. Emmerson has been cleared by the Secretary after full field investigation by the FBI under procedures relating to Presidential appointees."

The Nigerians always wondered why it took so long for me to be able to announce my personal rank of minister. They never knew the story.

As the date for Nigerian independence approached—October 1, 1960—it became clear that I was to move on. Another African post was proposed, that of consul general to the Federation of Rhodesia and Nyasaland, again with the personal rank of minister. (This time the investigation and clearance took only three months.) We would go to the other side of Africa, where the black-white problem existed in a form never known in Nigeria. Nineteen-sixty had been the year of Africa in which seventeen states had become independent. The United States was placing a priority on African–American relations, which it had never done before. The new president, John F. Kennedy, named G. Mennen ("Soapy") Williams as assistant secretary for African affairs before he named the secretary of state, terming the appointment "second to none" in importance for U.S. foreign policy. The Rhodesian Federation would be a trouble spot, and its unity, even then, appeared more fragile than that of Nigeria.

Salisbury, the capital, was a clean, modern city, with wide, straight downtown streets, blocks of solid business buildings, even skyscrapers. Residential streets were lined with flowering jacaranda trees, suggesting fragrant, lavender clouds. Ample houses were surrounded by English gardens, which often hid sparkling swimming pools. The modest homes were neat and well kept. This was the whites' city. The blacks lived outside, in separated African townships, in well-built, uniform houses, row upon row. Recreational, health, and welfare services were provided, and the white Rhodesians failed to understand why their well-cared-for, but carefully segregated, black Africans could possibly be discontented.

All of this was in utter contrast to the disorganized, happy-go-lucky scenes of Lagos: snaking, unkempt streets swarming with pushing pedestrians, bicycles and honking cars, where rundown concrete-and-mud buildings leaned against rough shacks, and shops spilled their wares before them. Nigeria's prospect of independence had, however, brought ambitious building programs and clean-up efforts so that the center of the city around the racecourse was already, by the end of 1960, taking on a modern, cosmopolitan air. Lagos was rampant, whereas Salisbury was static, orderly, and groomed.

The Rhodesian Federation was formed in 1953 on the principle of partnership, in contrast to the apartheid of South Africa. Its motto was brave: Let Us Deserve to Be Great. Cynics called the partnership one between a rider and his horse but the prime minister, Sir Roy Welensky, and the white governors of the two protectorates, Northern Rhodesia and Nyasaland, and of the self-governing colony, Southern Rhodesia, claimed to believe in the principle of partnership and the durability of federation. However, they did not recognize the strength and persistence of the African nationalist movement.

Although there were conflicts among Africans, by 1961 three individuals already had established credentials for leadership— Kenneth Kaunda in Northern Rhodesia, president of the United National Independence party (UNIP); Dr. Hastings Kamuzu Banda, president of the Malawi Congress party in Nyasaland; and Joshua Nkomo, then president of the National Democratic party in Southern Rhodesia. Kaunda's father had been a Christian preacher, and he grew up in a mission environment, early becoming a teacher and joining the nationalist movement. He had visited London and India and had served prison sentences in Northern Rhodesia for his activities. Banda had likewise attended mission schools but had obtained medical degrees in both the United States and England. He had practiced medicine for twelve years in London and five years in Ghana, returning to Nyasaland only in 1958. He, too, had received his badge of imprisonment, having been incarcerated for a year during a state of emergency declared in Nyasaland. Joshua Nkomo was less well educated than either Kaunda or Banda, and impressed one as lacking essential qualities of leadership. His quarrels with rival leaders and the strict suppression of nationalist activity by the Southern Rhodesian government had made independence movements in Southern Rhodesia disunited and ineffective.

The position of the United States toward the Federation of Rhodesia and Nyasaland was a delicate one in 1960 and 1961. "Soapy" Williams had taken office in time to ride the wave of

African independence. His speech at Nairobi airport in February 1961—in which he shouted "Africa for the Africans!"—sent icy chills up the spines of Roy Welensky and his white associates. Whites in Southern Rhodesia at that time numbered less than three hundred thousand among three million blacks, and the populations of the other two members of the federation included only a sprinkling of white settlers. We, as American officials in Salisbury, as well as in the other capitals, Lusaka and Blantyre, had to deal with white governments, and the white leaders disapproved of our pro-black African policy. A typical editorial in Salisbury's *Sunday Mail,* headed DANGEROUS GAMBLE IN AFRICA, defined the gamble as "come what may the black man shall be paramount in Africa. It means that America is quite willing to destroy her white friends in the hope of gaining the loyalty and affection of black majorities." The whites, nevertheless, welcomed our aid programs and an American presence. They disapproved of the British as well, although with perhaps less intensity. After all, Prime Minister Harold Macmillan had, on February 3, 1960, proclaimed, "The wind of change is blowing through the continent." When the British High Commissioner and I would meet, we would joke, "Which of us is enemy number one this week?"

I wrote to the department in May 1961, "Sir Roy is fighting for his political life and for the life of the federation, and he sees American interest in Africa and black Africans as a challenge to his position, his authority, and to the position of the white man in Africa. Reasoning and logic are replaced by emotion, bitterness and anger." Yet Sir Roy was an attractive character, big, burly, rough-hewn, an untypical prime minister. He had risen from the slums, had become a locomotive engineer, a trade union organizer, and Rhodesian boxing champion. He spoke bluntly and directly, but without personal animus. We became good friends. He had a deep faith in the white man's responsibility in Rhodesia and believed that federation would be good for both black and white. He was a moderate in comparison with his predecessor and with the successors who, upon the breakup of the federation of 1963, declared Rhodesia's unilateral independence from Great Britain.

In 1961 both Kenneth Kaunda and Hastings Banda visited the

United States. President Kennedy, fascinated with Africa, asked to see Kaunda. The black nationalist leader of Northern Rhodesia was ushered, overwhelmed, into the White House to meet the American president. When Banda went to Washington, we saw to it that he, too, would shake hands with the chief executive of the United States. After this episode, Sir Roy called me to his office. "What do you mean," he stormed, "by inviting those two black rebels to meet your president? What would your government think if I were to shake hands here in my office with Fidel Castro?"

The Congolese war boiled over into the Federation, which shared part of its northern border with Katanga, the rebel Congo province. White Rhodesian mercenaries jumped at the chance to help Moise Tshombe and his Katangan separatist movement, which America opposed. Tshombe would secretly come to Salisbury for meetings with Welensky. In the midst of this tension, "Soapy" Williams decided to visit the Federation in the course of an African tour. He and his wife Nancy were to spend six days with us, visiting Salisbury, Blantyre (Nyasaland) and Lusaka (Northern Rhodesia). I dreaded the meeting between "Soapy" and Sir Roy. "Africa for the Africans" was still ringing in Welensky's ears and I expected a confrontation, if not cold silence. When I introduced the two, they shook hands and, with a few cool, polite words, each sizing up the other, gradually drifted into animated conversation. No fur flew; they got along famously. In the corridor on the way out, Sir Roy whispered to me, "You know, I like that Williams bloke!"

The schedule we had worked out went smoothly. The speech in Salisbury, respectful and discreet, was received with polite applause. Williams had explained that by "Africa for the Africans" he had of course meant *all* Africans, black, white, and of other hues. With the calls on officials, visits to chiefs and institutions, Nancy Williams's genuine interest in nurseries and hospitals, the trip began auspiciously. In Nyasaland Banda turned his population out to greet the man who came to save the Africans; his mission-bred eloquence swayed his followers as he piled encomium upon encomium in praise of the United States, President Kennedy, "Soapy" Williams, and all Americans. In Northern Rhodesia Kenneth Kaunda welcomed the Williamses with warmth, and calls on both white and black officials and visits to schools and copper mills moved without a hitch. I began to breathe more easily as the six days neared their end.

The final function was a black-tie dinner given by the white governor of Northern Rhodesia at his official residence. "Soapy" and Nancy were to depart after the dinner. The ranking officials accompanied the Williamses to the airport where their U.S. Air Force plane was waiting. Suddenly, while formally attired Rhodesians were shaking hands and speaking polite words of farewell to the assistant secretary and his wife, out of the darkness staggered a bulky, white, shirt-sleeved figure. Before anyone knew what was happening, he approached "Soapy," drew back his fist, and landed a blow to Williams's face, shouting in blurred words, "We *love* Americans!" I had been standing slightly apart from the Williamses and did not see the blow; I first glimpsed the governor, small of stature, grappling with a huge white man, while his dumbfounded aide helped him usher the man off the tarmac. "Soapy," knocked back on his heels but unhurt, reacted as if nothing had happened, continuing to shake hands. Boarding the aircraft with Nancy, they flew off into the night, while I was left with an incident.

Police instantaneously whisked away the culprit, who turned out to be a mercenary fighting for Katanga; the governor apologized profusely, and we left the airport. The fellow was tried, convicted and fined fifty pounds. The irony of it was that political enemies of "Soapy"'s in Michigan wrote letters of support for the mercenary to the editor of the Lusaka paper; one said in effect, "Sock him again!" and enclosed twenty dollars to help pay the fine.

Years later, long after Northern Rhodesia had become the Republic of Zambia, Kenneth Kaunda was again at the White House, this time as chief of state and official guest of the U.S. government. In a toast to President Ford at a White House dinner, on April 19, 1975, President Kaunda, after expressing dismay at the "current posture of America toward Africa," referred to the incident of 1961:

> We cannot but recall that America did not wait for and march in step with the colonial powers but, rather, boldly, boldly marched ahead with the colonial peoples in their struggles to fulfill their

aspirations—an America undaunted by the strong forces of reaction against the wind of change, whose nationals helped teach the colonial settlers about the evils of racial discrimination; an America whose Assistant Secretary for African Affairs, "Soapy" Williams, could be slapped in the face by a white reactionary on our soil and yet, undaunted, still smile, still stand by American principles of freedom, justice, and national independence based on majority rule.

A month after the Williamses' visit to the federation, on September 18, 1961, Dag Hammerskjold, secretary general of the United Nations, was killed in a plane crash near Ndola in Northern Rhodesia. Why the accident happened has never been satisfactorily explained. Hammarskjöld's death focused world attention on events in Central Africa. Great Britain and the United States supported the unity of the Congo, including Katanga, which the UN was trying to bring about. Sir Roy Welensky pretended to be neutral but vainly hoped that Katanga would become a buffer state between the black nationalists of the Congo and his own white-led federation. London's *Economist* wrote in January 1962, ". . . The time has come to face the music in central Africa. There is still an appalling danger that the whole thing might blow up this year." In the following year, 1963, the Federation of Rhodesia and Nyasaland ceased to exist.

American policy satisfied neither blacks nor whites in Rhodesia. White officials winced at our insistence on maintaining relations with black nationalists; the blacks distrusted us because of our support of the white governments of the Federation and of Southern Rhodesia and of our ineffectiveness in furthering their independence. Our residence in Salisbury became a unique meeting ground for blacks and whites; we insisted on entertaining them together. White Rhodesian politicians shook hands in our house for the first time with black nationalists. I received in my office Joshua Nkomo and the Reverend Ndabaningi Sithole, both black nationalists in Southern Rhodesia, visited black leaders *and* white settlers in the country areas, and made numerous trips to Lusaka and Blantyre where we maintained consulates. But the Federation was doomed to disintegration. Northern Rhodesia had to become Zambia and Nyasaland, Malawi. Southern Rhodesia would remain a troubled country for a good many years. Two things would prolong white rule: an efficient army and police force and the lack of unity and direction in Rhodesia's African nationalist movement. Unlike Nigeria, there was no core of capable, university-educated black leaders; Africans in Rhodesia had been conditioned to be hewers of wood and carriers of water and had been denied the opportunity for education abroad.

The experience in the Federation was a frustrating one: no sense of accomplishment and none of the color, élan, fervor, and sprawling good humor of the Nigerians.

Our wanderings in exile from East Asia had brought us face to face in five countries with crises and problems which were testing the ability of man to live with himself. In Pakistan we observed the inheritance of partition—a divided country separated by a thousand miles of India and an obsession with Kashmir. Two future presidents of Pakistan, Iskander Mirza and General Mohammed Ayub Khan, sat in our living room in Karachi, their hands stretched out in gestures of despair, asking, "What are we ever going to do with those East Bengalis?" Yet neither would have admitted the inevitability of a Bangladesh. Kashmir, claimed by both India and Pakistan, seemed to be a permanent running sore. Paul Hoffman, one of many mediators, came to Karachi while I was there, to indulge in a pale and unsuccessful version of shuttle diplomacy between New Delhi and Karachi. The Pakistanis and Indians would be at each other's throats, and no outsider could prevent it.

Next, Lebanon, a tiny, beautiful, critically located country, caught up in an impossible network of seventeen sects of Islam and Christianity, in the middle of the Arab-Israeli dispute, buying and selling the products of others. Many Lebanese insisted, in self-defense, that they were Phoenicians, not Arabs, but this fact made them out-Arab the Arabs in their hatred of Israel. Eric Johnston indefatigably tried to forge an agreement on the use of the waters of the Jordan River, which would have made the desert bloom for both Israelis and Arabs, yet neither would sign the same piece of paper. Blood would surely run.

France was a different scene. We witnessed one of the last gasps of colonialism and saw the crisis of Algeria turn into the crisis of Gaullism. Americans had little leverage over Algeria and certainly none over de Gaulle; as the general intimated to the ambassador, what did Algeria have to do with us? De Gaulle saved France, and she became more prosperous than ever.

To be in Africa in 1960, the year of Africa, was a privilege. Our hopes were too high for Nigeria. We were carried away by the buoyancy and the promise. Nevertheless, I am convinced that our aid programs, scattered in effect, helped the Nigerians. But the Ibos had to fight for a Biafra, and to stop that conflict was beyond the power of the United States.

The Federation of Rhodesia and Nyasaland was bound to break up into three countries. The Kennedy policy toward Africa may have hastened independence for Zambia and Malawi, but it could incur only ill will in Rhodesia. Only in 1976 did Henry Kissinger discover that there were yet problems to be solved in southern Africa.

No foreign service officer can be an isolationist; our craft is internationalism. I was an enthusiastic supporter of our economic, educational, cultural, and informational programs in the countries in which I served. In spite of stupid mistakes, inept personnel, and wasted funds, I believe we brought useful help to many of the developing countries. Except for Rhodesia, the prestige of the United States was high during the years I served in these five nations. Uncle Sam was always a good guy to kick around, and the press was often unfriendly, but one did not have to hide the flag, and terrorists had not yet discovered that diplomats were fair game. We may have helped to speed the process of modernization and, in Africa, the progress toward independence, but the direction of events was an historical one which we did not nor could control.

On February 15, 1962, I received a telegram in Salisbury from George Ball, then under secretary of state, which began: "Am delighted inform you President wishes appoint you as first Ambassador to Tanganyika. Would appreciate telegraphic confirmation this appointment agreeable to you. If it is, will request your *agrément* immediately." It ended, "My congratulations on your selection for this position." After receiving my reply, "Soapy" Williams cabled: "Immensely pleased your acceptance and prospect your good services."

Because of the necessity for Senate confirmation, I could not publicly announce the new appointment, but I was authorized to inform Sir Roy Welensky confidentially. Meanwhile the *agrément* was requested of the Tanganyikan government, and the acceptances of Prime Minister Julius Nyerere and the Queen of England came promptly. Days went by, and I was puzzled that no announcement came from Washington. The department, after yet another full field investigation, had by this time decided that my security clearance was valid and anticipated no difficulties from the Senate Foreign Relations Committee. I said my farewells in the Federation, being necessarily coy about my next post, and arrived in the department only to be told by the deputy under secretary of administration, "We've got problems."

Senator Bourke Hickenlooper, ranking minority member of the Foreign Relations Committee, had decided to oppose my appointment as ambassador to Tanganyika. Senior officials in the department were apparently astonished and embarrassed. They would never have asked for the *agrément* had they expected difficulties in the Senate. The Secretary of State Dean Rusk, an old friend since CBI days in 1944, was sympathetic and assured me he would personally take the responsibility for persuading Hickenlooper to change his mind. Meanwhile I had been acting as though I were going to Dar-es-Salaam. Appointments were set up for me to meet the responsible officers for Tanganyikan affairs, not only in the State Department, but in the Agency for International Development (AID), and other agencies of government. I read reports from the embassy in Dar-es-Salaam and briefed myself on the problems of the new country in which I was to serve. The chargé d'affaires in Tanganyika cabled the department that an early announcement of the appointment would be in U.S. interest because an ambassador from the People's Republic of China was to be accredited momentarily.

Time went on. Finally, Dean Rusk called me into his office to inform me, as he expressed it, of the "failure of a mission." In a conversation of over an hour, the secretary had been unable to convince Hickenlooper that John Emmerson would stand up to the Communists in Tanganyika, a very important country in Africa. The senator's theme was "As goes Tanganyika, so goes Africa!" He would approve my assignment to Luxembourg or to some other country where communism was not an issue. Whether Hickenlooper had ever read the transcripts of my 1952 hearings and the testimony about my attitudes toward communism by Charles Bohlen, Walter Bedell Smith, Dean Rusk himself, and many others, I never knew. I had never met the senator from Iowa, and he refused to see me when I tried to make an appointment.

Many years later I learned that the withdrawal of my nomination had been decided at high administration levels on the grounds that it would produce a "floor fight" in the Senate and "damage the country." Senator J. William Fulbright was then chairman of the Senate Foreign Relations Committee. I recalled this when I read in 1972 his article in *The New Yorker* magazine entitled "In Thrall to Fear," in which he staunchly defended American officials in China "who provided a more objective, less ideologically colored view of the Chinese Communists back in the days before they won the civil war. Not only did the observations of these men go unheeded," Fulbright wrote, "they themselves were subsequently denounced and persecuted."

Secretary Rusk offered me the choice of any position in the foreign service that would not require Senate confirmation. I was to discover later, with gratification, that Chester Bowles, who had been under secretary of state and later special representative to President Kennedy, had written to Rusk in 1962, "In my opinion, the previous administration was wrong in not giving Emmerson the Nigerian embassy and we were right in planning to assign him to Tanganyika.... In any event, through speeches and public statements we have committed ourselves to firm support of public servants who have been unjustly accused, and I view the Emmerson nomination as an important test of our commitment."

My ties with Japan had become tenuous during my years of meandering in the wilderness. I tried to keep up with Japanese events through reading and became good friends with the respective Japanese ambassadors and consuls general in the posts in which I served. My Japanese became rusty with disuse. At diplomatic receptions and dinners, inevitably the wife of the Japanese chief of mission and I would spot each other from across the room and would soon be engaged in earnest Japanese conversation. Wives of Japanese diplomats do not always speak fluent English and, living lonely lives far from their native land, sparkle with animation when someone converses with them in their native tongue. Japanese diplomats themselves feel an obligation to speak English, as a mark of achievement in their profession. (I find that one has to deal gingerly with a Japanese in the matter of which language to speak. If his English is patently superior to my Japanese, there is no problem; if it is the other way around, one must tread lightly. Respect for his pride may require some sacrifice in communication.)

I learned that the post of deputy chief of mission and minister in Tokyo might be available. The Kennedy Administration had appointed as ambassador to Japan, Edwin O. Reischauer, a personal friend of mine from Kyoto days and the outstanding authority on Japan in the United States. I knew that we would be compatible and that the assignment would permit me finally, after sixteen years, to return to the land where my career began. And by 1962, the State Department would, I hoped, have lost its qualms about returning me to the Far East.

Alex Johnson was deputy under secretary for political affairs and Averell Harriman was assistant secretary for Far Eastern affairs. Both agreed that the assignment to Tokyo would be appropriate, and Harriman wrote to Reischauer making the proposal. Reischauer replied promptly, welcoming me as his deputy. The chargé in Dar-es-Salaam was informed by cable that "owing urgent need John Emmerson's services in another position, White House has reluctantly decided not appoint him Ambassador Tanganyika." I began to brief myself on Japan, bought an up-to-date character dictionary, and tried to pull from the depths of my memory the thousands of Japanese word-signs I had learned so many years before.

My appointment as deputy chief of mission and minister to Japan was announced by the White House on June 18. News of my congressional testimony in 1957 had been reported in Japan and right-wing circles had kept alive the stories of my meetings with Nosaka, Tokuda, and Shiga. Herbert Norman was well known in Japan, not only for the official positions that he had held, but for his writings, which had made him popular among intellectuals. The *Asahi* correspondent in Washington cabled his newspaper on the day of the announcement that I had been criticized at the time of the so-called "McCarthy storm" and had "pushed forward many progressive policies, including immediate release of political prisoners." In July, one Hashimoto Tetsuma, head of the Purple Cloud Society, became active in opposing my appointment. He, it will be remembered, was a *soi-disant* "peacemaker" in 1941, who had been distrusted by Ambassador Grew and taken seriously by Eugene Dooman and Stanley Hornbeck. He had undertaken a futile, single-handed mission to Washington. After the war, Hashimoto had attacked American Occupation policies and the peace treaty. In 1961, still promoting right-wing causes, he had tried unsuccessfully to call on the president, Secretary Rusk, and Treasury Secretary Douglas Dillon. Before my arrival in Japan, in 1962, Hashimoto wrote a letter of protest to Ambassador Reischauer, with copies to numerous Japanese businessmen, politicians, journalists, and other prominent citizens, as well as translations to some two hundred Americans, including members of Congress. The document was a scurrilous one, terming me a "proved ultra leftist" and quoting me as having stated that the only Japanese I could believe in were the imprisoned Communists who should take the leadership in reconstructing Japan. Mr. Hashimoto went on then to write that, among well-thinking circles in Japan, there was a rising sentiment of doubt regarding the true policy of the United States, that in the early stage of the Occupation, the Americans had joined with the Soviets to emasculate Japanese patriots and that in the same period, General George C. Marshall had tried to force a Kuomintang–Communist coalition and turn China into a Communist regime. Consequently, he wrote, my appointment had given rise to worries that similar incidents might take place during Ambassador Reischauer's tenure in Japan.

On July 15, a hot, blazing day in Tokyo, our plane touched down at Haneda airport. I was on Japanese soil again for the first time since February 15, 1946, and Dorothy for the first time since January 4, 1941. Burton Fahs, an old friend who was then minister for cultural affairs in the embassy, boarded the plan to greet us and to warn us that there might be a rightist demonstration against me. Because of the bright sunshine, I wore dark glasses, not expecting photographers and forgetting that in Japanese iconography, dark glasses suggest gangsters and suspicious persons. There were photographers but no demonstrations.

It became clear that not only Hashimoto, but other ultraconservatives, including a well-known columnist and commentator and a notorious prewar minister of Home Affairs (and thus supervisor of the well-known special police) had tried to mount a campaign to have me recalled. Reischauer refused to dignify these criticisms with an acknowledgment. The gist of replies to inquirers by the department and the embassy was that the accusations were unfounded, that to question the anti-Communist posture of the United States was presumptuous. Furthermore, to impugn the American government with respect to the caliber of its chosen representatives abroad was discourteous at the very least.

The State Department heard from a number of senators and representatives on Hashimoto's mailing list. Replies put Mr. Hashimoto in perspective, noting that at the age of seventy-three he was a "rather well-known ultraconservative figure of minor influence in Japan" and that his *Shiunsō* (Purple Cloud Society) had been founded in 1924 and was reputed to have no more than four or five members. My appointment was given unequivocal support. Dean Rusk personally wrote a reassuring four-page letter with a four-page enclosure to Representative Francis E. Walter, chairman of the House Committee on Un-American Activities.

In Japan Obama Toshie, a television news commentator, devoted a program to castigating me and one of the sensational right-wing weekly magazines, *Zembō*, published an article entitled "Repercussions Created by Minister in Dark Glasses. . . ." Obama opened his television news broadcast on July 18 by reporting: "When [U.S. Minister Emmerson] arrived at the airport, he was wearing sunglasses and looked like an espionage agent or a detective." In *Zembō*, Obama and Hashimoto discussed my "leftist tendencies" and the expectation that I would associate only with "progressive men of culture" and with Socialists and Communists, avoiding Japan's conservatives. Reischauer himself came in for criticism: "Some powerful leaders in the United States feared that Reischauer was leftist-inclined." Hints of Reischauer's so-called leftist orientation had surfaced at the time of his appointment, and ultraconservatives saw my addition to the embassy staff as a confirmatory signal that U.S. policy toward Japan was moving toward the Left.

By August 7 Reischauer was able to inform the department that "the whole matter is already blowing over." He believed, however, that the attack on me was symptomatic of two more basic problems: that right-wing conservatives still deeply resented the purge and certain other Occupation reforms and, furthermore, feared that the virtual monopoly of contacts with the American embassy, and of American friendship, which they thought they possessed, would now vanish. Reischauer, whose name had come to Washington's attention in 1960 through an article in *Foreign Affairs*, "The Broken Dialogue with Japan," had instituted a policy of wider relationships for the embassy to include more intellectuals, moderate opposi-tionists, Socialists and labor leaders. His point had been that American officials had lost touch with large and important segments of the Japanese population, and that as a result, our knowledge and judgment of people and events had become clouded. During the Reischauer period, more historians, artists, professors, journalists, politicians (of both Left and Right), and representatives of women's, labor, educational, cultural, and other organizations went through the doors of the ambassador's residence than at any time before or since. Nor did the embassy neglect relationships essential to diplomacy—those within the three prongs of Japan's power system, government, business, and bureaucracy.

We took advantage in Tokyo of opportunities to correct the image of a Red minister maneuvering behind the scenes to bring Socialists and Communists into a coalition government. I did not meet Mr. Hashimoto, who incidentally failed to respond to Reischauer's expressed willingness to talk with him. I had lunch with the television commentator, Obama, without my dark glasses, and we arranged suitable introductions to prominent businessmen, industrialists, and conservative politicians. As time went on, I did not confine my political contacts to conservatives, but cultivated acquaintances in the Socialist, Komeitō, and Democratic Socialist parties. In view of my widely and distortedly publicized wartime association with Nosaka, who by the 1960s was chairman of the Central Committee of the Japanese Communist party, I made no effort to see Communists. But with all other parties, we in the embassy maintained constant and profitable communication. Within a few months, the minor furor over the minister in dark glasses disappeared, and I was able to do my job without harassment.

Tokyo was a different city and Japan a different country from what I had seen in 1945 and the early months of 1946. Shock and confusion had been transformed into confidence and order. The Occupation had been over for ten years, but the American presence was evident in our numerous military bases and in our continued administration of Okinawa. An Occupation psychology of official deference lingered, but irritation over bases and the retention of Okinawa was growing. The rush for ever greater production was on. Prime Minister Ikeda's ten-year, "doubling the income" plan sounded bold; no one in his wildest fantasy would have dreamed that after another ten years, by 1970, Japan's GNP would have quintupled.

It was a privileged experience to be a part of the Reischauer embassy, as it had been to serve on the staff of Ambassador Grew. Reischauer had the perspective of an historian—he knew Japan and the language, and yet he had a practical sense of how to handle the immediate problems of political relations, security, economics, cultural affairs, and informational activities. His wife, Haru, a granddaughter of a Meiji prime minister of Japan, Matsukata Masayoshi, played a role no other ambassador's wife could undertake. Her language, her charm, her sense of public relations born out of a journalistic career, and her dedication were known and respected by enormous numbers of Japanese as well as Americans. The United States got two ambassadors for the price of one.

It took a while to get back into the Japanese scene. I studied the language with a tutor daily (as did Reischauer), and gradually recovered my newspaper-reading knowledge and my ability to converse on substantive subjects. It was like returning to a world that I had known before and yet did not recognize. A few old prewar friends turned up, and Kyoto, at least, looked the same. There one could lapse back into time and reconstruct the walks, the excursions, and even the mood of those prewar years. This was Japan, and I was back.

The thread had returned to its beginning.

14

Japan 1962–66

The Tokyo embassy in 1962 occupied the same site and buildings that we had known in 1941. From the entrance to the chancery, one could look across the reflecting pool to the wooded hillside and the ambassador's residence at the top. The zigzag path up the hill and past the ginkgo tree, which I had trod as a young third secretary, carrying telegrams and papers for Ambassador Grew's approval, was still there. The two apartment buildings, now almost entirely converted to office space, stood to the right and to the left. The swimming pool was behind the latter. The green grass and trees set off the white buildings. The high ceilings and marble fireplaces of the chancery were reminders of a day of more leisurely diplomacy, and, for me, the ghosts of Joseph Grew and Eugene Dooman walked the halls. The MacArthur interlude, with GIs billeted downstairs and the mud on the floors, which I had seen in 1945, seemed as though it had never happened. Now the embassy was again an embassy, and I was Rip van Winkle returning after twenty-one years.

The expanding functions of a diplomatic establishment of the 1960s had far outgrown the modest confines of the prewar compound. Before the end of the Occupation, in 1952, we had purchased for $827,500 the Manchurian Railway Building (Mantetsu Biru), just down the street, which in the 1930s had been the towering symbol, all of six stories high, of Japan's vast enterprise on the China mainland. It became the annex and, together with the chancery and offices in several other buildings in Tokyo, housed the embassy family. By 1973 the rise in land values had made the Mantetsu, by then battered, unwashed, and unimposing, sell for $47,170,000. This must have been one of the State Department's more profitable financial transactions.

I had a sixteen-year historical gap to fill. Japan's peace constitution, outlawing war, had gone into effect on May 3, 1947, but premonitions of the cold war and the reverse course in Occupation policy, were already evident. The Korean police action (it was not called a war), beginning in 1950, resulted in a spurt in economic recovery as well as a security problem for Japan. MacArthur ordered the formation of a National Police Reserve, shortly to become the Self-Defense Forces. The peace and security treaties effective April 28, 1952, marked the return of Japan's independence but left legacies of American military bases and the continued occupation of Okinawa. Fears bred at Hiroshima and Nagasaki were revived in 1954 by nuclear tests on Bikini Island, where the fallout inadvertently injured and killed crewmen of the fishing vessel *Lucky Dragon* and created an incident that took a year to settle.

The confused beginnings of postwar Japanese politics, which I had witnessed in 1945, had led ten years later to the formation of a united Liberal Democratic party that was to begin an uninterrupted period of rule. In the same year—1955—moderate and radical socialists had combined, only to split again in 1960. Yoshida Shigeru, the prewar Foreign Office bureaucrat who had served as prime minister during 1946–47, took the office again in 1948, to lead Japan for a then-unprecedented period of six years. The man who had stood up to MacArthur with skill and courage began what was to be known as the Yoshida line, a succession of prime ministers picked by him: Kishi Nobusuke, Ikeda Hayato, Satō Eisaku, and Fukuda Takeo. All took the reins of power in due course, with an unplanned and unexpected interruption between 1972 and 1976, when upstart Tanaka Kakuei spent himself into office, and the maverick Miki

Takeo received the mantle by default after a deadlock between top party leaders.

Japan's most serious postwar crisis had erupted in 1960, when rioting against the revision of the United States–Japan security treaty had caused the fall of the Kishi government and the cancellation of a visit to Japan by President Eisenhower. Although the moment was a critical one for Japanese–American relations, the leftist-inspired student demonstrations were more anti-Kishi than anti-American, and in elections held only a few months later, the Liberal Democratic party was accorded a popular majority of 57.5 percent. (This majority had already begun to erode, however; by 1967 it was to fall to 48 percent and by 1976 to 41 percent.) The Communists in 1962 had three seats in the House of Representatives, two fewer than they had won in the first postwar elections in 1946. It was 1964 before they claimed a membership of one hundred thousand, which was the number I was supposed to have added to their party roster by parading Tokuda and Shiga through the streets of Tokyo in October 1945.

Ikeda Hayato, when he assumed the prime ministership after the explosive events of the summer of 1960, called his policy a "low posture" *(teishisei)* and directed the nation's attention to economic growth. As early as 1950 Japan had recovered its prewar economic position, and by 1962 the GNP was three times that of the period 1934–36. The phrases *economic animal* and *economic miracle* were beginning to appear in foreigners' appraisals of Japan's rapidly advancing industrial power.

During the period 1962–66, the embassy was concerned with three main areas within the Japanese–American relationship: restoration of the dialogue, economics, and security. The word *partnership* became our theme, and every speech, toast, panel discussion, press conference, or statement, whether originating in Washington or Tokyo, evoked this concept. Its purpose was to rid the relationship of the Occupation psychology, to prod the Japanese into regarding themselves as equals and into playing a more important role in the *Free World*, a phrase descriptive of the then-accepted, bipolar nature of our globe.

The idea of being equal partners was not a new one. As early as 1910, when tensions had arisen between Tokyo and Washington following the Russo–Japanese war, a Japanese professor wrote about "a new relationship between Japan and the United States," observing that a change was occurring from a "superior–inferior" relationship to one based on "friendship between equals." A contemporary commentator, quoting this 1910 statement in 1976, asked somewhat cynically, "How many times since then has this 'new' relationship been proclaimed?"

As for Japan's role in the world, Americans have continually expressed dissatisfaction over the too low posture of the affluent Japanese and their failure to assume international responsibilities commensurate with their status as a leading industrial nation. Japan has been called a reluctant dragon, a timid colossus, a country "in neutral," and by Reischauer, the tongue-tied "big boy who prefers to sit in the back row of the classroom in the hope that no one will notice him."

The embassy's efforts to promote partnership and repair the dialogue were labeled by Japan's mass media as the Kennedy-Reischauer Offensive. Reischauer was an indefatigable lecturer and his reputation as an historian reinforced his statements as ambassador. Robert Kennedy visited Japan twice, once in 1962 and, again, in 1964. His youth and vigor captured the imagination of the Japanese, already fired by the Kennedy image established by his brother, the president. The RFK Committee, formed by a group of active young Japanese businessmen and politicians, took charge of the visits and saw that Robert Kennedy met new faces, people who did not necessarily speak English and who were presumably the future political and economic leaders of the country. A trip to Japan by President Kennedy was in the planning stages when he was assassinated. It would have been a stupendous success.

The developing dialogue met obstacles. The turbulence that had created riots in 1960 had not disappeared. Opposition to the security treaty, fed by the multitude of leftist and left-of-leftist student organizations, inspired sporadic demonstrations which were further fueled by demands for the return of Okinawa and by America's increasing involvement in Vietnam. Reischauer regretted that he was never able to speak on the campuses of Tokyo and other national universities. College deans and presidents, trembling at the thought of violence for which they would be held responsible, did not welcome American government officials on their campuses. Robert Kennedy incited a near riot with an appearance at Waseda University in 1962 and, determined to be heard out when he returned in 1964, did successfully make a speech there, but only after the most careful and elaborate precautions had been taken.

Our second preoccupation was economic. Japanese–American trade reached $3.2 billion in 1962, and four years later it had nearly doubled. The two-way exchange of goods was almost even in 1962, with a slight edge in favor of the United States. But Japan's export push was on and, by 1966, the balance had shifted in her favor, to go on to greater and more troublesome heights in later years. The Japanese were marching ahead, thanks to their ingenuity, high productivity, and a certain amount of protection. American manufacturers smarted under multifarious Japanese restrictions on trade and investment, and their representatives in Tokyo continually complained that the embassy was doing little to help them. The fact was, that for the Japanese, to export was to live, and only when they gained confidence in their economic strength would they relax restrictions, which in due course they did. Japan was then only seventh among the world's economic powers but was well on her way to the number three position—after the United States and the USSR—which she soon captured.

The most prickly problems that the embassy had to handle were in the third area—security—and arose out of the U.S.-Japanese mutual security treaty. Put simply, the United States guaranteed the defense of Japan in return for bases on which American military personnel and equipment could be stationed. Additionally, the two nations had agreed that no major changes in this personnel or equipment would be made without prior consultation between them. This compact meant that no nuclear weapons would be introduced into Japan nor would troops be dispatched into combat directly from American bases in Japan. Elements of controversy were ever present. The conduct of American soldiers was exceptionally good, but some rapes and murders occurred, planes crashed, and drunken brawls broke out. Such events were natural subjects for colorful journalism. The policy of the Japanese government was to support the treaty and to cooperate with the American military. Foreign Office officials constantly reminded us, however, of the political problems they faced, produced by an alert, energetic, and hostile opposition, and by something they described as *kokumin kanjō*, or "feelings of the people." These feelings grew out of a natural psychological resentment against foreign troops occupying home soil and from fear of involvement in someone else's war.

Beginning in 1964 the visits of American nuclear-powered submarines (called SSNs by the Navy) to Japanese ports produced such agitation that the benefits gained by the navy in refueling, provisioning, and affording rest and recreation for the crews, sometimes seemed hardly worthwhile. The government and the Liberal Democratic Party (LDP) approved the port calls, hoping that, as they became customary, they would diminish the so-called nuclear allergy still strong twenty years after Hiroshima and Nagasaki. The submarines were nuclear-powered but not nuclear-weaponed. Nevertheless, the Communists, Socialists, and cooperating leftist organizations found in the visits dramatic opportunities for protest. The embassy and the Foreign Office, in cooperation with the navy, played a game in scheduling arrivals and departures, picking days on which it would be most inconvenient to assemble marchers, either at Sasebo or Yokosuka, the two ports used, and assuring that as little advance notice as possible was given. Information leaked rapidly, however, and sizable crowds showed up, manning docks and rowboats, for the first succession of port calls. It was several years before the expectations of the Liberal Democratic Party were borne out, and the appearance of an SSN became so routine that no public notice was taken of it.

Okinawa became the fester that would not heal. American occupation of the Ryukyu Islands was the last reminder to the Japanese that they had lost the war. The Pentagon saw our continuing administration of the islands as essential to American security. The Japanese, who felt no threat, did not share the American preoccupation with the security of Southeast Asia. Prime Minister Satō announced that the postwar era would not end until

Okinawa had been returned, and when President Kennedy, in March 1962, recognized the Ryukyus as part of the Japanese homeland, reversion became a question of timing. The military wanted to hold on as long as possible, but Reischauer early saw the political importance of ending U.S. hegemony over this bit of foreign territory. The State Department was sympathetic, and a tug-of-war characterized American handling of the Okinawa problem.

Lieutenant General Paul W. Caraway, high commissioner for the Ryukyus from 1961 to 1964, epitomized the army's desire to perpetuate complete control over the islands. He resisted Japanese influence within his domain, whether in the form of advisers or aid programs. He suspected the Ikeda and Satō governments of trying to penetrate piecemeal the Okinawan administration, threatening the American governance. The military expressed their views in descriptive clichés: "salami tactics," "nibbling," and the "camel's nose under the tent." One concession would lead to another concession, in this view, and the strategic value of the bases would be impaired. It was not until Caraway was replaced by Lieutenant General Albert Watson that we were able to begin a process of increasing Japanese–American cooperation on Okinawan problems. General Watson had a sense of public relations, and he liked the Japanese. The embassy's relations with the high commissioner's office measurably improved upon his appointment.

I was chargé d'affaires in April 1964 when we were able finally to inaugurate a joint Japanese–American committee for economic aid to the Ryukyu Islands. The formation of this cooperative body was recognition of the fact that Japan would eventually exercise sovereignty over the islands and that, in the meantime, Japan and the United States would share responsibility for the welfare of the inhabitants. Foreign Minister Ōhira Masayoshi and I signed and exchanged the notes setting up the committee. At the ceremony in the Foreign Office, I read an innocuous statement referring to cooperation between our two governments as the essence of the agreement and stated its purposes: to provide economic and technical assistance to the Ryukyus, and to promote their economic development and the welfare and well-being of their inhabitants. The word *reversion*, a battle-cry for its proponents, was not mentioned. It took another eight years before Okinawa was finally returned to Japan, in May of 1972.

Publicity given to the signing of the agreement stirred up the old ghosts. Art Goul, a columnist, wrote, "What's This About the Ryukyus?" in the *Oakland Tribune,* a newspaper owned by William Knowland, the former senator from California, and "from Formosa," whom I had met at the United Nations in 1956. Goul called it "significant" and "unusual" that John K. Emmerson "should be speaking for the United States with regard to relinquishment of our front line defense in the Pacific." He reminded readers that this same Emmerson had been questioned "behind closed doors" in 1957 because of slanted reports in favor of Communist aims. The State Department, in replies to congressional inquiries about the column, affirmed that statements I had made were identical with U.S. policy and quoted President Kennedy's 1962 promise, "I recognize the Ryukyus to be a part of the Japanese homeland and look forward to the day when the security interests of the Free World will permit their restoration to full Japanese sovereignty." I had now won the perhaps unique distinction of being accused of losing China, the Middle East, and the Ryukyu Islands.

The assassination of John F. Kennedy, on November 22, 1963, shocked the Japanese as if the president had been one of their own. I got the news at two o'clock on the morning of the twenty-third (Tokyo time) from Burton Fahs, cultural minister and director of the Information Service. Members of the U.S. cabinet, headed by Secretary of State Dean Rusk, were in the air over the Pacific on their way to Tokyo for an annual Japanese–American ministerial conference. We were to meet the group at the airport later in the morning. They turned back to Washington in midair. The ambassador and I consulted by telephone and decided to meet at once at the chancery.

In the early predawn hours, as I drove through the embassy gates, little clusters of newsmen had already gathered. We set aside a small room on the ground floor, put up a photograph of the president and laid out a book for signatures. The line of visitors began forming early and remained unbroken for hours, continuing for several days. The outpouring of genuine grief and respect, in the form of mass media eulogies, personal calls, communications, gifts, and the unending file of mourners at the special memorial service, together with similar manifestations throughout the country, proved Japanese goodwill for the United States.

My own most touching experience was a chance encounter a few weeks later while on a walk in the outskirts of Nikkō, near our mountain home where we spent occasional weekends. Three small boys, probably nine or ten years old, were strolling along, and we began a conversation. When they learned I was an American, one spoke solemnly, "I know about President Kennedy. And you know, he was exactly the same age as my father."

Four months later another event was to demonstrate the esteem of Japanese for Americans. A few minutes after noon on March 24, 1964, an embassy officer suddenly opened my office door, shouting, "The ambassador has been stabbed!" I rushed into the hall and down the steps to the chancery entrance. A policeman and an embassy officer were scuffling with a young Japanese boy. The ambassador was sitting on a bench near an enlarging pool of blood. John Ferchak, a junior embassy officer, was trying, along with Reischauer, to apply a tourniquet to the latter's leg, the only article available being a woman's flimsy scarf. Within a few minutes other embassy employees, who happened to be nearby, helped the ambassador to enter his car, already waiting at the doorway. Fortunately, Toranomon Hospital was only two blocks from the embassy.

A mentally retarded nineteen-year-old youth, dressed like a laborer, had jumped over the compound wall and, escaping the notice of the Marine guards, had dashed up to the entrance. As Reischauer walked out the door to get into his car to go to lunch, the boy had suddenly plunged a knife into the ambassador's thigh, inflicting a long, deep cut. Recalling that his brother had died from loss of blood when injured in the bombing of Shanghai in 1937, Reischauer shouted for a tourniquet. Ferchak responded instantaneously.

Again, the embassy was overwhelmed with visits and messages. This time the latter were of apology, sympathy, and respect for the ambassador and for the United States. We set up a special staff to take care of the press, communications, and presents, and for the ambassador's protection, to screen the many visitors who wished to pay hospital visits in person. The *Sankei* newspaper typified media reaction: "He is the first ambassador who has been given so much sympathy and probably no one will be the second."

Reischauer's thoughts were, first, to try to prevent the resignation of any high official, which would be expected under such circumstances and, second, to issue a statement to express his own feelings. We immediately communicated the hope that no one would resign. It became clear, however, that this would be impossible; the Japanese public would expect an official admission of responsibility. The minister of Home Affairs, who was also director of Public Safety, announced, with the prime minister's sanction, that he would step down from the cabinet. I sat by Reischauer's bedside, and we worked out the release which he wanted issued to the press. I read it to assembled journalists and before television cameras in the lobby of the chancery at 9:30 on the evening of the stabbing. In his statement the ambassador expressed gratitude for messages of friendship and for the care being ministered by kind and efficient Japanese doctors and nurses. He recognized "the sad fact that unfortunate, unbalanced people exist in all the world," and referred to the recent tragic example in the United States. His sole concern about "this small incident was that to some people it might seem to mar the deep friendship and cordial relationship existing between our two countries." He had every confidence, however, that our partnership would continue to grow closer and stronger.

On the following day, the twenty-fifth, the first television transmission by satellite from Japan to the United States was to take place. Ironically, the first America-to-Japan broadcast had also occurred on an inauspicious occasion, November 23, 1963, hours following the assassination of President Kennedy. Prime Minister Ikeda, the minister of communications, and Ambassador Reischauer were to speak briefly on a program timed for live reception in the United States during the morning of March 25. The telecast went on the air as planned, the prime minister using the opportunity to apologize to the American people for the stabbing incident. I took Reischauer's place and reiterated our conviction that the unfortunate event could have no possible effect on Japanese–American cooperation.

The nineteen-year-old would-be assassin, a victim of Ménière's disease of the inner ear and with a history of mental disturbance, had harbored confused ideas about the distortion of education by American Occupation policy and its deleterious effect on his life. His condition and his act directed public attention to the state of mental care in Japan. Mental hospitals were few, and understaffed and ill-equipped. In Japanese society, families often looked upon such illness with shame and hid their retarded children at home rather than sending them to institutions. A Japanese columnist pointed out that of 1.5 million "abnormal" boys known to the police, only 130,000 were under legal protection. Another journalist discovered that juvenile delinquency had increased by 50 percent between 1962 and 1963. My most unnerving experience was the call paid on me by the father, mother, and elder brother of the boy who had tried to kill the ambassador. They lived in a town at some distance from Tokyo and made the trip by train to visit the embassy. Entering my office, they presented a letter of apology for their son's crime and for their failure to supervise him adequately and then prostrated themselves on the floor in front of me. I tried to calm them as best I could, assuring them that neither the ambassador nor Americans harbored rancor against them or their unfortunate son.

The ambassador's leg wound healed normally, but his blood loss necessitated massive transfusions, which led him to remark that he felt closer than ever to the Japanese people, since Japanese blood now flowed in his veins. Unfortunately, he contracted hepatitis, which inspired journalists to investigate and write about a flourishing market in bad blood, or *yellow blood* as it was termed, being sold for transfusions, and which could have been related to the complications which followed. Reischauer's recovery was long delayed, and on April 15 he left with his wife for Hawaii for several months of rest and recuperation.

The Olympic Games, held in the fall of 1964, were a symbolic turning point in Japan's postwar history. I could remember the flags bearing the Olympic emblem—the five interlaced rings—which flew throughout the country when the games had been scheduled for Tokyo in 1940. Their cancellation due to wars in China and in Europe made the Japanese determined that their second chance would produce a smashing success. The nation mobilized to show the world that Japan had reentered the international community as a respected power. For more than a year before the event, Tokyo was torn up in a frenzy of construction and preparation. Nobody believed that the elevated freeways would be ready, the facilities erected, and the debris removed from the streets in time. Tange Kenzō, already an internationally famous architect, designed sweeping buildings which remained as monuments. The last nail must have been driven as the participants began to arrive, but all was ready on the opening morning. The Japanese Rising Sun flag, in hiding for years after the end of the war, flew confidently.

Prime Minister Ikeda, suffering from cancer, presided over the games but died shortly thereafter. He was succeeded in November by Satō Eisaku, next in the Yoshida line, who broke his mentor's record by serving as head of government for more than seven and a half years.

Developing hostilities in Vietnam impinged more and more on our consciousness. The Tonkin Gulf incident occurred on August 2, 1964, and two days later the Japanese learned that President Johnson had ordered the bombing of torpedo-boat bases in North Vietnam. Tokyo's *Sankei Shimbun* commented, "It seems that the United States has finally gone into full-scale intervention in the Indo-China war; it has finally been dragged into the bog of Asia." The Japanese government maintained consistently a "correct" attitude on Vietnam, "understanding" American policy in Southeast Asia. After all, Japan had expressed in the security treaty with the United States a "common concern in the maintenance of international peace and security in the Far East." At the same time the leaders of government could not hide their uneasiness about the American war. LBJ was so intent on getting "more flags" in Indochina that the State Department repeatedly instructed us to urge the Japanese to give aid to South Vietnam. Our efforts were not eminently successful. About the best the Japanese ever did was to send a small field hospital unit which was stationed near Saigon.

When the Chinese detonated their first atomic weapon on October 16, 1964, the Japanese government promptly condemned the test and even the Socialists were unhappy over it. Public reaction, however, was not so strong as we had anticipated. As one Japanese remarked, "We have long been living next door to the Russians and their much more powerful nuclear weapons, so why should we be concerned over the explosion of a little device by the Chinese?" Some time later, on Washington's instructions, Ambassador Reischauer and I called on Foreign Minister Ōhira and briefed him with top-secret data on the nature of the Chinese weapon and the location of Chinese nuclear installations. Ōhira, craggy and heavyset, who often resembled a meditating Buddha, listened to our sensational revelations with half-closed eyes and without visible reaction. If the object had been to scare him into closer security cooperation with the United States, we patently failed.

In the summer of 1965, I was in charge of the embassy during one of the ambassador's trips to the United States. On July 27 we received an urgent message to inform the Japanese government that a group of B-52 bombers, normally stationed in Guam, would land at Itazuke, an American base in Kyūshū, in order to escape a typhoon. The Foreign Office agreed that no prior consultation for such a movement was necessary since the purpose of the flight was refuge from a storm and had nothing to do with combat. The weather changed, however, and instead of flying to Kyūshū, the B-52s landed on Okinawa, where treaty restrictions did not apply. I was next instructed to inform the Japanese that the bombers would take off from Okinawa on a combat mission to Southeast Asia. On the twenty-ninth I telephoned the director of the American Affairs Bureau at 7:30 A.M.. When the news hit the press, the outcry was deafening. I was waited on by top officials of the Socialist and Democratic Socialist parties, by friends of America, and by the press. Needless to say, the session with the Socialists was stormy. Legally we were in an unassailable position because the bases in Okinawa were outside the purview of the treaty, but to the Japanese, Okinawa was part of their territory, and they feared that its use for missions to bomb Vietnam would involve Japan in an unwanted war. Our friends in the Foreign Office were forced to explain the circumstances to the Diet and, in self-defense, testified that they had tried to get us to stop the bombing mission. This was not true, but they pleaded with us to remember in the future *kokumin kanjō* ("people's feelings") and not to put them in such a difficult position again. I irritated our military by recommending to Washington that, unless military considerations should be paramount, we refrain from dispatching B-52s on bombing missions from Okinawan bases, in order to avoid the kind of damaging political reaction that had just ensued.

Vietnam became an all-consuming problem. We were not policymakers in Tokyo; our job was to explain Japanese attitudes to the State Department and, through our relations with the government and in public statements, to communicate and interpret U.S. policy. It must be recorded, of course, that Japanese discomfort over escalating hostilities in Southeast Asia was tempered by the economic benefits of American procurement of Japanese goods used to prosecute the war. Such benefits were not, however, appreciated by the Japanese public in general and, therefore, they had little effect upon political opinion in the country. Some of our conservative, strongly anti-Communist friends would have liked to unfurl a Japanese flag along with our own, but they were a small minority.

Since I was in charge of the embassy during the extended period of Reischauer's illness, as well as at other times, I had the opportunity to become acquainted with Japan's political and business leaders. Two such were Satō Eisaku and Ōhira Masayoshi. Satō, prime minister after 1964, was typical of the Yoshida line of bureaucrat-politicians. Born in Yamaguchi, the westernmost prefecture of Japan's main island, home of the Chōshū clan from which rose many of the founding Meiji leaders, Satō graduated from Tokyo Imperial University and entered the Railway Ministry. His older brother, Kishi Nobusuke (adopted into the Kishi family), also became a bureaucrat and served as prime minister from 1957 to 1960.

Satō's family ties form an ideal example of the phenomenon called *keibatsu* in Japanese. *Keibatsu* can be translated as "nepotism" or "clan by marriage"; literally, the characters mean "clique-out-of-the-bedroom." Through marriage, alliances can be traced among many of Japan's leading politicians and industrialists. Satō, for example, married the niece of Matsuoka Yōsuke, prewar foreign minister; his son married the daughter of Anzai Hiroshi, president of

Tokyo Gas Company and a power in industrial circles. Anzai's brother married a sister of the wife of Miki Takeo, a recent prime minister, and his son married a sister of the crown princess. Satō was indirectly related to the Yoshida family. And so on. A genealogical chart would reveal an amazing network of blood links among Japan's leaders. These connections are not without influence on the integration of business and government in Japan and on the methods by which things get done.

Satō was a genial person, forthcoming, and always accommodating. On one occasion I had to see him urgently. A telegram from Washington instructed me to inform the prime minister and *only* the prime minister in the strictest secrecy about certain actions we were preparing to take in Vietnam. A sudden call by the chargé on the prime minister would incite the press to wild speculation. How to keep it secret? I put the problem to Satō's private secretary. I could hear on the telephone his prolonged "Saa!" indicating a predicament. After a silence, he replied carefully, "It will not be easy. Don't leave the embassy. I'll come for you in my car without a government license plate." I met him at the embassy entrance; he was driving and asked me to get in the back seat. As we neared the prime minister's official residence, he asked me to crouch on the floor. Reporters assigned to cover the prime minister would be watching visitors from upper-story windows. We stopped at a little-used back entrance. I unwound myself from my undignified posture, entered, and was escorted down back corridors to a small office. Presently Prime Minister Satō appeared, smiling. We had our conference. I left by the same way I had come, and no one ever knew that the American chargé d'affaires had met the prime minister. On our return to the embassy, my friend sighed with relief. "Let's not try that too often." When in 1971 the State Department gave the Japanese embassy thirty minutes' notice that President Nixon would go to China, thus producing the first "Nixon shock," the excuse was that by informing the Japanese in advance, the news would leak. I had satisfied myself that, if necessary, the most secret information could be transmitted safely to the top level of the Japanese government.

Ōhira Masayoshi, another bureaucrat turned politician, was foreign minister during much of the time I was in the embassy. He had come up through the Finance Ministry and, as a long-time member of the House of Representatives and the governing Liberal Democratic party, held successively most of the important cabinet and party positions leading to the prime ministership. Good-humored, his small eyes usually twinkling, he always had a jovial crack to make, ingenuously mixing English with Japanese. One day, during a period when we had had an unusual number of problems and incidents, he threw out his hands, imploring, "Don't give me another headache!" While the Vietnam war raged on, we seemed always to be asking for Japanese indulgence for our military activities in Japan and Okinawa, which, while legal under the treaty, aroused the opposition parties and caused political and public relations problems for the government. At the same time, Americans, especially the military, were often exasperated because they could not understand why the Japanese failed to realize that they had as much stake as we in securing Southeast Asia from Communist aggression. The simple fact was that Communist "aggression" was a long way from their shores.

With four hundred American and six hundred Japanese employees, the Tokyo embassy was a substantial establishment. We were a transplanted, but transient, Washington bureaucracy to which was added the Japanese component, our faithful and permanent local employees. Ambassadors and foreign service officers came and went, but the Japanese continued quietly to perform their jobs, which they knew well. One of these workers was Ishikawa Daisuke, whose first arrival at our Tokyo home when a boy of eighteen in 1936 I have previously described. He celebrated his thirty years of service to the American government in 1975. Efforts were made to bring the Japanese into the embassy family, to brief them on American policy, and to show interest in their welfare, recognizing that they were indispensable in the fulfillment of our responsibilities.

As for the Americans, the embassy was a conglomerate of agencies. The State Department core (ambassador, deputy chief of mission, political, economic, administrative, and consular sections) was dwarfed in numbers by the multitude of representatives of other government departments and bureaus. Name it, and we had it. We protested, usually in vain, at the addition of yet another office. The case was always made that the growing variety of our relations with Japan required the presence of more specialized bureaucrats. Indeed, the Japanese–American relationship had expanded far beyond the classic concepts of the diplomat's profession. One could scarcely conceive of my answer to the inquirer in 1940, "The embassy does not engage in propaganda." The embassy's activities were a reflection of the modern world, particularly its electronics and its copying machines.

For us, the embassy job could be said to have two shifts, day and night. Dorothy joined me for the night shift, which usually began at six o'clock. With more than seventy countries represented in Tokyo, one could attend a national holiday reception on about one out of every five evenings in a year. Yet if neither the ambassador nor the minister showed up at one of these affairs, no matter how small the country, it would be noticed. American relations with Kuwait hung in the balance one time when, for some reason, no American appeared at the Kuwaitis' celebration. Congressmen like to blast the so-called whiskey fund, by which they mean the rather niggardly representation allowances accorded for official entertaining in the foreign service. They forget that receptions and dinners are not given nor attended for pleasure (both the feet and the liver suffer); indeed, these social events often provide an informal meeting place and atmosphere for substantive discussions. Ambassador Horace Hildreth, a political appointee to the embassy in Karachi, had come to me one morning, saying, "John, I got more business done last night at that reception than I could have managed in a week of appointments. I solved a problem with the prime minister, talked over an important issue with the foreign minister, spoke to the etc., etc." And it was Hildreth who in his Senate confirmation hearings had announced that he would not go abroad to spend the taxpayers' money on cocktail parties.

The diplomatic corps was a minor element in our representational responsibilities. It was more important to keep in touch with politicians, businessmen, cultural and educational leaders, and representatives of organizations playing significant roles in Japanese society. The American businessmen were a special category; we arranged an all-day briefing in the embassy once a year for them and actively cooperated with the Tokyo American Chamber of Commerce.

Relations with the press were delicate but essential; two-way exchanges could be beneficial to both sides. Frequently, it was a battle of wits, the embassy officer wishing to be accommodating but exercising his ingrained bureaucratic restraint, while the correspondent prodded for an indiscretion. At a farewell party given me by the Foreign Correspondents Club, I put the diplomat's point of view in the form of a poem, later published in the *Japan Times*:

> When diplomat meets correspondent, results can never be
> foretold;
> a meeting of the minds can be no meeting and no minds if I
> may be so frank and bold.

> You want to know if policy's changed,
> But you must know that we must say that policy
> Never, never, never, never changes.
> So we with words in lovely patterns ranged
> Denote, describe, depict, declare
> And thus we ring the changes

> But then the questions from the press!
> What and why and who, what for, and when?
> We deviate, extrapolate, interpolate, perambulate
> We answer brilliantly—off the record—
> And then!

> What comes out in the papers sends us running to our bosses,
> Mumbling denials, disclaimers, demurrers, derogations—
> Any relation to our uttered words is *so* coincidental,
> That we gnash our teeth and sink in gloom that's wholly
> transcendental.

So let us cheer the minds that meet and those that slide right by.
   'Ere long the need will disappear. The diplomat will speak no
     more.
His craft is being futurized, mechanicized, computerized.
   The input in, the output out—
No more the friendly, bloody bout!

And diplomats again will tilt their tea and wear their spats
   And neatly creaséd stripéd pants.
While correspondents sit and think, and as the think piece smooth
     unwinds
   They dream of days of other kinds,
When kicking live diplomats was more fun than bashing the
     damned computer.

Reischauer submitted his resignation in the autumn of 1966, and it appeared that, after four and a half years, I also would leave Japan. Before departure, I took advantage of an opportunity to visit Vietnam, just to get a feel of the place.

I was surprised by the pessimism I found among the political officers in the Saigon embassy. They agreed that we were "wrestling with democracy," but that there was no unity, no solidarity, no national movement, no consensus in the country. There was no leadership, no one with real support; General Nguyen Cao Ky had the backing of the army but nothing else. Reports of our military successes did not tell the whole story; we were coping with regional forces, but the Vietcong were still masters of much territory at night and continued to pour people in. My colleagues spoke of the pressures to invade, bomb, and smash the enemy, but, remembering Korea, always came back to the key question, What would China do? Some believed the Chinese would come in if the Americans bombed North Vietnam.

Ambassador Henry Cabot Lodge, for whom I had worked at the United Nations in 1956, saw no neat end to the war. He believed there would be no peace conference and no negotiated settlement as such. No one would be able to say, "We won the war." Instead, the fighting would gradually die away. After six months of quiet, we would realize that it was all over. Americans could win a regular war but, unquestionably, a guerrilla war would require new methods and a long time. But it would end.

Before I left Saigon, I talked with the Dutch ambassador, who disagreed with Lodge, "American talk about a 'petering out' of the war is just not realistic. There is no sign that the Vietcong are tired. They continue to recruit manpower and have an enormous untouched source in the delta. They lack neither ammunition, food, nor people." This was the military side. As for the other war, the one for people's minds, it was far more difficult. The ambassador saw no end in sight.

Commanders and foreign service officers in the field were dedicated to their jobs and had to believe they were making progress in pacification and economic improvement—"country building," as it was called. I was impressed by the enormity of the effort: the vast air bases, the acres of tanks and trucks, as seen from the air, and American uniforms everywhere. It was hard to conclude that, with all this power, plus our moral commitment to democracy, we could not overcome the persistent, derogated, so-called bedraggled enemies fighting in the bush. Statistics on body counts and defections kept our hopes up. I came away from Vietnam discouraged but certainly unable to imagine that we would be directly engaged militarily in Indochina for another six years and three months.

The Reischauers had departed on August 19 and his successor, U. Alexis Johnson, arrived with his wife Pat on October 29. Alex had twice been deputy under secretary of state for political affairs, from 1961 to 1964 and again in 1965–66. In between he had served in Saigon as deputy to the ambassador, General Maxwell Taylor, who had been with us as an army language officer in prewar Tokyo. In January 1936, Pat and Alex had met Dorothy and me at Tokyo station on the night we first arrived in Japan. Now, thirty years later, Dorothy and I were welcoming Pat and Alex back to the embassy, where we had all started our careers together. Johnson was the first and only one to become ambassador to Japan out of the valiant band of eight young foreign service officers, who simultaneously attacked the Japanese language in those dim and distant prewar years.

We left our second country with pain and pleasure. There had always been a mixture of feelings when the day of transfer came, and it had come often during the thirty years we had followed our career. This time the pain came from knowledge that our official connection with Japan was ended. The pleasure came from knowing that the thread would not be broken, that only a knot had been tied.

15

The White Thread

In the mid-third of the twentieth century, the United States was involved in four wars—with Germans and Japanese, with North Koreans and Chinese, with Vietnamese, and in a continuing struggle with Communists—the cold war. This was the historical setting out of which grew the foreign service career that spanned those years.

When I think of prewar Japan, I see the bicycle-filled streets of Tokyo with honking *en-taku* ("yen taxis") prodding wooden-clogged and kimono-clad pedestrians; quiet country villages with clear air faintly tinged by smells of drying *daikon* ("giant radish") and "honey-bucket" carts transporting human manure. As wartime fuel shortages began to hurt, the Datsuns, which we derided as jerry-built, became wood-burning, and drivers would stop their cars to stoke the fire in the converted trunks at the back. Foreigners in those days patronized the Japanese; they called the emperor "Charlie" and laughed at the pathetic *boku-enshu* ("air raid drills"), which required hanging black cloths over windows, and at the early morning lines of sober citizen-members of the *tonari-gumi* ("neighborhood associations"), mechanically performing in the streets their patriotic calisthenics to blaring radio drill masters.

Behind all this regimented human activity was always the ineffable, unchangeable beauty of Japan. Our sojourn in Kyoto

introduced us to the quietude of the Japanese garden, that careful
positioning of each rock and each grain of sand to simulate and
suggest nature with a backdrop of real mountains in the distance.
We learned the eloquence of spaces in painting, the philosophy of
the unexpressed, of nothingness, of transiency. An eighth-century
Japanese priest compared this world to "the white wake behind a
ship that has rowed away at dawn." This passionate passivity of the
Japanese can, however, be sharply broken by the flash of a sword.
The duality in Japanese character has been an eternal enigma for
foreigners. Part of it may have to do with the Japanese concept of
death, Mishima's "beauty is death." Falling cherry blossoms symbolize the beautiful death of the samurai. Nagano-san, the geisha we
knew in occupied Tokyo, found beauty in the shining B-29s, which
rained death on her compatriots. This does not mean that the
Japanese do not suffer or do not grieve. It may mean that belief in
the passage of all worldly things and in the continuity of life and
death makes the threshold between life and death less terrifying.

My assignment to the China-Burma-India theater of war
brought me face to face with the kind of ordinary Japanese whom I
had never known before. Their attitudes as prisoners of war
emphasized an acceptance of destiny. They offered a clue to the
behavior of the Japanese nation after a defeat that had never been
imagined in the lore of the superpatriots who guided Japan in the
1930s. The same energies mobilized in an imperial crusade seemed to
turn instantaneously to the construction of a new and prosperous
Japan.

From the vantage point of a minor actor, I watched the
unfolding, or, more accurately, the studied improvisation of
American policy during these periods. Somehow American sights on
Asia blurred. We were unable to put China and Japan into accurate
and clear perspective. Pearl Buck's *The Good Earth* and American
missionaries taught us to admire the hard-working peasant Chinese,
while the Japanese, caricatured as buck-toothed and bespectacled,
came out as the sneaky, untrustworthy bad guys. Few Americans
recognized coldly that Japan then, as today, could not live without
resources and markets and that China and Southeast Asia were the
logical areas of opportunity. The Japanese discovered that a land war

in China was a mistake (we also later found out about land wars in Asia), that colonialism was outmoded, and that sending armies and navies for resources and markets did not work. Ambassador Grew in 1941 clung tenaciously to an old-fashioned faith in diplomacy as a means for solving international disputes. True, our two navies had traditionally trained to destroy each other, and militarism had gained an upper hand in Japan. Yet if Americans had not been so encumbered by the emotional cloud that surrounded our approach to China and Japan, diplomacy might have had a better chance.

Diplomacy likewise failed at the war's end. We misjudged the desperate plight of the Japanese in the spring and summer of 1945 and failed to communicate our terms to them. Those Japanese who were trying to make peace, bereft of encouragement or clarifications from our side, were unable to prevail. The accepted conviction in Washington that Japan would not surrender without atomic bombing and without Russian entry into the war, blocked the vigorous pursuit of diplomacy. Finally, the failure of American policymakers, except Under Secretary Grew, to recognize the essentiality of a guarantee that the emperor would be preserved, albeit shorn of his prerogatives, postponed the surrender, inviting the dropping of the atomic bombs and the unnecessary Soviet declaration of war.

The take-over of China by the Communists in 1949 produced effects on my own life that I could not foresee at the time. Three years later, when the hysteria of McCarthyism had paralyzed the organs of government as nothing had done before, activities that I had carried out with ardor in wartime Yenan and in postwar Tokyo suddenly became cast in a suspicious light. At the time I was interviewing Nosaka Sanzō, and making policy and action recommendations to the State Department, I was impelled by two motives only: to end the war quickly and to prepare for a democratic postwar Japan. Encouraged by my associates and superiors, both in the field and in Washington, I not once dreamed that what I was doing would one day be questioned. In Yenan in 1944 we believed that Communist control of China was inevitable, but that Soviet domination was not. Communication, if not goodwill, with a postwar Communist Chinese government would be in the national interest of the United States. If we were able successfully to encourage the establishment in Japan of a free, representative system of government, Communists would be able to compete, as would all other political parties. However, knowing something about prewar Japanese politics and the deep-rooted antipathy of Japanese for Soviet Russia and communism, I was convinced that communism would not win in Japan.

When, seven years later, I was accused of pro-Communist attitudes and of having written slanted reports, I had to look at my wartime and immediate postwar activities from a new vantage point. Every conversation, meeting, and line of writing had to be examined under the microscope of 1952. What was revealed was an enthusiastic young foreign service officer pounding away at his typewriter in the rarefied air of Yenan and in the charged atmosphere of bombed-out, occupied Tokyo, an eager reporter pouring forth ideas in which he strongly believed. He was not philosophizing about the ideology of communism or about its threat to the world. Marxism–Leninism was alien to his experience and to his way of life. Yenan was a headquarters for war. Soldiers of the Eighth Route Army tramped through the streets. Shirtless in the sun and open air, he tapped out dispatches and sent them on. They were not the studied ruminations from a book-lined study or embassy chancery, and bore the marks of an ardent, youthful, on-the-spot reporter.

Lillian Hellman has sensitively described this "scoundrel time," when the convulsion of China

> gave us the conviction that we could have prevented it if only. If only was never explained with any sense, but the times had very little need of sense. . . . It was not the first time in history that the confusions of honest people were picked up in space by the cheap baddies who, hearing a few bars of popular notes, made them into an opera of public disorder, stated and sung, as much of the congressional testimony shows, in the wards of an insane asylum.

The Loyalty Security Boards set up in the State Department were products of these times. The officers who manned them were, certainly in my case, honest and fair. They had a disagreeable task to perform, which they carried out in the line of duty, to make a record that would either show guilt and require dismissal, or would refute the charges and clear the defendant.

My unanimous clearance sent me off to Karachi with enormous relief, reinforced by subsequent promotion and an award for meritorious service. But not for long. In the hands of the bloodhounds of the Senate Subcommittee on Internal Security, old charges sprang to life, embellished, turned into a Lillian Hellman opera, and this time, after the fact, played in public. When asked to submit to a lie detector test, I thought I had reached the nadir of indignity. But it never occurred to me to question the procedure or to hesitate to undergo the examination; besides, it would be a novel experience. The administrator of the operation admonished me after it was over, "You're pretty sensitive to this machine. If you are ever guilty of anything, don't submit to the polygraph!"

I remained in the foreign service until retirement age. I might have resigned, after my clearance, to deplore and view with alarm from the outside. Such a course I never considered. The foreign service was my life; it had brought great satisfactions—interests, study, contacts with people, inspiration from foreign cultures, and some small involvement in history. In all assignments during and subsequent to the security investigations, the thought of altering an opinion, a position, or a recommendation to suit some superior or some line of policy, never crossed my mind. The past did not inhibit the future.

A government official is an organization man, and there is something to the connotation of conformity suggested by the French definition of bureaucrat as a *rond-de-cuir*, the round piece of leather on which the official sits. The flamboyant, impatient, innovative, crusading individualist is often restive in the foreign service and seeks greater satisfaction in the freedoms of journalism or academia. Diplomats are constantly constrained by the art of the possible, confronting alternatives that must be judged not only by acceptability but by feasibility. Our concern with the feasible may on occasion lead caution to overcome instinct, and then we can be wrong. We must, however, confront the real world as we see it; we are making history, not just looking at it.

The foreign service has been much maligned. We are the cookie-pushers, the striped-pants boys, the cocktail tipplers, or the envoys sent abroad to lie for our country. Unlike the diplomatic services of other nations, which are almost uniformly professional and career, the American foreign service has been fair game for campaign contributors, and the best plums have often gone to the wealthy politicos. Over the years a competent foreign service has nevertheless evolved with a professionalism of which we can be proud. Forty years ago we were a small corps, called smug and elitist by some.

Whatever our competence, those who took the oath of office in my day were no longer of the eastern Ivy League establishment, as our predecessors had been accused of being; we were boys from small towns and from cities and villages in all parts of the United States. We took our calling seriously and expected to go wherever sent. Our wives were a part of the service and shared our careers. Unlike the businessman who sheds his office cares when he comes home at the end of the day, the diplomat carries his burden and his job with him. In a foreign country the foreign service officer and his wife are on stage perpetually. They both represent their country, as do their children. An enriched home life is one of the advantages; the children have unique opportunities to learn languages, tolerance, and an adaptibility that can serve them well in later life. The right temperament is essential, the temperament of the curious, the inquisitive, the people-lover, of the person who endures heat, cold, mountains, deserts, who relishes disruption, discontinuity, abrupt shifts in languages, customs, and climate, who can be at home in a bazaar or a palace, and zestfully! I tell my students, "Without such a temperament, the foreign service is not for you!"

The foreign service today has expanded to meet the responsibilities of a compressed and complex world. Like other government bureaucracies, however, the expansion has often outdistanced the need. Still required is the small corps of professionals who can cut through the distracting detail and discern the interests of the United States. Thirty years of history have taught us that while these interests are legion, and while almost every aspect of our national life has its international dimension, our power is limited. From isolation we went to the opposite extreme, to assurance in our ability to solve any problem, anywhere.

In one of his last statements before leaving the office of secretary of state, Henry Kissinger remarked that "the 1960s were the last full flowering of these impulses—the belief in our omnipotence, in our self-sufficiency, in our ability to remake other societies in our image." For Japan, these same years brought faith in unlimited growth. Before the end of the decade, glimmerings of doubts had begun to appear in both countries. Americans were discovering the limitations of power, and the Japanese, the inadequacies of the GNP. During the first half of the sixties, Japan was still feeling her way tentatively toward great power status. Absorption in production left little time to ponder a future role in the world. It was enough to export in order to import in order to live, and the United States would defend the country in case of danger. Americans, meanwhile, becoming more enmeshed in the tangle of Indochina, were impatient with Japan, failing to understand why a prospering country would not assume more of the burden of security for the non-Communist world. Americans were also annoyed that Japanese seemed to be flooding our markets with automobiles and television sets, while guarding their own frontiers with restrictions on trade and investment. Perceptions were not always consonant with reality. In spite of barriers, which have been disappearing, trade has continued to mount between the two countries.

We are indeed in a period of shifting values and shifting relationships. The quality of life has replaced production as a goal for the Japanese. This means better housing, cleaner air and water, and better relations with close neighbors: China, the Soviet Union, the two Koreas, and Taiwan. Ties with the United States remain fundamental, but the equality posited in 1910 is goal, not fact. Communication between Japan and the United States is still not perfect, and perception by each of the other's vital interests in a changed world is still not complete. These are tasks for the years ahead.

Coda

Walk with me through the red gate of Akamon in Nikkō and follow the ancient stone path that leads up to Takio Jinja, the mountain "shrine of the tail of the waterfall." Cryptomeria trees, like giant redwoods, line the path that winds up through the forest. Before we begin the climb, we come to the Kaisandō, a modest, red-lacquered temple dedicated to the founder, Shōdō Shōnin, the itinerant priest who discovered that Nikkō was a sacred mountain in 766 A.D. To the left is a smaller wooden structure, in the form of a traditional shrine, with hundreds of wooden blocks in the shape of Japanese chess pieces, arrayed on the steps. Pregnant women come here to pray for the successful delivery of their children, and, after having kept one of the chess pieces under their pillow, and having given birth safely, return to express thanks by depositing a newly inscribed block bearing the baby's name, birthdate, and birthplace. Nearby is the tomb of Shōdō Shōnin, its five shaped stones piled one upon the other to denote the five elements—earth, water, fire, air, and space. Behind the tomb is the mountain with a great, jagged, open-rock face. According to legend, the rock once resembled Buddha, but an earthquake destroyed the natural image. Beneath the open, cavelike aperture now stand stone figures of grotesque guardians, watching over the Buddha rock. Tourists seldom visit here. It is quiet. Continuing up the uneven path, we pass the almost-hidden grave of the faithful horse of Ieyasu, the first Tokugawa shogun, whose seventeenth-century mausoleum is the showplace of Nikkō. After the battle of Sekigahara, which completed the unification of Japan in 1600, Ieyasu is said to have set free in this restful grove the horse that had accompanied him in battle. The steed outlived his master; almost indecipherable characters on the lichened monument identify the sacred horse. A little farther on, between the towering trees, we come to a fork in the road. The path to the left climbs the mountain; straight ahead is a venerable giant of a tree, almost hollow at its base. A moss-covered, rough-hewn stone stands prominently, with dim, chiseled characters urging the pilgrim not to defile the sacred precincts of Takio shrine, which we are now about to enter. Around a bend, and suddenly, cool air, like a freshet, fills the lungs. Back in a cove, always in shadow, the waterfall of the white thread tumbles down over the rocks.

It is recorded that a trio of Buddhist monks first saw the waterfall on July 16, 820 A.D. and likened it to cloth being bleached. They called it the waterfall of the white thread.

Since few people, even Japanese, visit the waterfall, it is always a place of cool, serene tranquility. The old, broken sign standing at the foot of the falls bears the poem attributed to an old book:

> The end of the white thread of the
> Waterfall of Takio,
> A bond from one generation to another—
> Forever.

Notes

The following abbreviations are used in the notes:

JWC   *Japan Weekly Chronicle,* Kobe, Japan

HP   Hornbeck Papers, unpublished documents, Hoover Institution, Stanford University, Stanford, California

FRUS   *Foreign Relations of the United States,* Department of State publication, United States Government Printing Office, Washington, D.C.

IMTFE   International Military Tribunal for the Far East, Hoover Institution, Stanford University, Stanford, California

POLAD   Political Adviser to Supreme Commander for Allied Powers (SCAP), Tokyo, Japan

Security   U.S., Congress, Senate, Committee on the Judiciary,
Subcommittee Hearings before the Subcommittee to Investigate the
Hearings   Administration of the Internal Security Act and Other Internal Security Laws

        SF Emmerson Security File
        SP Stilwell Papers, unpublished documents, Hoover Institution, Stanford University, Stanford, California

Japanese names are written according to Japanese usage, last names first.

Chapter 1

12 The United States ... a French colony: Frederick Lewis Allen, *Only Yesterday* (New York and London: Harper & Brothers, 1931), p. 241.

13 "... letter to Santa Claus": Thomas A. Bailey, *A Diplomatic History of the American People* (New York: Appleton-Century-Crofts, 1964), p. 650.

Chapter 2

29 "... the extent of our own Embassy ...": Joseph C. Grew, *Ten Years in Japan* (New York: Simon and Schuster, 1944), p. 162.

32 The Japanese language!: Kurt Singer, *Mirror, Jewel, and Sword: A Study of Japanese Characteristics* (New York: George Braziller, 1973), p. 126; and "Sixteen Ways to Avoid Saying 'No' in Japanese," in John C. Condon and Mitsuki Saitō, eds., *Intercultural Encounters with Japan* (Tokyo: Simul Press, 1974), pp. 185–192.

34–35 Franklin D. Roosevelt's 1936 New Year's message ... was termed "plain speaking": *JWC*, 9 January 1936, p. 23; and Grew's comments on the message: Grew, *Ten Years*, pp. 163–164.

35 Senator Pittman's speech: *Domei* (news service) dispatch, *JWC*, 20 February 1936, p. 236; *Asahi*, on Pittman, ibid., p. 237; and Grew, *Ten Years*, pp. 164–165.

36 "... anomalous character of Tokyo's streets ...": Singer, *Mirror, Jewel, and Sword*, p. 70.

36   The snowfall was reported . . . : *JWC*, 13 February 1936, p. 198.

37   Announcement of February 26 incident censored: *JWC*, 5 March 1936, p. 293.

38–39   Assassination of Ii Naosuke: Kōno Tsukasa, *Ni-ni-roku Jiken* [Two-two-six Incident] (Tokyo: Nihon Shūhō Sha, 1957), p. 94; and Ben-Ami Shillony, *Revolt in Japan* (Princeton, N.J.: Princeton University Press, 1973), pp. 133–134. See also, James Murdoch, *A History of Japan* (London: Kegan Paul, Trench, Trubner, 1926), 3:699–700.

39   Japanese foreign policy in the 1930s: James B. Crowley, *Japan's Quest for Autonomy* (Princeton, N.J.: Princeton University Press, 1966), preface, p. xvi, and chap. 4, p. 191.

40   Young officers' ideas on reform: Masao Maruyama, *Thought and Behaviour in Modern Japanese Politics* (London, Oxford, New York: Oxford University Press, 1969), p. 55.

40   "Killing traitors is not a crime . . .": Shillony, *Revolt*, p. 59.

40–41   Suicide of Lt. Aoshima Kenkichi: *JWC*, 12 March 1936, p. 322.

41   Mishima's fictional description of suicide based on that of Lt. Aoshima Kenkichi: Yukio Mishima, "Patriotism," in *Death in Midsummer and Other Stories* (New York: New Directions, 1966), p. 117.

41   Mishima on patriotism and the Shōwa restoration: In *Runaway Horses*, the second novel of his final tetralogy, *The Sea of Fertility*, Mishima dwells at length on the theme of patriotism and sacrifice for the emperor, by placing in the context of 1933 a rebellion that actually took place in 1876. Mishima's fictional students take the name of their Meiji models, The League of the Divine Wind, and prepare a proclamation similar to the manifesto of the young warriors of 1936: "The purpose of our Shōwa restoration is to place finance and industry under the direct control of his Imperial Majesty, to uproot capitalism and communism, those doctrines of western imperialism, and thus deliver our people from their misery and here beneath the bright light of the sun to seek the direct rule of the Emperor that will glorify the imperial way." Although the students are apprehended before they are able to consummate their plot, the leader-hero fulfills his destiny at the end by killing one corrupt financier and then by committing suicide in the prescribed fashion. As described by Mishima: "The instant that the blade tore open his flesh, the bright disc of the sun soared up and

exploded behind his eyelids." Yukio Mishima, *Runaway Horses*, trans. Michael Gallagher (New York: Alfred A. Knopf, 1973; Rutland, Vt. and Tokyo: Charles E. Tuttle, 1971; *Homba*, original Japanese edition, Tokyo: Shinchosha, 1969). Above quoted references are to Tuttle edition, pp. 256 and 241 respectively.

41 The emperor and the February 26 incident: For references to Yukio Mishima's *Eirei no Koe* [Voices of the Heroic Dead], see Donald Keene, *Landscapes and Portraits* (Tokyo and Palo Alto, Calif.: Kodansha International, 1971), p. 219.

41 ". . . insurgent army, . . .": Crowley, *Japan's Quest*, p. 273; and Kido Kōichi, *Nikki* [Diary] (Tokyo: Tokyo Daigaku Shuppansha, 1966), vol. 1, p. 464.

42 Emperor's instructions to war minister: Richard Storry, *The Double Patriots* (Boston and New York: Houghton Mifflin, 1957), pp. 187–188.

43 February 26 incident reported in *The Saturday Evening Post:* J. P. McEvoy, "Honorable Revolution," *The Saturday Evening Post,* 25 April 1936, p. 6.

44 university professors and journalists were bravely publishing denunciations of the military . . . : Hashikawa Bunsō, "Teikōsha no Seiji Shisō" [Antiwar Values—the Resistance in Japan], in Hashikawa Bunsō and Matsumoto Sannosuke, eds., *Kindai Nihon Seiji Shisō* [The Political Thought of Modern Japan] (Japan, 1971), 1: 399–413. A translated version by Robert Wargo appears in *Japan Interpreter,* vol. 9, no. 1 (Spring 1974).

47 Hideyoshi at Kiyomizu temple: William Elliot Griffis, *The Mikado's Empire* (New York: Harper & Brothers, 1876), p. 242.

47 Tōjō's "jump" from Kiyomizu temple: Robert G. Butow, *Tōjō and the Coming of the War* (Stanford, Calif.: Stanford University Press, 1969), p. 267.

50 ". . . slender margin between the real and the unreal": Chikamatsu Monzaemon, "On Realism in Art," in Tsunoda Ryusaku, William Theodore de Barry, and Donald Keene, eds., *Sources of Japanese Tradition,* 2 vols. (New York: Columbia University Press, 1958), 1:439.

51–52 *The Love Suicides at Amijima* at the Bunraku-za: Chikamatsu Monzaemon, *Shinjū Ten no Amijima* [The Love Suicides at Amijima]. For Japanese text, see Kitani Hōgin, ed., *Dai*

Chikamatsu Zenshū [Complete Works of Chikamatsu], 16 vols. (Tokyo: Dai Chikamatsu Zenshū Kankō Kai, 1922), 1:549–632; and for English translation, see Donald Keene, *Major Plays of Chikamatsu* (New York: Columbia University Press, 1961), pp. 387–425. Quotations are from author's translation.

Chapter 3

54 Ilha Formosa ("the beautiful isle"): T. Philip Terry, *Guide to the Japanese Empire Including Korea and Formosa,* rev. ed. (Boston and New York: Houghton Mifflin, 1928), p. 762.

58 His dramatic exploits served Chikamatsu ... : Chikamatsu Monzaemon, *Kokusenya Kassen* [The Battles of Coxinga]. For an English translation, see Donald Keene, *Major Plays of Chikamatsu* (New York: Columbia University Press, 1961), pp. 202–269; and Keene, *The Battles of Coxinga* (London: Taylor's Foreign Press, 1951), pp. 114 and 143.

58–59 "... Thus the island, which China had torn from Coxinga's descendants . . .": Takekoshi Yosaburo, *Japanese Rule in Formosa,* trans. George Braithwaite (London: Longmans, Green, 1907), p. 86.

59 Li Hung-chang, on Formosa: James W. Davidson, *The Island of Formosa, Past and Present* (New York and London: Macmillan, 1903), pp. 276–277. See also, Baron Gotō Shimpei, "The Administration of Formosa (Taiwan)," in Count Okuma Shigenobu, ed., *Fifty Years of New Japan* (London: Smith, Elder, 1909), p. 530.

59 Armed revolts by Formosan Chinese: Joseph W. Ballantine, *Formosa, A Problem for United States Foreign Policy* (Washington, D.C.: Brookings Institution, 1952), p. 25.

59–60 Influence of religion in colonial policy: Gotō, "The Administration of Formosa," p. 531.

60 Headhunting as "the most glorious thing in their life": Government of Formosa, Bureau of Aboriginal Affairs, *Report on the Control of Aborigines in Formosa* (Taihoku, 1911), p. 2.

60–61 Musha incident: *JWC,* 6 November 1930, pp. 524 and 536; and George H. Kerr, *Formosa: Licensed Revolution and the Home Rule Movement, 1895–1945* (Honolulu: University Press of Hawaii, 1974), pp. 151–152.

62 "the greatest and richest treasurehouse of the Empire": Gotō, "The Administration of Formosa," p. 553.

62 Coxinga's "bridge of boats": Kerr, *Formosa,* p. 210.

62 Kodama report: Ibid., p. 49.

63 Admiral Kobayashi's three points: *JWC,* 25 May 1939, p. 625.

64 Educational statistics: U.S., Navy Department, *Civil Affairs Handbook, Taiwan (Formosa),* OPNAV 50E-12 (Washington, D.C.: Navy Department, 15 June 1944), pp. 35–37.

64–65 Purposes of *kominka:* Taiwan Government General, *Taiwan Jijō* [Situation] *1939* (Taihoku, 10 December 1939), p. 211.

65 Japanese historian, quoting Canadian missionary: Takekoshi, *Japanese Rule,* p. 300, quoting Dr. George L. Mackay's *From Far Formosa* (New York: Fleming H. Revell, 1896).

66 Formosan gods: John K. Emmerson, "Kominka or the Japanization of the People of Taiwan," report sent by the U.S. Consulate, Taihoku, to the Department of State, 2 December 1939, file no. 849A.00/27, pp. 32–41.

68 Governor General Kobayashi on Formosans in China. Statement to the press: *JWC,* 25 May 1939, p. 625.

68 ". . . appendix of human resources, . . .": Tai Kuo-hui, Nihonjin to Taiwa [Dialogues with Japanese] (Tokyo: Shakai Shisōsha, 15 August 1971), p. 91.

68 Coal production: U.S., Navy Department, *Civil Affairs Handbook, Taiwan (Formosa)—Economic Supplement,* OPNAV 50E-13 (Washington, D.C.: Navy Department, 1 June 1944), p. 39; and John K. Emmerson, "The Industrialization of Taiwan," report sent by the U.S. Consulate, Taihoku, to the Department of State, 16 September 1939, file no. 850, p. 8.

68–69 Coal production, 1974: Han Lih-wu, *Taiwan Today* (Taipei: Institute of International Relations, July 1974), p. 34.

69 Sun and Moon Lake dam and power plant: Kerr, *Formosa,* p. 138.

71 Secret police sending agents to see American officials: The then American naval attaché in Tokyo, Capt. H. H. Smith-Hutton, described this prewar practice in an article published in 1973: "The Japanese secret police made each Naval Attaché pass a test within a few months after he arrived. A voice, almost a whisper over the telephone, would ask for an appointment but the caller would not give his name nor tell why he was calling. When the man appeared at the appointed time, he would

propose that he be hired as an undercover agent or he would offer to sell the plans of a naval base or an air station." H. H. Smith-Hutton, "Tokyo, December 1941," *Shipmate,* vol. 36, no. 11 (December 1973), p. 14. This is a monthly magazine published by the U.S. Naval Academy Alumni Association, Annapolis, Md.

73 Chiba Shin-ichi: letter of Chiba Kazuo, Consul General, Atlanta, Ga., to Emmerson, 11 February 1976.

73–74 Matsuo Chūhei case: Joseph C. Grew, Diary, Personal Notes, July 1940, p. 4440, HP; and note to Foreign Office (oral), re: Matsuo Chūhei, 17 December 1940, HP.

Chapter 4

77 Open Door policy and preservation of territorial and administrative integrity of China: George F. Kennan, *American Diplomacy 1900–1950* (Chicago: University of Chicago Press, 1951), p. 39; and A. Whitney Griswold, *The Far Eastern Policy of the United States* (New Haven, Conn.: Yale University Press, 1962), p. 326.

77 Stimson and Manchurian crisis: Henry L. Stimson, *The Far Eastern Crisis* (New York: Harper & Brothers, 1936), p. 162.

77–78 Roosevelt's speech advocating a "quarantine": FDR recognized a champion of the "quarantine" idea in Adm. H. E. Yarnell, who, on 15 October 1937 wrote to Adm. William D. Leahy that an effective plan would be one which would take advantage of Japan's dependence on external sources of raw materials by forming a common front among China, the United States, Great Britain, France, the Netherlands, and Russia in order to encircle and cut off all Japan's trade except in China, north of the Yangtze. Yarnell called this a war of "strangulation," which could be waged economically. Leahy passed Yarnell's recommendation on to FDR, who replied, "Yarnell talks a lot of sense ... it goes along with the word 'quarantine' which I used in the Chicago speech last month." See also Waldo H. Heinrichs, Jr., "The Role of the United States Navy," in Dorothy Borg and Shumpei Okamoto, eds., *Pearl Harbor as History: Japanese–American Relations 1931–1941* (New York: Columbia University Press, 1973), pp. 212–213.

78 Hull on FDR's "quarantine" speech: Cordell Hull, *The Memoirs*

of Cordell Hull, 2 vols. (New York: Macmillan, 1948), 1:544–545.

78   Ambassador Grew's 1936 recommendations: Embassy Tokyo dispatch 1665, 7 February 1936; and *FRUS, 1936,* vol. IV, pp. 7–8 and 42–49. See also Waldo H. Heinrichs, Jr., *American Ambassador* (Boston: Little, Brown, 1966), pp. 223–224.

78–79   Embassy–Roosevelt Administration disagreement: Heinrichs, *American Ambassador,* p. 245.

79   Grew, on duties of embassy: Joseph C. Grew, Diary, Personal Notes, no. 129, November 1939, p. 4141, HP; and Grew, *Ten Years in Japan* (New York: Simon and Schuster, 1944), p. 300.

79   "two points on the Far East . . .": Hull, *Memoirs,* 1:270.

79   Hornbeck's writings of 1914 and 1916: Marlene J. Mayo, "Anti-Japanism: The Eastern Education of Stanley K. Hornbeck 1904–1919" (1974), pp. 30–31 and 39.

80   Hull's four principles: *FRUS, Japan, 1931–1941,* vol. II, p. 332.

81   a policy of sanctions could lead to war: Grew's statement and Hornbeck's comment. Memorandum given by Grew to Dooman (counselor), Creswell (military attaché), and Smith-Hutton (naval attaché) after Grew's return to Tokyo. Grew, Diary, Calendar, 19 October 1939, p. 4127, HP.

81   "some sort of major operation . . .": Grew, Diary, Personal Notes, no. 128, October 1939, p. 4108, HP.

81   "brass tacks" . . . , not "Jovian thunderbolts": Grew, Diary, Calendar, 15 October 1939, p. 4120, HP.

81   Horse's mouth speech: Grew, Diary, Personal Notes, no. 128, October 1939, p. 4108, and Calendar, 19 October 1939, p. 4127, HP. For text of speech, see Grew, *Ten Years,* pp. 289–294, especially p. 293.

82   "very deep impression . . .": Grew, Diary, Calendar, October 1939, p. 4135, HP.

82–84   "the outlook . . . does not now appear to be bright," and following discussion of embassy dispatch of December 1, 1939: Grew, Diary, Personal Notes, no. 129, November 1939, pp. 4141–4199, HP. See also Grew, *Ten Years,* pp. 299–305, for abbreviated text.

84   U.S. attitude toward a new treaty: *FRUS, Japan, 1931–1941,* vol. II, pp. 190–195; Grew, Diary, Calendar, 20 and 22 December 1939, p. 4225, HP; and Heinrichs, *American Ambassador,* p. 300.

84–85   Grew's New Year's prediction: Grew, Diary, Calendar, December 1939, p. 4247, HP.

87   Yonai . . . assured Grew that he need have no further anxiety . . . : Grew, Diary, Items, 14 January 1940, p. 4256, HP.

87   Treaty date passed "without too many local fireworks": Grew, Diary, Personal Notes, January 1940, p. 4253. Hornbeck had scoffed at Grew's preoccupation with the date of the termination of the treaty, stating that he was "overanxious" and explaining away his attitude by Tokyo influences. "He is functioning in the Tokyo environment and atmosphere, where there prevail conditions of strain, uncertainties, apprehensions, tensions. He is subjected to a great variety of impacts from Japanese minds and his diplomatic colleagues' minds and other minds all functioning in a disturbed and disturbing environment." Memorandum by Hornbeck, "A 'reviewer's review' of Mr. Grew's thesis," 12 January 1940, HP.

87   "the most critical period . . .": Grew, Diary, Personal Notes, no. 129, November 1939, pp. 4141–4199, HP.

87   Grew confident that Japanese efforts toward conciliation were "on an upward curve . . .": Grew, Diary, Personal Notes, February 1940, p. 4282, HP.

87   "steadily coming home to the great majority . . .": Grew, Diary, Personal Notes, March 1940, HP.

87   Ozaki Hotsumi and the New Structure: Civil Intelligence Section, GHQ, SCAP, "The Brocade Banner, The Story of Japanese Nationalism," 23 September 1946, unpublished, unsigned report written in G-2, Headquarters of Supreme Commander for Allied Powers, Tokyo, copy in Hoover Institution, Stanford, California, p. 112; and Chalmers Johnson, *An Instance of Treason: Ozaki Hotsumi and the Sorge Spy Ring* (Stanford, Calif.: Stanford University Press, 1964), p. 120.

87–88   Prince Konoye and the Imperial Rule Assistance Association: John K. Emmerson, Embassy Tokyo dispatches 5315, 22 January 1941, "The Organization of the Imperial Rule Assistance Association," and 5402, 28 February 1941, "The Present Status and Significance of the Imperial Rule Assistance Association."

88   Ozaki Yukio and IRAA: Emmerson, "The Present Status," p. 5.

88   ". . . totalitarianism *sui generis*": William T. Turner, Embassy

Tokyo dispatch 4946, 5 September 1940, "The New 'National Structure' in Japan," pp. 3–6.

88 Under the all-embracing rubric of the New Structure ... : William T. Turner, Embassy Tokyo dispatch 4928, 30 August 1940, "Comments on the 'New Structure,' " pp. 3–6.

88–89 Ambassador Grew's sixtieth birthday: The Po Chu-i poem, translated by Arthur Waley, appears in Grew, Diary, May 1940, p. 4399, HP.

89 that a typhoon could hardly have more effectively demolished ... : Grew, Diary, Personal Notes, no. 137, July 1940, p. 4430, HP.

89–90 "now ... the process of 'teetering'...": Ibid., p. 4436, HP.

90 "talk of principle": Heinrichs, *American Ambassador*, p. 311.

90 In his famous green-light telegram, ... : *FRUS, The Far East, 1940*, vol. IV, pp. 599–603; Joseph C. Grew, *Turbulent Era: A Diplomatic Record of Forty Years*, 2 vols. (Boston: Houghton Mifflin, 1952), 2:1224–1229.

90 This retaliation ... might take the form of "sudden stroke ...": Grew, Diary, Personal Notes, no. 141, November 1940, pp. 4616–4617, HP.

90 Kennan's red-light telegram ... of 22 February 1946: George F. Kennan, *Memoirs, 1925–1950* (Boston: Atlantic-Little, Brown, 1967), pp. 292–297; and for text of telegram, see pp. 547–559.

90 Grew recommends economic force: *FRUS, Japan, 1931–1941*, vol. II, pp. 201–218.

91 Kissinger on strangulation: Henry Kissinger, in an interview with *Business Week:* "I am not saying that there's no circumstance where we would not use force. But it is one thing to use it in the case of a dispute over price, it's another where there is some actual strangulation of the industrialized world." *Business Week*, 13 January 1975.

91 Imperial conference on adherence to Axis pact, September 19, 1940: Nobutaka Ike, *Japan's Decision for War* (Stanford, Calif.: Stanford University Press, 1967), pp. 3–13; for Hara's statement, see p. 13.

91–92 Prince Konoye on the Axis: Handwritten memorandum by Prince Konoye, undated [probably 1945], pp. 208–210, Konoye Papers (copy, from original in Yōmei Bunko, Kyoto, Japan), Hoover Institution, Stanford University, Stanford, Calif.

93–94 Frank Williams's election dinner: Grew, Diary, Personal Notes, no. 141, November 1940, Entertainments, p. 4661, HP.

94 Japan's 2600th anniversary, November 11, 1940: Grew, *Ten Years*, pp. 352–353.

94–95 Grew's letter to Franklin D. Roosevelt: Grew, Diary, Personal Notes, no. 142, 14 December 1940, pp. 4673–4674, HP.

95 "I can never hear . . .": Grew, Diary, Items, 31 December 1940, HP.

Chapter 5

96 Group photograph of embassy staff: Joseph C. Grew, Diary, 24 April 1941, p. 5001, HP.

96 Grew had great confidence in him and his judgments: In a diary entry, Grew stated, "With all due modesty on behalf of our Embassy . . . I think it will be found that over the last several years our reports, analyses and diagnoses have in general been consistent and sound and have usually proved accurate in the long run. If that is true, a very large share of the credit must go to Dooman." Grew, Diary, Items, 10 June 1941, p. 5219, HP.

98 nuances . . . and trends in official policy: Grew, in his diary for July 1941, stated, "For the present we may assume that Japan will adopt an increasingly independent attitude toward all nations, including her allies in the Axis, and that if there is to be some new orientation of policy it will be revealed gradually by efforts on the part of the Government to prepare public opinion through the doctored press. Therefore, in order to watch any new trends, we shall most carefully study the vernacular press." Grew, Diary, July 1941, Items (paraphrase of telegram to the State Department), 23 July 1941, p. 5360, HP. For text of telegram, see *FRUS, The Far East, 1941*, vol. IV, pp. 336–338.

98 Circulation figures for newspapers: *The Japan Yearbook, 1943–44* (Tokyo: Foreign Affairs Association of Japan, 1943), p. 753.

99 When he read Grew's description of the long Memorial Day weekend, . . . : Grew, Diary, May 1941, Items, 29 May 1941, p. 5101, HP.

100 "Gentlemen do not read each other's mail": Henry L. Stimson and McGeorge Bundy, *On Active Service in Peace and War* (New York: Harper & Brothers, 1947), p. 188.

100 Ushiba statement, on reading American telegrams: *FRUS, The Far East, 1941,* vol. IV, pp. 364–365; and Grew, Diary, 7 August 1941, p. 5514. This memorandum also appears in Joseph C. Grew, *Ten Years in Japan* (New York: Simon and Schuster, 1944), pp. 414–415. Grew, in *Turbulent Era,* attributes Ushiba's revelation directly to Prime Minister Konoye: "We had little doubts that Prince Konoye was reflecting information received from the Japanese military police, and was passing it on to us in view of certain types of intelligence which it was not in his interest to have known to the police. I duly communicated this statement to the Department." Joseph C. Grew, *Turbulent Era: A Diplomatic Record of Forty Years,* 2 vols. (Boston: Houghton Mifflin, 1952) 2:1275.

100–101 Grew's speculation on ability of Japanese to read U.S. codes: Grew, Diary, 10 June 1941, pp. 5219–5220, HP.

101 Japanese Foreign Office's Code Research Section: David Kahn, *The Codebreakers* (London: Weidenfeld and Nicolson, 1967), p. 495.

101–102 "How *infra dignitatem* ... !": Grew, Diary, 30 April 1941, pp. 5505–5506, HP.

101–102 Telegram to Sumner Welles complaining of Washington failure to keep embassy informed: Grew, Diary, 10 July 1941, pp. 5346–5347, HP.

102 "Our telegrams ... even the ripples": Grew, *Turbulent Era,* 2:1273.

103 War resulted from a major Japanese conspiracy ... : Richard H. Minear, *Victors' Justice, The Tokyo War Crimes Trial* (Princeton, N.J.: Princeton University Press, 1971), pp. 125–159; and David Bergamini, *Japan's Imperial Conspiracy* (New York: William Morrow, 1971; Pocket Books, 1972) pp. xxxv–xxxvi.

103 "Precisionist that he was, ... ": Waldo H. Heinrichs, Jr., *American Ambassador* (Boston: Little, Brown, 1966), p. 341.

103 Plan Dog: James MacGregor Burns, *Roosevelt: The Soldier of Freedom* (New York: Harcourt Brace Jovanovich, 1970), p. 85.

104 "a man of weak physique, ... ": Grew, Diary, Personal Notes, August 1940, p. 4463, HP.

104 "many masks beside him": E. H. Norman, memorandum, "Prince Fumimaro Konoye as a War Criminal Suspect," 5 November 1945, p. 2, enclosure to dispatch 58, 17 November

1945, from the acting U.S. political adviser to the Supreme Commander for the Allied Powers, Tokyo, Japan.

104 Konoye a "complex and ... contradictory character ... a shy squirrel ...": Kase Toshikazu, *Journey to the Missouri* (New Haven, Conn.: Yale University Press, 1950), pp. 5 and 43.

104–105 "congenitally a hypochondriac ...": Norman, memorandum, 5 November 1945.

105 "a loose talker ... to his lights": Grew, Diary, Personal Notes, August 1940, p. 4463, HP.

105 Matsuoka, "by all criteria ... mentally ill-balanced": Grew, Diary, Items, May 1941, p. 5099, HP.

105 Nomura ... met FDR in 1915 ... : Nomura Kichisaburō, *Beikoku ni Tsukai Shite: Nichibei Kōshō no Kaiko* [Envoy to the United States: Reminiscences of the Japanese–American Negotiations] (Tokyo: Iwanami Shōten, 1946), p. 3; the letters from FDR to Nomura are reproduced as frontispieces to the book.

105 Hull's first impression of Nomura ... : Cordell Hull, *The Memoirs of Cordell Hull*, 2 vols. (New York: Macmillan, 1948; 2: 987.

106 "too much evidence that ... and comprehensively": Grew, Diary, 7 August 1941, p. 5517, HP.

106 staff of Japanese Embassy in Washington was "painfully weak": Grew, ibid., p. 5514.

106–107 Hashimoto Tetsuma, a former member of the nationalist Black Dragon Society, ... : Herbert Feis, *The Road to Pearl Harbor* (Princeton, N.J.: Princeton University Press, 1950), p. 174n. The name *Shiunsō* ("Purple Cloud Society") was an allusion to "clouds lighted by the dawning sun as an augury of good weather."

106 Half-page advertisement by Shiunsō in Tokyo press: "Reply to Ambassador Grew." "Ambassador Grew and Americans should reread their American histories. . . ." Grew, Diary, Personal Notes, no. 129, 10 November 1939, HP.

106 In 1940 Grew had a chance to tell Hashimoto what he thought of him, . . . : Grew, Diary, Personal Notes, 29 March 1940, HP. Grew wrote at the time, "I suddenly realized that this was the Hashimoto who runs the *Shiunsō*, that one-man patriotic and ultra-chauvinistic society which issues period [*sic*] printed blasts against foreign countries and sometimes against the Japanese government itself as being weak-kneed and as

truckling to foreign interests. I promptly took occasion to tell Hashimoto that I deeply resented some of the things he had written about my country in times past. Dooman says, however, that lately Hashimoto has been less virulent and is apparently genuinely seeking a way out of the Japanese–American impasse."

106 Ballantine wrote that Hashimoto . . . : Memorandum by Joseph W. Ballantine, 5 February 1941. *FRUS, The Far East, 1941,* vol. IV, pp. 27–29. Hornbeck apparently did not share Ballantine's skepticism. When Ambassador Grew reported in his diary a call by Hashimoto and an associate after their return from Washington, Hornbeck wrote in the margin, "The Department's talks with them were excellent and *well* worthwhile." Grew, Diary, Calls and Callers, 17 March 1941, pp. 4911–4912, HP.

107 "their backdoor diplomacy . . .": R. J. C. Butow, *The John Doe Associates: Backdoor Diplomacy for Peace, 1941* (Stanford, Calif.: Stanford University Press, 1974), p. 319.

107 "From start to finish . . .": Ibid., p. 44.

108–109 "the outlook . . . has never been darker": Grew, Diary, Personal Notes, no. 143, January 1941, p. 4716, HP.

109 on the threat to Singapore, . . . : Embassy Tokyo telegraphed the Department of State on February 7, "The capture of Singapore would virtually predicate the fall of the Chinese government. The taking of Singapore by a hostile power would necessarily have grave repercussions against Britain's position in the Near East and in the Eastern Mediterranean." Hornbeck underlined this passage in the copy of Grew's diary that was sent to him. Grew, Diary, February 1941, p. 4850, HP, quoting from Embassy Tokyo telegram 180, 7 February 1941, 11:00 P.M.

109 was impressed by the views of Hugh Byas . . . : Grew, Diary, January 1941, Miscellaneous Notes, p. 4768, HP.

109 At the same time . . . to save Singapore: Grew, in Diary, Items, 30 January 1941, HP, quotes article by Ludwell Denny in the *New York Telegram.*

109 Rumor about Pearl Harbor attack: Grew, Diary, 27 January 1941, p. 4740, HP; and Grew, *Ten Years,* p. 368. For text of telegram, see *FRUS, Japan, 1931–1941,* vol. II, p. 133.

109 Peruvian ambassador's account of Pearl Harbor rumor: Embassy Lima dispatch no. 148, 7 February 1949, "Dr. Ricardo

Rivera Schreiber, Peruvian Ambassador to Italy, makes statement that he informed United States of Japanese Plan to attack Pearl Harbor." Dispatch transmits clipping from *El Comercio* (Lima), 5 February 1949, reporting interview with Rivera Schreiber.

110 Admiral Yamamoto Isoroku and the Pearl Harbor attack: Roberta Wohlstetter, *Pearl Harbor: Warning and Decision* (Stanford, Calif.: Stanford University Press, 1962), p. 368.

110 Japanese-American relations "couldn't be worse": Grew, Diary, Items, 18 January 1941, p. 4733, HP.

110 Matsuoka's surprise at Axis neutrality pact: Grew quoted the American ambassador in Moscow, Lawrence Steinhardt, as reporting after a conversation with Matsuoka about the neutrality treaty, "Nobody, apparently, was more surprised than Matsuoka." Grew, Diary, 22 April 1941, p. 4993, HP.

110 "no probability" of Japan–USSR agreement: Grew, Diary, Items, 22 February 1941, p. 4816, HP.

110 Matsuoka and Stalin at the station: I. Deutscher, *Stalin: A Political Biography* (New York and London: Oxford University Press, 1949), pp. 452–453.

110-111 Sir Stafford Cripps delivers Churchill's questions: Grew, Diary, 22 April 1941, pp. 4996–4997, HP.

111 "perhaps the most important telegram": Grew, Diary, 27 May 1941, p. 5101, HP. For text of telegrams, see *FRUS, The Far East, 1941*, vol. IV, Department of State telegram no. 297, 24 May 1941, p. 224, and Embassy Tokyo telegram no. 743, 27 May 1941, pp. 231–232.

112 Hornbeck's opposite view: Memorandum by the adviser on political relations (Hornbeck), 23 May 1941, *FRUS, The Far East, 1941*, vol. IV, pp. 212–215.

112 Bohlen, on German–Soviet war, memorandum for the ambassador: Grew, Diary, Miscellaneous Notes, 25 June 1941, pp. 5277–5278, HP.

112 "Dog eat dog . . .": Grew, Diary, Items, 22 June 1941, p. 5233, HP.

113 Konoye-Roosevelt meeting: First proposed by Father Drought, Butow, *The John Doe Associates*, p. 34; proposal for meeting, *FRUS, Japan, 1931-1941*, vol. II, pp. 346–347; Juneau instead of Hawaii, ibid., pp. 571–572.

114 Grew-Konoye meeting on September 6: *FRUS, Japan, 1931-1941*, vol. II, pp. 604–606.

115 An imperial conference convened on September 6: Nobutaka Ike, *Japan's Decision for War* (Stanford, Calif.: Stanford University Press, 1967), pp. 133–163. See Ike, for later conferences as well.

115 "Why, then, do the winds ...": Ibid., p. 151.

115 "Time is of the essence": Grew, Diary, 6 September 1941, pp. 5695–5699, HP.

116 Hornbeck's leave of absence: Grew, Diary, memorandum of conversation, Dooman–Terasaki (Foreign Office), 20 September 1941, pp. 5747–5748, HP.

117 Grew's warnings to Washington: In his autobiography, Grew devotes an entire section to listing "warnings by the embassy." Grew, *Turbulent Era*, 2: 1282–1289.

117 "... dangerous and dramatic suddenness": Embassy Tokyo, telegram no. 1736, 3 November 1941, *FRUS, Japan, 1931–1941*, vol. II, p. 704.

117 Hornbeck's "reviewer's review": Memorandum by Hornbeck, "A 'reviewer's review' of Mr. Grew's thesis," 12 January 1940, HP.

117 Hornbeck's memorandum on the day before Pearl Harbor: Untitled memorandum, 6 December 1941, Autobiography, Box 464, HP.

118 Hornbeck's no-war prediction: See Hornbeck, memorandum, with attached "Covering Memo to Secretary," 27 November 1941, Autobiography, Box 464, HP; and for Hornbeck's post-Pearl Harbor explanation, see ibid.

119 "The United States would hesitate to fight in the Pacific": Grew, Diary, April 1941, p. 4990, HP. Grew quotes Ishihara Kōichirō, president of the Ishihara Industrial Company, writing in the *Hochi* newspaper.

119 Darling cartoon: Accompanies article by Capt. Paul B. Ryan, "How Young We Were," U.S. Naval Institute *Proceedings*, vol. 94, no. 12, December 1968.

120 Hornbeck's comment on the United States urging Japan to disregard the Axis pact: Hornbeck, memorandum analyzing conversation on November 12 between the secretary of state and Ambassador Nomura, 13 November 1941, Autobiography, Box 464, HP.

120 "read between the lines": *FRUS, Japan, 1931–1941*, vol. II, p. 716. On November 10, 1941, Ambassador Nomura called on the president, who was accompanied by the secretary of state,

and read a communication, which was reported by Secretary Hull. In the course of the communication the following appeared with reference to Japan's obligations under the Tripartite Pact: "... Japan would decide entirely independently in the matter of interpretation of the Tripartite Pact between Japan, Germany, and Italy, and would likewise determine what actions might be taken by way of fulfilling the obligations in accordance with the said interpretation. ... The present circumstances under which Japan is placed do not permit my Government to go any further to write in black and white than what is proposed in the draft of September 25th which I have just quoted. All I have to ask you is 'read between the lines' and to accept the formula as satisfactory." This last sentence was later deleted by Admiral Nomura.

120 Japanese position on withdrawal of forces and nondiscrimination: See "Document Handed by the Japanese Ambassador [Nomura] to the Secretary of State on November 7, 1941, 'Disposition of Japanese Forces and Principle of Non-Discrimination'," *FRUS, Japan, 1931–1941*, vol. II, pp. 709–710; and Kurusu statement, *FRUS, The Far East, 1941*, vol. IV, p. 620. With respect to the Japanese November 7 statement of the principle of nondiscrimination in international commercial relations, Hull questioned the qualification that this principle should be applied "uniformly to the rest of the entire world as well." Such a provision might lead to misunderstandings, namely, that the United States would be required to assume responsibility for nondiscriminatory practices outside its national jurisdiction or that the consent and cooperation of all other governments would be a condition for the activation of the principle. After a lengthy description of the American trade agreements program, the secretary urged deletion of this clause and proposed a draft declaration on economic policy. *FRUS, Japan, 1931–1941*, vol. II, pp. 734–737.

120 "things are automatically going to happen": Hull, *Memoirs*, 2:1074.

120–121 *modus vivendi:* For text of Final Draft, 25 November 1941, see *FRUS, The Far East*, vol. IV, pp. 661–664. For Hull's account, see Hull, *Memoirs*, 2:1074–1082. For Hornbeck's version, see Hornbeck, Autobiography, 1941, Box 464, HP.

121 U.S. note of November 26: *FRUS, Japan, 1931–1941*, vol. II, pp. 766–770.

121–122 Japanese note of December 7, 1941: Ibid., pp. 787–792.
121–122 Final meeting of Nomura, Kurusu, and Hull, on December 7, 1941: Hull, *Memoirs*, 2:1095–1097.
123–124 Grew interview with Hull: This description of Grew's call on Hull is based on the recollections of Robert A. Fearey. See also Heinrichs, *American Ambassador*, p. 362, and fn. 18, p. 436. The gist of the report can be found in Grew, *Turbulent Era*, chap. 34: "Pearl Harbor: From the Perspective of Ten Years," 2:1244–1375.

Chapter 6

126 Emergency advisory committee for political defense: Edward N. Barnhart, "Japanese Internees from Peru," *Pacific Historical Review*, vol. 31, no. 2 (May 1962), p. 171. In his article, Barnhart cites Emergency Advisory Committee for Political Defense, *First Annual Report Submitted to the Governments of the American Republics* (Montevideo, 1942), p. 73; English edition (Washington, D.C., 1944), p. 133.

127 Special Intelligence Service (SIS): Don Whitehead, *The FBI Story: A Report to the People* (New York: Random House, 1956), pp. 211–212.

128 "From island to island ...": Bernardin de Saint-Pierre, *Studies of Nature*, abridged from translation of Henry Hunter (London: J. F. Dove, n.d.), p. 343.

128 Saint-Pierre's reliability as an historian: Gustave Lanson, *Histoire de la Littérature Française*, 19th ed. (Paris: Librairie Hachette, n.d.), pp. 827–831.

128 Theory that Incas were Japanese: Fr. A. Loayza, *Manko Kapac, El fundador del Império de los Inkas fué japonès* (para, 1926), pp. 67 and 71–79, as cited in J. F. Normano and Antonello Gerbi, *The Japanese in South America* (New York: John Day, 1943), p. 63.

129 "Our ancestors must indeed ...": Comisión organizadora del monumento a Manco Capac, *La Independencia del Perú y la Colonía Japonesa* (Lima, n.d.), p. 47.

129 In 1845 the Council of State, ... : Juan de Arona, *La Inmigraçíon en el Perú, Monografía Historico-Critica* (Lima: Imprenta del Universo, de Carlos Prince, 1891), flyleaf.

129 *"Sin brazos"*: Ibid., p. 36.

129   Pizarro and his black slaves: Mario E. Del Rio, *La Inmigraçion y su Desarrollo en el Perú* (Lima: San Martin, 1929), p. 38.

129   Chinese in Peru: de Arona, *La Inmigraçion en el Perú*, p. 54.

129   Chinese population of Peru in 1940: Ministerio de Hacienda y Comercio, *Extracto Estadistico del Perú*. (Lima, 1940), p. 61.

130   ". . . a whip across the buttocks of a Chinese": Manuel Gonzales Prada, "Nuestra Aristocracia" (1904), in *Horas de Lucha* (Lima: Editores Latinoamericanos, n.d.), p. 133.

130   *Maria Luz:* Ota Mosaburō, "Peru Imin Shiryaku" [Historical Sketch of Japanese Immigrants in Peru], *Kaishi* (April 1939), p. 55. *Kaishi* is a publication of Japanese Central Society of Peru.

130   Garcia mission: Jorge Bailey Lembcke, "La primera misión diplomâtica del Perú al Japón," *El Comercio* (Lima), 26 October 1941.

130   Sakura Maru: Ota, "Peru Imin Shiryaku," p. 58.

131   Foreign minister's admission of corruption: Alberto Ulloa, *Posiçíon Internaçional del Perú* (Lima: Imprente Torres Aguirre, 1941), p. 349.

131   Immigration statistics: These have been compiled from variety of sources—Del Rio, *Inmigraçion;* the Japanese Central Society's publication *Kaishi;* and the Peruvian Ministry of Foreign Affairs.

131–132   Japanese doctors and dentists for Peru: Ibid.

132   "The whole weight of the imperial Japanese government . . .": Carleton Beals, *America South* (Philadelphia, New York, London: J. B. Lippincott, 1937), p. 441.

132–133   They dominated certain classes of small business—the bazaar . . . : Normano and Gerbi, *The Japanese in South America*, p. 93.

134–135   Government step to deprive nisei of their Peruvian citizenship: Barnhart, "Japanese Internees," p. 170.

136   Manuel Gonzales Prada on Peruvian aristocrats: Prada, "Nuestra Aristocracia," *passim.*

137–138   Economic warfare against the Japanese: John K. Emmerson, "The Japanese in Peru," dispatch no. 8065 from Embassy Lima, 9 October 1943, p. 72. Much information in this chapter derives from this dispatch.

138–145   Expulsion of Axis nationals: Barnhart, "Japanese Internees," p. 172. Also, author's dispatch no. 8065 and personal experience.

148–149   Postwar treatment of Peruvian Japanese. Ibid., pp. 173–177.

Chapter 7

153 Purposes for warfare in China area: Conversation by Secretary of War Henry L. Stimson, quoted in Charles F. Romanus and Riley Sunderland, *U.S. Army in World War II: China-Burma-India Theater, Stilwell's Mission to China* (Washington, D.C.: Department of the Army, 1953), p. 64.

153 Stilwell on his prospective command: Theodore H. White, ed., *The Stilwell Papers* (New York: William Sloane Associates, MacFadden Books, 1962), p. 33.

154 "I claim we got a hell of a beating ...": Barbara W. Tuchman, *Stilwell and the American Experience in China, 1911–1945* (New York: Macmillan, 1971), p. 300.

154–155 Stilwell, on Stalin, Roosevelt, Churchill, and Chiang Kai-shek: Joseph W. Stilwell, *The Black Book*, 12 November 1943, Diary, pp. 86 and 93, SP.

155 "Coast, boys ...": Stilwell, ibid., undated, p. 56.

155 Churchill ... "quite willing to see China collapse": Tuchman, *Stilwell and the American Experience*, p. 382.

155 "The only way to beat the enemy ...": John Paton Davies, Jr., *Dragon by the Tail* (New York: W. W. Norton, 1972), p. 286.

155 Col. Lewis Andrew Pike, on the Ledo Road: Leslie Anders, *The Ledo Road* (Norman, Okla.: University of Oklahoma Press, 1965), p. 89.

156 "like dead giant voles with their paws in the air": Charlton Ogburn, Jr., *The Marauders* (New York: Harper & Brothers, 1959), pp. 73–74.

156 Currie's recommendation to replace Stilwell: Romanus and Sunderland, *Stilwell's Mission to China*, p. 186. "Mt. Batten [Mountbatten] tried to ditch me": Stilwell, Diary, 4 September 1944, SP.

156–157 Chennault, on bringing about the downfall of Japan. Claire Lee Chennault, *Way of a Fighter* (New York: G. P. Putnam's Sons, 1949), p. 213.

157 Chennault, on Stilwell's obsession with ground warfare: Ibid., p. 221.

157 Churchill, on fighting in Burma: Winston S. Churchill, *The Second World War: Closing the Ring* (Boston: Houghton Mifflin, 1951), p. 560.

157   "out at the end of the thinnest supply line of all": *General George C. Marshall's Biennial Report, July 1, 1943 to June 20, 1946*, quoted in Fred Eldridge, *Wrath in Burma* (Garden City, N.Y.: Doubleday, 1946), p. 160.

159   "A Jap's a Jap …": Testimony by Lt. Gen. John L. DeWitt, commander of the Western Defense Command, quoted in Bill Hosokawa, *Nisei, The Quiet Americans* (New York: William Morrow, 1969), p. 260.

159   Interviewers found that only 3 percent … : Ibid., p. 397.

159   A nisei sergeant's first contact with enemy: Staff Sgt. Edgar Laytha, "Nisei," *CBI Roundup* (New Delhi), vol. III, no. 1 (September 14, 1944), p. 3.

159–160   GI's letter about nisei: Patricia Davies, "Horizontal Hank."

161   GI's letter on Henry Gosho: Ibid.

162   "as a red flag to a bull …": Ogburn, *The Marauders*, p. 279.

162   "Nuts to you, General Stilwell": Col. Charles N. Hunter, *Galahad* (San Antonio, Tex.: Naylor, 1963), p. 1.

162   We four political advisers … developed our own code … : Later this code was to come under suspicion. Richard Deacon, in his book *The Chinese Secret Service* (New York: Taplinger, 1974), states, "Service had worked out a code for the use of the network … Chiang Kai-shek was 'Snow White' and the Chinese Communists were referred to as 'Harvard.' Davies, not Service, devised the code, and the 'network,' consisted of Davies, Service, Ludden, and Emmerson."

164   The team leader was … Koji Ariyoshi, … : Laytha, "Nisei."

164–165   "nisei Sergeant York": Laytha, "Nisei"; and interviews with witnesses.

165   Civil affairs problems in Hukawng valley: Dispatch from John Davies, Jr., enclosing "Memorandum on Civil Affairs in the Hukawng Valley," by John K. Emmerson, 3 July 1944, State Department file 740.0011 PW/7-344.

166   "Burma Night" leaflet: Scrapbook of leaflets prepared by Psychological Warfare Team, U.S. Office of War Information, APO 689, book II issued to Lt. Proctor Mellquist.

166   "in the ring": White, *Stilwell Papers*, p. 236.

167   "You will defend Myitkyina to the death": Ushiro Masaru, *Biruma Senki* [Burma War Diary] (Tokyo: Nihon Shuppan Kyōdō, 1953), p. 58.

167   "Over at last …": White, *Stilwell Papers*, p. 247.

167 "Almost every weapon of war ...": Dispatch to the secretary of state, "Transmission of Memoranda on Psychological Warfare and Civil Affairs Problems in Myitkyina, North Burma," by John K. Emmerson, 27 July 1944, State Department file 740.0011 PW/7-2744.

167 Japanese propaganda leaflet addressed to "General Merrill ...": Scrapbook, Psychological Warfare Team, U.S. Office of War Information, APO 689.

168–169 First broadcast at front lines: Emmerson memorandum, 27 July 1944.

169–170 Interviews with twelve prisoners of war: Dispatch to the secretary of state from John Davies, Jr., enclosing memorandum "Interrogations of Japanese Prisoners of War for Purposes of Psychological Warfare," by John K. Emmerson, 8 April 1944, State Department file 740.0011 PACIFIC WAR/3874.

170 "Graveyard of North Burma": Ushiro, *Biruma Senki,* p. 47.

171 Description of wounded evacuees from Japanese field hospital: Emmerson report of July 27, 1944.

171 "seven hundred men against four divisions": Fujino Hideo, *Shi no Idaka* [Raft of Death] (Tokyo: Ryokuchi-sha, 1956), pp. 204 and 209.

171–172 Ledo prisoners of war: "Use of Japanese Prisoners of War," by OWI Psychological Warfare Team in William E. Daugherty, in collaboration with Morris Janowitz, *A Psychological Warfare Casebook* (Baltimore: Johns Hopkins University Press, 1958), pp. 201–211.

172 "It would be difficult to find anywhere a group more enthusiastic ...": Ibid., p. 204.

173–174 POW discussion sessions: Transcripts of the conferences, handwritten, in Japanese, October 1944, in possession of the author.

173 "To compare hunger ...": Handwritten poem in author's file.

175 "the thought popped into my mind": James MacGregor Burns, *Roosevelt, the Soldier of Freedom, 1940–1945* (New York: Harcourt Brace Jovanovich, 1970), p. 323.

175 "Roosevelt has threatened to wipe every last Japanese from the face of the earth": Yamanaka Minetarō, *Yōki Amerika* [Western Devil America] (Tokyo: Takunansha, 1943), as quoted in translated excerpt, *The Japan Interpreter* (Tokyo), vol. XI, no. 1 (Spring 1976), p. 30.

175-176 Japanese troops and surrender: John K. Emmerson, "Resistance of Japanese Forces After the Fall of the Central Government," 27 July 1944, State Department file 740.0011 PW/7-2744.

176 "A Policy Toward Japan": Dispatch to the secretary of state from John K. Emmerson, Headquarters, United States Army Forces, China–Burma–India, "Transmitting Memorandum Entitled 'A Policy Toward Japan,'" 18 August 1944, State Department file 740.0011 PW/7-1844.

176 Captain Zacharias's first broadcast, May 8, 1945: Ellis M. Zacharias, *Secret Missions, The Story of an Intelligence Officer* (New York: G. P. Putnam's Sons, 1946), pp. 399–401.

176 President Truman's statement on unconditional surrender: Harry S. Truman, *Memoirs*, vol. 1, *Year of Decisions* (Garden City, N.Y.: Doubleday, 1955), p. 207.

Chapter 8

177 Significance of invasion of Saipan: The U.S. Bombing Survey immediately at the end of the war asked a selected number of Japanese, When did you first anticipate that Japan would surrender or lose the war? Those in their twenties or thirties replied "the fall of Okinawa" or the "first experience of bombing"; however, most of the respondents in their forties or fifties set the loss of Saipan as the moment they expected defeat. Itokawa Daikichi and Kuno Osamu, "Tennō sei to Nihonjin: Sono Shinjō to Ronri" [The Emperor System and the Japanese: Feelings and Logic], *Ushio* (Tokyo), September 1975, pp. 82–83. Effect of China-based B-29 raids on Japan: Charles F. Romanus and Riley Sunderland, *U.S. Army in World War II: China-Burma-India Theater, Stilwell's Command Problems* (Washington, D.C.: Office of the Chief of Military History, Department of the Army, 1956), p. 370.

178 "I confess there is nothing . . .": *FRUS, China, 1944*, vol. VI, p. 101.

178 Walter Judd on the "four Johns": Rep. Walter Judd testified before the Senate Subcommittee on Internal Security, 31 May 1956. *Report of the Subcommittee for the Year 1956*, Sect. XI, pp. 191–192.

179 Service recommendation on observers to Communist areas:

Joseph W. Esherick, ed., *Lost Chance in China: The World War II Despatches of John S. Service* (New York: Random House, 1974), p. 176.

179 Chiang Kai-shek's first reply to Wallace on observers to Communist areas: U.S., Department of State, *United States Relations with China, with Special Reference to the Period 1944–1949* (Washington, D.C.: Department of State, Publication 3573, Far Eastern Series 30, August 1949), p. 554. This document is also known as *The China White Paper* under which title it was published in 1967: *The China White Paper, August 1949*, 2 vols. (Stanford, Calif.: Stanford University Press, 1967), 2:554.

179 "That can be done": *U.S. Relations with China*, p. 555; *The China White Paper*, 2:555.

180 Kaji Wataru and his Anti-War League: Shioda Shobei, "Sokoku ni Somuite" [Against the Motherland] *Asahi Janaru* (Tokyo), 5 December 1965.

181 Stilwell, "THE AXE FALLS": Theodore H. White, ed., *The Stilwell Papers* (New York: William Sloane Associates, Mac-Fadden Books, 1962), p. 273.

181–182 Service's first report from Yenan: Esherick, ed., *Lost Chance*, pp. 178–182.

184–185 [Forman] asked Mao why he did not change the party's name: Harrison Forman, *Report from Red China* (New York: Henry Holt, 1945), pp. 179–180.

185 Service . . . identified three Russians: Esherick, ed., *Lost Chance*, pp. 351–353.

186 Vladimirov, on messages to Moscow: Diary entry for 18 December 1944, in P. P. Vladimirov, *Osobi Raion Kitaya 1942–1945* [China's Special Area 1942-1945] (Moscow: Novosti Press Agency, 1974), p. 401. For an English translation, see Peter Vladimirov, *The Vladimirov Diaries* (Garden City, N.Y.: Doubleday, 1975), p. 311. The citations are from the Russian original.

186 ". . . Kolya transmits while I am sleeping": Diary entries for 27 June 1944 and 21 August 1944 in Vladimirov, *Osobi Raion*, p. 321.

186 Service memorandum of August 27, 1944: Esherick, ed., *Lost Chance*, p. 295.

186 Vladimirov entry of August 30, 1944: Vladimirov, *Osobi Raion*, pp. 324–325.

186 Vladimirov's description of Service: Ibid., pp. 335–336 (diary entry of 10 September 1944), and p. 359 (diary entry of 8 October 1944). For his description of Davies, see ibid., p. 371 (diary entry of 4 November 1944); and for Barrett, see ibid., pp. 341–342 (diary entry of 15 September 1944) and p. 359 (diary entry of 8 October 1944).

187 "My earlier contacts with American servicemen ...": Ibid., p. 310 (entry of 1 August 1944).

187 "For China, United States policy ...": Ibid., p. 256 (entry of 21 January 1944).

187 "no matter what ... our revolution will eventually turn against the imperialists": Ibid., p. 306 (entry of 20 July 1944).

187–188 Chinese Communists' attitudes toward Russians: Embassy Chungking dispatch no. 63, 9 January 1945, "Transmission of Memorandum 'Interviews with Chinese Communist Leaders' by John K. Emmerson."

188 Mao-Service interview, August 23, 1944: Esherick, ed., *Lost Chance,* p. 306.

188 Khrushchev, on K'ang Sheng: Nikita Khrushchev, *Khrushchev Remembers: The Last Testament* (Boston: Little, Brown, 1974; New York: Bantam Books, 1976), p. 287 (321 paperback).

188 K'ang Sheng had "grave doubts about Russian loyalty to the Chinese cause": Richard Deacon, *The Chinese Secret Service* (New York: Taplinger, 1974), p. 261.

188–190 Interview with K'ang Sheng: Author's memorandum, 14 December 1944.

191 Nosaka on Ryū: Nosaka Sanzō, *Fusetsu no Ayumi* [Walk Through Wind and Snow] (Tokyo: Shin Nihon Shuppansha, 1975–), 2:24.

192 "In 1930 he petitioned ... for leave": Some former members of the prewar Japanese special police believe that, although no documentary evidence is said to exist, Nosaka in some form renounced Communist activities *(tenkō shimashita)* or cooperated with authorities in order to obtain release from prison for medical treatment.

194 Policy of Eighth Route Army toward Japanese prisoners: Memorandum by John K. Emmerson, Yenan, 10 November 1944, SP, file 123.

195 Telephone communication across enemy lines: *Asahi Janaru* (Tokyo), 5 December 1965, p. 75.

195 The stated purpose of the Peasants and Workers School: Tech.

Sgt. Koji Ariyoshi, "The Japanese Peasants and Workers School: A Study," 1945, report for Office of War Information, the author's notes.

196　Poll of Japanese prisoner attitudes: Memorandum by John K. Emmerson enclosed in dispatch no. 25 from Embassy Chungking, "Transmission of Memoranda prepared by Mr. John K. Emmerson on General Subject of Psychological Warfare," 20 December 1944, State Department file 740.0011, PW/12-2044.

197　Factors influencing changes in POWs: John K. Emmerson, "The Mind of a Japanese Prisoner of War," 21 November 1944, enclosure to dispatch no. 25 from Chungking.

199　Nosaka on leadership and help of Comintern: Nosaka Sanzō, *Senshū Senji-hen, 1933-1945* [Selected Works of Nosaka Sanzō: War Period] (Tokyo: Central Committee, Japan Communist Party, 1964), p. 5.

200　Nosaka's program: Memorandum by F. MacCracken Fisher, Office of War Information, Chungking, "The Program of the Japanese Communist Party, discussion by Okano Susumu, 6 September 1944." Note that Okano was another name used by Nosaka.

200　Nosaka on the emperor: Okano Susumu (Nosaka Tetsu), representative of the Japanese Communist party, "The Construction of Democratic Japan," report presented to the Seventh National Delegates Conference of the Chinese Communist party, May 1945, trans. Koji Ariyoshi, Office of War Information in Yenan, report no. 71.

201　a brief history of the Japanese Communist party . . . : John K. Emmerson, "The Japanese Communist Party," U.S., Congress, Senate, Committee on the Judiciary, *The Amerasia Papers: A Clue to the Catastrophe of China*, 2 vols., 91st Cong., 1st sess., 26 January 1970, 2:1219-1225. Also published in Jon Livingston, Joe Moore, and Felicia Oldfather, *Imperial Japan, 1800-1945* (New York: Random House, 1973), pp. 397-405. Also see, John K. Emmerson, "The Japanese Communist Party After Fifty Years," *Asian Survey*, vol. XII, no. 7 (July 1972), pp. 564-579.

202　Dispatches proposing "statements" on Japan: The dates of these dispatches were 18 August 1944, New Delhi, "Policy Toward Japan: An Outline Statement"; 16 September 1944, New Delhi, "Japan Since Koiso," proposing imperial rescript declaring the war ended; 7 November 1944, Chungking, "A Statement on Japan"; 21 November 1944, Chungking, "Propaganda Theme for Japan: A U.S. Statement"; and 23 December 1944, Chungking, memorandum to General Wedemeyer, "official statement urgently needed."

206   Mao's proposal to visit Washington: Barbara W. Tuchman, "If Mao Had Come to Washington: An Essay in Alternatives," *Foreign Affairs,* vol. 51, no. 1 (October 1972), pp. 44–64.

208   ". . . was a husk, . . . democracy an illusion": Barbara W. Tuchman, *Stilwell and the American Experience in China 1911– 1945* (New York: Macmillan, 1971), p. 656.

209   "Eyes only for Wedemeyer" messages on proposed visit by Mao Tse-tung and Chou En-lai to Washington, and on alleged secret negotiations between the Chinese Nationalist Government and the Japanese: Both of these were army messages from Dixie Mission to Chungking, nos. 322 and 324, 9 and 19 January, respectively. See Chungking's telegram no. 180, 7 February 1945, *FRUS, The Far East, China, 1945,* vol. VII, p. 209.

210–211   Author's memorandum on Communist "revelations": John K. Emmerson, "Communist Report of Kuomintang–Japanese Agreement," Embassy Chungking, 13 January 1945, top secret.

211   Hurley's reports to President Roosevelt: Embassy Chungking telegram no. 141500 NCR 6810, 14 January 1945, in *FRUS, The Far East, China, 1945,* vol. VII, p. 176. See also Embassy Chungking telegram no. 180, *FRUS, The Far East, China, 1945,* vol. VII, p. 209.

211   Roosevelt "baffled yet acutely fascinated" with situation in China: Tuchman, "If Mao Had Come to Washington," p. 63.

Chapter 9

215   Only Stettinius, Harriman, and Bohlen knew about Yalta: Charles E. Bohlen, *Witness to History, 1929–1969* (New York: W.W. Norton, 1973), p. 198.

215   Ballantine learned about the Yalta accords six months after the conference: Joseph W. Ballantine, Diary, Ballantine Papers, Hoover Institution, Stanford University, Stanford, Calif., chap. XI, p. 261.

215 Defeat of Japan eighteen months after that of Germany: Combined Chiefs of Staff, CCS 776/3, 9 February 1945, in Ray S. Cline, *Washington Command Post: The Operations Division* (Washington, D.C.: Office of the Chief of Military History, Department of the Army, 1951), p. 340.

215 "The American planners did not think . . .": Cline, *Washington Command Post*, p. 342.

216 "There seems to be no feeling that he is a traitor to his own country . . .": Report by John K. Emmerson, enclosed in dispatch to State Department from Embassy New Delhi, "A Policy Toward Japan," 18 August 1944, State Department file 740.0011 PW/8-1844.

216 State Department impressed by "thoroughness and initiative . . .": It was State Department practice to send comments to officers who had submitted dispatches and memoranda to Washington. The commendation quoted: "The Department is impressed by the thoroughness and initiative Mr. Emmerson is displaying in his work . . ." was sent to Embassy Chungking 7 February 1945 by the Division of Japanese Affairs, Department of State; the text can be found in U.S., Department of State, Loyalty Security Board, *Transcript of Proceedings, In the Matter of: John Kenneth Emmerson,* 13 vols. (Washington, D.C.: U.S. Department of State, 20 March 1952), 7:1. Subsequently referred to as Emmerson Transcript.

216 Postwar planning for Japan: Hugh Borton, *American Presurrender Planning for Postwar Japan* (New York: Columbia University Press, 1967), p. 18.

217 Harrison Forman, on Chinese Communists: Forman, *Report from Red China* (New York: Henry Holt, 1945), p. 1.

218 Amerasia case: Security Subcommittee, U.S., Congress, Senate, *The Amerasia Papers: A Clue to the Catastrophe of China,* 2 vols., 91st Cong., 1st sess., 26 January 1970.

220-221 Conversation with Chen Chia-kang: Memorandum of conversation, 28 April 1945, *FRUS, The Far East, China, 1945,* vol. VII, p. 369.

221 Recommendations on indoctrination of prisoners of war: John K. Emmerson and Dr. C. W. Hepner, "The Indoctrination of Japanese Prisoners of War," memorandum to the Secretary of State and the Provost Marshal General, Washington, D.C., 12 April 1945.

222-223   Prisoner's view of the Texas indoctrination program: Moriji Yamaga, *American Democracy and Its Ways* (Tokyo: Iwanami Shōten, 1947), pp. i-iii.

223   "We may expect the resistance of the Japanese . . .": Dispatch to the secretary of state from John K. Emmerson, "Transmitting Memorandum entitled 'An International Organization of "Free" Japanese,'" 9 February 1945, State Department file 740.0011, PW/2-945.

224   Organization not to be Communist-inspired: Ibid.

224   Inter-Divisional Area Committee for the Far East: Minutes of meeting of the Inter-Divisional Area Committee for the Far East, 23 February 1945.

225-226   Information on Ōyama Ikuo, from a who's who of proletarian parties: Noguchi Yoshiake, *Musan Undō Sō Tōshi Den* [Biographies of Leaders of the Proletarian Movement] (Tokyo: Shakai Shisō Kenkyū-jo [Research Institute for Social Thought], 1931), pp. 55-59.

226-227   Interview with Ōyama Ikuo: Bureau of Far Eastern Affairs, memorandum of conversation, subject, Japanese Postwar Problems; participants, Ikuo Ōyama, Northwestern University, Evanston, Ill., and John K. Emmerson, 14 April 1945.

228   Ishigaki, on Ōyama: Ishigaki Ayako, *Kaisō no Sumedore* [Reminiscences of Smedley] (Tokyo: Misuzu Shōbō, 1967), p. 145.

229   Ishigaki, on Miyako lunch: Ibid., pp. 140-141.

230   Battle of Leyte Gulf: Kase Toshikazu, *Journey to the Missouri* (New Haven, Conn.: Yale University Press, 1950), p. 95.

231   Hull, "one of the most difficult questions" . . .: Cordell Hull, *The Memoirs of Cordell Hull*, 2 vols. (New York: Macmillan, 1948), 2:1591.

231   Memorandum on the emperor, January 1944: Emmerson Transcript, 18 March 1952, 3:A-86-87.

231   State Department memorandum of May 9, 1944: Hull, *Memoirs*, 2:1591-1593.

231   Grew, on the emperor, in response to Robert Sherrod, 3 January 1945: *FRUS, The British Commonwealth, The Far East, 1945*, vol. VI, pp. 515-516.

231-232   Dean Acheson on the emperor: Dean Acheson, *Present at the Creation: My Years in the State Department* (New York: W. W. Norton, 1969), pp. 112-113.

232 Drew Pearson on the emperor: Pearson column of 10 June 1950, quoted in Joseph C. Grew, *Turbulent Era: A Diplomatic Record of Forty Years,* 2 vols. (Boston: Houghton Mifflin 1952), 2:1408.

232 Public opinion poll on the emperor: Memorandum to Undersecretary Grew by Joseph W. Ballantine, 6 August 1945, *FRUS, The British Commonwealth, The Far East, 1945,* vol. VI, pp. 588–589.

232 Kido's 1942 advice to the emperor: Robert J. C. Butow, *Japan's Decision to Surrender* (Stanford, Calif.: Stanford University Press, 1954), p. 14, 15*n.*, and Kido Kōichi, *Nikki* [Diary], 2 vols. (Tokyo: Tokyo Daigaku Shuppansha, 1966), 2:944.

232 Koiso felt the war lost; Butow, *Japan's Decision,* pp. 37 and 43.

232 Admiral Takagi's studies: Ibid., pp. 21 and 38–39.

232 Konoye's memorial to the throne: Ibid., pp. 47–50.

233 Tōgō refused to take the post . . .: Shigenori Tōgō, *The Cause of Japan* (New York: Simon & Schuster, 1956), p. 276.

233 Suzuki "understood" the emperor's desire to make peace: IMTFE, Suzuki Kantaro, affidavit, pp. 35 and 590.

233–234 Joint Intelligence Committee estimate: Cline, *Washington Command Post,* p. 343.

233–234 Grew's case for the emperor: *FRUS, The British Commonwealth, The Far East, 1945,* vol. VI, pp. 546–547.

234 Grew memorandum of May 29: Ibid., p. 548.

234 Use of atomic weapon: Henry L. Stimson and McGeorge Bundy, *On Active Service, in Peace and War* (New York: Harper & Brothers, 1947), p. 617.

234 Tōgō–Yonai exchange: Tōgō, *Cause of Japan,* p. 292.

234 Kido's "tentative plan to cope with the situation": Kido, *Nikki,* 2:1208–1209.

234 Supreme Council decision, June 18: Tōgō, *Cause of Japan,* p. 296.

235 Grew's proposed statement of June 18 to coincide with victory on Okinawa: Harry S. Truman, *Memoirs,* vol. 1, *Year of Decisions* (Garden City, N.Y.: Doubleday, 1955), p. 417.

235 Joint Chiefs' desire to await a Japanese refusal: Ibid., p. 417.

235 Satō's despairing telegram: Satō Naotake, *Kaisō Hachijūnen* [Memoirs of Eighty Years] (Tokyo: Jiji Press, 1963), p. 497.

235 Truman's objective to confirm Stalin's declaration of war on Japan: Bohlen, *Witness,* p. 229.

236   Truman plays the piano for "old Stalin": Merle Miller, *Plain Speaking: An Oral Biography of Harry S. Truman* (New York: Berkley, 1973), p. 85.

236   Authors of Potsdam Proclamation, Eugene Dooman and Douglas Fairbanks, Jr.: Security Subcommittee Hearings, Dooman's testimony, 14 September 1951, pp. 731–733.

236   Sentence on emperor in original draft proclamation, May 28, 1945: Grew, *Turbulent Era*, 2:1433.

236   Hull asks deletion of reference to emperor: Hull, *Memoirs*, 2:1593–1594.

236–237   Tōgō and the Potsdam Proclamation: Tōgō, *Cause of Japan*, pp. 311–314.

237   *Mokusatsu:* IMTFE, Sakomizu Hisatsune, affidavit, pp. 35 and 608. Interview with Sakomizu (20 April 1974): Ōmori Minoru, *Sengo Hishi: Tennō to Genshi Bakudan* [Secret Postwar History: The Emperor and the Atomic Bomb] (Tokyo: Kodansha, 1975), 2:248.

237   Molotov's declaration of war to Satō: Satō, *Kaisō Hachijūnen*, pp. 498–499.

237–238   Ballantine learned at 7:00 A.M.: Ballantine, Ballantine Papers, chap. XI, pp. 264–265.

238   White House meeting of August 10: Truman, *Memoirs*, 1:428; Walter Millis, ed., *The Forrestal Diaries* (New York: Viking Press, 1951), pp. 82–83; Stimson Diaries, 10 August 1945, pp. 72–73, Yale University, New Haven, Conn.; Forrestal Diary, 10 August 1945, p. 428, Princeton University, Princeton, N.J. For a perceptive discussion of this meeting see Barton J. Bernstein, "The Perils and Politics of Surrender: Ending the War with Japan and Avoiding the Third Atomic Bomb," *Pacific Historical Review*, vol. XLVI, no. 2 (February 1977), pp. 4–6.

238–239   Byrnes on drafting of U.S. statement on the emperor: James F. Byrnes, *Speaking Frankly* (New York: Harper & Brothers, 1947), p. 209.

Chapter 10

251   Admiral Nomura, on war: Elliott R. Thorpe, *East Wind, Rain: The Intimate Account of an Intelligence Officer in the Pacific, 1930–49* (Boston: Gambit, 1969), p. 199.

251–252   Grew, on proffered appointment as political adviser to General MacArthur: Joseph C. Grew, *Turbulent Era: A Diplomatic Record of Forty Years*, 2 vols. (Boston: Houghton Mifflin, 1952), 2:1522.

252   Grew recommends Dooman or Ballantine: Joseph W. Ballantine, Diary, Ballantine Papers, Hoover Institution, Stanford University, Stanford, Calif., chap. XII, pp. 266–268.

252   Acheson queries Ballantine on Atcheson: Ibid.

252   New group in ascendance in State Department: Ibid.

252   "New Deal economists . . .": Ibid.

253   "Thorpe . . . arrest General Tōjō . . .": Thorpe, *East Wind, Rain*, p. 184.

254   Recommendations of United Nations Commission on War Crimes: *FRUS, The British Commonwealth, The Far East, 1945*, vol. VI, pp. 911–918.

254   SWNC policy on war criminals in the Far East: Ibid., pp. 926–936.

254   Arrest of thirty-nine war criminals: Ibid., p. 974.

255   conspiracy to dominate the whole world: Count 1 of the indictment charged a common conspiracy to secure the military, naval, political, and economic domination of East Asia and of the Pacific and Indian oceans, and of all countries and islands therein or bordering thereon. Count 5 charged a conspiracy of Germany, Italy, and Japan to secure the military, naval, political, and economic domination of the whole world. Count 5 was thrown out by the tribunal but all twenty-five defendants except two were judged guilty on Count I. Richard H. Minear, *Victors' Justice, The Tokyo War Crimes Trial* (Princeton, N.J.: Princeton University Press, 1971), pp. 24–25, 193, 197, 198, 203.

255–256   Atcheson telegram of February 28, 1945: *FRUS, The Far East, China, 1945*, vol. VII, p. 244.

256   "forcing to be free": John D. Montgomery, *Forced to Be Free: The Artificial Revolution in Germany and Japan* (Chicago: University of Chicago Press, 1957).

257–258   Visit to political prisoners at Fuchū: POLAD dispatch no. 7 from George Atcheson, Jr., political adviser to Supreme Commander for Allied Powers, Tokyo, 10 October 1945, enclosing memorandum by John K. Emmerson, "Visit to Fuchū Prison," 5 October 1945.

258   Report of visit to Fuchū prison by Tokuda and Shiga: Tokuda

Kyūichi and Shiga Yoshio, *Gokuchū Jū-hachi Nen* [Eighteen Years in Prison] (Tokyo: Jiji Press, 1947), p. 161.

258–259 Interrogation of Tokuda Kyūichi: POLAD dispatch no. 22, 19 October 1945, enclosing "memorandum by John K. Emmerson, 'Interrogation of Tokuda Kyūichi, released political prisoner, conducted at General Headquarters, Tokyo, 7 October 1945, under the auspices of the Counter Intelligence Section.'"

259 "transfer of Reds to Tokyo ...": Harry Emerson Wildes, *Typhoon in Tokyo: The Occupation and Its Aftermath* (New York: Macmillan, 1954), p. 269.

260 "for years afterward to prove ... special privilege to Communists": Walt Sheldon, *The Honorable Conquerors: The Occupation of Japan, 1945–1952* (New York: Macmillan 1965), p. 133.

260 "In the latter part of the war ...": Ōmori Minoru, *Sengo Hishi: Akhata to GHQ* [Secret Postwar History: Red Flag and GHQ] (Tokyo: Kodansha, 1975), 4:26.

260 Japanese Communist party membership reached six hundred in November 1945: POLAD dispatch no. 74, 24 November 1945; five thousand in January 1946: report to State Department by John K. Emmerson, "Political Factors in the Present Japanese Situation," 8 February 1946.

261 Communists' *Appeal to the People: Akahata*, [Red Flag], no. 1 (Tokyo), 20 October 1945.

262 Yoshida, on "leniency" toward the Communists: Yoshida Shigeru, *The Yoshida Memoirs* (Boston: Houghton Mifflin, 1962), p. 38.

262 Konoye on communism: Konoye's memorandum of conversation between himself and General MacArthur, General Sutherland, George Atcheson, Jr., on 4 October 1945, Konoye Papers, Hoover Institution (copy), Stanford University, Stanford, Calif.

263 Nosaka's trip from Yenan to Tokyo: "Nosaka Gichō ni Kiku: Yenan kara Tōkyō made" [Listening to Chairman Nosaka: from Yenan to Tokyo], *Akahata* (Tokyo), 15 August–6 September 1971.

264 "the Communist Party and Nosaka agree ...": POLAD dispatch no. 226, "Political Parties in Japan: Developments During the Week Ending 19 January 1946," 25 January 1946.

264 in 1975 ... Nosaka ... affirmed ...: Author's interview with Nosaka, Tokyo, 22 September 1975.

265 Konoye–MacArthur interview, October 4, 1945: Japanese text of memorandum of conversation, Konoye Papers, Hoover Institution (copy), Stanford University, Stanford, Calif., pp. 340–348.

265 Author's memoranda of October 20 and 23, 1945: POLAD dispatch no. 27, "Procedure for Revision of Japanese Constitution," 24 October 1945, enclosing two memoranda to the Supreme Commander, drafted by John K. Emmerson.

266 State Department's principles for Japanese constitution: *FRUS, The British Commonwealth, The Far East, 1945*, vol. VI, pp. 757–758.

266 MacArthur advises Atcheson to break relations with Konoye group: SCAP press release of 1 November 1945; *Nippon Times* (Tokyo) 3 November 1945; letter from George Atcheson, Jr., to Dean Acheson, undersecretary of state, 7 November 1945, *FRUS, The British Commonwealth, The Far East, 1945*, vol. VI, p. 837; and telegram from Atcheson to secretary of state, 8 November 1945, ibid., p. 841. Atcheson on November 5, in the course of a letter to President Truman (ibid., p. 327), referred to a "curious story," according to which the interpreter at the MacArthur–Atcheson meeting of 5 October mistranslated the general's phrase *administrative machinery* as *constitution*. Atcheson describes his own subsequent meeting with Konoye on 7 October and comments that "it would not seem the part of wisdom to interfere at this juncture with an individual so engaged who is in the confidence of the emperor and carries weight among the reactionaries because he himself is a feudal lord." Certainly, no effort was made to correct the alleged mistranslation or to discourage Konoye from pursuing his tasks of constitutional revision until the press release of 1 November and the notification by MacArthur of Atcheson that our office should terminate discussions with Konoye.

266 ". . . Konoye was fighting against fearful odds, . . .": Takagi Yasaka, *Toward International Understanding* (Tokyo: Kenkyusha, 1954), p. 119.

266–267 Norman, on Konoye: Memorandum dated 5 November 1945, by E. H. Norman, enclosure to POLAD dispatch no. 58, 17 November 1945. For text of dispatch only, not including enclosure, see *FRUS, The British Commonwealth, The Far East, 1945*, vol. VI, pp. 971–972.

267   Konoye's suicide: Sheldon, *Honorable Conquerors,* p. 99.

268–269   Founding of Socialist party: POLAD dispatch no. 43, 7 November 1945, "Political Parties in Japan: Developments During Week Ending 3 November 1945," by John K. Emmerson.

269   Inauguration of Liberal party: POLAD dispatch no. 53, 14 November 1945, "Political Parties in Japan: Developments During the Week Ending 10 November 1945," by John K. Emmerson.

269–270   Inauguration of Japan Progressive party: POLAD dispatch no. 60, 17 November 1945, "Political Parties in Japan: Developments During Week Ending 17 November 1945," by John K. Emmerson.

270   Tsurumi Yūsuke . . . assured us . . .: POLAD dispatch no. 72, 26 November 1945, "Report of Joint Interview with Tsurumi Yūsuke Held at SCAP Headquarters, 17 November 1945."

270–272   Meeting with university students: POLAD dispatch no. 119, 22 December 1945, "Conversation with Japanese University Students," by John K. Emmerson, held 19 December 1945.

274–275   Dispatch written on board S.S. *Mount McKinley:* John K. Emmerson, report on "Political Factors in Present Japanese Situation," 8 February 1946, transmitted to State Department, 25 February 1946, State Department file 740.0019, Control (Japan) 12-2546, 0510.

275   this "American interlude": See Kawai Kazuo, *Japan's American Interlude* (Chicago: University of Chicago Press, 1960).

277   British comment on dispatch, "Political Factors in Present Japanese Situation": Foreign Office document F 7365/95/23, letter from Chancery, British Embassy, Moscow to Far Eastern Department, Foreign Office, London, 13 May 1946, covering memorandum, London, 17 May 1946. Document used by permission of Her Majesty's Stationery Office, London.

278   "The General's words . . .": Herbert Norman, quoted in Charles Taylor, *Six Journeys: A Canadian Pattern* (Toronto: Anansi, 1977), p. 129.

278   Muragi Tamotsu, the general's barber; his interview: *Mainichi Shimbun* (Tokyo), 6 April 1964.

Chapter 11

281 Stalin's proposal to occupy the northern half of Hokkaido: Stalin's message to President Truman, 16 August 1945, *FRUS, The British Commonwealth, The Far East, 1945,* vol. VI, p. 668; and Truman's reply, 17 August 1945, ibid., p. 670.

281 "I have to say that I and my colleagues . . .": Stalin to Truman, 22 August 1945, ibid., pp. 687–688.

281 Harriman advises that Soviets would be uncooperative in Europe . . . : Ibid., p. 756.

281 "The Soviet Union had become an American satellite . . .": *Ibid.*, pp. 789–790.

282 Harriman, in 1977, on Stalin and Hokkaido: FROM THE MOUTH OF THE "CROCODILE," *Women's Wear Daily,* quoted in *San Francisco Chronicle,* 23 February 1977, p. 14.

283 Stalin's speech, February 9, 1946: Walter Millis, ed., *The Forrestal Diaries* (New York: Viking Press, 1951), pp. 134–135.

283 Kennan's red-light telegram, February 22, 1946: George F. Kennan, *Memoirs, 1925–1950* (Boston: Atlantic–Little, Brown, 1967), pp. 547–559.

283 "A shadow has fallen . . .": Louis J. Halle, *The Cold War as History* (New York: Harper & Row, 1967), pp. 103–104.

283 Mark Gayn on Soviet–American war: Mark Gayn, *Japan Diary* (New York: Sloane, 1948), p. 239.

283 Tokyo dispatch: Memorandum by Robert Fearey, "Reappraisal of United States Security Interests and Policies in Regard to Japan," POLAD dispatch no. 384, Tokyo, 23 April 1946, and comment by Emmerson, 15 May 1946, State Department file 740.00119 Control (Japan) 4-2346.

283–284 John Davies's memorandum: "Comments of the embassy at Moscow on the Policy and Information Statement concerning Japan, Dated 1 June 1946," Embassy Moscow, 10 August 1946, *FRUS, The Far East, 1946,* vol. VIII, pp. 285–286.

284–285 Emmerson's comments on Davies's memorandum: "Memorandum by the Assistant Chief of the Division of Japanese Affairs (Emmerson)," 9 October 1946, ibid., pp. 337–339.

285 By March of 1947 a small group in the State Department . . . : Memorandum (Top Secret—Eyes Alone) to General MacArthur from George Atcheson, Jr., 18 March 1947, enclosed in letter of same date to General John J. Hilldring, assistant secretary of state, State Department file 740.0011 PW (Peace) 3-1847.

285 MacArthur's comments on treaty proposals: Douglas Mac-Arthur, "Memorandum Concerning Drafts of Chapter V (Interim Controls) and Chapter VI (Disarmament and Demilitarization) of a Treaty of Peace with Japan in Process of Preparation by the State Department, and Draft of Treaty on the Disarmament and Demilitarization of Japan," 21 March 1947, State Department file 740.0011 PW (Peace) 3-2147.

286 Emmerson's transfer to Moscow: Embassy Moscow telegram no. 98, 15 January 1947, from Ambassador Walter Bedell Smith to Department of State, Control 4232.

288–289 Description of dacha: Paraphrased from Dorothy Emmerson, "Embassy Wife in Moscow," *Foreign Service Journal* (June 1952), vol. 29, no. 6, pp. 18–19.

295 "The Monkey Wrench": Cited by Robert Magidoff, *In Anger and Pity, A Report on Russia* (Garden City, N.Y.: Doubleday, 1949), pp. 207–209; and Walter Bedell Smith, *My Three Years in Moscow* (New York: J. B. Lippincott, 1950), pp. 299–302.

295–296 Turgenev on the Russian language: Ivan Turgenev, *Senilia* [Poems in Prose], cited in Bernard Guilbert Guerney, *A Treasury of Russian Literature* (New York: Vanguard Press, 1943), frontispiece.

297 Annabelle Bucar's book: Annabelle Bucar, *The Truth About American Diplomats* (Moscow: Literaturnaya Gazeta, 1949).

297 "All that was done for me by the U.S. Embassy ...": Alexander Dolgun with Patrick Watson, *Alexander Dolgun's Story: An American in the Gulag* (New York: Alfred A. Knopf, 1975), p. 354.

298 Bucar, on intelligence gathering: Bucar, *Truth About American Diplomats*, p. 86.

298–299 Trip to Tiflis: Embassy Moscow dispatch no. 331, 7 June 1949, "Transmitting Report of Trip to Tbilisi, Kharkov, Stalingrad, and Saratov, taken by John K. Emmerson and D. Eugene Boster," State Department file 861.00/6-749.

300 Soviet press denounced unilateral action of the U.S. in initiating peace treaty negotiations ... : Embassy Moscow telegram no. 2486, 23 July 1947, State Department file 740.0011 PW (Peace) 7-2347.

300 "American protectors of Japanese imperialists ...": Embassy Moscow airgram no. A-954, 18 September 1947, State Department file 740.0011 PW (Peace) 9-1847.

300 Embassy estimate of Soviet actions on Japanese peace treaty: Embassy Moscow telegram no. 3310, 2 December 1947, State Department file 740.0011 PW (Peace) 12-247.

300 Kennan's recommendations: Kennan, *Memoirs 1925-1950*, p. 391.

300 "force of a blockbuster bomb": Millis, *Forrestal Diaries*, p. 387.

300-301 "There is an element of tragic irony ...": Marshall D. Shulman, *Stalin's Policy Reappraised* (Cambridge, Mass.: Harvard University Press, 1963), p. 63.

301-302 "We produced a ... top secret report ...": Embassy Moscow dispatch no. 315, 1 April 1948, "Transmitting Report 'Soviet Intentions,'" top secret, State Department file 761.00/4-148.

301 Khrushchev estimated Soviet armed forces at 2.8 million in 1948: Shulman, *Stalin's Policy Reappraised*, p. 27.

302-304 Missing document: Embassy Moscow dispatch no. 253, 9 March 1948, "Possible Breach of Security," State Department file 124.616/3-948.

304 Kennan's "Mr. X" article: X, "The Sources of Soviet Conduct," *Foreign Affairs* (July 1947), vol. 25, no. 4, pp. 566-582.

304 "There were few messages ...": Smith, *My Three Years*, p. 187.

306 "We will serenade our transfers ...": Words of a song written by Richard M. Service, to the tune of the Yale "Whiffenpoof Song."

Chapter 12

307-308 I was presented with a letter ...: Letter to author from Conrad E. Snow, chairman, Loyalty Security Board, Department of State, Washington, D.C., 29 December 1951, author's file.

308-309 War College report: John K. Emmerson, "Comparative Communist Policies in Europe and the Far East," in *Individual Studies* (Washington, D.C., National War College, 28 October 1949).

309-310 Dean Acheson's War College speech: David S. McLellan, *Dean Acheson: The State Department Years* (New York: Dodd, Mead, 1976), pp. 173-174.

310 Chou En-lai's warning to Pannikar, and MacArthur's assurances that China would not enter war: Truman, *Memoirs,* vol. 2, *Years of Trial and Hope, 1946-1952* (Garden City, N.Y.: Doubleday, 1955), pp. 361-362 and 365. See also Allen S. Whiting, *China Crosses the Yalu* (Stanford, Calif.: Stanford University Press, 1968), p. 108.

311 Truman's standards and procedures for investigation of government employees: "Executive Order 9835, Prescribing Procedures for the Administration of an Employees Loyalty Program in the Executive Branch of the Government," signed: Harry S. Truman, The White House, 21 March 1947.

311 McCarthy's speech of February 9, 1950: Richard H. Rovere, *Senator Joe McCarthy* (New York: Harcourt Brace, 1959), p. 123.

311 Father Walsh suggested communism: Ibid., pp. 122-123.

311 Alsop brothers on McCarthyism and the cold war: Ibid., p. 265.

311-312 Act of Congress on security: U.S. Congress, House, Public Law 733, chap. 803, H.R. 7439, 81st Cong., 2nd sess., 26 August 1950, H. Rept., p.1.

312 Loyalty Security regulations of 1951: U.S., Department of State, "Loyalty and Security of Employees," *Manual of Regulations and Procedures; Administrative Operations* (Washington, D.C.: U.S. Department of State, 21 September 1951), sect. 5, pp. 390-396.

312 FBI investigation of October 20, 1950: Loyalty Security Board, memorandum, "Rationale: Emmerson, John Kenneth," 26 June 1953, p. 2.

312 Communication from General Willoughby: "To Assistant Chief of Staff, G-2, Department of the Army, Washington, D.C., from C.A. Willoughby, Major General, GSC, Asst. Chief of Staff, G-2, General Headquarters, Far East Command, March 3, 1951. 27 enclosures," SF.

313 Editorial, "Career versus Conscience": *Foreign Service Journal,* vol. 28, no. 7 (July 1951), pp. 23 and 50; and *The Providence* (R.I.) *Journal,* 9 August 1951.

314 "Dooman says Left-Wingers Ran Jap Policy": *The Washington Post,* 15 September 1951; and Dooman's testimony before Senate Subcommittee, 14 September 1951, Security Subcommittee Hearings, pp. 703-754.

314-315 Exchange of letters with Dooman: Emmerson to Dooman,

Washington, D.C., 26 October 1951; and Dooman to Emmerson, Litchfield, Conn., 30 October 1951, author's file.

315 Grew, "I . . . never lacked confidence in you": Letter from Joseph C. Grew to Emmerson, Washington, D.C., 31 October 1951, author's file.

315 Wedemeyer testimony: Security Subcommittee Hearings, 18 September 1951, pp. 755–836. For Wedemeyer, on advice of four political advisers, see ibid., p. 831.

315–316 Exchange of letters with Wedemeyer: Emmerson to Wedemeyer, Washington, D.C., 26 October 1951; Wedemeyer to Emmerson, New York City, 26 November 1951, copy of letter from Wedemeyer to Sen. Pat McCarran, New York City, 11 November 1951, author's file.

316 Reference to Emmerson in Wedemeyer's book: Gen. Albert C. Wedemeyer, *Wedemeyer Reports* (New York: Henry Holt, 1958), p. 314.

317 The allegations . . .: Letter from Snow to Emmerson, 29 December 1951; supplementary memorandum, 22 January 1952, author's file.

317–318 Dooman testimony at Emmerson hearings: Emmerson Transcript, 26 February 1951, 13 vols., 1:1–57. This transcript is the source for quotations of Dooman's testimony.

318 Communist success in changing Japanese attitudes: Ibid., 1:85–86.

319 "These Far Eastern experts are a penny a dozen . . .": Peter A. Adams, "Eugene H. Dooman, a 'Penny-a-dozen Expert': A Thesis Prospectus" (University of Maryland, n.d.).

319 "Threw himself body and soul": Emmerson Transcript, 26 February 1951, 1:90.

319 "Now, Mr. Chairman, you have the choice . . .": Ibid., 1:130.

320 "persons responsible had an affinity for communism?": Ibid., 1:69–71.

321 The report which drew most attention . . .: John K. Emmerson, "The Japanese Communist Party," U.S., Congress, Senate, Committee on the Judiciary, *The Amerasia Papers: A Clue to the Catastrophe of China*, 91st Cong., 1st sess., 26 January 1970, 2:1219–1225.

322 Bohlen's testimony: Emmerson Transcript, 19 March 1952, 5:1951, 1:90, A-34–35.

323 Nosaka's departure from Yenan: Letter from Arnold Dadian,

Cambridge, Mass., 14 March 1952; and Emmerson Transcript, 11: B–21–22.

323–324 Nosaka's letter to General Hodge: Letter dated 19 December 1945, to Lt. Gen. John R. Hodge, commanding general of the U.S. Army in Korea, Seoul, Korea, signed Okano Susumu (Nosaka Tetsu). Note that Okano was another name used by Nosaka. Also note, enclosures to Willoughby letter of 3 March 1951, previously cited on p. 312.

324 Tokyo headquarters sent a sergeant to interview Service and Emmerson: Memorandum, "Check Sheet," from Sergeant Selznick to Lieutenant Colonel Marcum, 10 January 1946, reporting interview with Service and Emmerson on 30 December 1945. SF.

324 Search of ATC records: State Department memorandum from John W. Sipes, Personal to Mr. Nicholson, Security, 11 March 1952: "The Board requests that SY [Division of Security] review the records of the Army Transport Command to ascertain if these records reflect any information as to how Nosaka arrived in Tokyo either from Yenan or Heijo, and whether Mr. Emmerson initiated, assisted, supported, or facilitated this transportation in any way." Memorandum from Division of Security to Chief Investigations Branch, Omaha, 25 April 1952: "A search of the records required to complete this case was started with the Kansas City Records Center AGO, Kansas City, Mo., on April 24, 1952.... The searchers are encountering voluminous material." SF.

324–325 Political prisoner interrogation: See testimony in Emmerson Transcript by Colonel Stewart (vol. 7, pp. 2–19); and affidavits by General Thorpe (vol. 10, pp. 13–14), Herbert Norman (vol. 10, p. B–35), and Lieutenant Colonel Davis (vol. 10, p. B–24).

325–326 "There was nothing which would lead me to think ...": Testimony by Gen. Walter Bedell Smith, Emmerson Transcript, 6:5–6.

326 He would employ me in the CIA ... : Ibid., 6:9.

326 "You will shake hands with anybody": Ibid., 6:6–7.

326–327 Quotes on personality: SF.

327–328 Osborn affidavit: Emmerson Transcript, 9:58.

328 Report of January 5, 1945, and attitudes toward communism: Emmerson's testimony, Emmerson Transcript, 13:1–33.

328 "no reasonable doubt ...": Memorandum of 19 May 1952,

signed by members of Loyalty Security Board—Henry H. Kelly, chairman, Homer M. Byington, Jr., and Francis T. Murphy, members; "Rationale," 26 June 1952; letter of 30 August 1952 to John K. Emmerson from W. K. Scott, acting deputy undersecretary. SF.

330 In 1954 my entire security file . . . : Memorandum from Dennis Flinn, Security, to Scott McLeod, Office of Security and Consular Affairs, dated 29 January 1955, enclosing "Summary and Analysis" of Emmerson case and making favorable recommendation. SF.

332–333 Senator Jenner's statement: U.S., Congress, Senate, *Congressional Record*, 85th Cong., 1st sess., 1957, 103, pt. 3: 2905–2906.

334–335 Hearings of March 12, 1957: Security Subcommittee Hearings, 1957, "Scope of Soviet Activity in the United States," pt. 56:3645–3666.

335 Testimony regarding Herbert Norman: Ibid., pp. 3656–3666.

335 Senator Jenner's admonishment regarding executive session: Ibid., p. 3666.

336 Headlines after hearing: SENATORS PROBE CANADIAN ENVOY, *Washington Star*, 15 March 1957; and CANADA TO PROTEST SENATE GROUP'S RELEASE OF "SLANDEROUS TESTIMONY," *The Washington Post and Times Herald*, 16 March 1957.

336 Pearson said Canada would protest: *The Washington Post and Times Herald*, 16 March 1957.

336 State Department statement: STATE AGENCY REPUDIATES CANADA ENVOY "SLANDER," *Sunday Star* (Washington, D.C.), 17 March 1957.

336 "When is the Senate going to put a bridle . . .": SMEAR, INC., editorial, *The Washington Post and Times Herald*, 16 March 1957.

336–337 March 21 hearing: Security Subcommittee Hearings, 21 March 1957, pp. 3667–3685.

337 my testimony on the twenty-third had "cleared the air": Memorandum to file from SY/E, Raymond P. Levy, 17 February 1959. SF.

337 March 23 hearing: Senate Security Subcommittee, *Amerasia Papers: A Clue to the Catastrophe of China*, "Testimony of John K. Emmerson, March 23, 1957," 2:1679–1762.

338 Canadian students burn Morris in effigy: *Sunday Star*, 7 April 1957.

338   Hon. Lester B. Pearson may be next ... : Article in *Toronto Star*, 5 April 1957, quoted in Canadian House of Commons, 6 April 1957, by Mr. Stanley Knowles. "The Strange Case of Herbert Norman," *U.S. News and World Report* (26 April 1957), vol. 42, p. 140.

338   Pearson revealed on April 12 that ... : Testimony by Secretary of State for External Affairs Lester B. Pearson in Canadian House of Commons, ibid., p. 144.

338–339   "I was convinced of his loyalty ...": Ibid., p. 149.

339   Senator Javits's statement: *The Washington Post*, 13 April 1957.

339   Press editorial comment on Norman case: RECKLESS AND UNFAIR, *The New York Times*, 6 April 1957; SUICIDE AND SLANDER, *The Washington Post*, 5 April 1957; TRAGEDY IN CAIRO, *Evening Star* (Washington, D.C.), 5 April 1957; LICENSE TO DESTROY, *The Washington Post*, 9 April 1957; and DISGRACE-FUL HARASSMENT, *The New York Herald Tribune*, 10 April 1957.

339   RECKLESS PERSECUTION: *Times* (London) editorial, quoted in "The Strange Case of Herbert Norman," p. 139.

340   Exchange of notes between Canadian government, March 18, 1957, and U.S. government, 10 April 1957: For text see *The New York Times*, 11 April 1957, p. 4.

340   "if the United States administration had answered the protest ... promptly ...": Mr. Alistair Stewart in Canadian House of Commons, 10 April 1957, quoted in "The Strange Case of Herbert Norman," p. 143.

340–341   Norman had joined the Communist party ... : Charles Taylor, "Herbert Norman," *Six Journeys: A Canadian Pattern* (Toronto: Anansi, 1977), p. 117. I am indebted to Charles Taylor and also to the Rev. W. H. Norman, Herbert Norman's brother, for information about Norman's early life and for insights into his thinking.

341   "he had had mistaken beliefs ...": Ibid., p. 138.

341   none of his contacts or his actions "could in any way be questioned ...": Ibid., p. 138.

342   Notes left by Norman: Ibid., pp. 149–150.

Chapter 13

346 May 13, 1958, in Paris: Henry and Serge Blomberger, *Les 13 Complots du 13 Mai ou la Délivrance de Gulliver* (Paris: Librairie Arthène Foyard, 1959).

346 Senate Subcommittee on Norman: "The Norman Case," U.S., Congress, Senate, Committee on the Judiciary, *Report of the Senate Internal Security Subcommittee for the Year 1957,* 85th Cong., 1st sess., sec. VII, 31 December 1957, pp. 101–109.

346 "The footnote": Ibid., p. 107.

346 Press release issued by Senator Watkins: *The New York Times,* 6 April 1957.

346–347 "Emmerson ... in a staff car flying the American flag": Elizabeth Churchill, "How We Have Been Losing Japan," *The American Legion Magazine,* vol. 64, no. 3 (March 1958).

347 Letter to Dulles: Dated 19 May 1958 by unidentified sender, attached to State Department memorandum, 26 May 1958. SF.

348 "irresponsible southerners ...": Embassy Lagos, airgram no. 237, 27 October 1960, "The Outlook for Independent Nigeria," by John K. Emmerson, Leon G. Dorros, George Dolgin, p. 2.

348 "feudal and reactionary northern aristocrats." Ibid., p. 4.

350 We met the Fon of Bafut ... : See Gerald M. Durrell, *The Bafut Beagles* (New York: Viking Press, 1954).

350 the turmoil of transition: Chinua Achebe, *Things Fall Apart* (London: Heinemann, 1958).

350–351 seminar on ... federalism: Consulate General Lagos, airgram no. 118, 29 August 1960, "Seminar on Constitutional Problems of Federalism in Nigeria," signed, John K. Emmerson, consul general.

352 "... technical interrogation ...": Letter to John K. Emmerson from Loy W. Henderson, deputy undersecretary for administration, Department of State, Washington, D.C., 23 December 1958, author's file.

352–353 a day-long interrogation ... : Transcript of interrogation, 18 February 1959, pp. C-6 and C-17. SF.

353 Allen Dulles's refusal to administer lie detector test: Interdepartmental reference, 16 December 1958, to Roderic L. O'Connor, signed, E. Tomlin Bailey. SF.

354 Report of polygraphic examination: Headquarters, 902nd

Counter-Intelligence Group, Washington, D.C., 3 March 1959, "Technical Support," addressed to Director, Office of Security, Department of State. SF.

354 Approval of security clearance: Memorandum for the acting secretary from Loy W. Henderson, deputy undersecretary for administration, approved "C.D.D." (C. Douglas Dillon), undersecretary, 18 May 1959. SF.

354 Clearance: "Notification of Security Clearance under E. O. 10430," 25 November 1959. Form with typed statement: "This amends E. O. 10450 clearance of Feb. 18, 1955. Mr. Emmerson has been cleared by the Secretary, after full field investigation by the FBI under procedures relating to Presidential appointees." SF.

357 U.S. "gamble" in Africa: "Dangerous Gamble in Africa," *Sunday Mail* (Salisbury, Federation of Rhodesia and Nyasaland), 26 March 1961.

357 "The wind of change ...": Prime Minister Harold Macmillan in a speech to the South African Parliament, Capetown, 3 February 1960, Alan and Veronica Palmer, *Quotations in History, A Dictionary of Historical Quotations* (Hassocks, Sussex: The Harvester Press, 1976), pp. 144–145.

357 "Sir Roy fighting for his political life ...": Dispatch to Department of State, no. 1037, 31 May 1961, from John K. Emmerson, Consul General, Salisbury, p. 4.

359–360 Kaunda's toast to President Ford: U.S., Department of State, *Bulletin*, (12 May 1975), p. 616.

360 "The time has come to face the music in Central Africa ...": "A Message for Sir Roy," *The Economist* (London), 13 January 1962, pp. 103–104.

362–363 "Am delighted inform you President wishes ...": Department of State telegram no. 633 to consulate general Salisbury, 15 February 1962, signed RUSK. SF.

364 Fulbright, on China foreign service officers: J. William Fulbright, "Reflections: In Thrall to Fear," *New Yorker*, 8 January 1972, p. 49.

364 Chester Bowles's comment: Letter to Dean Rusk from Bowles, dated 11 March 1962. SF.

365 "... owing urgent need John Emmerson's services ...": Department of State telegram no. 903 to chargé d'affaires, Dar-es-Salaam, 1 June 1962, signed Rusk. SF.

365 Announcement of appointment to Tokyo: Department of State telegram no. 3180 to Embassy Tokyo, 18 June 1962, signed Rusk. SF.

366 *Asahi* article on Emmerson appointment: Dispatch by Matsuyama Yukio, dated Washington, D.C., 18 June 1962.

366 Hashimoto letter: "To Hon. Edwin O. Reischauer, U.S. Ambassador to Japan, Tokyo," dated Tokyo, 21 June 1962, signed Tetsuma Hashimoto, the *Shiunsō* [Purple Cloud] Society. Accompanying covering letter to Reischauer, addressed "Dear Sir," dated 13 July 1962, signed T. Hashimoto, Chairman, The *Shiunsō*.

367 Rusk letter to Walter: Letter addressed to the Hon. Francis E. Walter, chairman, Committee on Un-American Activities, House of Representatives, Washington, D.C., 7 December 1962, signed Dean Rusk, replying to four-page letter from Walter to Rusk, 8 November 1962. SF.

367 Obama opened his television news broadcast ... : Japan Broadcasting System in Japanese, 2050 GMT, 18 July 1962, reported by Foreign Broadcast Information Service (FBIS), Tokyo, 18 July 1962.

367–368 Article in *Zembō:* Department of State airgram no. 183, sent by Embassy Tokyo to Department of State, 8 August 1962, enclosing full translation of article appearing in *Zembō*, monthly magazine published in Tokyo, September 1962, entitled "Repercussions Created by Minister in Dark Glasses: A Slanderous Talk Between Tetsuma Hashimoto and Toshie Obama." SF.

368 "the whole matter is blowing over": Embassy Tokyo telegram (Limit Distribution) no. 365, 7 August 1962, signed Reischauer. SF.

368 Edwin O. Reischauer, "The Broken Dialogue with Japan," *Foreign Affairs,* vol. 39, no. 1. (October 1960), pp. 11–26.

Chapter 14

372 The Bikini incident: John M. Allison, *Ambassador from the Prairie or Allison Wonderland* (Boston: Houghton Mifflin, 1973), p. 265.

373 Japan's economic growth, 1950 and 1962: Hugh Borton, *Japan's*

Modern Century: From Perry to 1970 (New York: Ronald Press, 1970), p. 520.

374 "friendship between equals": Kamei Shunsuke, "Japanese See America: A Century of Firsthand Impressions," *Japan Interpreter*, vol. 11., no. 1 (Spring 1976), p. 8.

374 Japan . . . "in neutral": Philip W. Quigg, "Japan in Neutral," *Foreign Affairs*, vol. 44, no. 2 (January 1966), pp. 253–263.

374 "big boy who prefers to sit in the back row . . .": Edwin O. Reischauer, *Japan: The Story of a Nation* (New York: Alfred A. Knopf, 1970), pp. 315–316.

378 Emmerson accused of "losing Okinawa": Art Goul, "What's This About the Ryukyus?" *The Oakland* (Calif.) *Tribune*, 10 May 1964.

380 "He is the first ambassador to be given so much sympathy . . .": *Sankei Shimbun* (Tokyo), 30 March 1964.

380 Reischauer statement on stabbing: *Japan Times* (Tokyo), 25 March 1964.

380 First satellite broadcast from Japan to the United States: *Japan Times* (Tokyo), 26 March 1964.

381 Numbers of "abnormal" boys under legal protection: Inukai Michio, "A Shocking Deed," *Japan Times* (Tokyo), 28 March 1964.

381 Increase in juvenile delinquency: *Japan Times* (Tokyo), 28 March 1964.

382 Japanese Rising Sun flag: In 1964 the Japanese flag was not widely flown. A Tokyo newspaper noted that the Olympics were less than one hundred days away and that the time had come to examine the question of the national flag. An insurance company was distributing flags free of charge, and it was hoped that they would soon fly throughout the country. The newspaper commented, "Interest in the national flag must arise from the people themselves." *Nihon Keizai Shimbun* (Tokyo), 4 July 1964.

384–385 *Keibatsu* in Japanese society: Suzuki Yukio, *Keibatsu: Kekkon de katamerareru Nihon no Shihaisha Shūdan* [Nepotism: Japan's Ruling Group Solidified by Marriage] (Tokyo: Kobunsha, 1965). For chart of relationships with Satō Eisaku, see ibid., pp. 30–31.

388–389 Emmerson's poem on diplomats and the press: Ogawa Masaru, "Our Times," *Japan Times* (Tokyo), 12 December 1966.

390 "American talk about a 'petering out'. . .": Author's notes.

Chapter 15

393   An eighth-century Japanese priest . . . : The priest Mansei is
      quoted in Kurt Singer, *Mirror, Jewel, and Sword: A Study of
      Japanese Characteristics* (New York: George Braziller, 1973), p.
      52.
395   Lillian Hellman on McCarthy period: Lillian Hellman, *Scoun-
      drel Time* (Boston, Toronto: Little, Brown, 1976), p. 38.
398   Henry Kissinger, on the 1960s: Henry A. Kissinger, "Laying the
      Foundation of a Long-term Policy," address before the
      National Press Club, Washington, D.C., 10 January 1977.
      (Washington, D.C.: Bureau of Public Affairs, Office of Media
      Services, Department of State).

Index